MW01625554

Saloua Raouda Choucair

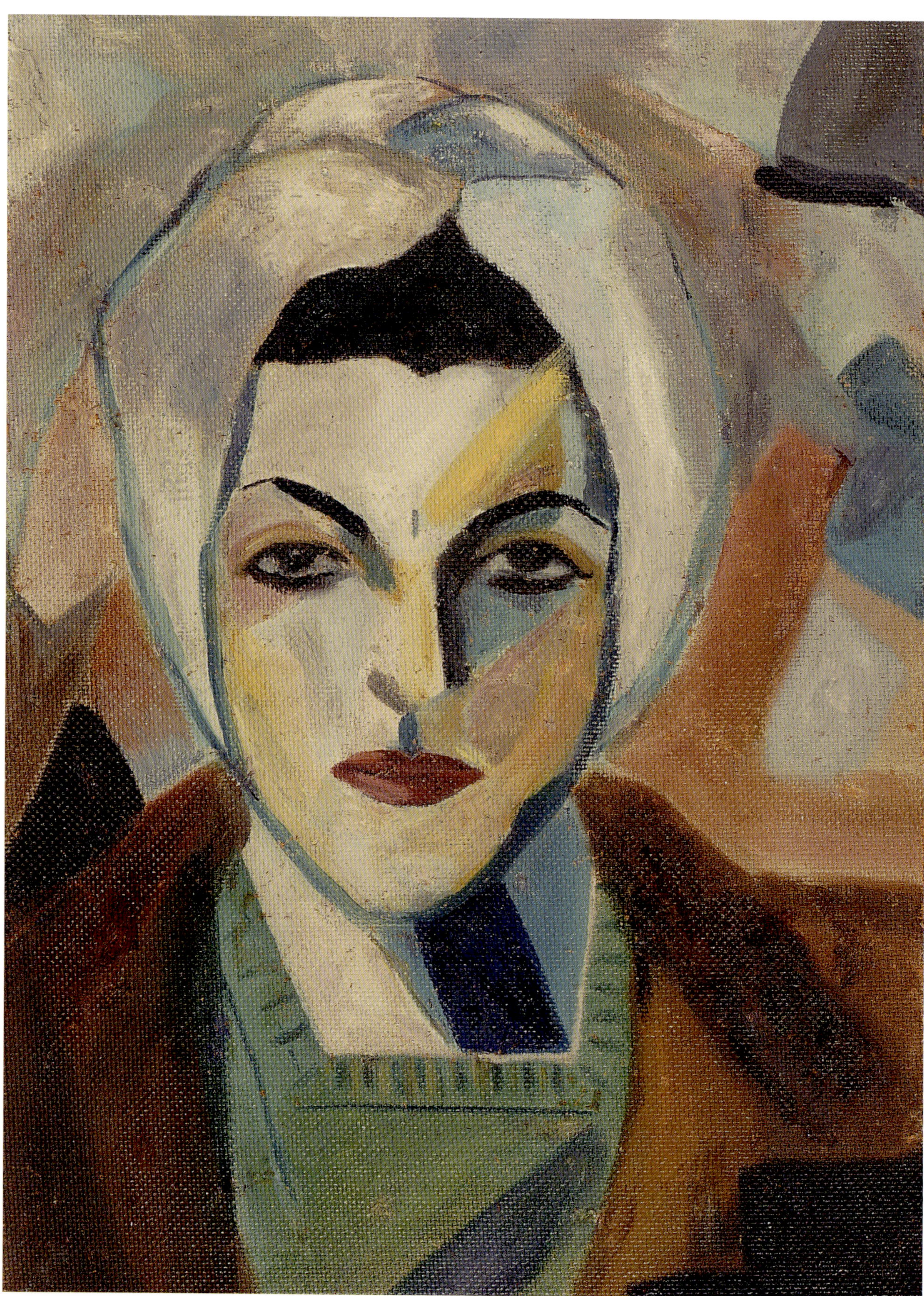

Saloua Raouda Choucair

Edited by Jessica Morgan

With essays by
Ann Coxon
Jessica Morgan
Kirsten Scheid
Kaelen Wilson-Goldie

Tate Publishing

First published 2013
by order of the Tate Trustees
by Tate Publishing, a division
of Tate Enterprises Ltd,
Millbank, London SW1P 4RG
www.tate.org.uk/publishing

On the occasion of the
exhibition
Saloua Raouda Choucair

Tate Modern
16 April–20 October 2013

Supported by

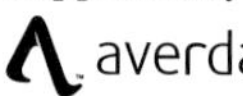

With additional support
from The Choucair
Exhibition Supporters Group:
Marwan T Assaf
Fondation Saradar
Mikati Foundation

A catalogue record for
this book is available from
the British Library

ISBN 978 1 84976 124 6

Distributed in the United
States and Canada by ABRAMS,
New York

Library of Congress Control
Number applied for

Designed by
Micha Weidmann Studio
Colour reproduction by
DL Imaging, London
Printed in Belgium by
die Keure

Jacket:
Saloua Raouda Choucair,
Poem 1963–5
(fig.65)

Fig.1, p.2:
Saloua Raouda Choucair,
Self-Portrait 1943
Oil paint on canvas
45.5 × 42

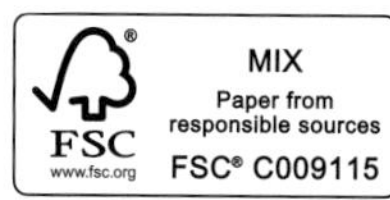

Measurements of artworks are
given in centimetres, height
before width and depth

Contents

Foreword

Saloua Raouda Choucair is in many ways an exceptional artist. A pioneer of abstract art in the Middle East, she spent nearly six decades following the courage of her conviction that principles of Islamic design and Arabic poetry could be explored and reinvigorated within a modernist, non-objective art. Her paintings and objects – and also her artist's displays and sculptural interventions – call into question our one-sided Western concept of modernity.

Though Choucair was inspired and informed by a period of study in Paris in the late 1940s, she returned to Beirut where she worked tirelessly, against the odds, to carve out her personal vision. A substantial body of work has remained in the possession of the artist – a fact made all the more remarkable given the physical and political circumstances through which these works have survived. One of her vibrant painted compositions from the late 1940s was pierced by shards of shattered glass in the artist's apartment during a bombing raid in the Lebanese civil war in the 1980s. The object bears witness to this history. Choucair's varied, experimental works on paper, painting and sculpture have rarely been exhibited outside Lebanon. We are therefore extremely grateful to the artist and her daughter Hala Schoukair for opening the doors to this treasure trove. All loans to the exhibition have been made courtesy of the Saloua Raouda Choucair Foundation. We hope that we are able to introduce the work of Saloua Raouda Choucair to many new audiences and to bring to the artist the long-overdue attention she deserves.

I would like to thank averda for their generosity in making the exhibition possible, and Marwan T Assaf, Fondation Saradar and the Mikati Foundation for their additional support. This exhibition reflects Tate's objective to acquire and exhibit works by artists from the Middle Eastern region and I would like to acknowledge the activities of the Middle East and North Africa Acquisitions Committee. Tate was able to acquire a group of key works by the artist in 2011 with funds provided by the Committee and with the generous support of the Saloua Raouda Choucair Foundation. Jessica Morgan, The Daskalopoulos Curator, International Art, has been instrumental in forming and supporting the Committee and researching artists from the region. We are very grateful to her for recognising the importance of Choucair's contribution and for presenting the artist's work with intelligence and enthusiasm. Ann Coxon has worked alongside Jessica in curating the exhibition for Tate Modern as well as contributing to the catalogue. They have been ably assisted by intern Sophie Partarreiu.

Many people have helped in establishing an awareness and understanding of Choucair's work. Saleh Barakat of Agial Gallery, Beirut

2
Choucair's old studio in Beirut

3
Some of Choucair's sculptures stored in the studio

has personally introduced Tate to the artist's oeuvre, for which we are most grateful, and we thank the catalogue contributors Kirsten Scheid, whose thesis undertook some of the first significant research into the artist, and Kaelen Wilson-Goldie for their excellent contributions. Rasha Salti and Joe Tarrab have provided meaningful insight into Choucair's many decades of work and we have benefited from their thoughtful analysis.

Tate's conservation team has provided essential expertise during the exhibition's preparation. In particular, Rachel Barker, Elizabeth McDonald and Rosie Feemantle are to be thanked for their contribution. The exhibition would not have been possible without the work of the team at Tate Modern, including Exhibition Registrar Carol Burnier Magno; Phil Monk, Rhona O'Brien and the installation team; Simon Bolitho and Corrine Scurr in Tate Learning; the Marketing and Press teams; and all at Tate Media.

Nicola Bion, Roz Young and Juliette Dupire at Tate Publishing have worked hard on the production of this catalogue. We would also like to thank Micha Weidmann for the elegant design.

The exhibition was made possible by the Government Indemnity Scheme. Tate Modern would like to thank HM Government for providing Government Indemnity and the Department of Culture, Media and Sport and the Arts Council England for arranging the indemnity.

Chris Dercon
Director, Tate Modern

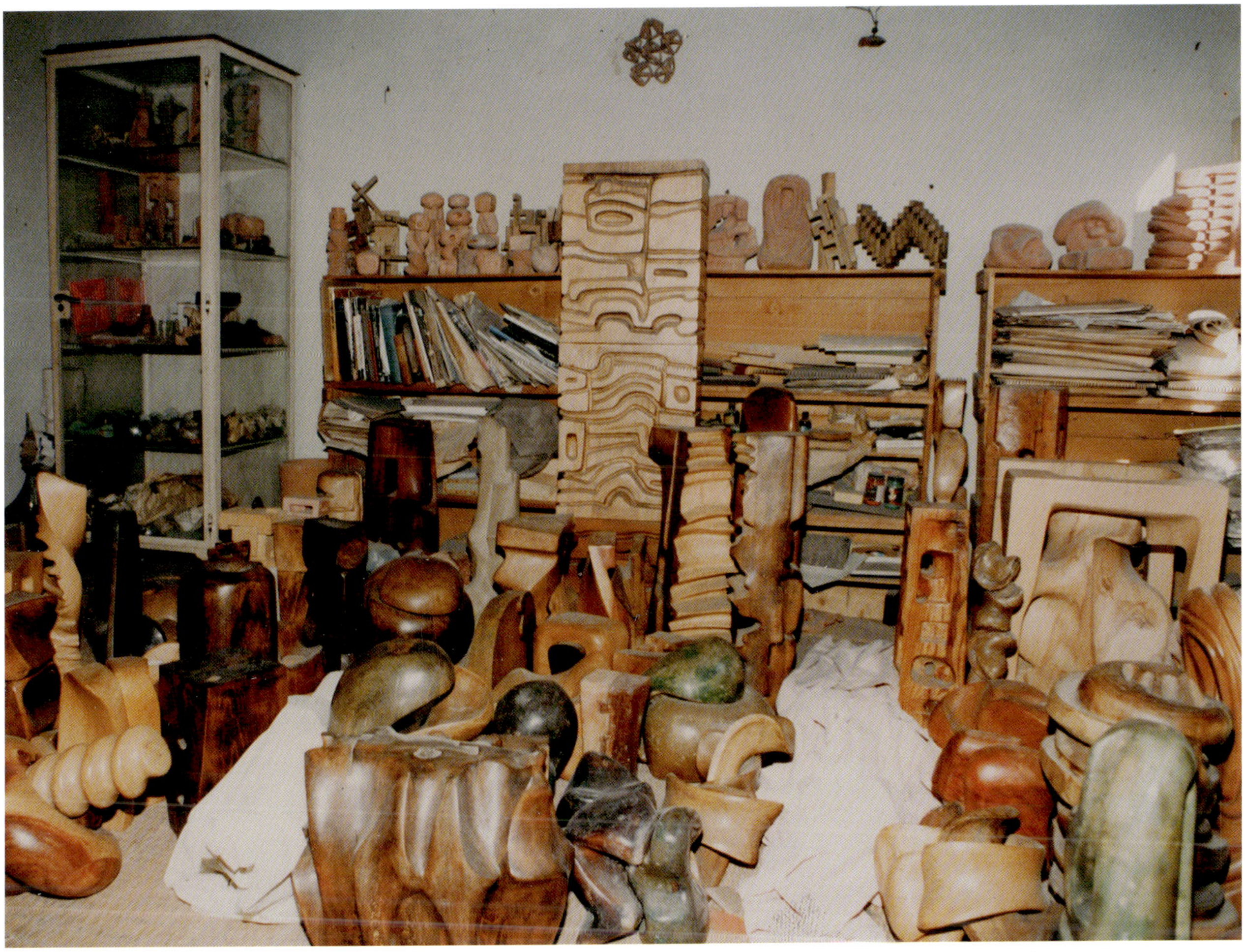

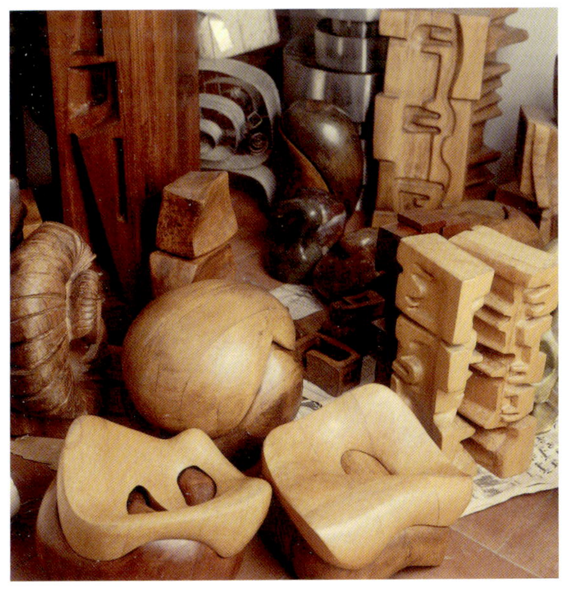

4
Two=one 1947–51
Oil paint on canvas
62×82

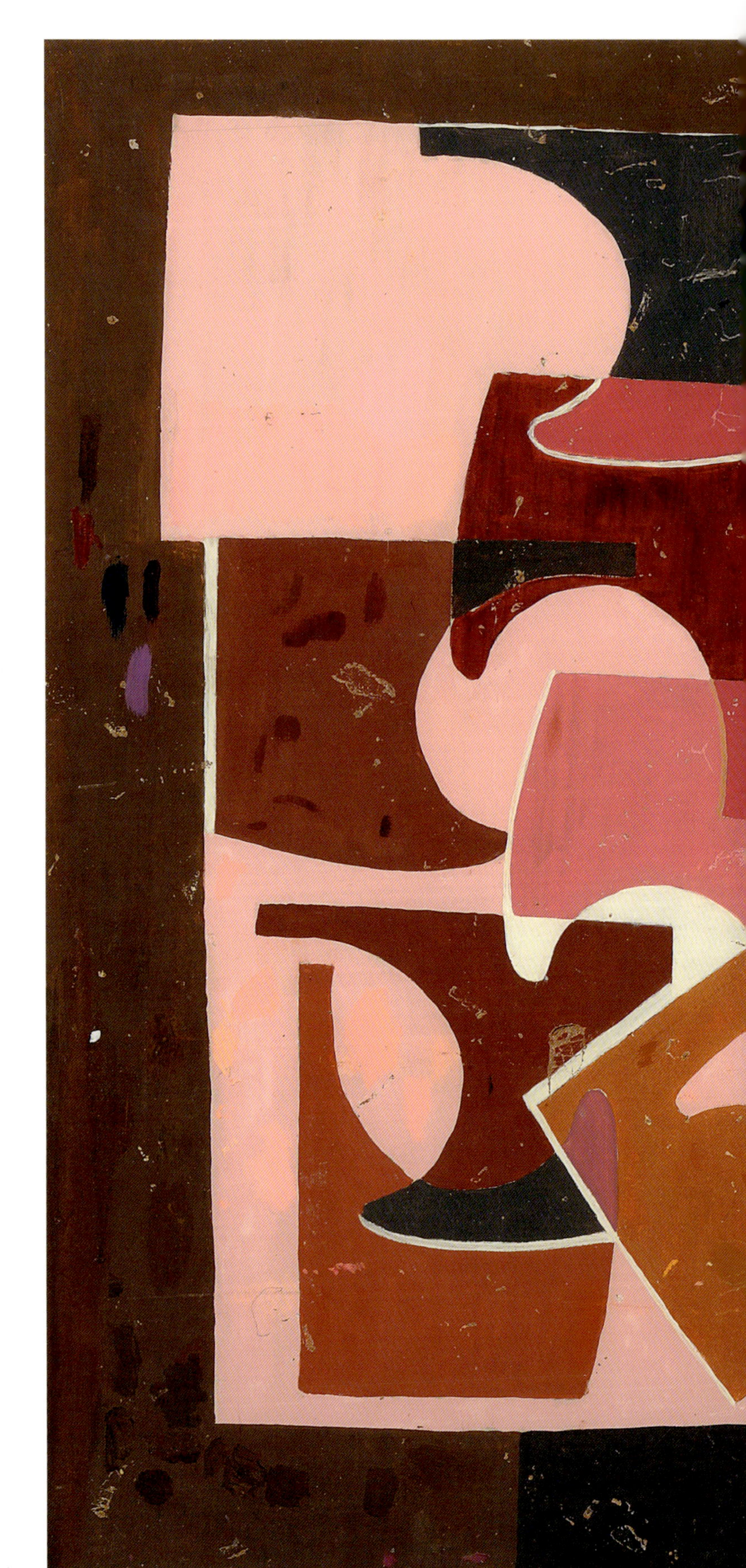

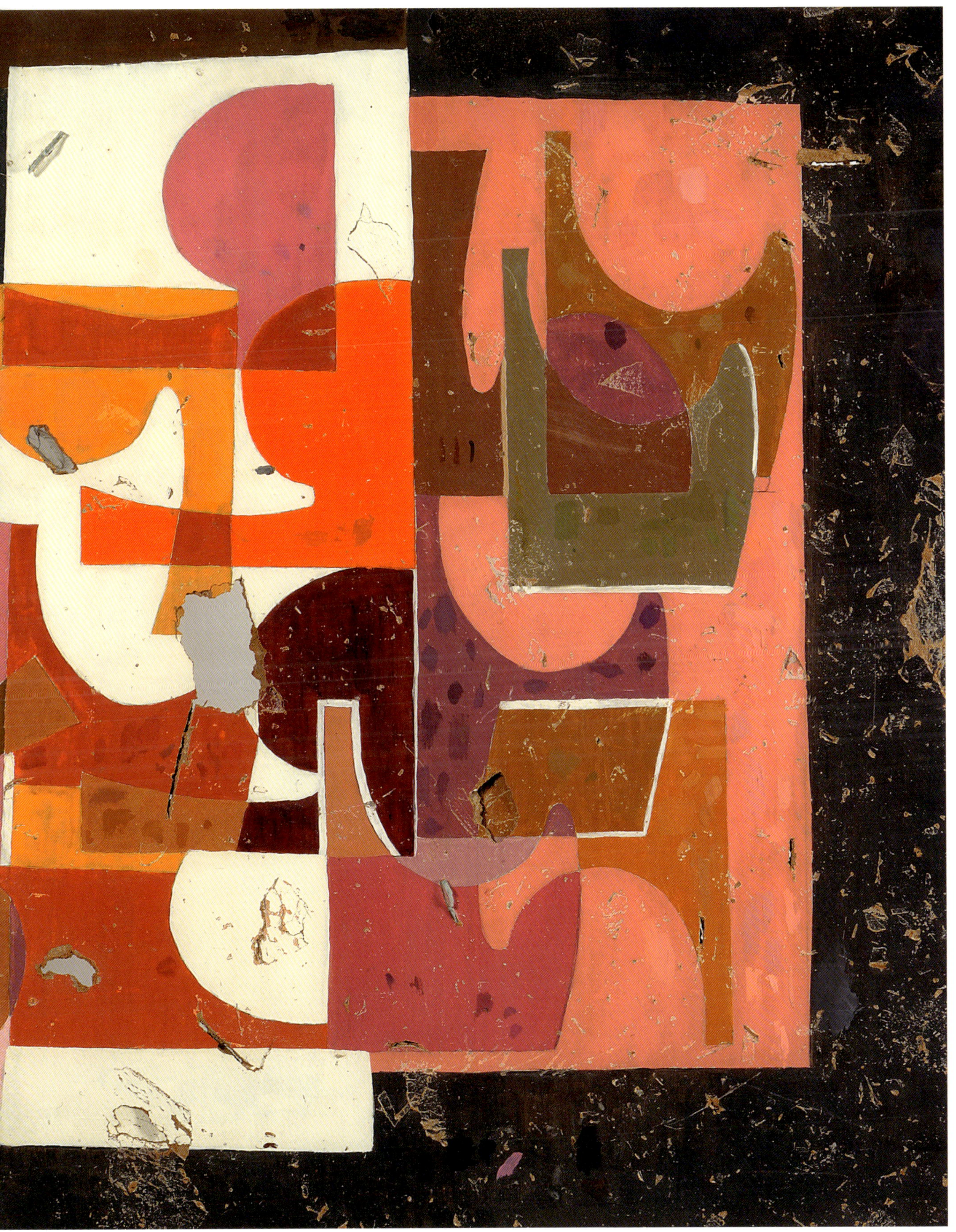

Introduction

In the late 1940s Saloua Raouda, as she was then, went from Paris to Marseille to visit the still unfinished Unité d'habitation, the first building of Le Corbusier's modernist residential housing project that became known later as the 'Cité radieuse' (1947–52). Le Corbusier's plans for the building included medical and athletic facilities, a restaurant, a playground on the roof and shopping facilities, in addition to housing for around 1,600 people. Choucair took copious photographs, some of which were in the spirit of 'heroic modernism' with stark light contrasts, but many acted as concrete and straightforward aides-mémoires, annotated on the back in Arabic with her observations of the site and the construction details (figs.5–7).

5
Corbusier's Cité radieuse in Marseille, 1940s

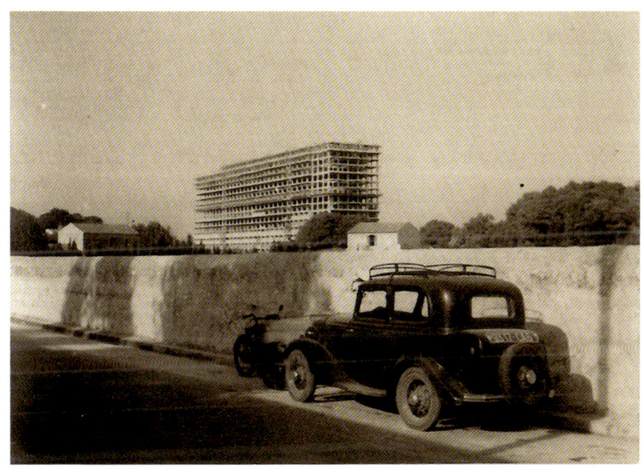

The striking modernity of the thinking behind this concrete housing complex is apparent in what may have been the first of Choucair's series of photographs. The image was taken at some distance from the construction at the side of the road and shows the rectangular honeycomb infrastructure of the building, as yet just a concrete shell. In the foreground is a car – perhaps the one in which the artist and her friends travelled to see this architectural revolution, the design of which seems to belong to another era. The disparity of engineering and design seen here – the futuristic housing block arising from an empty landscape and the old automobile whose design throws the viewer back to a scene from a silent movie – serves to make evident the excitement and engagement that Choucair felt on visiting the site. From her carefully written notes on the back of the photograph we learn that the two smaller buildings in front of the Cité radieuse were occupied by the architect and his building manager.

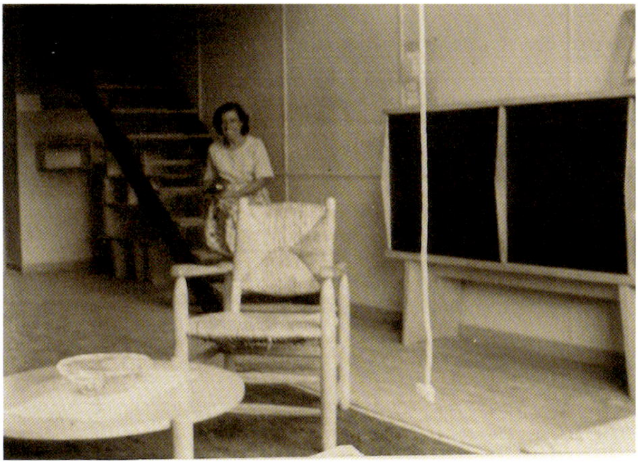

6
Choucair in the show apartment for the Cité radieuse, c.1949

Choucair's notes on the reverse of the other photographs from this visit reveal her attention to detail and design, the conceptual approach and the ideals of the architecture from which she evidently gained so much. Her images are intensely practical and were clearly taken in order to memorise what she had seen. The notes on the back, presumably written on her return to Paris once the images had been processed, document details of the apartment interiors, such as the manner in which partitions are used for dual purposes, the compact efficiency of the integrated furniture and the design of the foundations featuring Le Corbusier's emblematic 'Modular Man'. Choucair and her friends must have visited the show apartment, completed in 1949, as the finished interior in which we see her seated, smiling, at the foot of the stairs (in a picture perhaps taken by the friend we see in others in this series) bears no relation to the skeleton of a building in the photograph taken by the side of the road.

The aspects of the building and interiors to which Choucair is drawn and which she describes in her notes – the simple appearance of a solution to a complex issue of space and form – are, unsurprisingly perhaps, entirely in keeping with her absolute consistency in thought and experimentation throughout the extraordinary sixty years of her work as an artist. During her career she repeatedly returned to the unit or model and its potential for duplication, interrelation, fabrication and extension. Within the Cité radieuse she would have discovered Le Corbusier's modular units for living, each apartment spanning the width of the building and containing two floor levels. Fitting together like blocks, the design reduced the need for long corridors on every floor, limiting this to every third floor and thereby maximising living space. The 'vertical garden city', as the architect conceived of the structure, shared many characteristics with his better-known villas, here duplicated over and over again to create a communal collective housing structure, albeit with individual spaces.

7
Choucair's annotations on the back of two of the photographs of the Cité radieuse

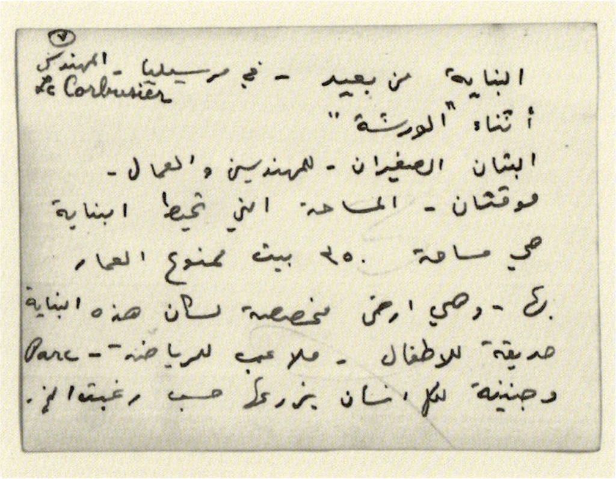

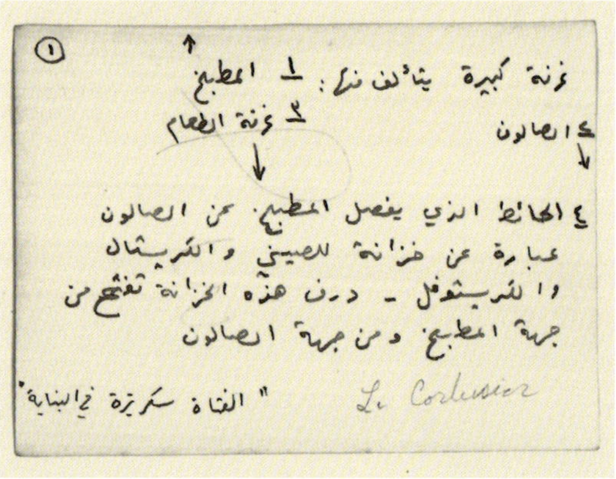

Alas, the many buildings Choucair was to have designed later in her career were not realised and remain unbuilt. Her architectural sensibility is, however, very evident from her earliest works in stone and wood that in some cases look remarkably like mid-rise structures. *Sculpture with One Thousand Pieces* 1966–8, for example, gives the impression of an occupied building, lit as it is from the centre in order to accentuate the varied positions of the wooden blocks like vertical brise-soleil placed irregularly on each 'floor' of the structure. Alongside Le Corbusier, a number of modern buildings in Beirut appear to have influenced Choucair on her return there in 1951. The façade of Dar al Sayad (1954), by the Polish emigré architect Karl Schayer (1900–1971) is characterised by a concrete cuboid grid structure providing shade for the entire building; this recalls the screen effect of Choucair's own sculpture. Antoine Tabet's Hotel Saint George, built in the 1920s, and the Pan Am building of 1955 by Georges Rayes would have been striking landmarks in the city and both are remarkable for their use of a simplified grid or modular system. Choucair's *Infinite Structure* 1963–5, which consists of multiple rectangular stone modules each with a slight variation of rectangular and spherical holes cut into the block, could similarly be compared with an architectural configuration, each unit appearing like an apartment or floor in a Brutalist-style concrete structure.

8
(opposite)
Infinite Structure 1963–5
Tufa stone
240 × 48 × 30

Unlike the architecture referenced here, however, Choucair's interest remains focused on difference within similitude rather than a strict replication of a module. Her structures and interlocking forms each comprise varied units combined to form a remarkable balancing act of formal and associative qualities. This dissimilarity between the units in

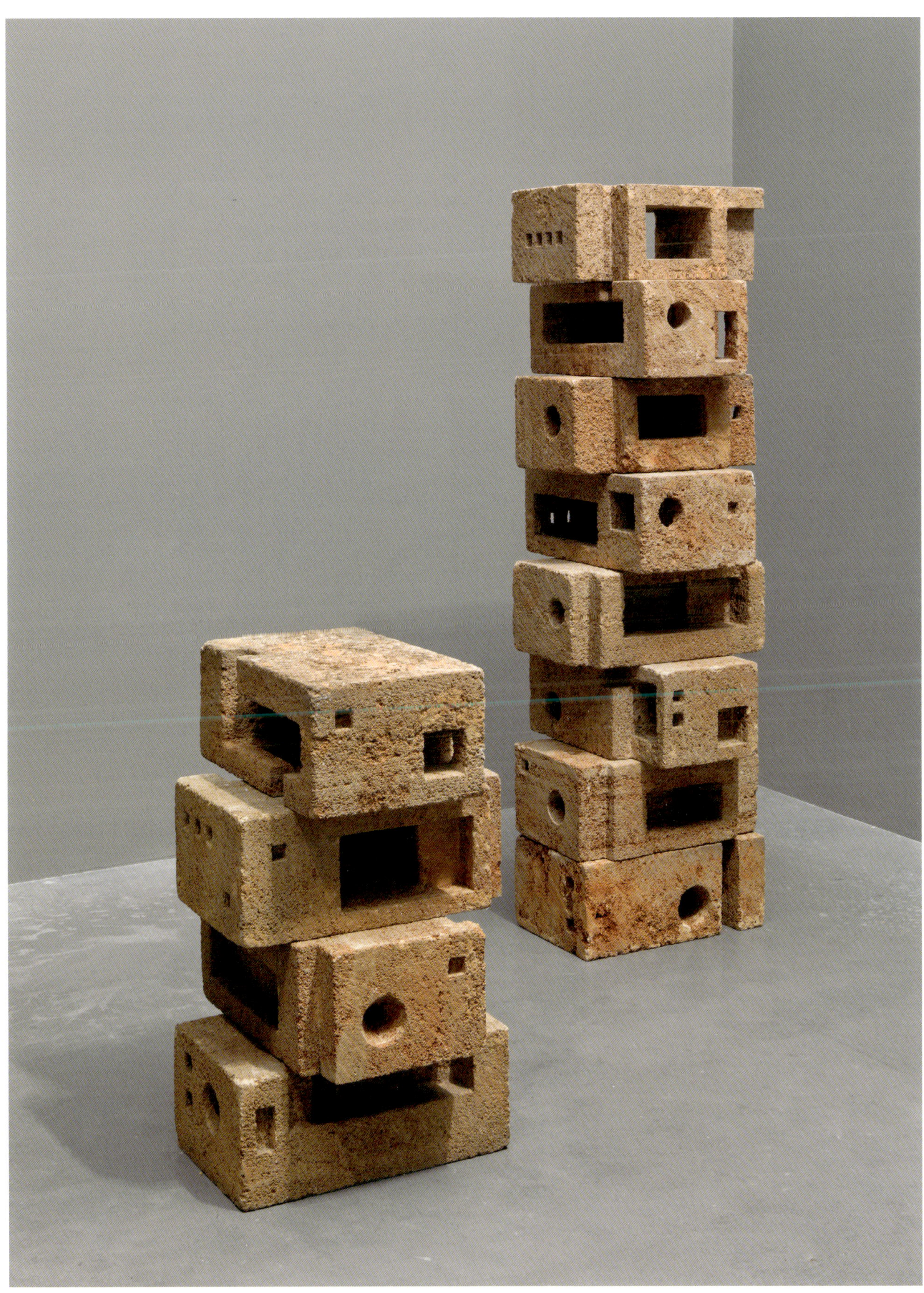

her work is perhaps closer to the repetition we see in nature, where each unit or form is as unalike as it is alike others of its kin. Her sculptural works have an organic quality that is borne out in her choice of materials, in particular stone and wood, and her ability to work with the inherent qualities of the material while encouraging them to take on new forms in their own internal language. This type of experimentation no doubt reflects Choucair's long interest in science and her approach to the limits and potential of an individual piece of wood or stone.

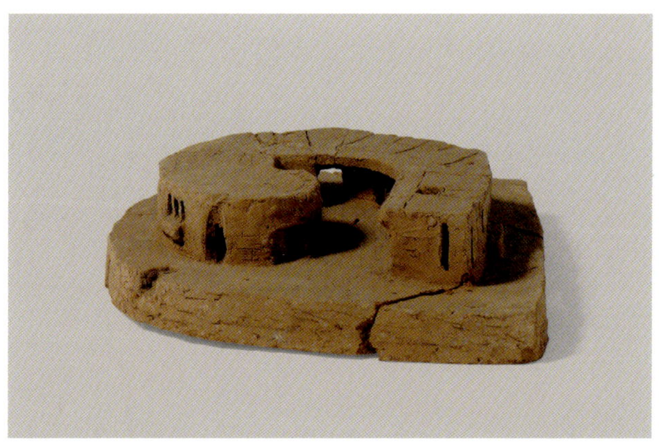

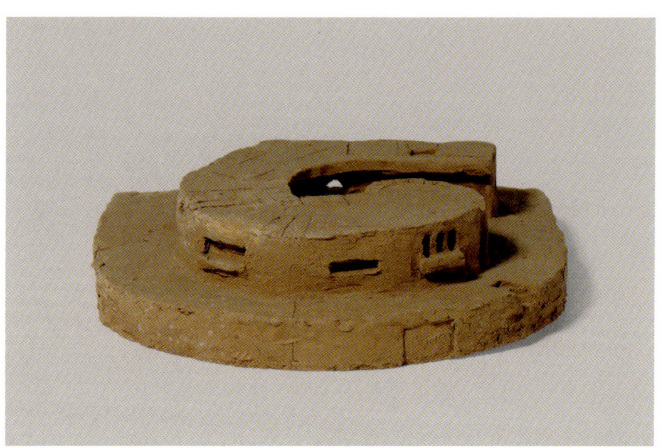

9
Clay model
of a house design
11×30×26
The tail could
be endlessly extended
with additional
units.

Her most developed architectural projects – all designed to be domestic homes with her own family in mind – are closely linked to her sculptural concerns. These projects are characterised by Choucair's interest in forms, materials and kineticism, and her desire to investigate modular and practical designs – a tendency that speaks to the mid-century ideals of economy and efficacy. According to her daughter Hala, and as documented in a humorous cartoon drawn by the architect with whom Choucair was collaborating (fig.10),one of her dreams was to construct a house that could turn – a kinetic structure relating closely to the many water sculptures that she designed in the 1970s (figs.66–7). These were carefully mapped out in drawing after drawing to establish the effect of air and water pressure on the resulting sprays or flows of liquid. Another plan, inspired by her love of the newly discovered moulded plastic – a material she used in sculptural form but which sadly did not survive a move from her studio in later years – was to produce an entire house from plastics with an interior made from the same material, which could be efficiently hosed down for ease of cleaning (a chore she hated, for it took her away from her work). This was a kind of feminist version of the Futuro House of 1968 by Matti Suuronen (of which she was unaware), itself coincidentally affected by the same events in the Middle East as impacted Choucair's career, as the rise in the cost of plastics due to the oil embargo in 1973 prevented the Futuro House from being anything more than a prototype. Events in Lebanon undermined Choucair's ambitions to build the synthetic house but did not prevent her from going on to design and model in clay another potential family home, this time based on a spiral formation whose tail could be endlessly extended with additional units as the generations were added to over time (fig.9).

The purpose of this book – and the exhibition it accompanies – is not, however, to dwell on what might or should have been in this extraordinary artist's career, constrained as it was by her gender and religion, and the effects upon her homeland of fractious events across the Middle East. On the contrary, it is an opportunity to begin to focus international attention on her work as she takes her rightful position as a significant figure in the history of twentieth-century art. Choucair's thinking – through painting and drawing, architecture and textiles, jewellery and furniture, as well as of course her prolific and experimental sculptural practice – places her among the few artists whose work expands beyond the parameters of the discrete art object. She approached her work as a total practice, applying the same analytical, mathematical and scientific thought to every series of artworks, each the result of studies in clay and drawing as well as careful calculations and engineering. Little or nothing was left to chance. Once a form or idea was settled upon, Choucair approached it through diverse media – stone, metals, wood, plastics, fibreglass – returning to particular ideas again as new possibilities were encountered in order to see how an idea might manifest itself differently according to the character of a new material. Like a scientist, she approached her ideas with the exhaustive aim of scientific analysis: systematic observation, measurement, experiment, formulation, testing and modification of a hypothesis.

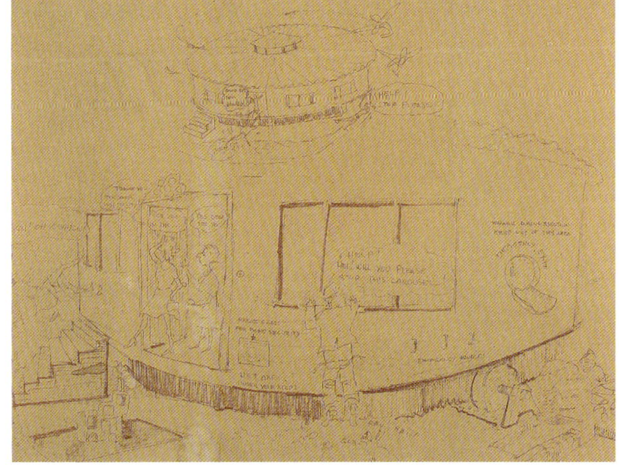

10
Comic strip by
the architect P. E. Deeb
after working
with Choucair on plans
for a house made of
fibreglass that could turn
48 × 64

We are fortunate here to have several voices to reflect on Choucair's work and to begin to add to the research and thinking about her practice that have been sorely missing over the years. Kirsten Scheid has been a pioneer in examining Choucair's practice and its complex relationship to an understanding of Arab modernism, as well as its conflicted relationship with a Western heritage. Her essay includes first-hand conversations with the artist about her work and life. Co-curator of the exhibition Ann Coxon places Choucair's oeuvre in the context of an international abstraction and is one of the first attempts to examine its formal associations in relation to the practice of others. Kaelen Wilson-Goldie reflects on the contemporary context of Choucair's work and embeds it in the city in which she remained for most of her life, Beirut. The exhibition spans the extraordinary breadth of Choucair's work, featuring pieces from the late 1940s to the 1980s. It is of course disappointing not to be able to exhibit her large-scale projects – and indeed her architecture – but there is no mistaking the ambitious and experimental spirit that underlines all her works, both planned and realised.

Jessica Morgan

11
(overleaf)
Subhan 1950
Gouache on paper
32 × 25

12
(overleaf)
Paris-Beirut 1948
Gouache on paper
32 × 23.5

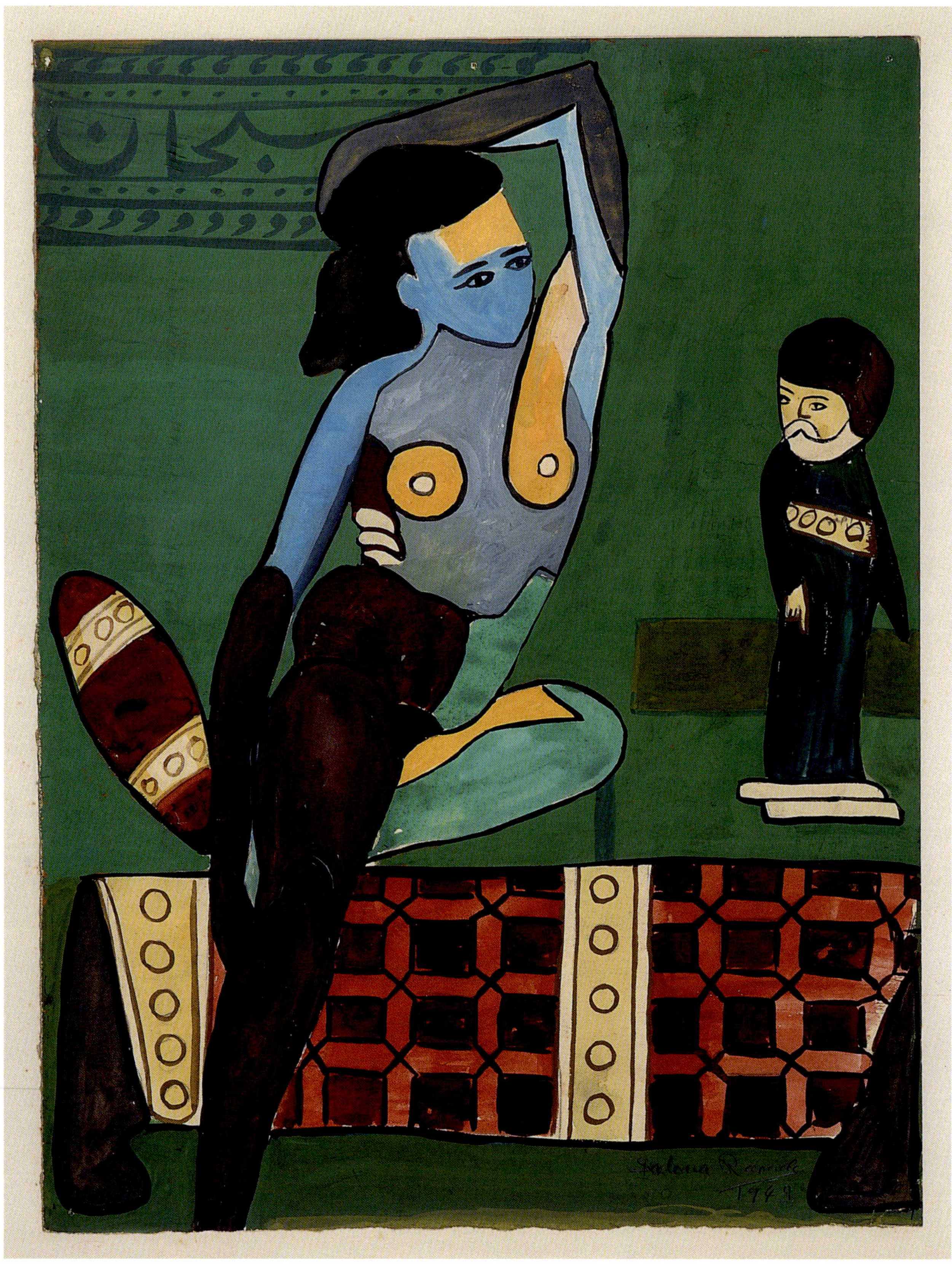

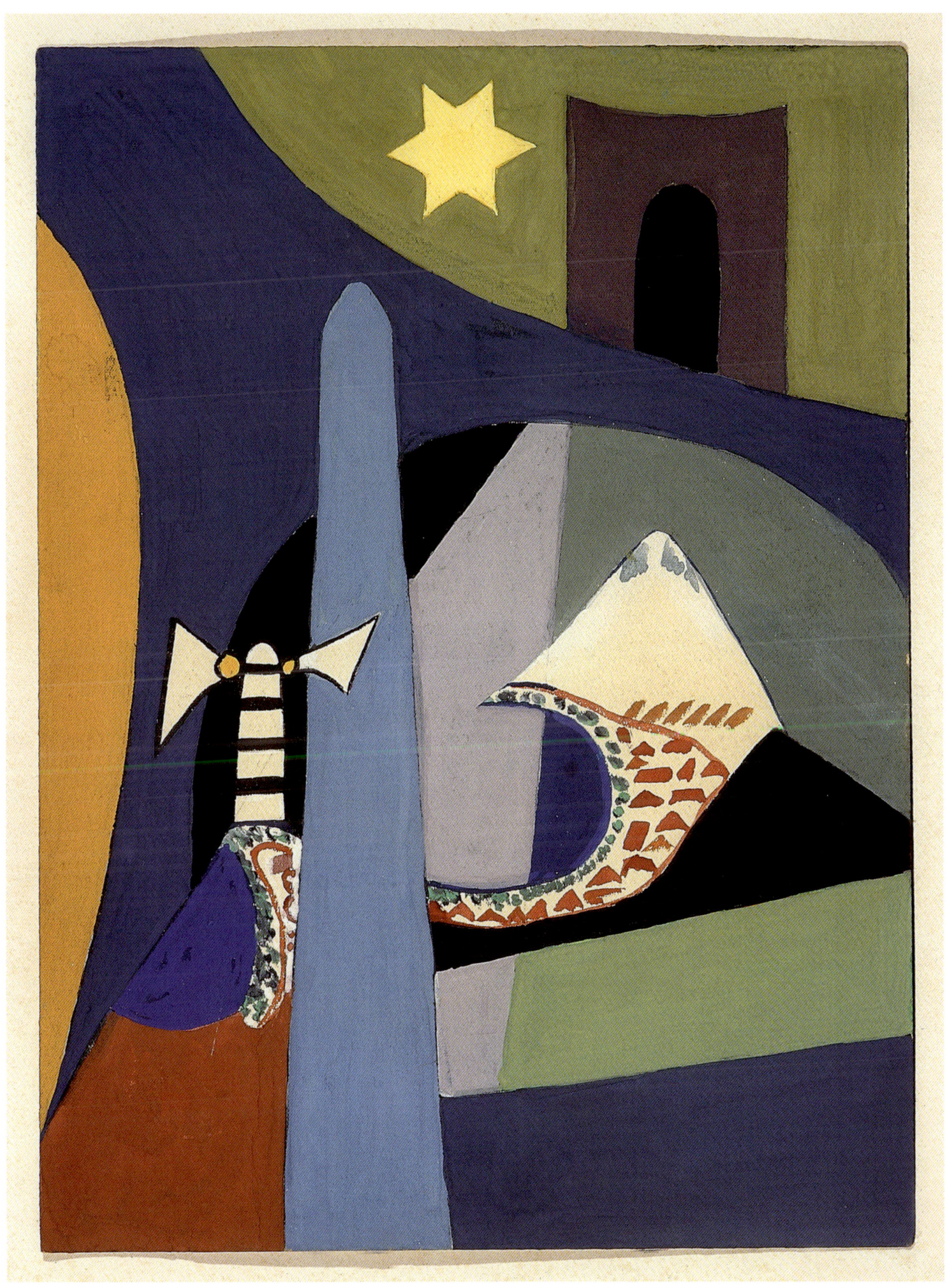

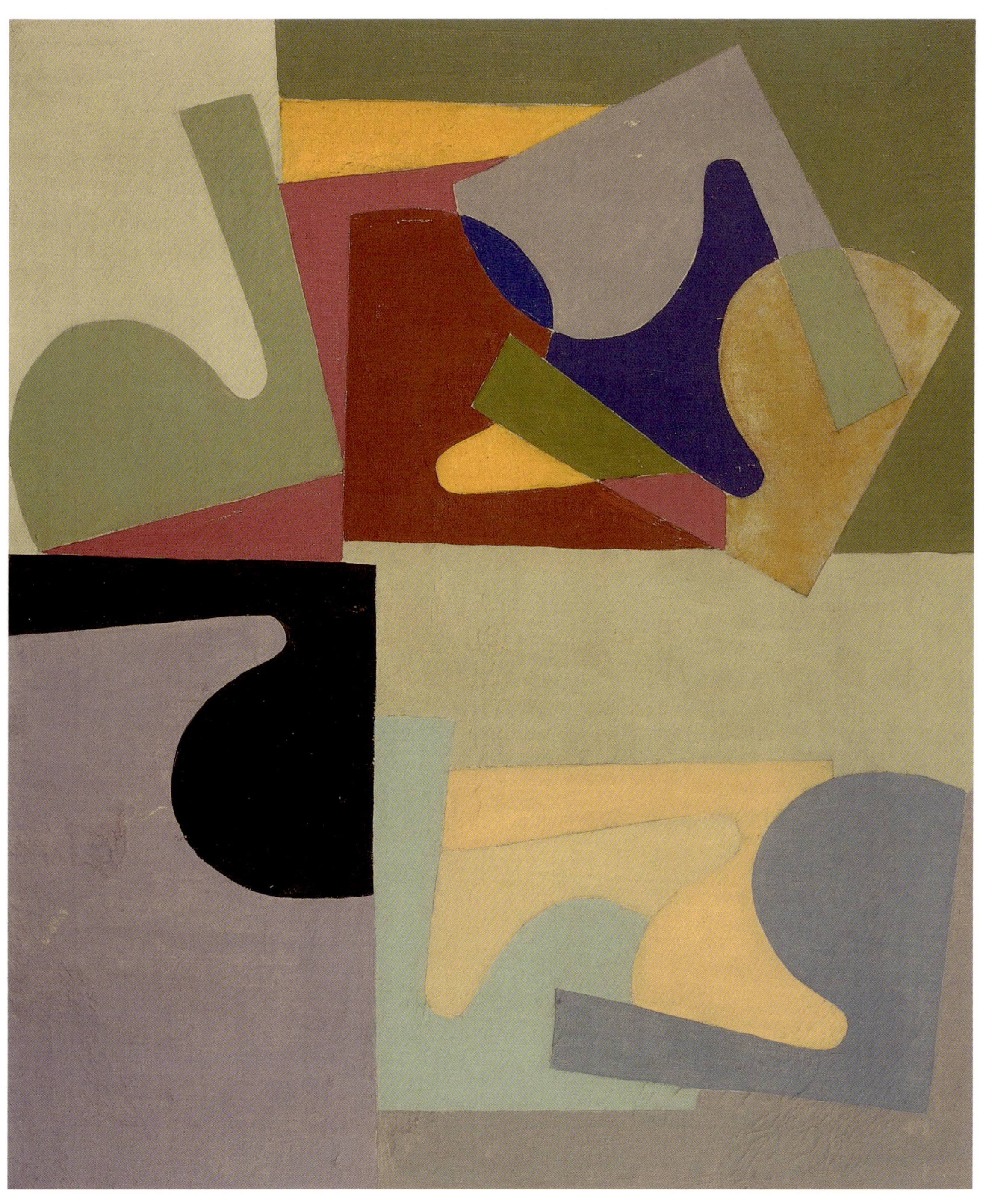

13
Fractional Module
1947–51
Oil paint on canvas
50 × 59

14
Fractional Module
1947–51
Oil paint on canvas
49 × 59.5

15
(overleaf)
Experiment with Calligraphy 1947–50
Gouache on paper
48 × 31

16
(overleaf)
Experiment with Calligraphy 1947–50
Gouache on paper
48 × 31

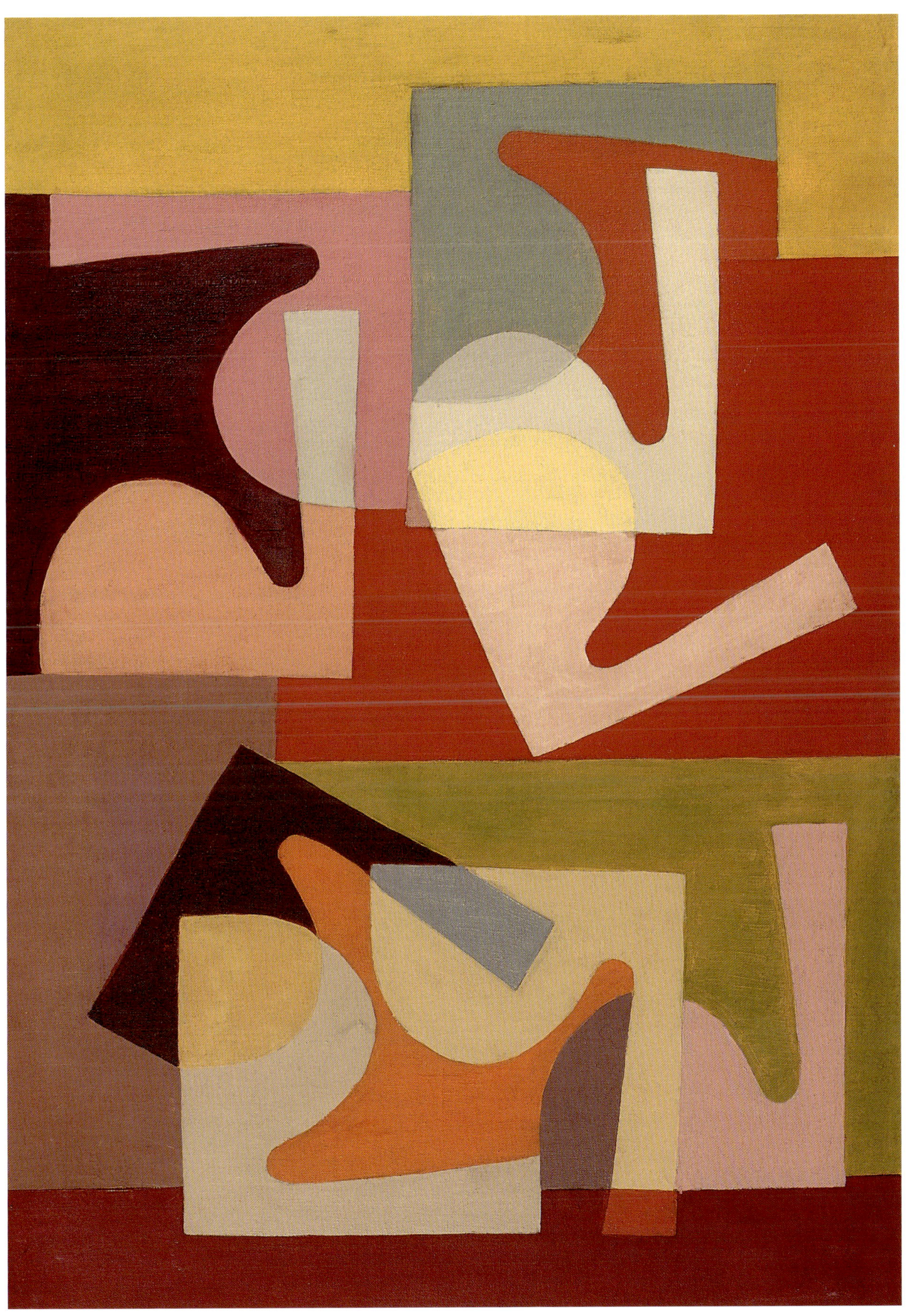

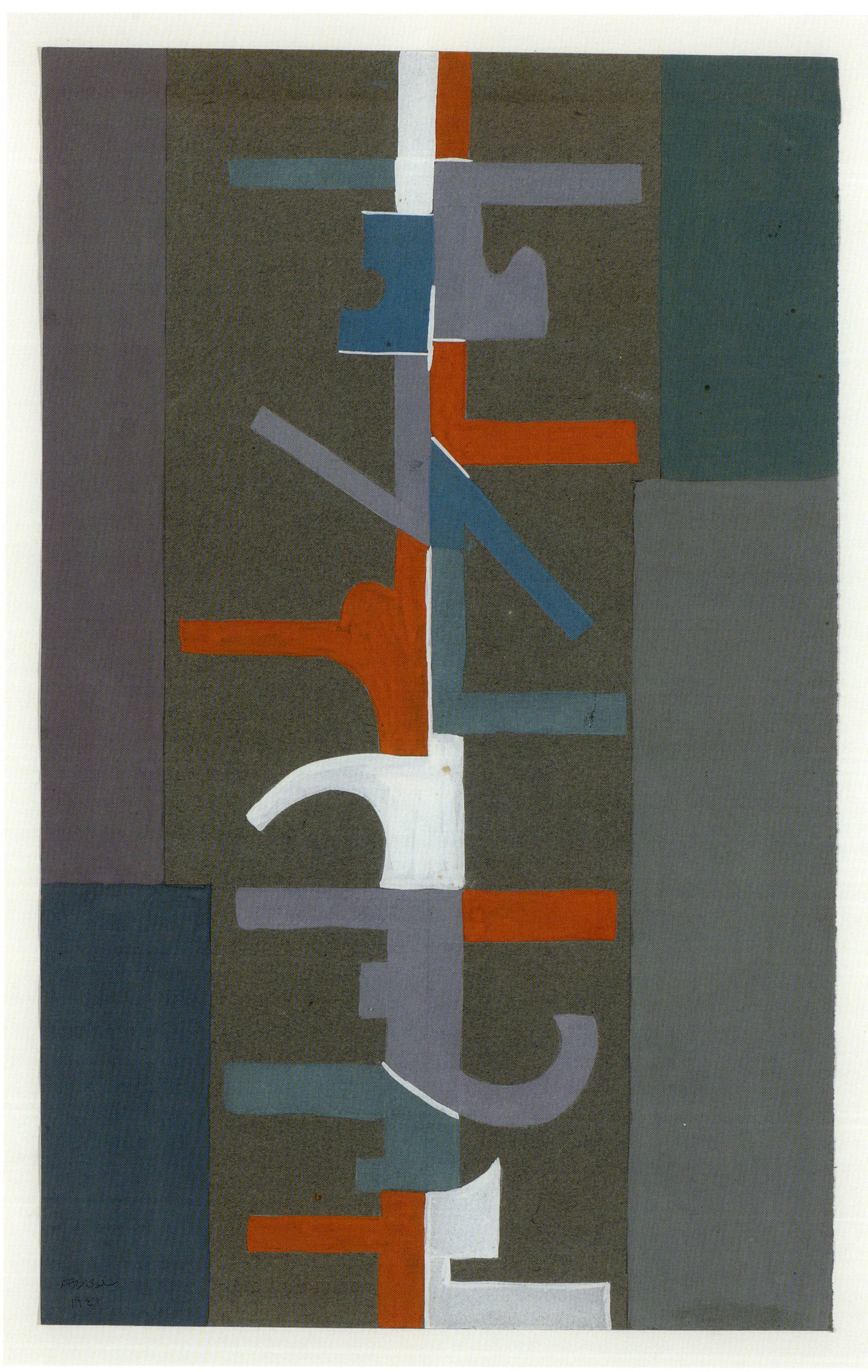

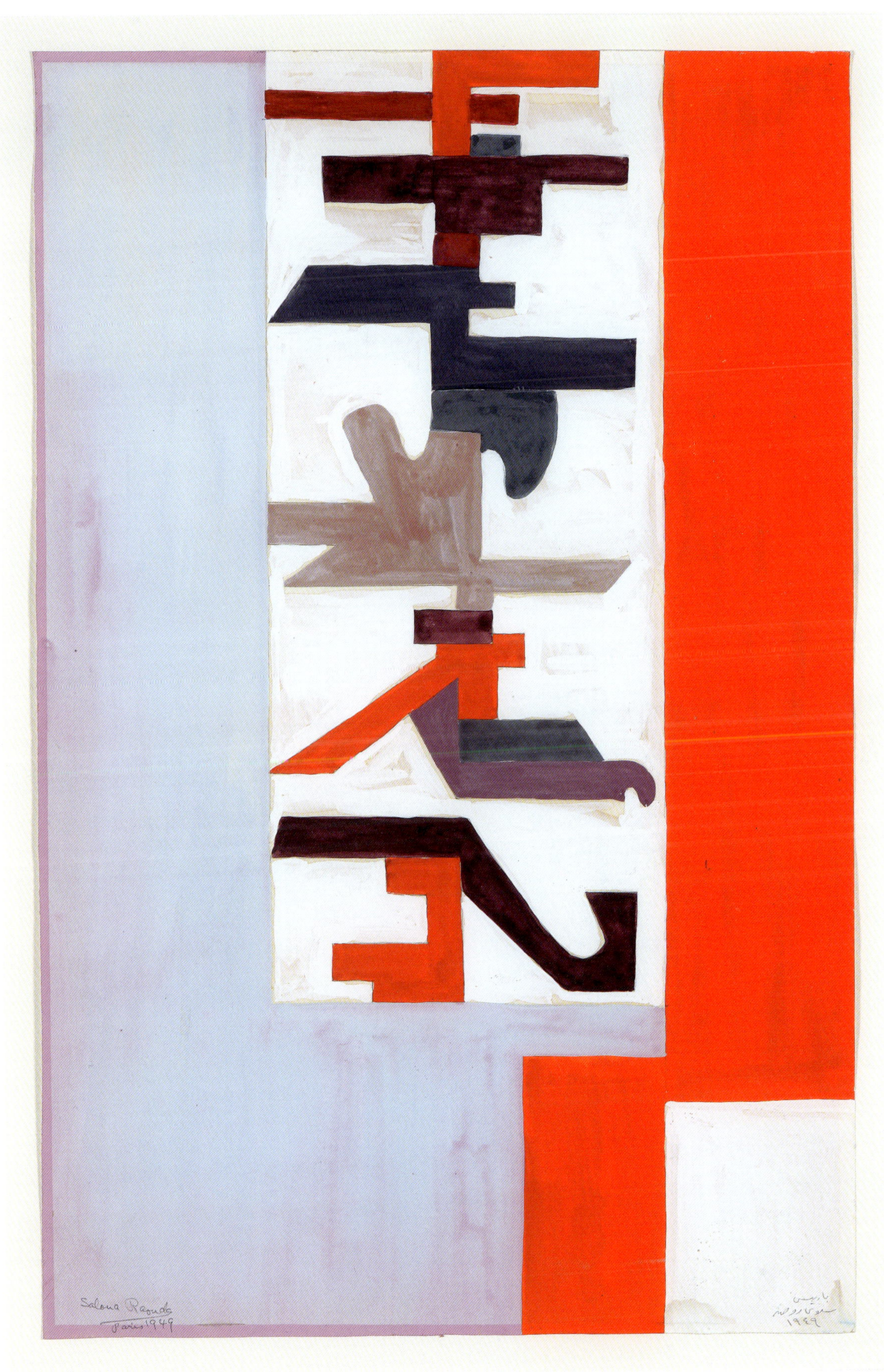
Saloua Raouda
Paris 1949

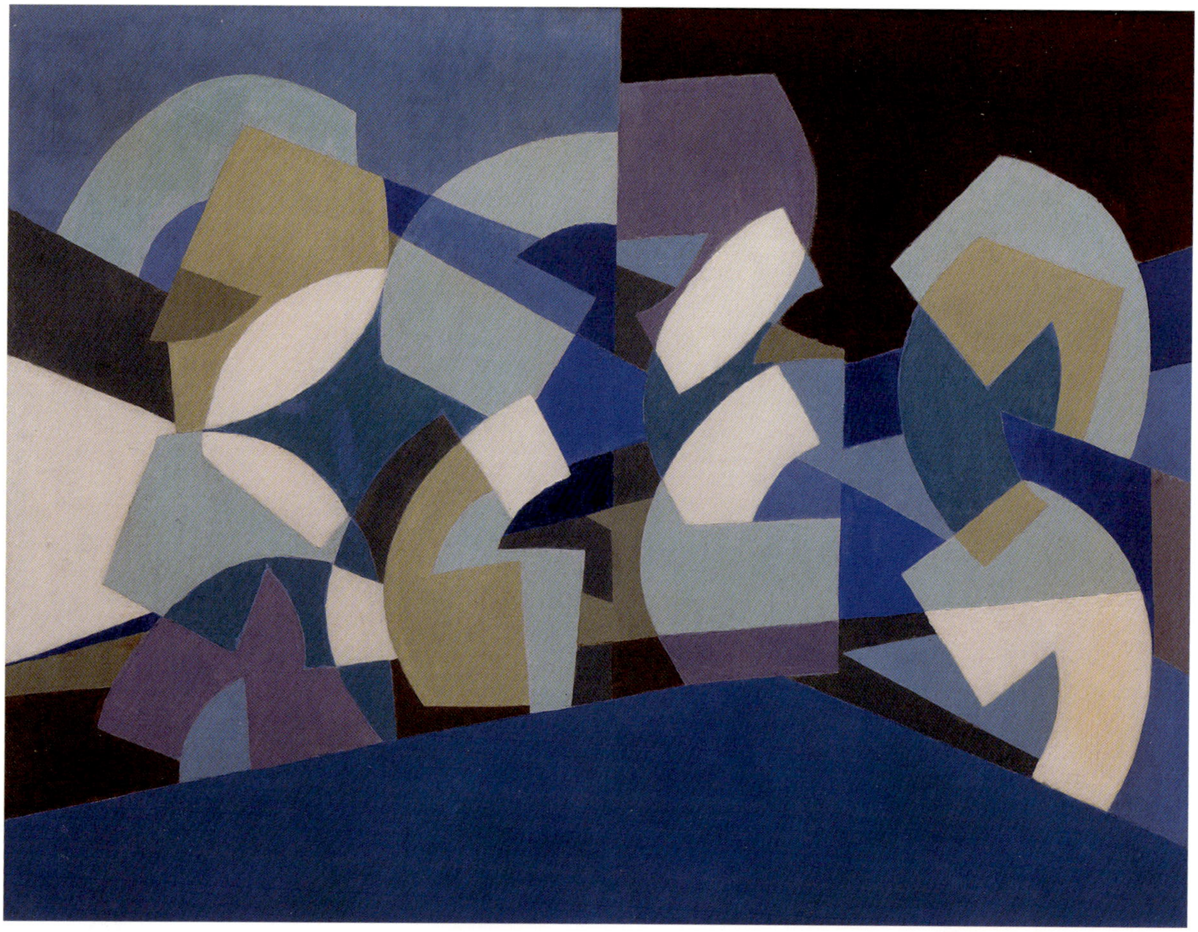

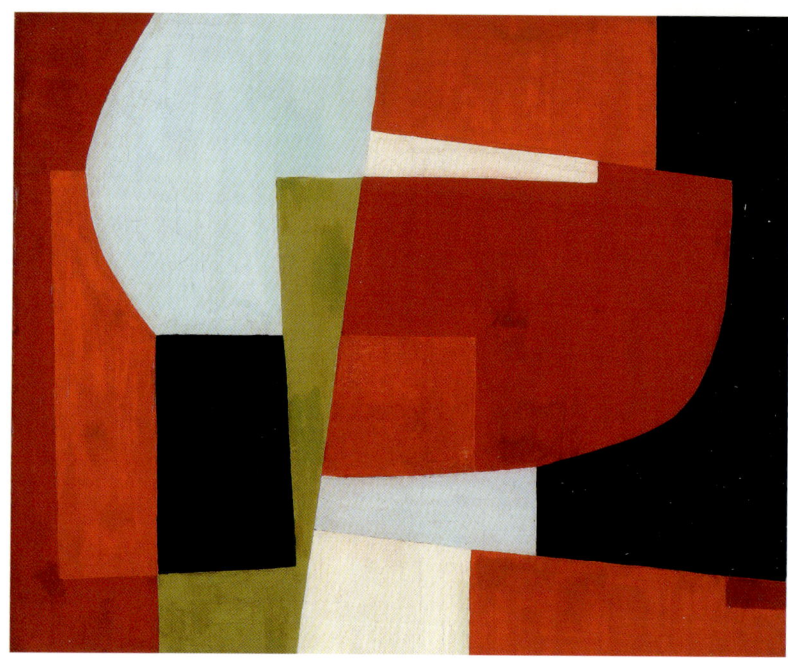

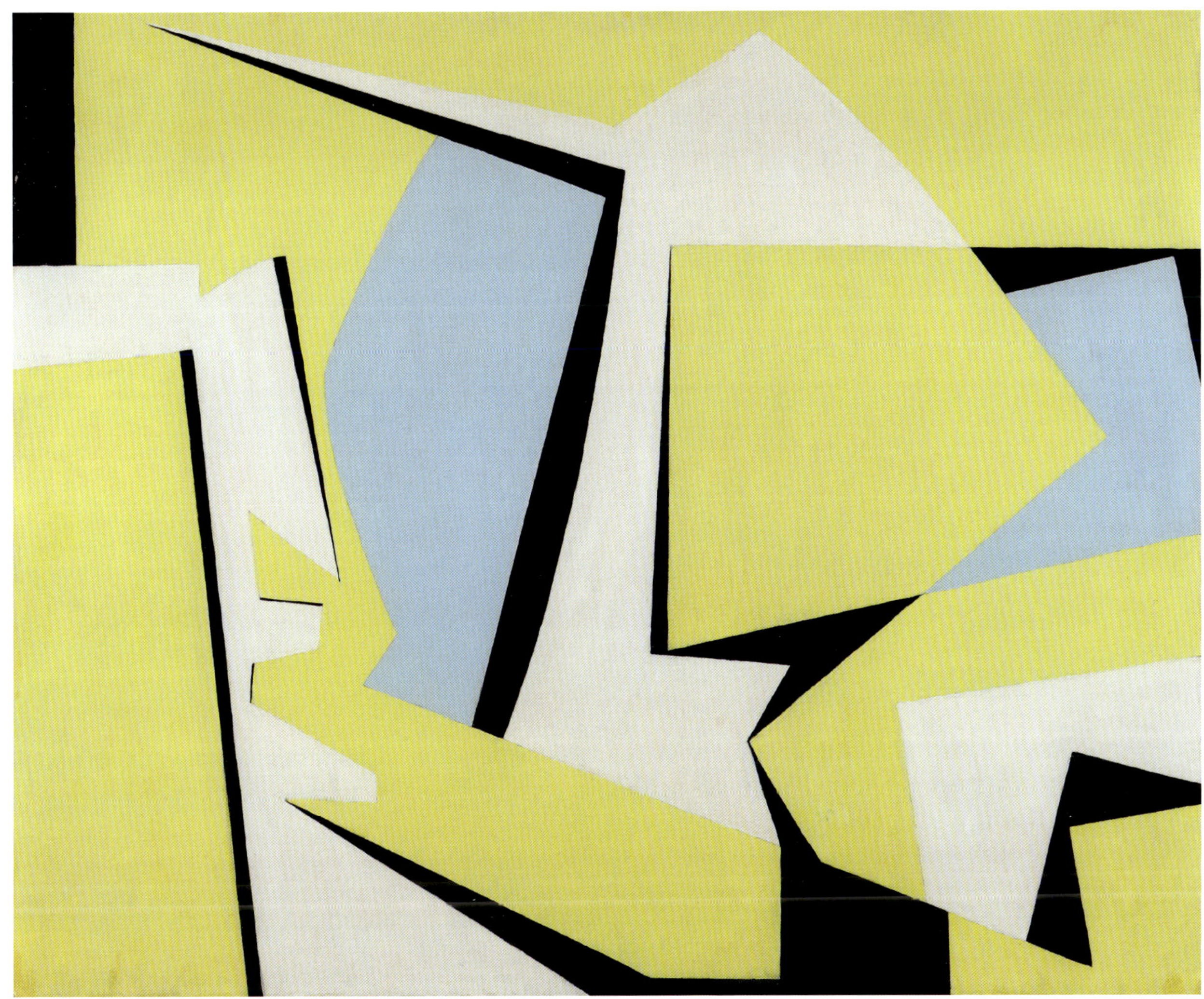

17
Composition in Blue Module 1947–51
Oil paint on canvas
59.5 × 80

18
Rhythmical Composition with Red 1951
Oil paint on canvas
24 × 31

19
Rhythmical Composition with Yellow 1952–5
Oil paint on canvas
100 × 124

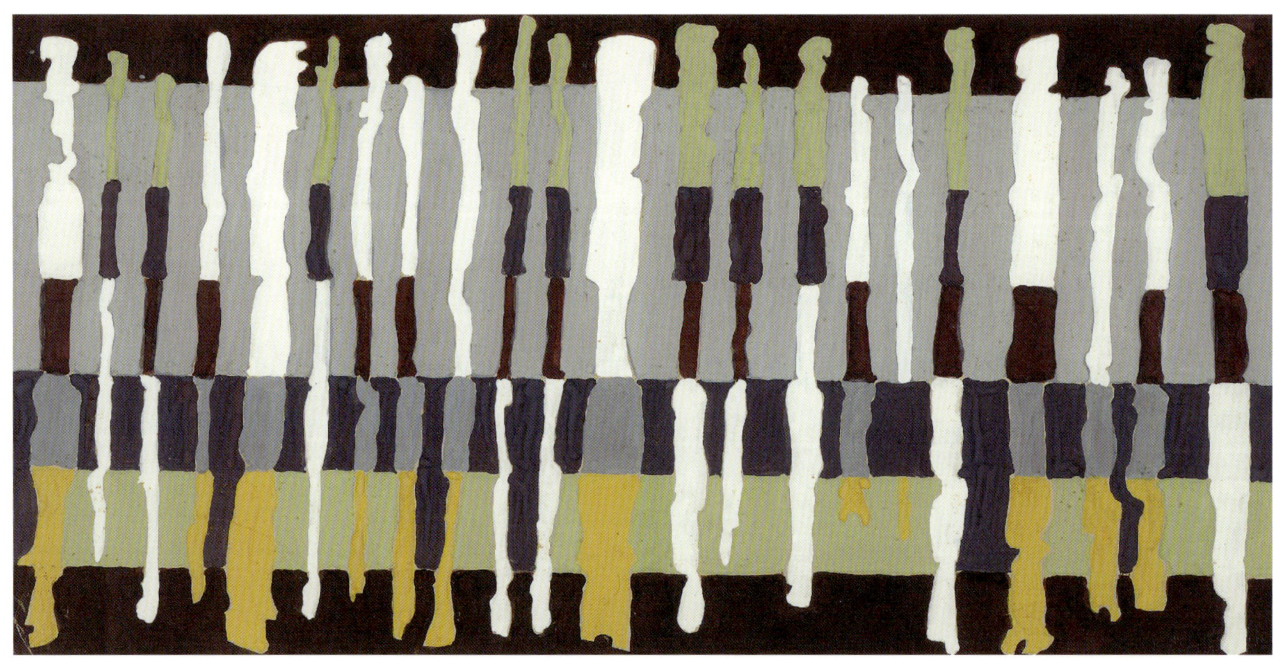

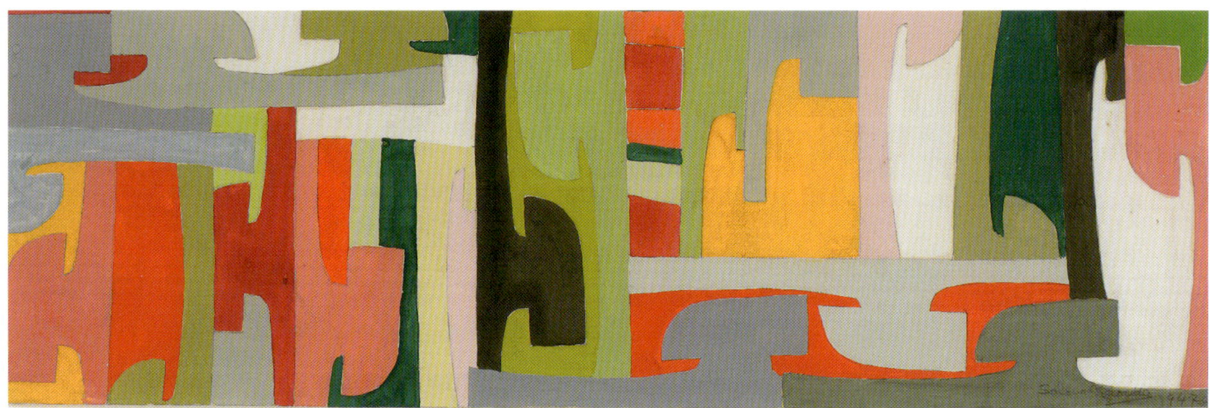

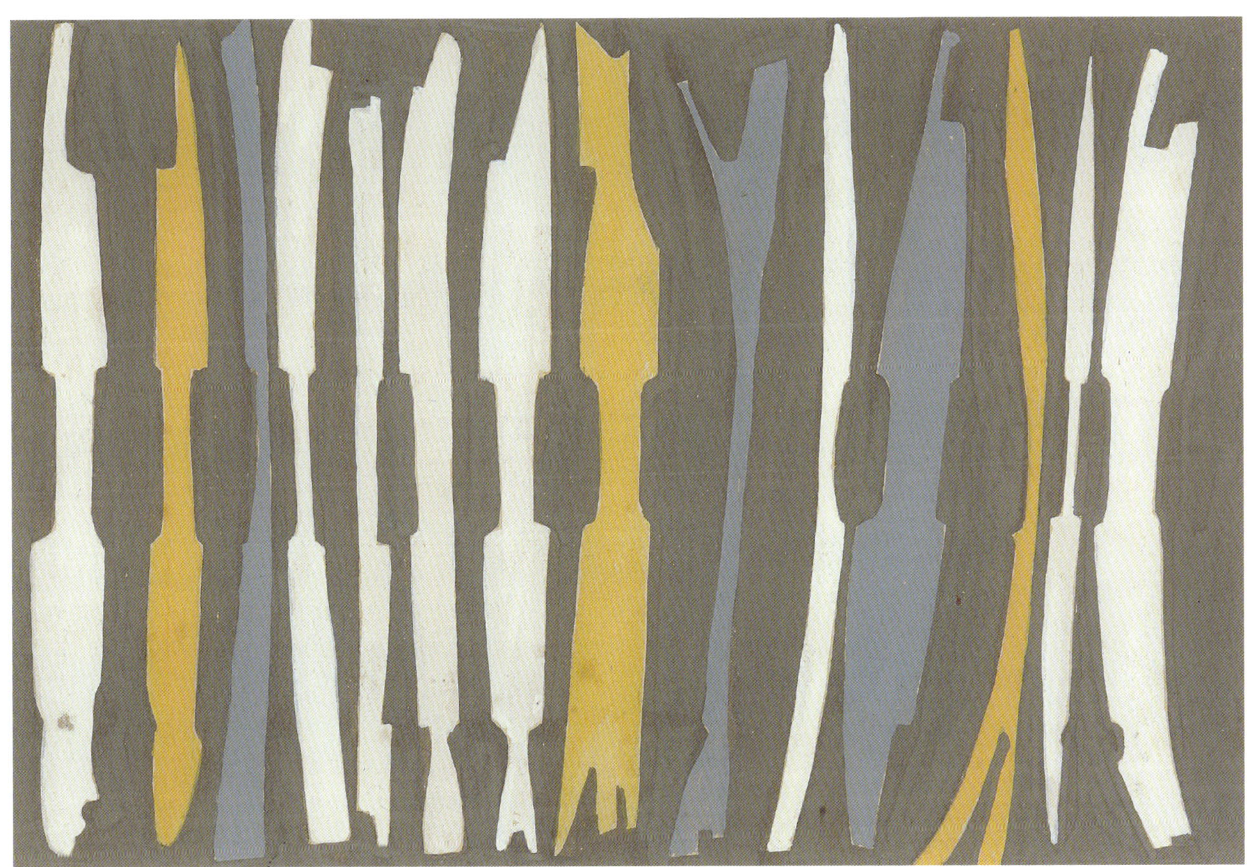

20
Visual Meter 1950s
Gouache on paper
25 × 50

21
Fractional Module (Sphinx) 1947–51
Gouache on paper
16 × 140

22
Visual Meter 1950s
Gouache on paper
20.5 × 29.5

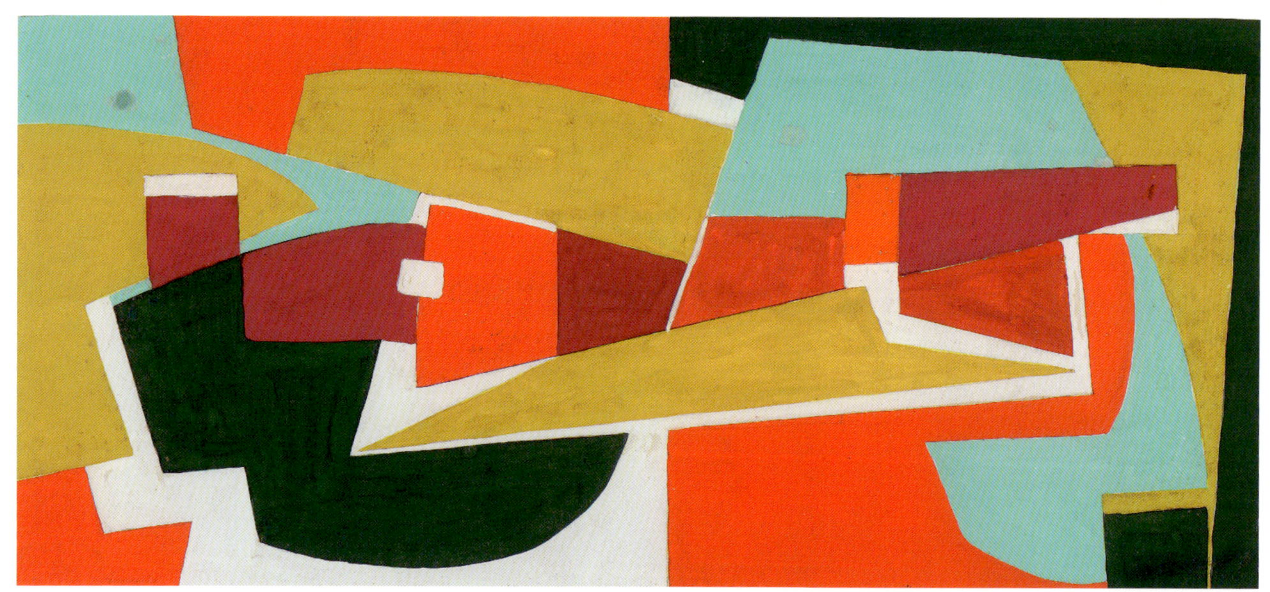

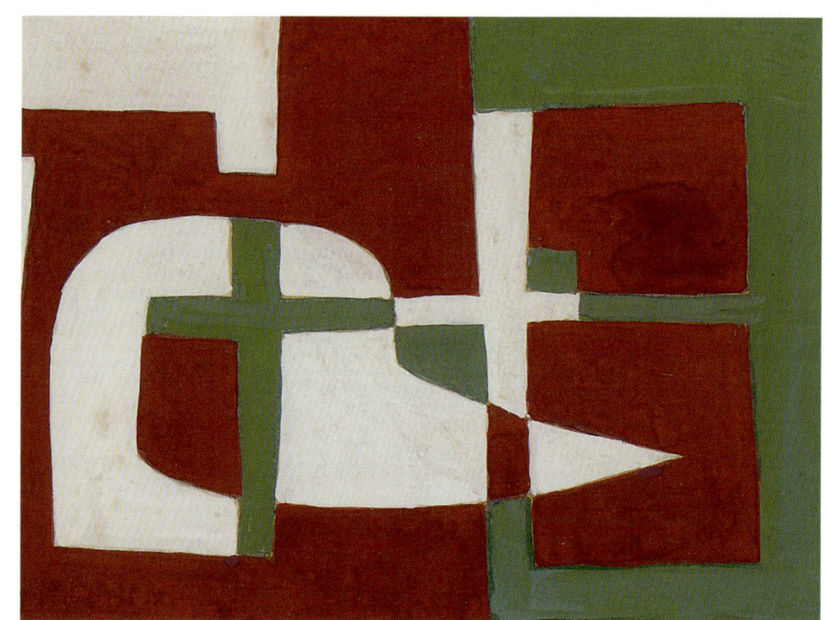

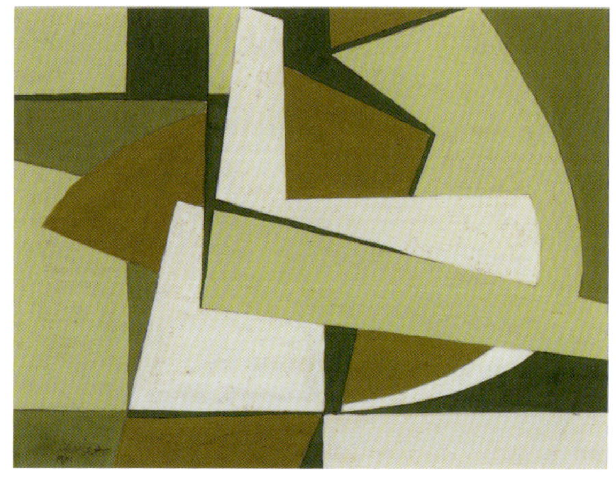

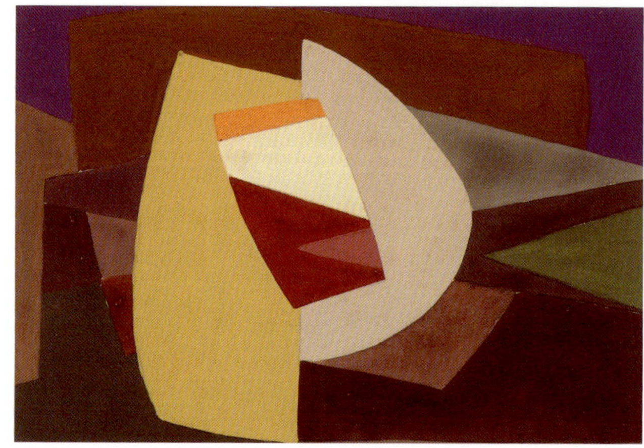

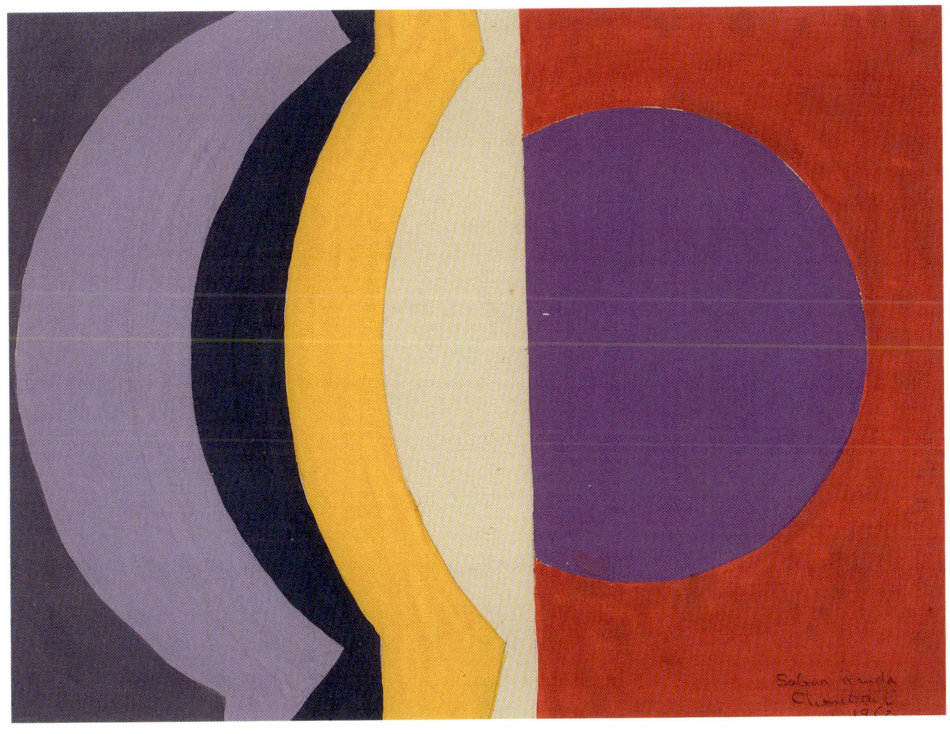

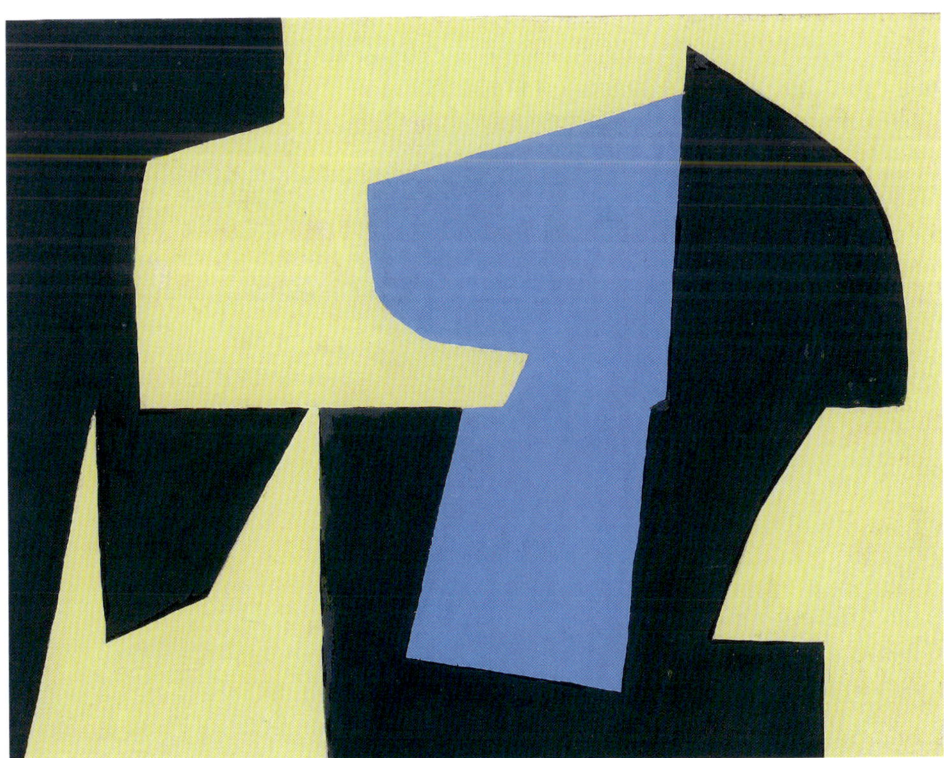

23
Gradual Rhythmical Composition 1959–60
Gouache on paper
22 × 50

24
Composition with Verticals 1952–5
Gouache on paper
10 × 13.8

25
Composition in Brown 1952–5
Gouache on paper
23 × 31

26
Rhythmical Composition 1952–5
Gouache on paper
17 × 25

27
Composition with a Circle 1956–8
Gouache on paper
25 × 32

28
Rhythmical Composition 1952–3
Gouache on paper
23 × 30

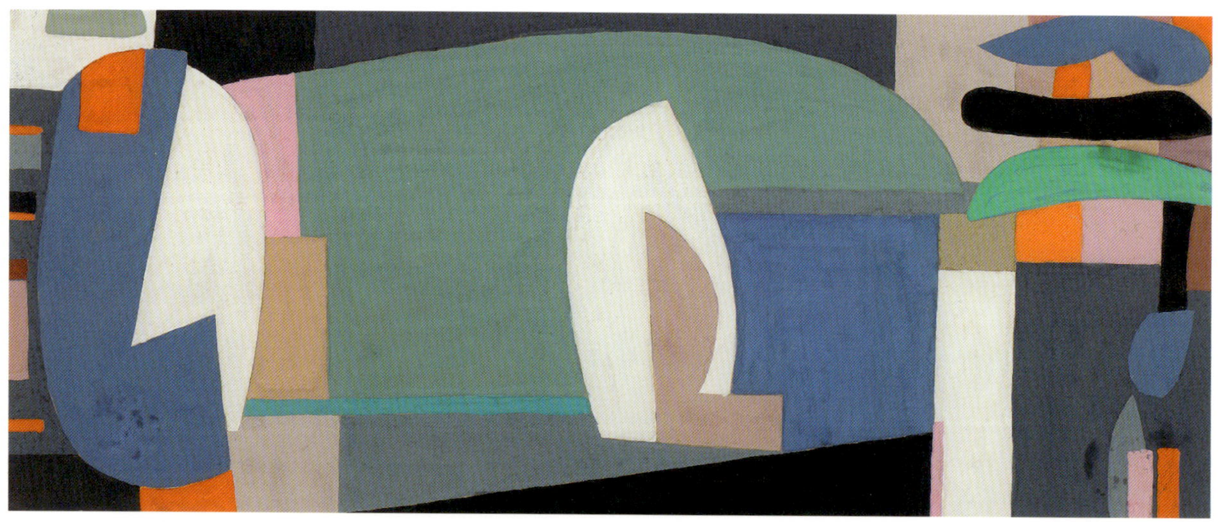

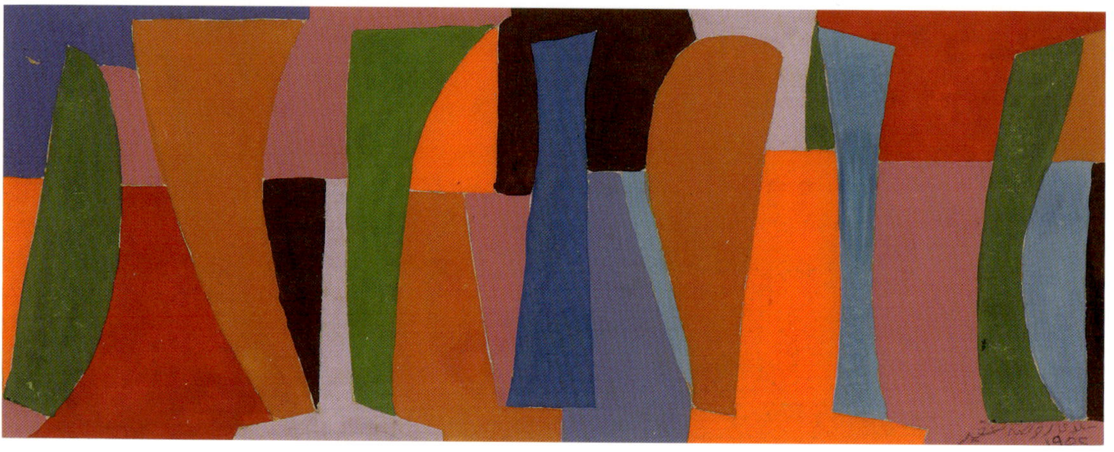

29
Composition for Tapestry 1956–8
Gouache on paper
20.5 × 49

30
Composition for Tapestry 1956–8
Gouache on paper
12 × 30.5

31
Rhythmical Composition with Blue
1956–8
Gouache on paper
33 × 24

32
(overleaf)
Composition in Yellow
1962–5
Oil paint on canvas
50 × 79.5

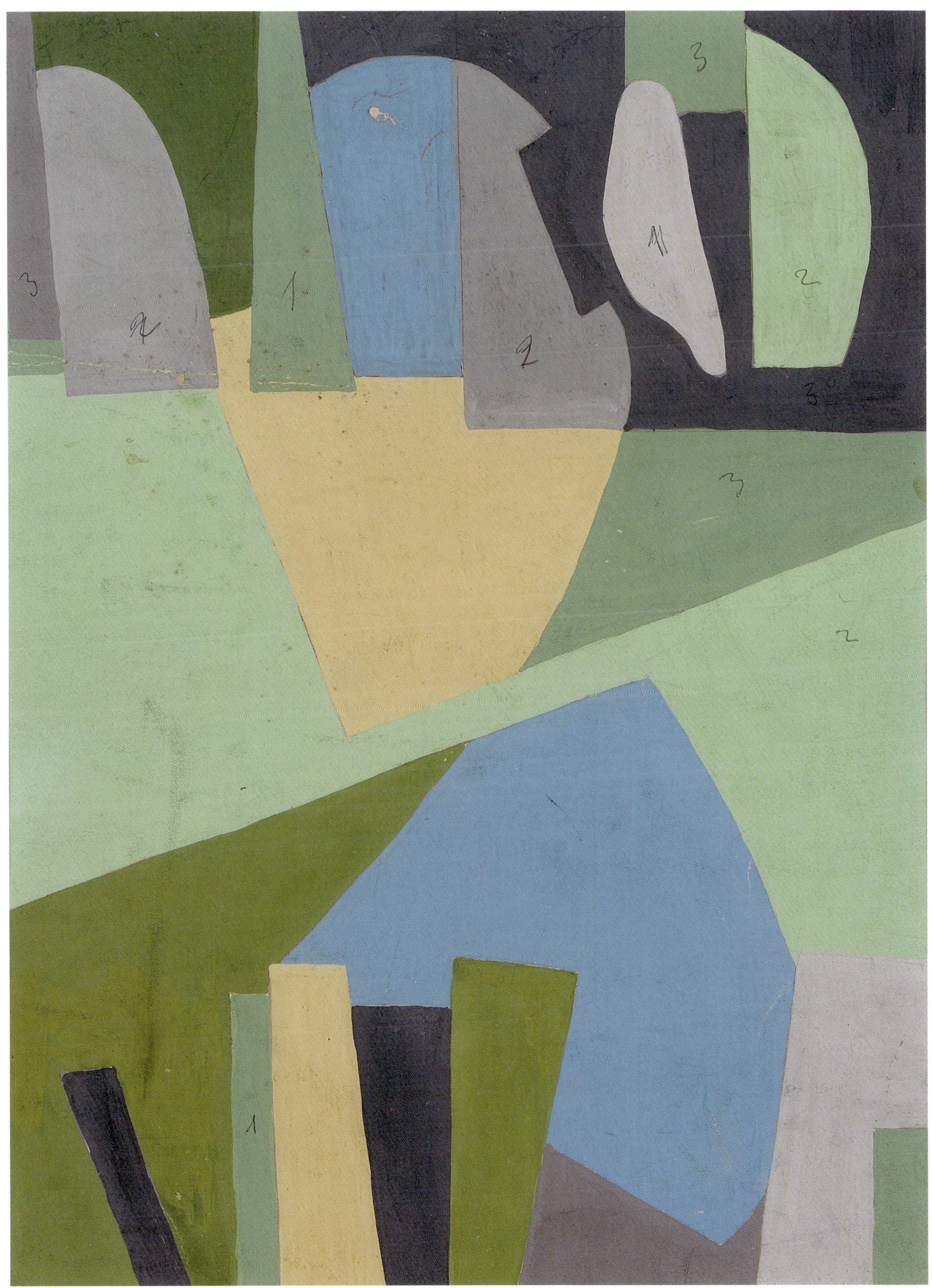

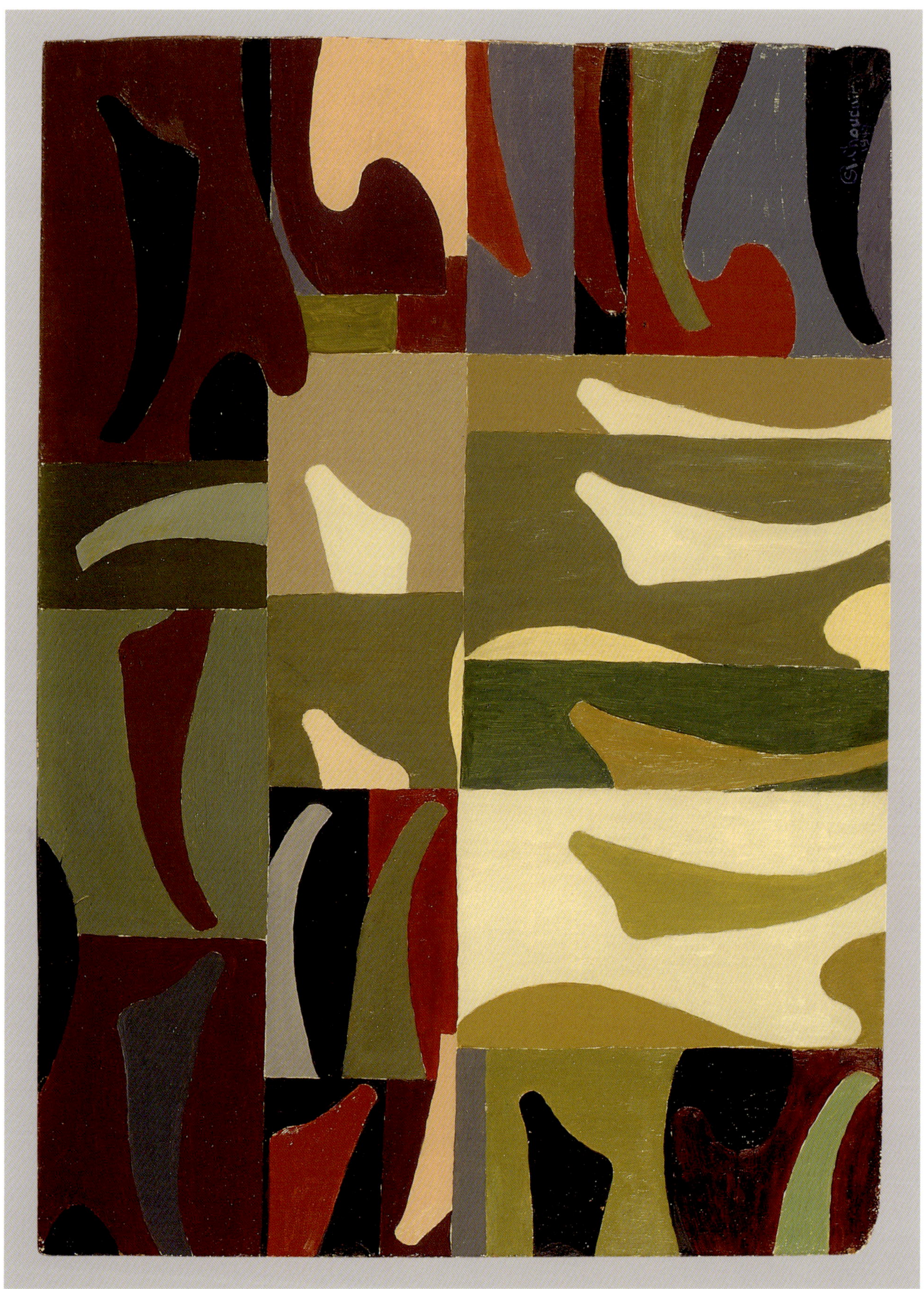

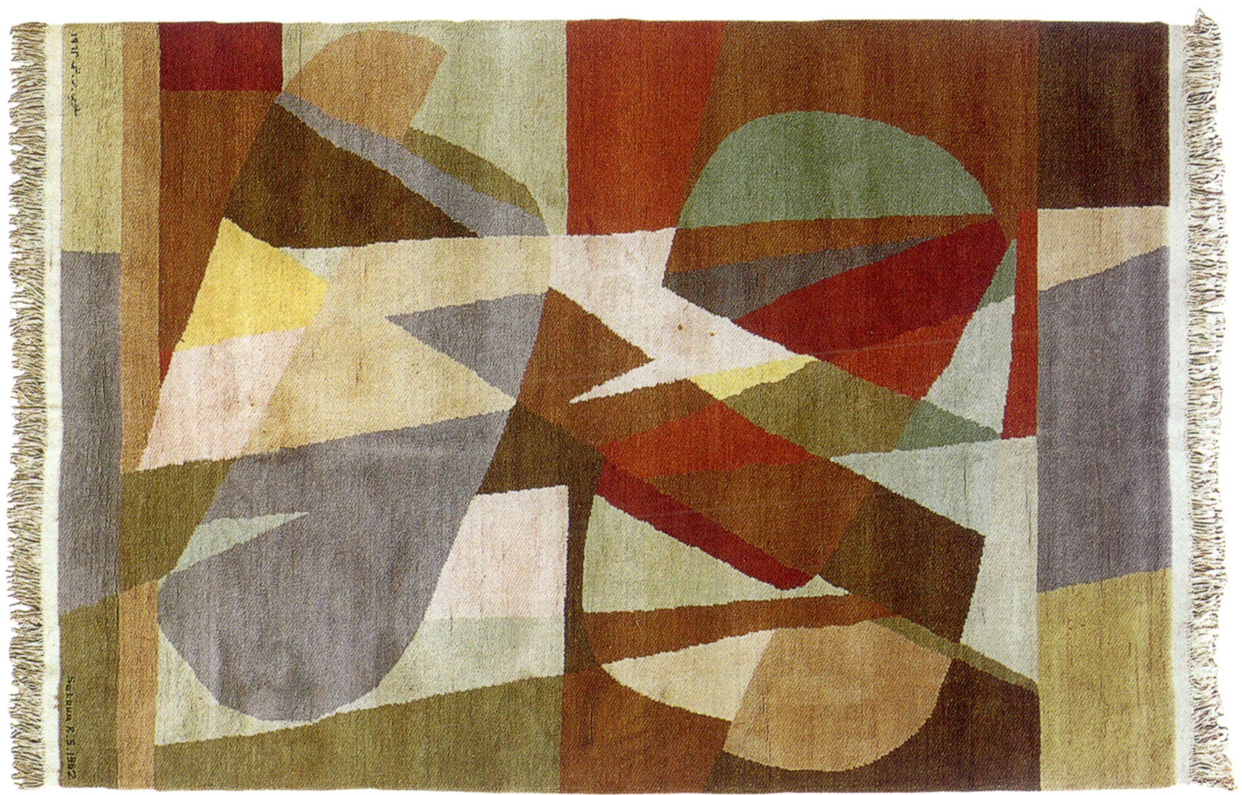

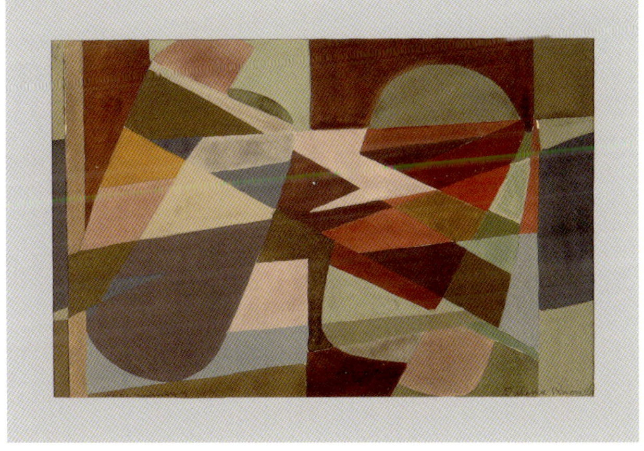

33
Fractional Module
1959–60
Oil paint on wood
60 × 45

34
Composition,
Two Forms 1961
Carpet, Persian point
178 × 275

35
Composition,
Two Ovals 1952–5
Gouache on paper
19 × 29.5

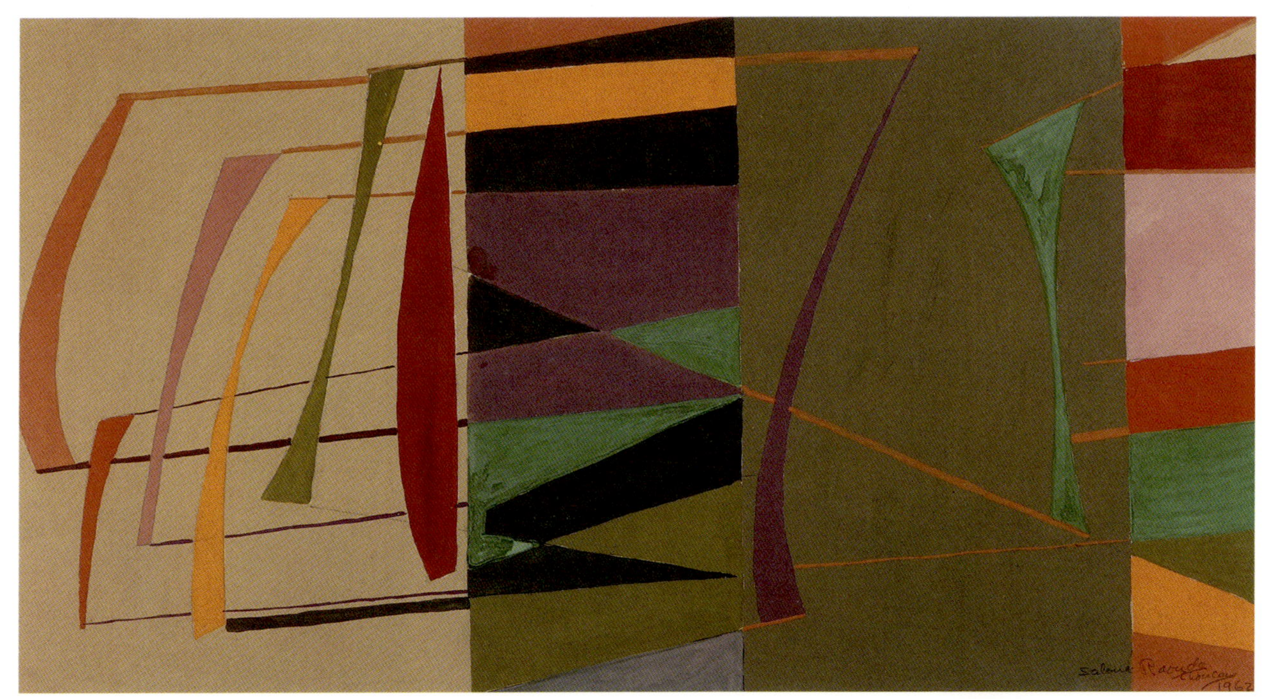

36
Composition with Arcs 1962–5
Gouache on paper
25 × 48

37
Composition with Arcs 1962–5
Gouache on paper
47 × 32

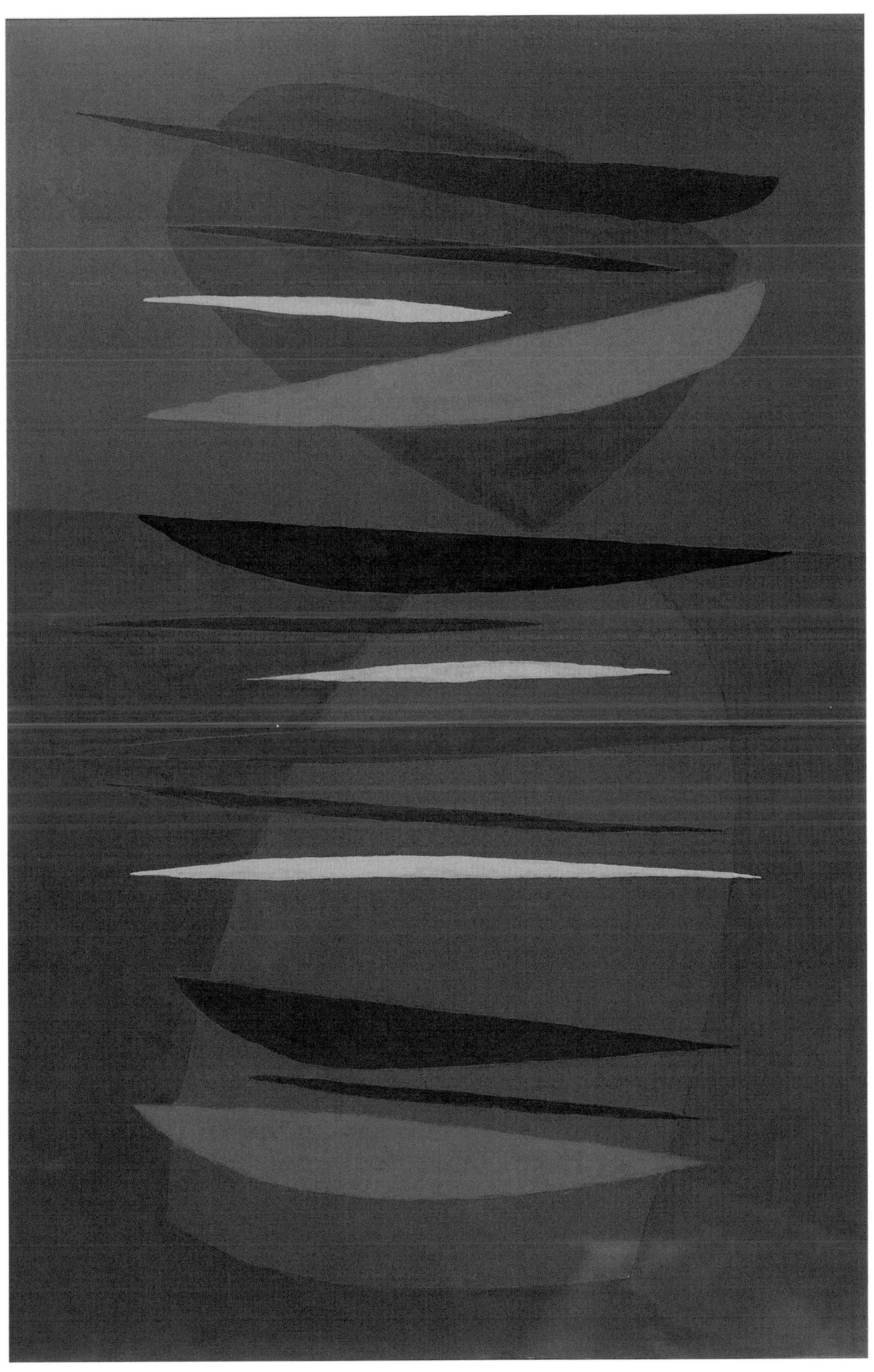

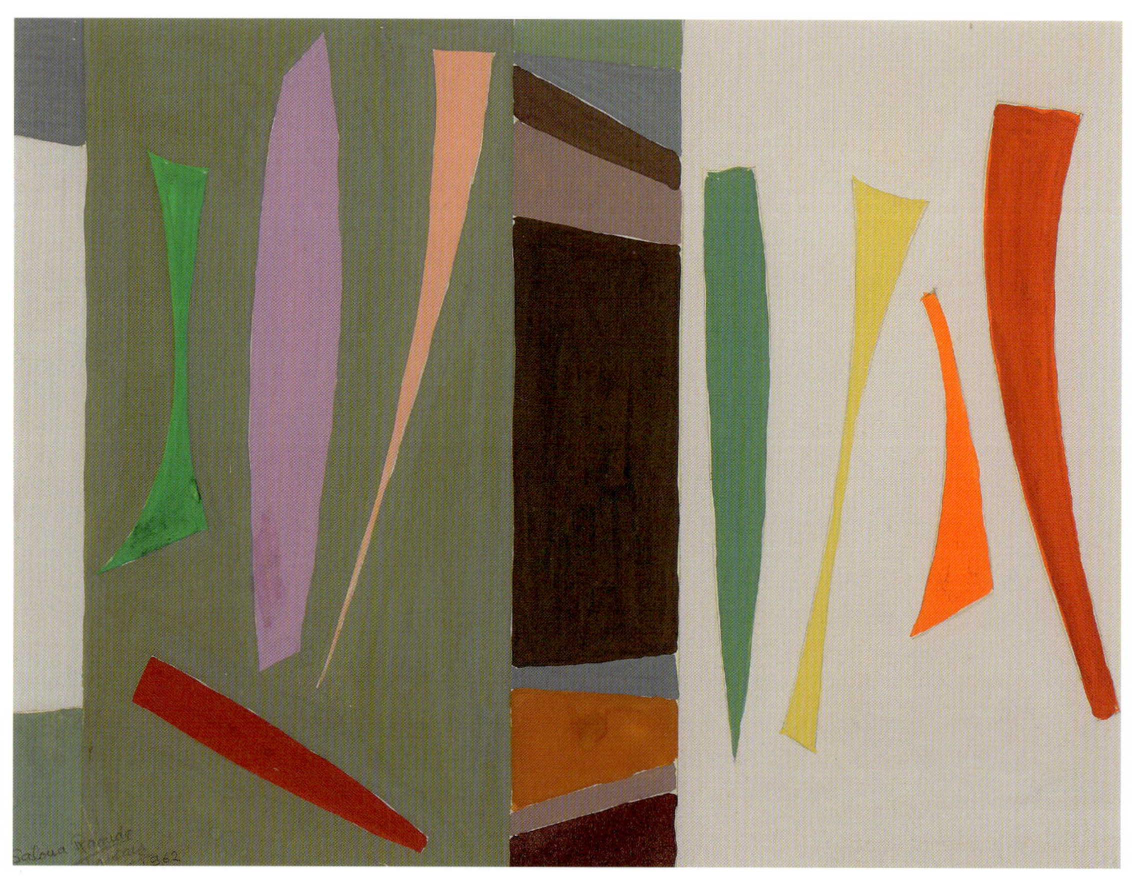

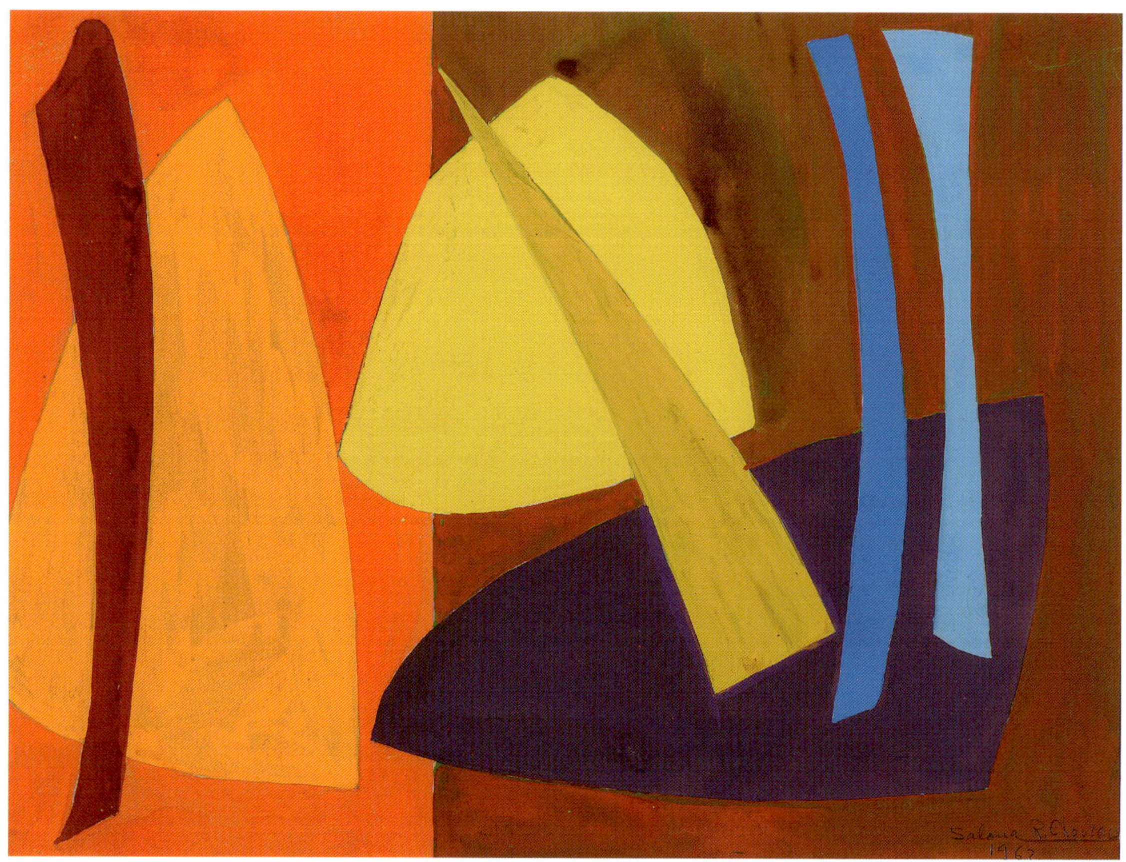

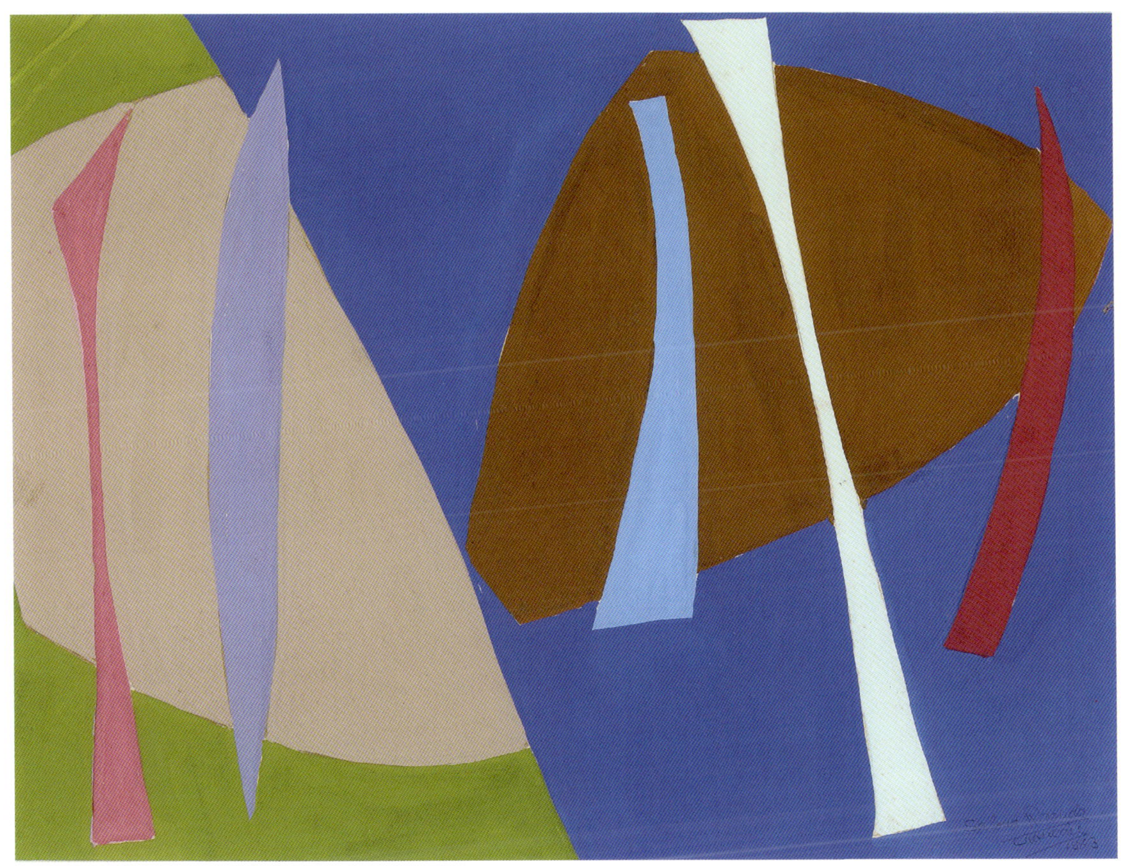

38
Composition with Arcs 1962–5
Gouache on paper
24×33

39
Composition with Arcs 1962–5
Gouache on paper
24×33

40
Composition with Arcs 1962–5
Gouache on paper
24×32.5

Distinctions That Could be Drawn *Choucair's Paris and Beirut*

A clear plastic bag, bursting with papers of various yellows and greys – this is what Saloua Raouda Choucair reached for in the cupboard next to her bed. She pulled out of it press reviews of her work and interviews conducted over forty years. Her favourites were at the top of the stack; below were the more objectionable ones, which she had scribbled over, sometimes in several different pens, crossing out 'wrong' phrases and correcting 'misinterpretations'. Interspersed were numerous photocopies which I, like other writers who had come before, could have to help me in my writing about her, along with copies of her own published writings. Sharing her personally gathered press dossier was the first thing that Choucair did when I informed the 80-year-old sculptor that I would like to focus my study on her career.

A definitive distinction between Beirut-based art-making prior to and after the 1930s can be seen in the way it came to be taken up in the local press (which was developing contemporaneously) and publicised for a wider audience than would ever enter an art gallery. With press reports of exhibitions were disseminated the ideas that people *should* enter special areas for seeing art (even if in reality they did not), and that they *should* develop special ways of relating to art and apply those experiences to reinterpreting their roles in society. In those early years of journalistic art writing an exhibition report could be front-page news, and although such reports gradually moved deeper inside the papers in the following decades, special staff were eventually hired by Beiruti papers just for writing about 'arts and culture'.[1] What these writers produced could have great impact on an artist's access to audiences, to commissions and awards. As Howard Becker has found in his study of art worlds, writing about art can reform standards for valuing art by revealing 'that [the previous] standard was too constricted, that there are in fact other things to enjoy'.[2] Beirut artists and gallery owners knew this for a fact, regularly preserving and propagating reviews of their work that upheld their own standards of value.

These texts become very important keys to understanding the role of art in society and its potential to influence, especially in situations where not a single but multiple, even conflicting, conceptions exist or are being brought deliberately into play in order to counter others. Such has certainly been the situation during the past sixty years of interpreting art in Lebanon. 'Traditional', 'European', 'Arab', 'universal', 'Ottoman', 'modern', 'Islamic', 'nationalist' and 'individual' notions of art were called upon by different protagonists to promote various projects designed to transform society. This is partly the reason why so much of the art produced seems to have existed simultaneously in categories as diverse as 'trash' and 'fine art': the same objects have been viewed at different points in history as 'traditional', 'European', 'Islamic' and 'modern'.

My interest in the stack of articles stored in Choucair's studio, whose counterparts lie in the homes of so many other locally active artists, is inspired by feminist theory that seeks to place the 'contradictoriness of socio-cultural systems center stage'.[3] Such a focus leads to an interest in 'cultural possibilities', where culture is not assumed to be shared, but contested.[4] By looking at Choucair's troubled fifty-year-long career, it is possible to study what art as a category – or what she has experienced as a 'lack' of art[5] – has meant for a Lebanon that has transformed in that time from a region mandated to France to a territorial state, from a largely feudal-agricultural economy to a cosmopolitan import-export one.[6]

The process of seeking to engage the conception of art that artists and their audiences hold when viewing art objects enables us to revisit Choucair's works with contextualised eyes. This is particularly significant when viewing pieces that appear familiar or assimilable by other standards. This is true of most socially portable objects, whose very portability gives them an ease of interpretation in various different contexts. In order to resist the temptation to take similarity of appearance, even when deliberately effected, to indicate similarity of meaning it is necessary to adopt, as far as possible, the viewpoint of the original intended audience.

Inside Beirut: importing audiences

March 1952, 'Greatly Admired in French Papers': Reception and production of a universal artist

> *Salwa Rawdah Exhibits in Paris*
> It was reported from Paris that the exhibition of paintings by Salwa Rawdah, a Lebanese artist, has met with success.
>
> Miss Rawdah graduated from Beirut College for Women in the early 40s. Then for three years she worked in the AUB library, after which she went to Paris to indulge in the field of art.
>
> Her work represents a new orientation. While impressed by the [*sic*] Western art she did not fail to give her own paintings an eastern touch.[7]

The first three words of this article (published in *Outlook* in May 1951), 'It was reported', defer judgment of Choucair's exhibition to an undefined Parisian viewer, *le tout Paris* perhaps, or 'Western art' (which apparently impressed but did not dominate Choucair). Other, less positive responses may have reached the ears of the former librarian's peers in Beirut, but the *Outlook* reviewer shouted them down by conjuring a strong French declaration of success. That the writer was in all likelihood a friend asked by Choucair to write a positive article points to the practicality of invoking an approving French audience.

Long before the days of computer simulation, a 'virtual audience' in France was able to follow Choucair back to Beirut and continue to view her shows via the journalist's pen until the late 1970s. In the first two decades of writing about Choucair's art, her compatriots almost uniformly described her oeuvre above all in terms of its relationship to the Parisian art world. 'As with Mondrian, for whom the strictest mathematical calculus orders the composition…';[8] her work is 'part of the school founded by Matisse to rebel against classical art';[9] she 'listens to the master Fernand Léger';[10] she 'was the personal friend of … Mr Plikoff, Sonia Delauney and Léger'.[11] Visitors to her latest exhibition were reminded that she had 'already held two shows in Paris',[12] had 'preoccupied the famous papers in Paris',[13] 'was greatly admired in French papers'[14] and had 'earned the admiration and appreciation of critics in France'.[15]

Perhaps most adroit in exploiting these virtual French viewers was Thuraya Malhas, another close friend of Choucair from their days together at al-Ahliyya National School for Girls. In March 1952 Malhas wrote for the widely read Arabic daily *Bayrut* on the subject of Choucair's first public exhibition, held on her return to Beirut. This was at the École supérieure des lettres just outside the old city walls, on the road leading from downtown to Damascus. Malhas' later accomplishments as a modernist poet and literary critic attest to the independence and originality of her insight. Yet what is interesting in this early exercise of her own literary talent is how she constructed her voice in relation to French art criticism. For her enthusiastic review she initially developed a very personal voice for describing Choucair's 'worldly' paintings as the result of a 'spiritual decision'. After a bold introduction, however, Malhas muted her own voice and devoted three quarters of her article to the assessments of three French critics. Their opinions, presented as the objective voice of universal art criticism, literally overwhelmed the author's own assertions. Malhas had deliberately constructed this imbalance because she considered it a sign of the 'talent enjoyed by our international Arab artists, and of (Choucair's) high stature in the world of modern art, that Julian Alvard and writers for the Parisian reviews *Art d'aujourd'hui* and *Combat, Art* should take it upon themselves to discuss Choucair's 1951 solo exhibition at Galerie Colette Allendy and her participation in the *Salon des Réalités Nouvelles* in June the same year. The concurring praise was also a sign, and one no less significant, that Malhas' own, very personal and unconventional take on Choucair's unusual art was itself valuable and valid.

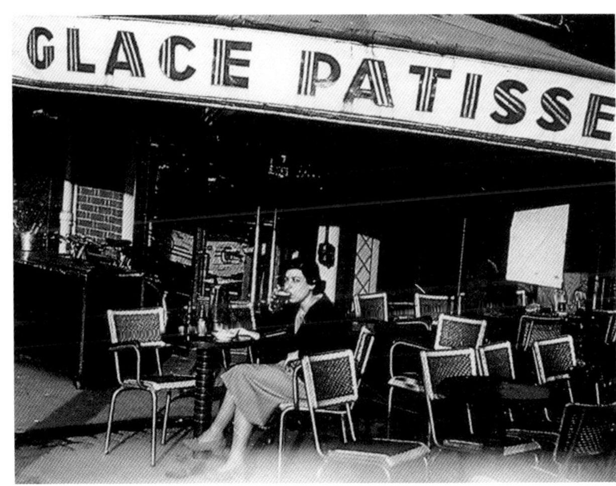

41
Choucair sitting outside a café in Paris, 1948

Recognising the invocation of French approval as a strategy for promoting Beiruti art does not invalidate judgments such as Malhas' about the work of Choucair. However, measuring the value of Choucair's art by the yardstick of modernist Parisian standards was not an entirely valid strategy. For one thing, the argument that art must inevitably change swiftly called to mind the opposite view, that it was about creating lasting beauty. This familiar view of art as an embodiment of beauty lurked in some reviews and threatened to elbow Choucair's work out of the category of art.

For the next two decades commentators in Beirut would struggle to evaluate Choucair's art in terms of the standardised metropolitan ideal of beautiful expression. The underlying assumption was that aesthetic splendour, whether naturalistic or abstract, should be understood as the rightful descendant of the nineteenth-century beaux-arts ideal with its Graeco-Roman pedigree. A second problem of this tactic of regarding Choucair's art in the light of contemporary French practice was that it disregarded two important factors: the distinctions Choucair made between her own work and that of her counterparts in Paris; and the tactics used by those in the Parisian art scene to distinguish their work from their peers as they jockeyed for position in their bid to define contemporary art. While art-writers of the 1950s chose to align Choucair's work with dominant Parisian schools, labelling her paintings either 'abstract' or 'expressive', looking again at her paintings can also spark consideration of her ability to cross boundaries within the Paris schools, where she was a student, establishing new lines between alternative approaches and, indeed, separating her own work from that of her peers.

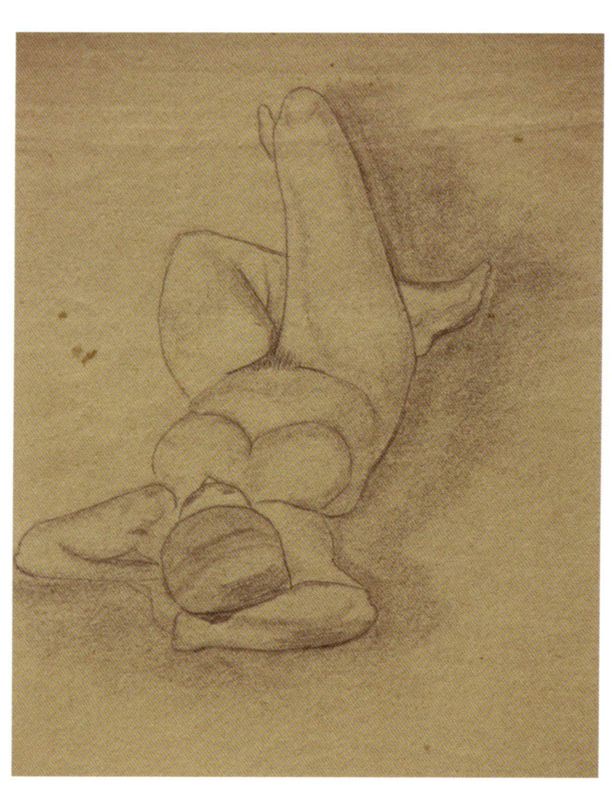

42
Reclining Nude 1948
Graphite on paper
29.5 × 23.5

Producing art and internal boundaries in Paris

A snapshot of Choucair having an espresso at an empty Parisian café in the autumn of 1948 has the sad air of a tourist in low season (fig.41). The appearance of this young woman surrounded by so many empty seats underlines French concerns about the country's new role in the aftermath of the Second World War. In late July 1948 Choucair accompanied her brother-in-law on a business trip to a Paris that was still reeling from the destruction of war, with a population struggling to cope with rationing of food, fuel, electricity – and coffee.[16] France stood clearly in second place to America, both economically and politically,[17] but French political leaders hoped that the country's cultural wealth would compensate for such lacks and that her great artistic resources would bring the world back to the 'universal fountain of art'.[18] Yet, as the photograph shows, most of the seats at that universal fountain were empty.

The postwar years were a tumultuous time for the Paris art scene. With strong competition from New York, artists active in Paris fought for the very future of artistic practice and strenuously resisted prescriptive directions and styles.[19] As a result, Choucair found herself presented with scores of options for studying art, and she seems to have set out to make the most of the opportunities open to her. While attending classes at the conservative École des beaux-arts, where she took lessons in drawing, mural painting, engraving and sculpture, she also frequented the more loosely structured Académie de la Grande Chaumière atelier, which welcomed amateurs, foreigners and others who were unable to enrol at the École. Thus she had one foot in the orthodox establishment and the other in its long-established alternative. Straddling this division, Choucair 'gained experience' (as she put it) and took up life-drawing (fig.42).[20] In 1949 she invited her friend Najla Tannus ʿAkrawi to attend a lecture given by Fernand Léger with her at the École des beaux-arts:

> One day she took me with her to Beaux-Arts to attend a lecture by Léger. He was already a renowned artist then. [He talked about] how the artist composes his tableaux, saying 'Don't assume that abstract art is far from nature; it isn't'. He picked up a branch and set it down. He got a piece of newspaper and placed it next to the branch. He got a piece of wood and put it next to them. He would use all of these elements in abstract art, except that he would have an idea to express without doing their 'portrait', without doing the art that the camera does today – 'it's not necessary to work that way', he explained.[21]

'Akrawi recalls that Choucair was impressed with Léger's ideas and it was probably following this lecture that she joined his atelier, crossing another boundary within the Paris art scene. John-Franklin Koenig, an American painter who arrived in France the same year as Choucair, has said that Léger, himself just back from a sojourn in New York, 'was one of the most "modernist" and well-known artists who operated an academy of painting, but all his students were forced to paint *à la Léger*'.[22]

Of all the artists mentioned by name in early discussions of Choucair's art, Léger occurs most frequently and appears as a sort of progenitor to Choucair's idiosyncratic style. Some of her works certainly demonstrate her facility for mobilising the visual tropes popularised by Léger. In examining the nature of Choucair's apparent affiliation to the famous painter, however, it is helpful to understand the workings of the atelier. A series of three gouaches by Choucair and originally shown at the École supérieure des lettres provides an unexpected vehicle for this (figs.50–2). These three were among the paintings identified by critics in 1952 as examples of 'expressive' (as opposed to 'geometric') art. In all three images four naked women are gathered awkwardly around a table (or couch?) covered in red-checked cloth, drinking tea and reading from a large tome titled *Les Peintres Célèbres*. Their rigid poses (one an odalisque!), signal that they are models. Whereas models are more usually summoned at the instigation of painters, in Choucair's scene it is the other way round: the models invoke the painters, making them the subject of *their* inquiry and *their* spectatorship. We are prompted to ask what they read about these celebrated painters. Looking at these inquisitive models, we are reminded that at this point in his career Léger was retreating from his purely geometric compositions, which had largely alienated him from the French public, and had begun to reintroduce figuration. This firmly re-established him in Paris as the hero of the French Communist Party.[23] By the time Choucair was studying with Léger he was held in the highest regard, as a figure whose status spoke to the shifting boundaries in avant-garde artistic practice in France. It is highly relevant that a significant set of the pictures Choucair made in Léger's studio deals explicitly with issues of artistic status and pedigree.

Choucair's curious scenes are probably based on one of Léger's most famous paintings, *Le Grand Déjeuner* 1921 (Museum of Modern Art, New York),[24] itself a take on Manet's scandalous picnic scene, *Déjeuner sur l'herbe* 1863 (Musée d'Orsay), which in turn alluded to the work of Titian. In Léger's composition three women and a cat crowd round a small table.[25] One holds an open book in her voluptuous lap, but she

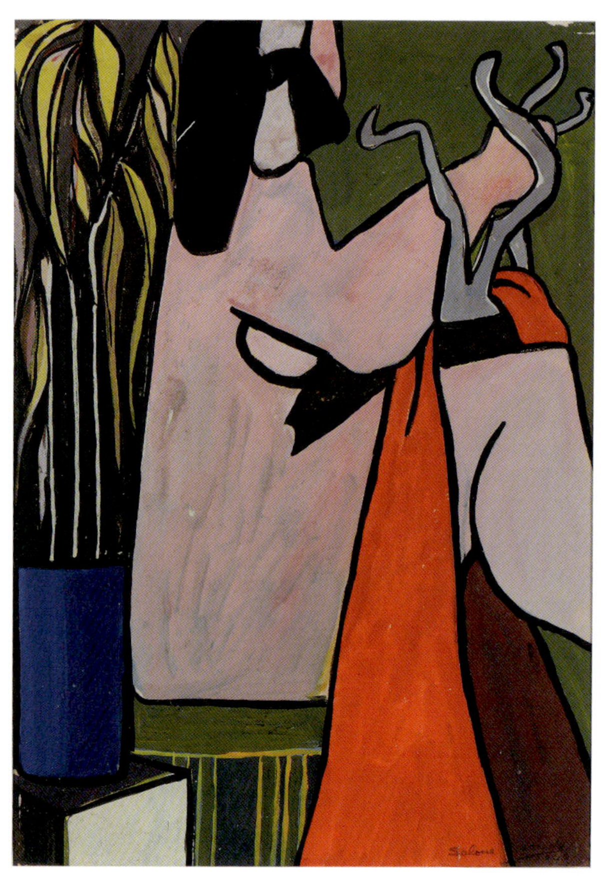

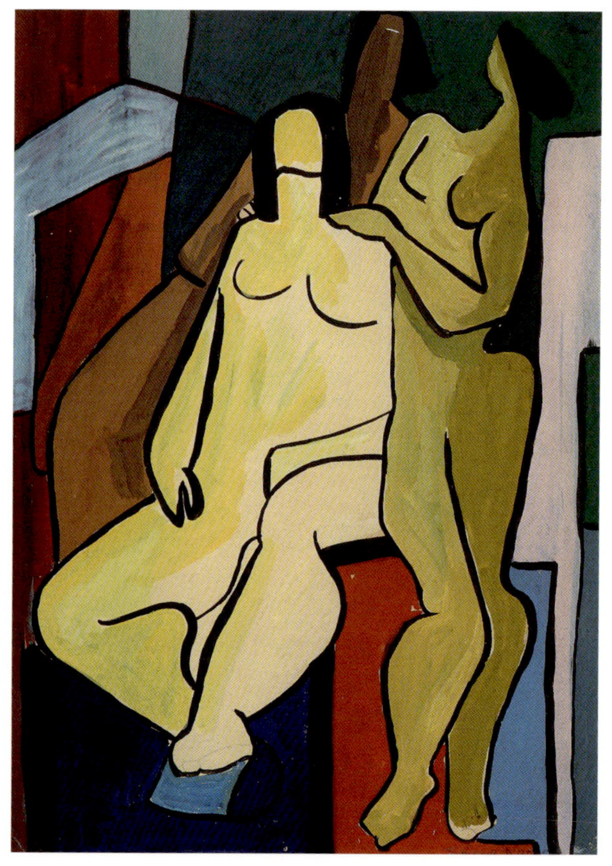

43
Nude with a Tree 1948–9
Gouache on paper
36 × 25

44
Les Trois Graces 1948
Gouache on paper
35.5 × 25

45
Untitled 1948–9
Gouache on paper
37 × 26

46
Nude with Roses 1948–9
Gouache on paper
25 × 36

47
Untitled 1948–9
Gouache on paper
36 × 25

48
Nude with Iris 1948–9
Gouache on paper
36 × 25

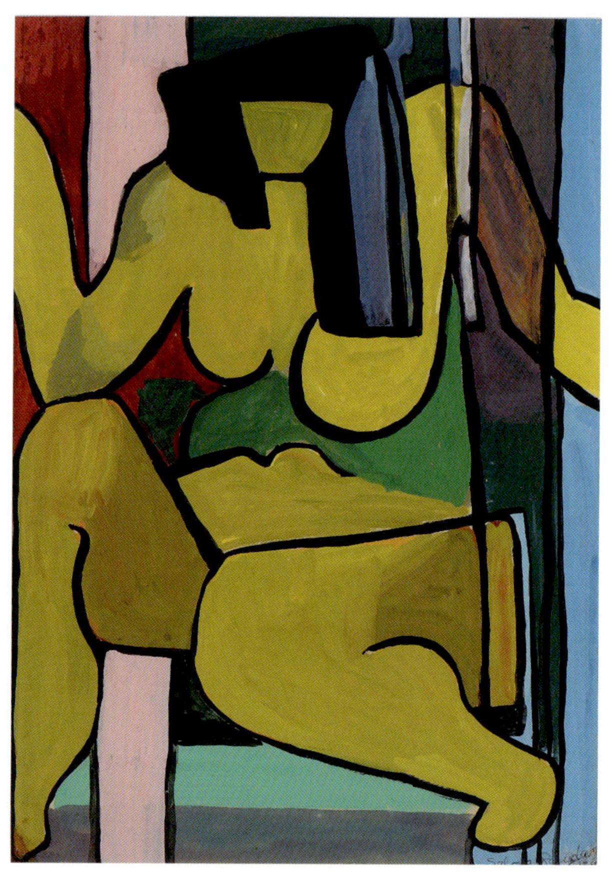

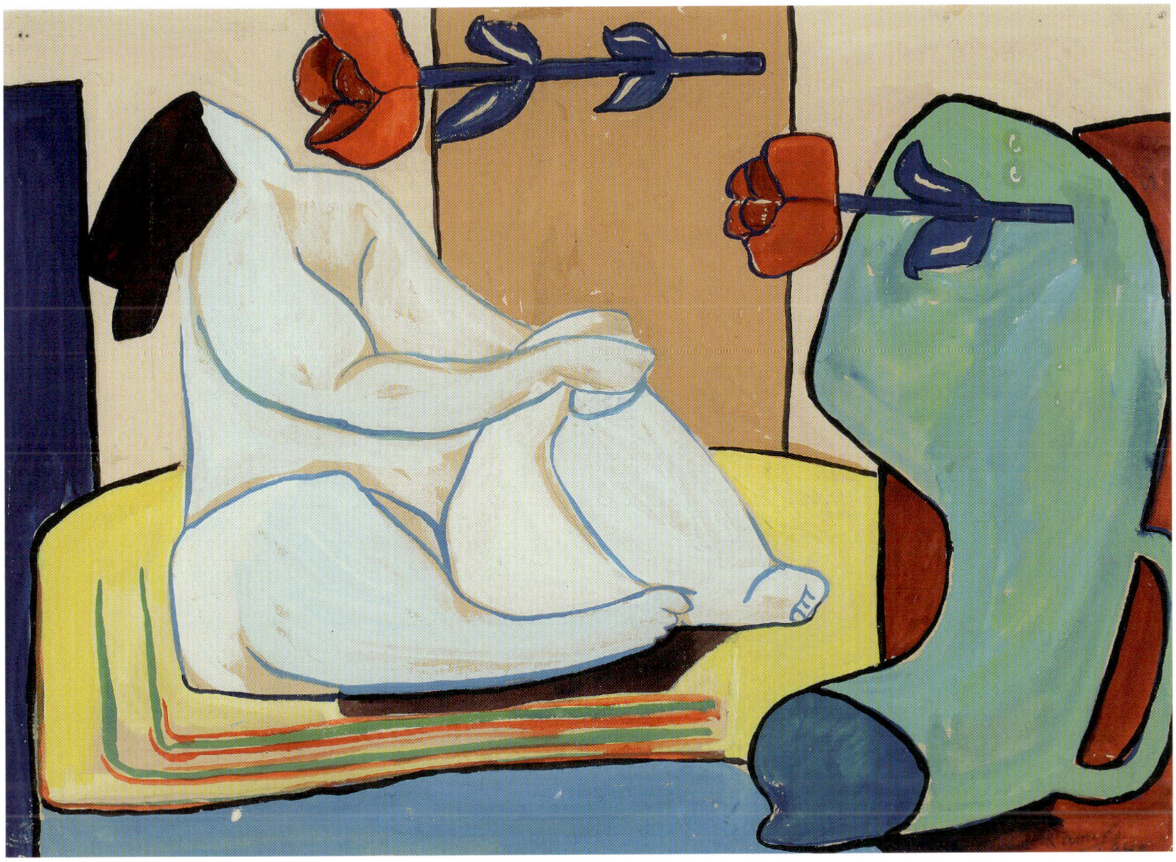

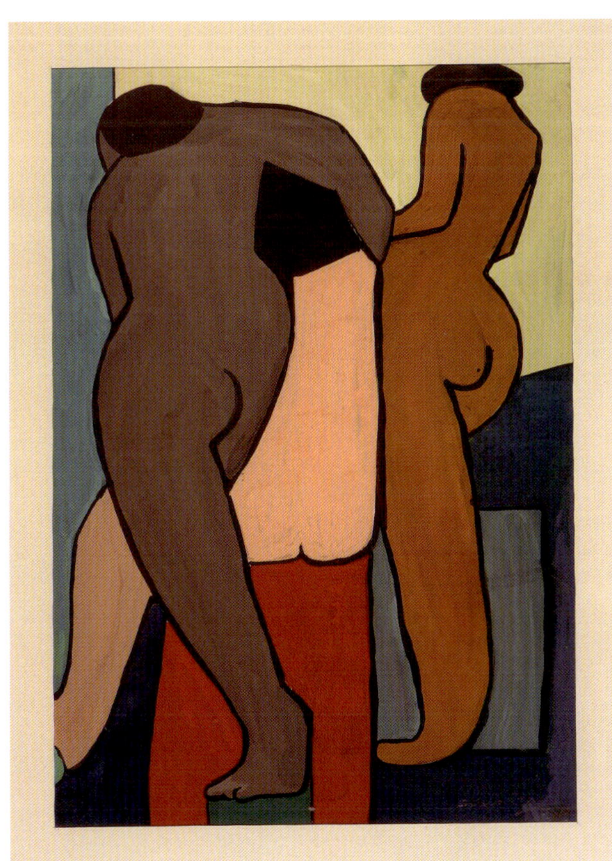

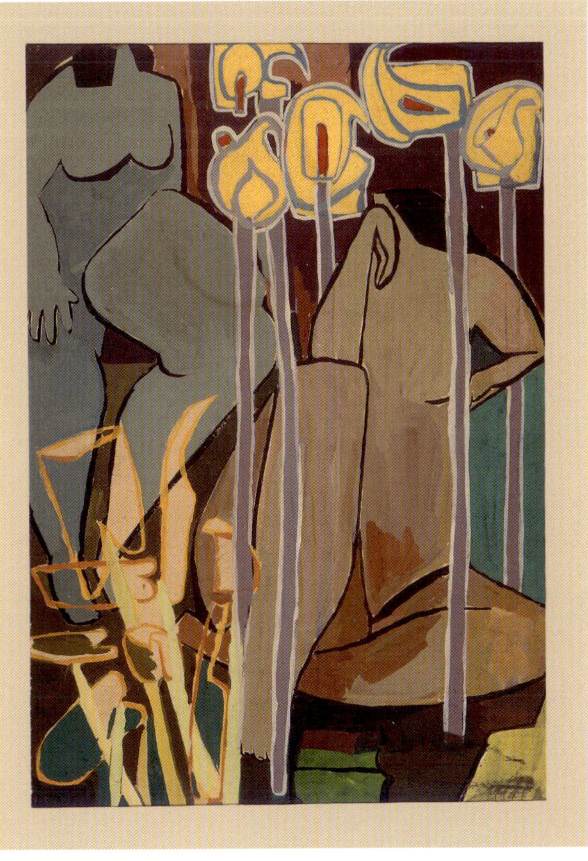

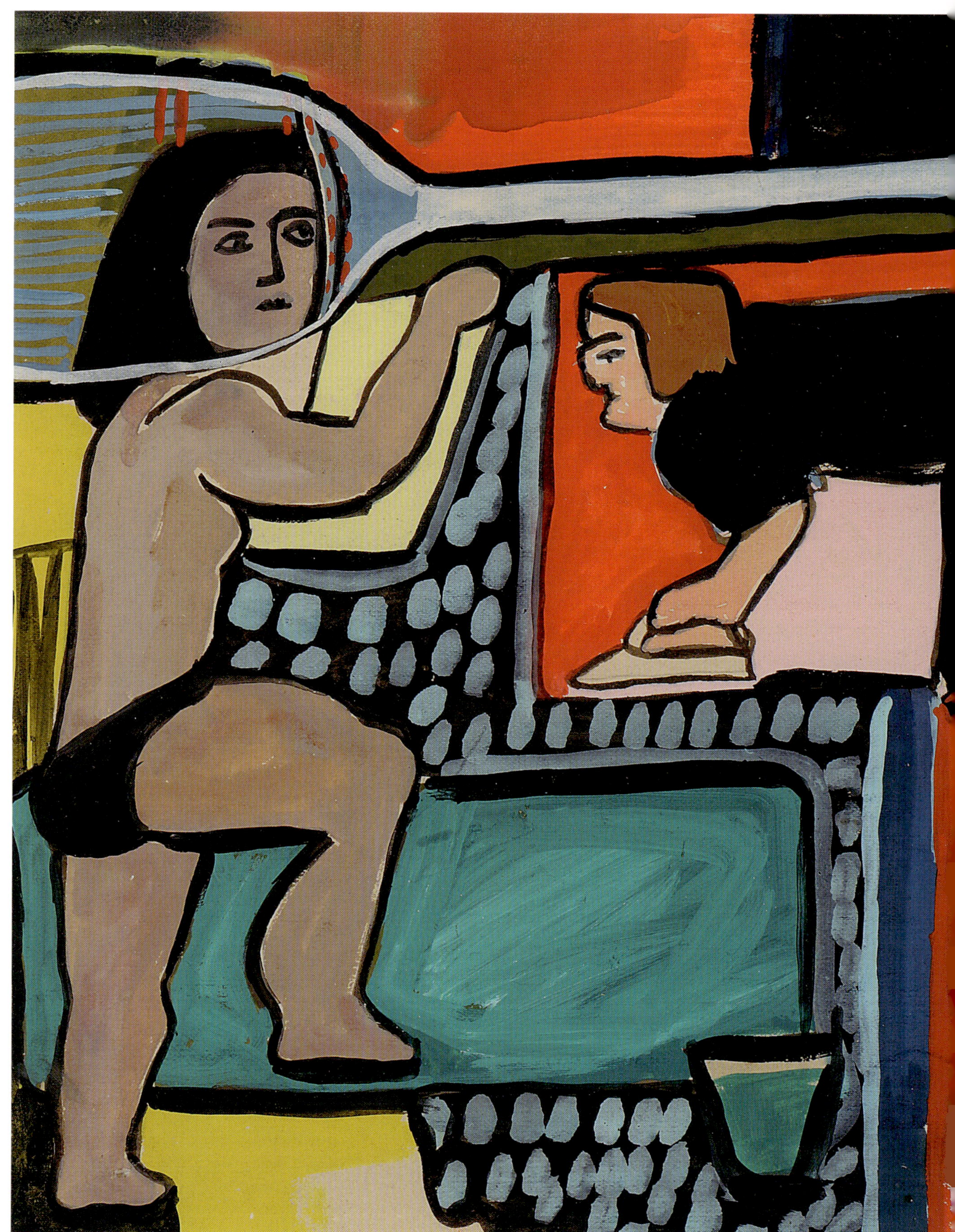

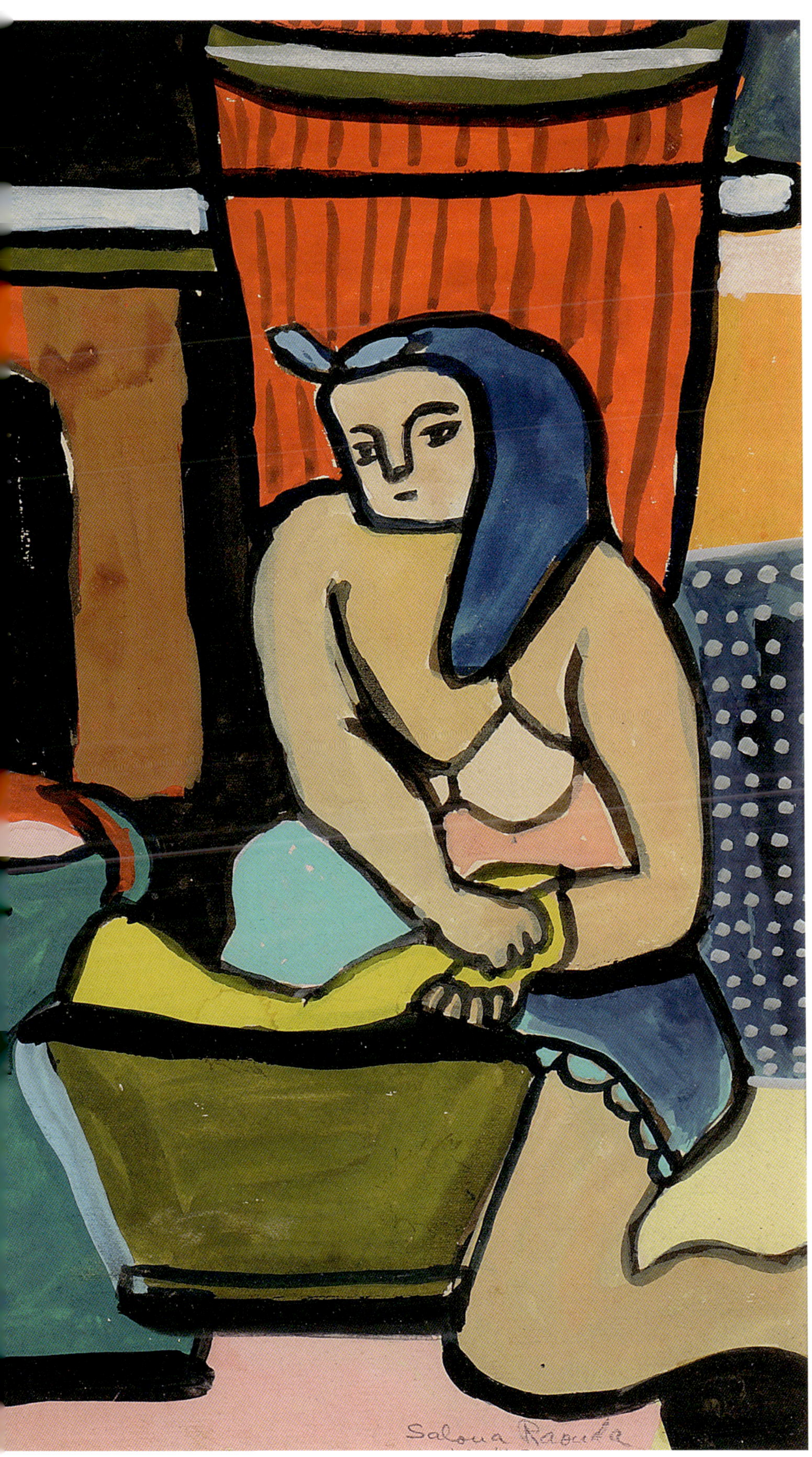

49
Chores 1948–9
Gouache on paper
25 × 35.5

is unable to read it, being more concerned with balancing her tea and sugar. Similarly, the other two women, odalisques whose bodies are mysteriously conflated, are unable to look at what they are doing. The decor has echoes of orientalism, even at this late stage in the French empire, and the composition has been recognised as a harem scene.[26] While the picture may be interpreted as an example of how in Léger's art 'traditional representational ideas like perspective do not play a role',[27] one should not overlook the presence of several perfectly perspectival elements, such as the table and the flooring, with geometric tiling reminiscent of a technique commonly used in Renaissance paintings to indicate spatial depth.[28] By conflating two systems for representing space, Léger declares his ability both to represent traditionally and to reduce wilfully. Significantly, it is his female models that have been reduced, distorted into a series of breasts and buttocks, arms and thighs, with the connecting parts removed. Even the cat on the couch has more spatial consistency than the two odalisques, whose arms are totally dislocated, their legs floating off to the side and their breasts seeming to merge with the pillows.

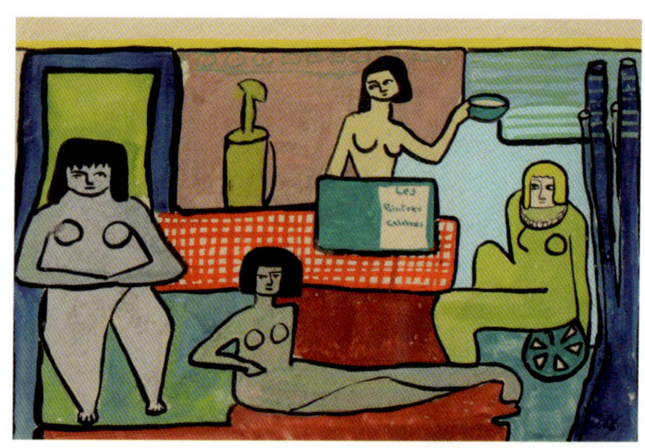

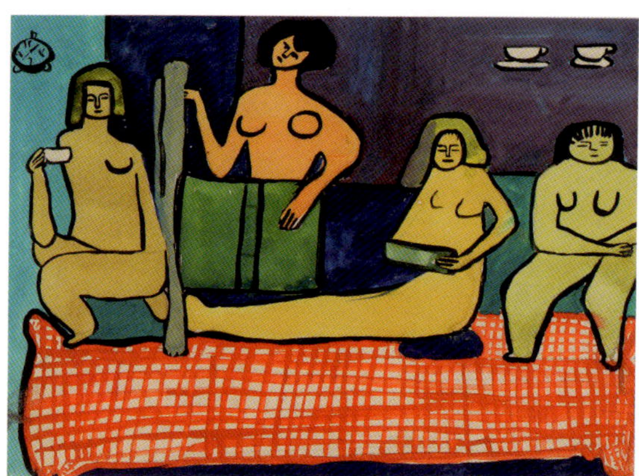

50
Les Peintres Célèbres
1948–9
Gouache on paper
25 × 36

51
Les Peintres Célèbres 1
1948–9
Gouache on paper
25 × 36

Choucair's versions of the scene make several important changes: the implicit harem rationale is gone; there is no couch but simply a red and white geometrical pattern to situate the women in space. Though perspectival space is not re-established, the integrity of the women's bodies is: each body claims its own part of the pictorial space, in one case sitting on the pillow instead of being subsumed by it.[29] Choucair's addition of a fourth woman moves the composition firmly away from the iconography of the Three Graces and their association with perfect feminine beauty.[30] The women no longer stare out at the viewer with that vacuous look that Nanette Salomon (1996) has defined as the sign of the nude's existential emptiness, but give an aggressive glare or avert their glances slightly to avoid eye-contact. The book they read is propped up so that its cover is legible, inviting the viewer to be aware of what they are reading and to position their actions in the realm of consciousness. There is a narrative explanation for their behaviour: they are workers who are reading up on the people who make a living out of distorting them. Implicitly, their very act of curiosity calls into question the painter's profession based on their cooperation.[31]

In all three compositions Choucair's handling of paint is playful, almost child-like – although we must not forget that, as seen in her figure studies, she was perfectly capable of handling human figures *à la Léger*. Rather than see this as an imperfect rendering of a scene in the style of Léger, we might more productively see it as Choucair's (repeated) 'de-Légerisation' of the scene. She reveals her decision not to impose geometricising schemes upon human form and its environment, but rather to discover the geometric principles they contain within themselves. For example, the legs of the lowest woman stretched in an odalisque's pose (fig.50) are defined by the angle that one makes crossing over the other. Seeing the women in these minimalistic but integrating terms, Choucair subverted Léger's way of viewing that had become rigorously stylised by the late 1940s. Given that the famed painter had become an imposing atelier-master, this series of gouaches can be read as an ironic comment on Léger's concurrent turn from conceptual abstraction to mechanistic representations of the human, and most often female, nude.

A new atelier opened down the street from La Grande Chaumière in October 1950. It was called L'Atelier d'art abstrait and was associated with two well-known artists, Jean Dewasne and its secretary-general, Edgard Pillet.[32] The Atelier's goal was to encourage discussion about abstract art, its evolution, purification and enrichment. The founders believed firmly that an abstract art totally opposed to figuration would have to be integrated into all aspects of life.[33] Their announcement in *Art d'aujourd'hui*, 'the best contemporary art magazine of its time',[34] explained that while art is always a collective activity in which the youngest build on the findings of their elders, 'those who come here will not content themselves to receive; they must know that they too will have to search, to discover, to throw themselves into the unexplored, the constant source of fecundity'.[35] As in an artisanal workshop, there would be no 'master' here, but rather the gathering together of useful experiences for the benefit of all. The proposed 'group quest' was a direct challenge to both the École des beaux-arts and, more provocatively, to Léger. Crossing yet another boundary of Parisian art-making, Choucair immediately volunteered to help with administration and to organise the twice-monthly debates (the same role that she had had at the Arab Cultural Club in Beirut in the late 1940s).[36]

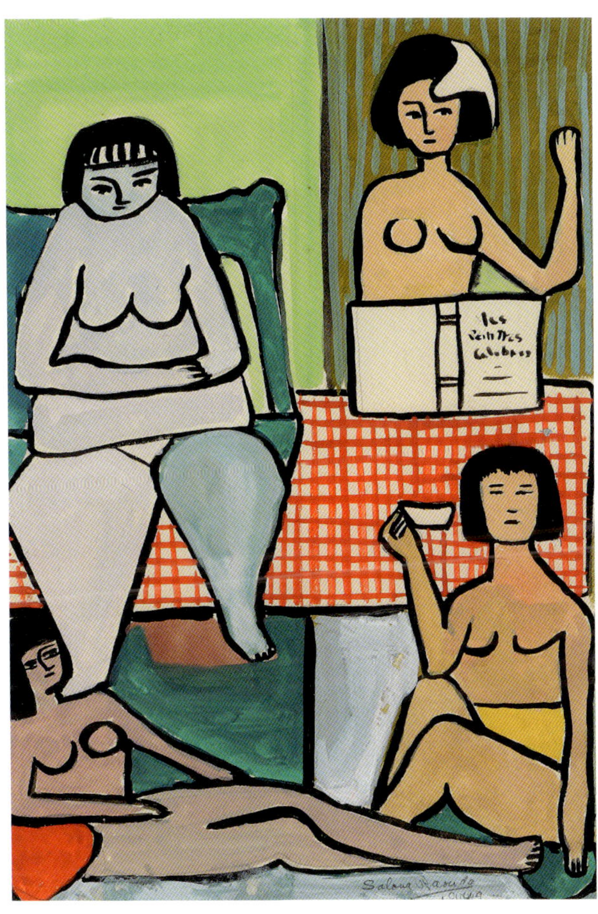

52
Les Peintres Célèbres 2
1948–9
Gouache on paper
35 × 24

Distinctions that could be drawn: universal art and local claims

In the workshop atmosphere of the Atelier d'art abstrait, it is relevant to note how Choucair was an active participant in the quest of the group, deliberately probing the experiments of the other members. She used the playfully jumbled patterns associated with Alberto Magnelli; the hectic but structured interaction of Jean Deyrolle; the tilting organic thrust of Jean Dewasne; the deliberate cold, outlined modules and resulting rational clarity of Edgar Pillet;[37] the shifting, restless energy of R. Mortensen; and Viktor Vasarely's balanced play of tonal and linear distinctions.[38] Though these artists differ in their handling of the paint, the geometric basis of their forms, their method of denoting three-dimensional space, and so on, according to Michel Seuphor they were all heirs of Kandinsky and the tradition of expressive, individualistic creation rather than constructivism exemplified by Mondrian.[39] What is striking is that for all the visual echoing and the exchange of ideas in the atelier atmosphere, none of the other members appears to have shared the mathematically generated method that was at the heart of Choucair's interpretation of modernism.[40]

The role of mathematics in Choucair's exploration of total anti-figuration reveals itself most clearly in her precise method of creation, by which she also distinguished her work from that of the others in the atelier. Her first step was to divide the canvas into areas, say four equal squares; she would then draw an irregular dividing line through one square, creating a curve to contrast with the rigidity of the square's corners. The resulting shape, which she called a 'module', is then traced, like a pattern, into a field opposite the first (in the upper right corner of *Module,* fig.53). The pattern, with its curved edge, is then mirrored and another piece cut from its interior, this time employing right angles. The new pattern is traced into a third region vertically adjacent to the second (in the lower right corner of the work. Diagonally facing that the curved edge is again traced, but now tipped in the opposite direction and minus yet another internal segment. This internal segment is dropped down to the first region (lower left) to interrupt the pristine starting square with a remnant of its interior. The divided square with which this method started has now moved across the sheet in an 'X', each time settling it a degree further from the central axis and losing a piece of its interior.

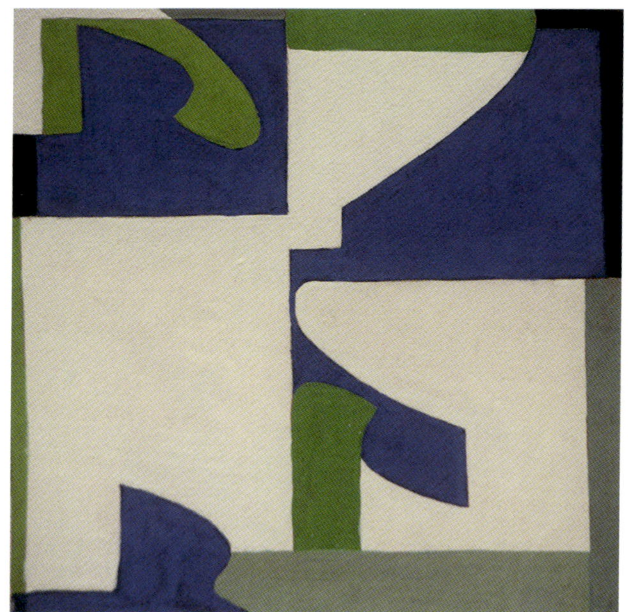

53
Module 1947–51
Gouache on paper
22×22

Through such a multi-step formula (and this piece probably represents the simplest version), Choucair used geometric form and contrasting curves to set up a centrifugal rhythm that she enhanced by applying tonal opposites to adjacent areas. The result is a visual ratio. Although the viewer may not fully appreciate the ratio-structure, the overall effect of the composition is one of perfect equilibrium achieved by continual movement: undeniably reminiscent forms appear to draw together, while their contrastive rhythm and colour seem to compel them apart. Logically, the process of composition is closely related to the notion of the perfect number whose proper divisors, when added, amount to the number. Just as 6 is the sum of 3+2+1 and the multiple of these same digits, so Choucair's compositions speak to unified wholes and their inner, elementary parts which can be variously combined to arrive at the original whole. In such works, decomposition and unity at once are premised and enacted.

With regard to the engagement of Islamic mathematics as an intellectual basis and method for Choucair's art-making, a distinction *may* be drawn between her 'geometric' work and that of other members of her atelier. Interestingly, this distinction has not hitherto been drawn by writers, whether in Paris or Beirut, examining the Atelier d'art abstrait or Choucair's experience there. Given that writing about art can reform standards for valuing it, the writings of Choucair's contemporaries led to her ambiguous art being written into each of the equally fraught Parisian and Beiruti scenes and was itself part of local struggles over the meaning of modernity. Choucair's abstract compositions were incorporated into Parisian art journals at a time when abstract art was by no means the popular or official favourite and when American art was receiving far greater institutional support on the metropolitan scene.[41]

In this contest, paintings could enter the fray as like-minded comrades, proving the validity of the Atelier d'art abstrait's collective quest: *Module* (fig.53) could certainly be seen to prove that a square could be painted without representing a square in the world outside, but rather existing for itself, in the context of the painting only, as Léon Degand argued in his rebuttal to the charges against the Atelier.[42]

Alternatively, works of art could be written into the cultural battleground as a pledge of foreign alliances. In so far as Choucair's works seemed to come from a different tradition altogether, they were at times taken by certain French critics to prove the international viability of 'l'École de Paris'. Thus Julian Alvard, writing on 'hard abstraction' at the Salon de Réalités Nouvelles in 1951, detected in Choucair's paintings 'a magnanimous Eastern spirit' that had 'intermingled with the deepest Western direction and its art concepts to reject Eastern traditions and carve out her own genius path'.[43] Léon Degand wrote:

> We would not be fair if we said only that Saloua Raouda is an innovative student in this modern school; rather, she is far from accepting lock, stock and barrel the known rules, because she rediscovered them after bending them according to her whims and mindset, so she colored them as she willed, bending them possibly according to her Arab mentality.[44]

The 'Arab mentality' that Choucair's work apparently exuded was an important factor in this appropriation. Indeed, it is clear that her work was an asset in the formation of a notion of a Paris School at a time when not only was the future direction of Parisian art insecure, but the world seemed altogether more interested in artistic developments in New York.[45] Simultaneously emphasising Choucair's connections and her apparent ethnic difference, supporters of the Atelier could hold to their assertion of two years earlier: 'More than ever, Paris is the capital of the arts.'[46]

When Thuraya Malhas imported the voices of French critics to Beirut through her own writing on art, she removed any sense of controversy among them. Similarly, she softened the sense of Choucair's ethnic distinctiveness in order to highlight the achievement of having joined a unified *'alamiyya* (universalism). This is not to suggest that Malhas devoted the majority of her article to translations because she herself had run out of things to say – or because she was inclined through background or education to admire French assertions uncritically. Nothing could be further from the truth. Both Malhas and Rose al-Ghurayib, who also wrote about Choucair's 1952 show, were committed Arab nationalists who believed in supporting the movement through cultural activity; al-Ghurayib led the Arab Association, which performed plays promoting an Arab heritage, at the American Junior College.[47] Rather than assuming that the trust in French approval resulted from a lack of respect for 'Arab cultural values', I regard Malhas' importation of the voices of French critics as a strategy whose role in newly independent Lebanon merits examination. An obvious way to appraise this strategy is to consider how it handled functionaries of the nascent Lebanese state.

Following a pattern established in the 1930s, Choucair's 1952 exhibition was sponsored and opened by Laure al-Khuri, the wife of

President Bishara al-Khuri, a fact not overlooked by art commentators. In Paris the Lebanese ambassador to France, Ahmad Da'uq, had attended the exhibition at Galerie Colette Allendy. According to legend elaborated years later, he made a perfunctory tour and then addressed Choucair with the words: 'Your type of work is curious, Miss Raouda. Have you not done any Lebanese works for us?'[48] Given the proximity in time of the two shows, it is most certain that many of the works hanging in the École Supérieure des Lettres were the same as those that had provoked such dismay from the 'ambassador, to the ambassador's wives, and on down'.[49] The point is that while the stories of official rebuke were recounted from 1951 on (and their being passed on by word of mouth is said to have prompted the *Outlook* notice of success), they did not appear in Beirut art commentary until decades later.

Although they were later to become a predominant motif in art writing generally, and about Choucair in particular, the scandalised voices of elite Lebanese audiences did not appear early on. The opinions that appeared instead, repeatedly translated and presented en masse, were those of French art critics, invoked to articulate how in Paris this art had been understood and to incite Arabic readers to lend their own understanding. Local audiences at all levels were enjoined to look not for the familiar but for the most contemporary, to show that they were part of the modern world. In this sense, nationalism, as referenced in the 'Lebanese-ness' of Choucair as a citizen and her patron as a state representative, was not separate from internationalism – or cosmopolitanism – but a step towards it. Contrary to the idea of art somehow appropriate to a certain nation or culture, the notion of art brought to life by the commentaries of Malhas and others suggests a universal, borderless entity defined by its relation to a widely acknowledged pedigree that had recently produced Picasso and Matisse. The other idea of art was certainly familiar enough to audiences of the time, but it was deliberately displaced by this strategy.

This tactic of deference to French audiences and their views was well established by scholars in Beirut long before Choucair's 1951 exhibition. As in previous years, their tendency was to give more attention to the views of an admiring public than to the works of art themselves. This is not to say that the look of the art was irrelevant. On the contrary, it mattered a great deal that people wanted to make vastly different objects and yet sought to fit them to a validated conception of art, so that the commentary had significant influence on output. It is important to emphasise that the tactic worked equally well – or equally ambiguously – for different styles of art production in the late 1940s and early 1950s, when the occupying French forces had been finally expelled from their former Mandate region and French authority had passed into local hands.

An illustration of this tactic in action may be seen at a local institution dedicated to cosmopolitanism's apparent opposite: Arab nationalism. It may seem ironic that at the Arab Cultural Club (ACC), the Arab nationalist organisation Choucair helped establish in the mid-1940s, the programme for the propagation of a modern Arab identity for the new nation of Lebanon included an appeal to local intellectuals and activists to appreciate and assimilate developments in contemporary 'French' art-making (and symphonic music, but that is another story). As Munah al-Sulh has put it, these were years when the state of Lebanon had been declared but the French army was still very much present and the populace was struggling to establish the character of the new entity.[50] Politically, the Lebanese people sought to define how their state would be independent from the regional colonial powers and how it would be affiliated with neighbouring states. Culturally, they sought to define its language, a programme and institutions for 'social revival', and development of common intellectual assets. Thrusting themselves upon this situation, ACC members had twin goals of strengthening local ties by promoting intellectual interaction between its members and the wider community, and at the same time providing the community with resources for local development.[51] In opposition to a subjugated colonial identity, a discredited Ottoman-Turkish affiliation or, most importantly, a self-limiting sectarian identity, Arab nationalists exploited as an asset the veneration of Paris-based *'alami* (worldwide or universal) art.

Thus Choucair and her colleagues at the ACC did not choose between 'Arab' and 'Western' identity; they used a sense of Arabness to create a culturally relative sphere that was distinct from the 'Western' one, connecting the artistic production of each culture to its own environment and mentality. 'Western' artistic culture represented modernity, held up to encourage ACC members to embrace specific social reform programmes. In other words, these apparently mutually exclusive identities were simultaneously evoked through media such as fine art to provide the citizens of the newly independent Lebanese Republic with ambiguous identities that were not limited to the previous moulds of 'Arab colonial subjects' or 'Western anti-Arab colonisers'.

In the 1950s Choucair's art benefited to a certain extent from having been apparently accepted among some of Paris's avant-garde circles. The key to its strangeness lay in the ambiguous identities being constructed by certain Lebanese intellectuals to deal with the necessities of nation-building during the Cold War. Their commentaries point to the conception of 'art' as a universal rather than national or local social entity, which can help people adapt to contemporary life. However, with this universalist conception of art, audiences deliberately limited their engagement with Choucair's work to its formal and conceptual traits which fit current aesthetic standards propagated by 'France'. Not France – the land of battling ateliers and abandoned academies, but the 'France' that was unified in Beiruti art-writing as an undisputed authority on good art. The elements of Choucair's oeuvre that did not fit a universalist conception of contemporary art were seen as secondary and received much less attention in art-writing of the period, either in Arabic or French. These elements received the attention they deserved in subsequent scholarship.

Kirsten Scheid
Based on the author's doctoral dissertation, *Painters, Picture-makers and Lebanon: Ambiguous Identities in an Unsettled State* (Princeton University, 2005).

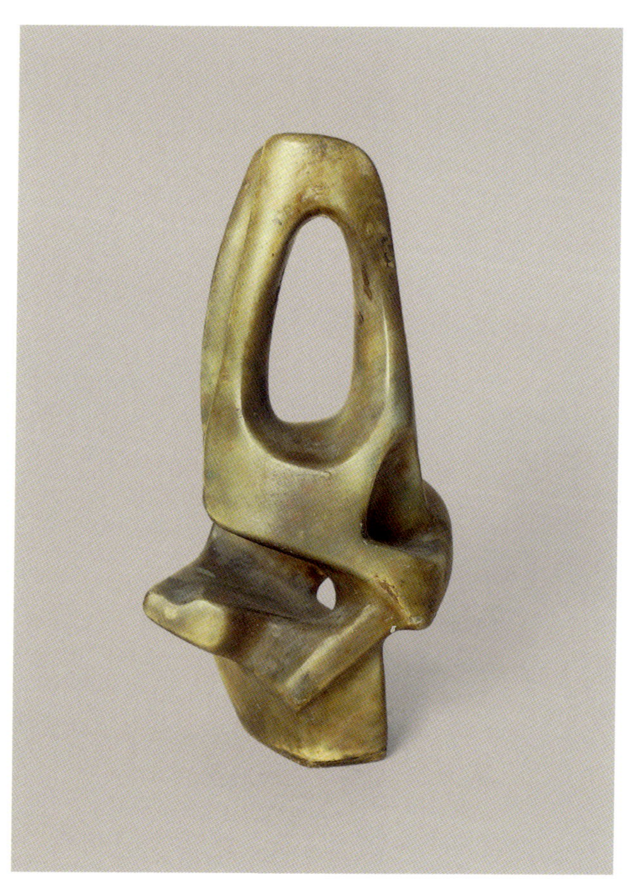

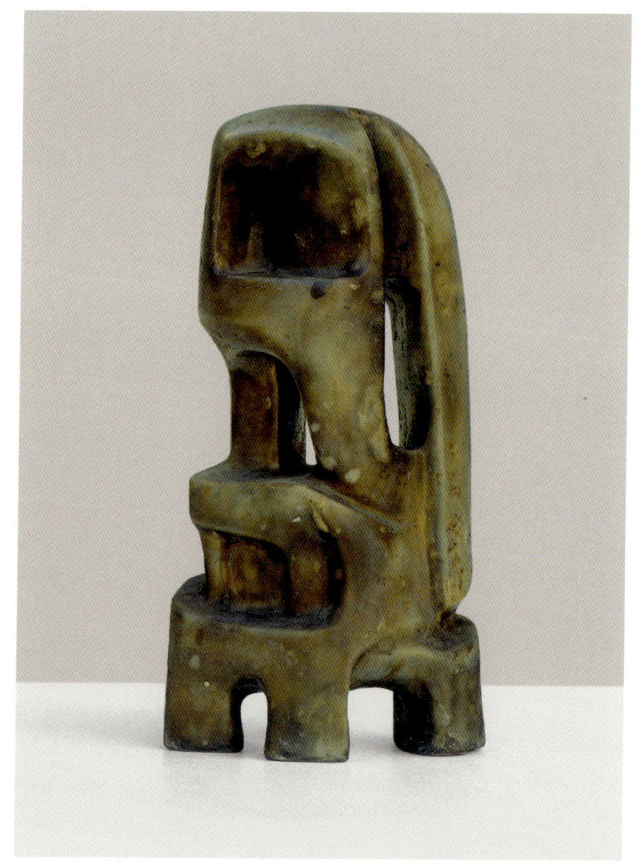

54
Trajectory of a Line, The Cave 1957–9
Fibreglass
37 × 24 × 22

55
Trajectory of a Line, Tripod 1957–9
Fibreglass
41 × 21 × 17

56
Trajectory of a Line 1957–9
Brass
19 × 7 × 7

57
(overleaf)
Interform 1960–2
Wood
49 × 12 × 12

58
(overleaf)
Secret of a Cube 1960–2
Wood
28 × 19 × 19

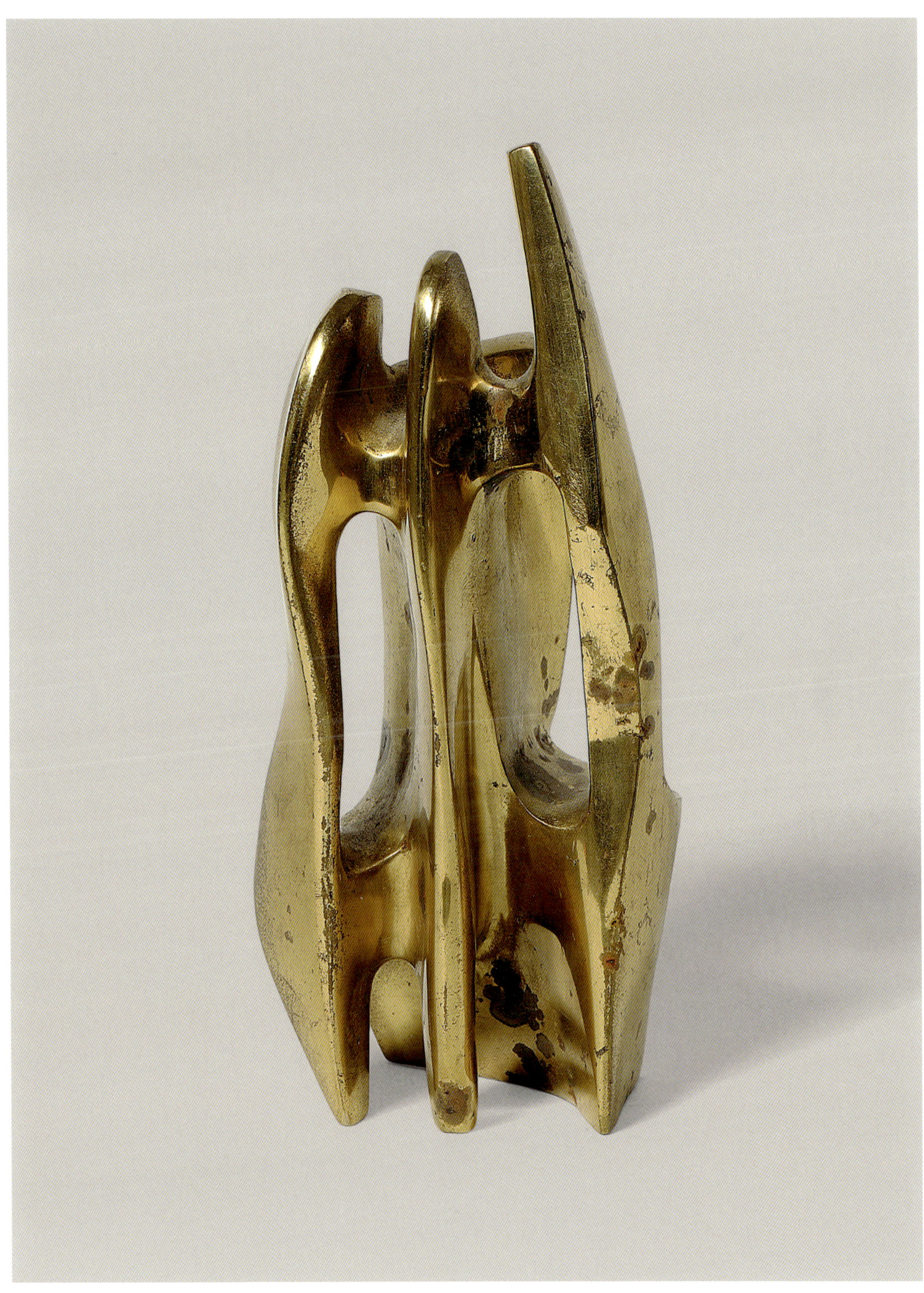

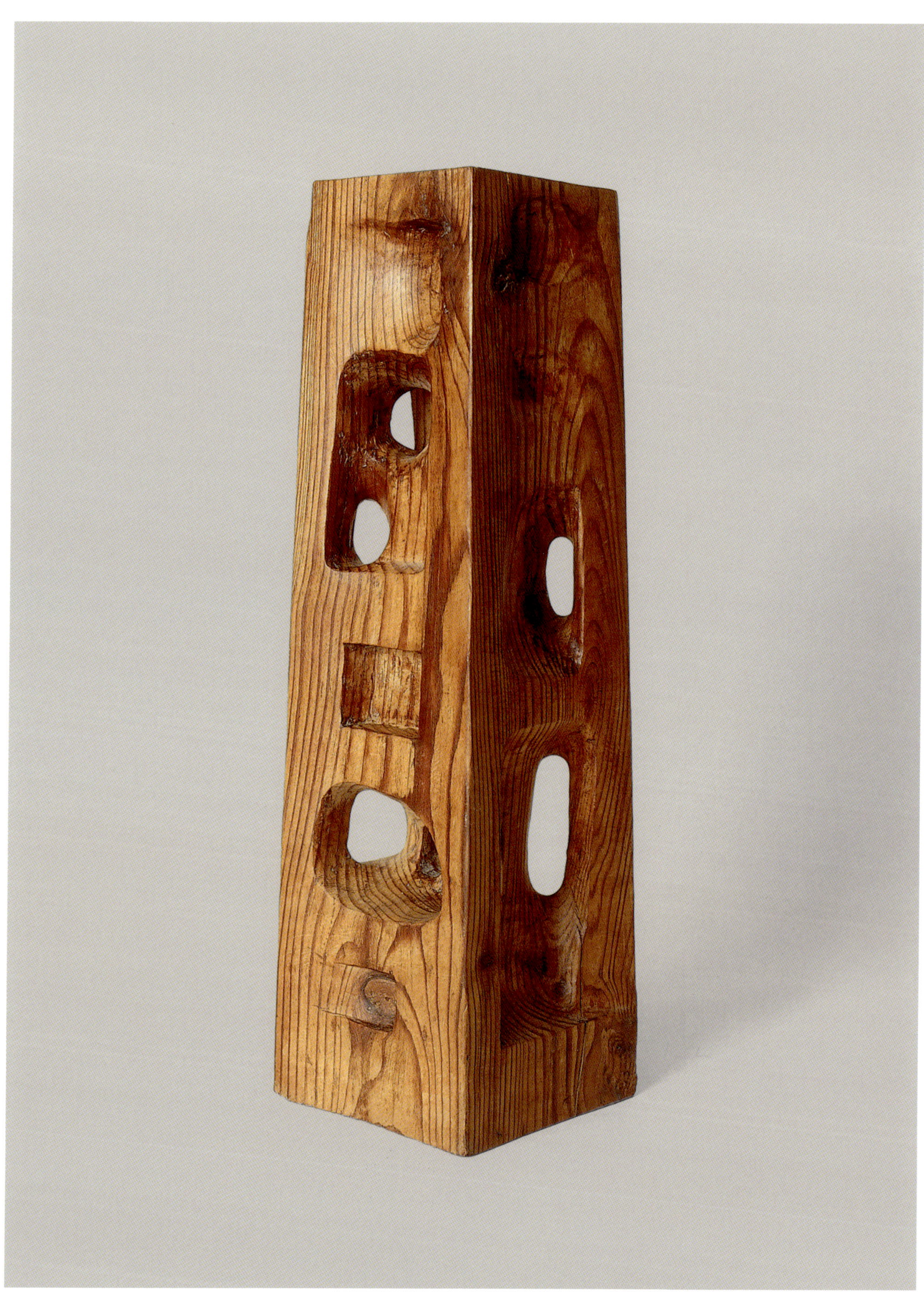

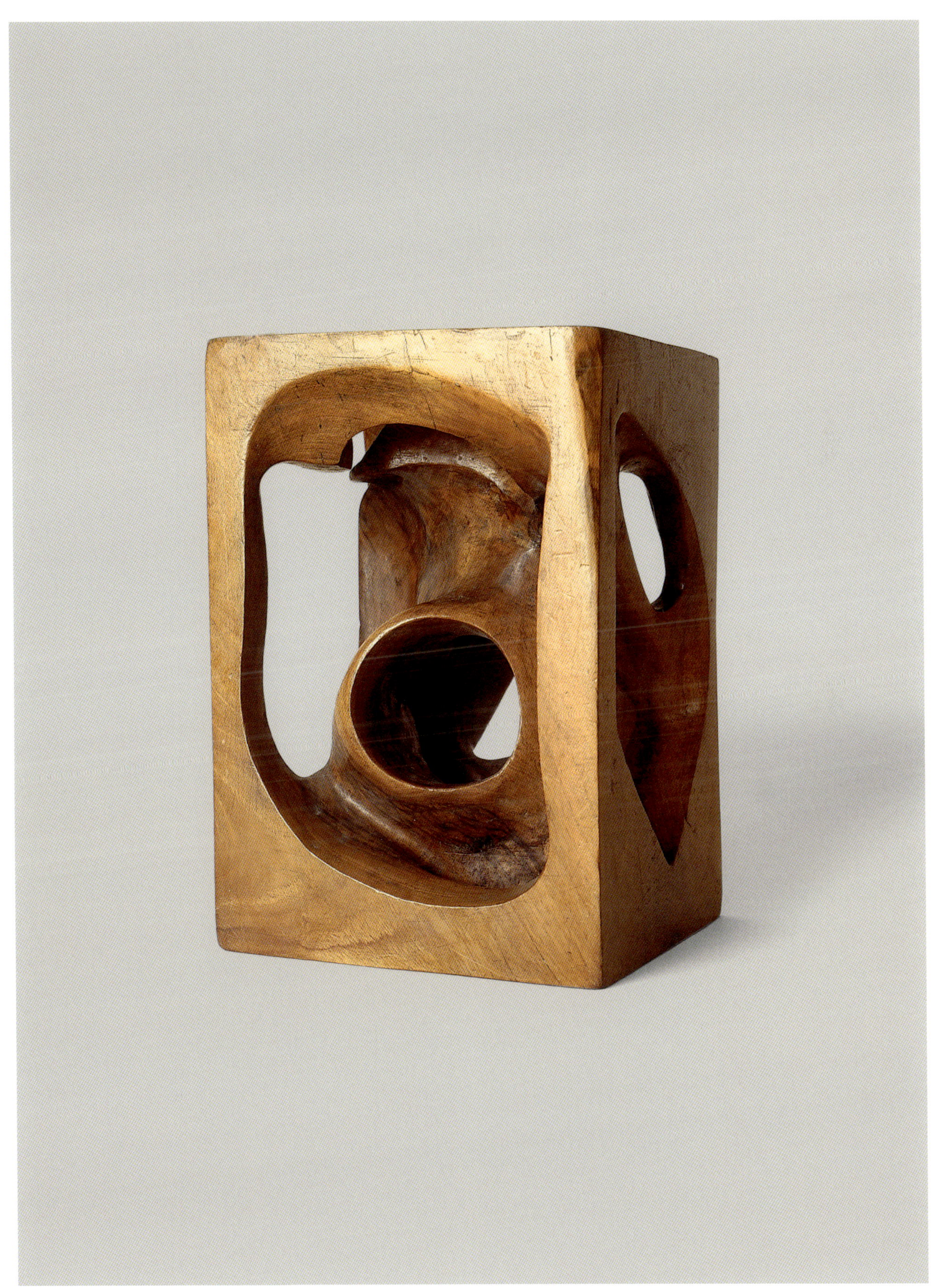

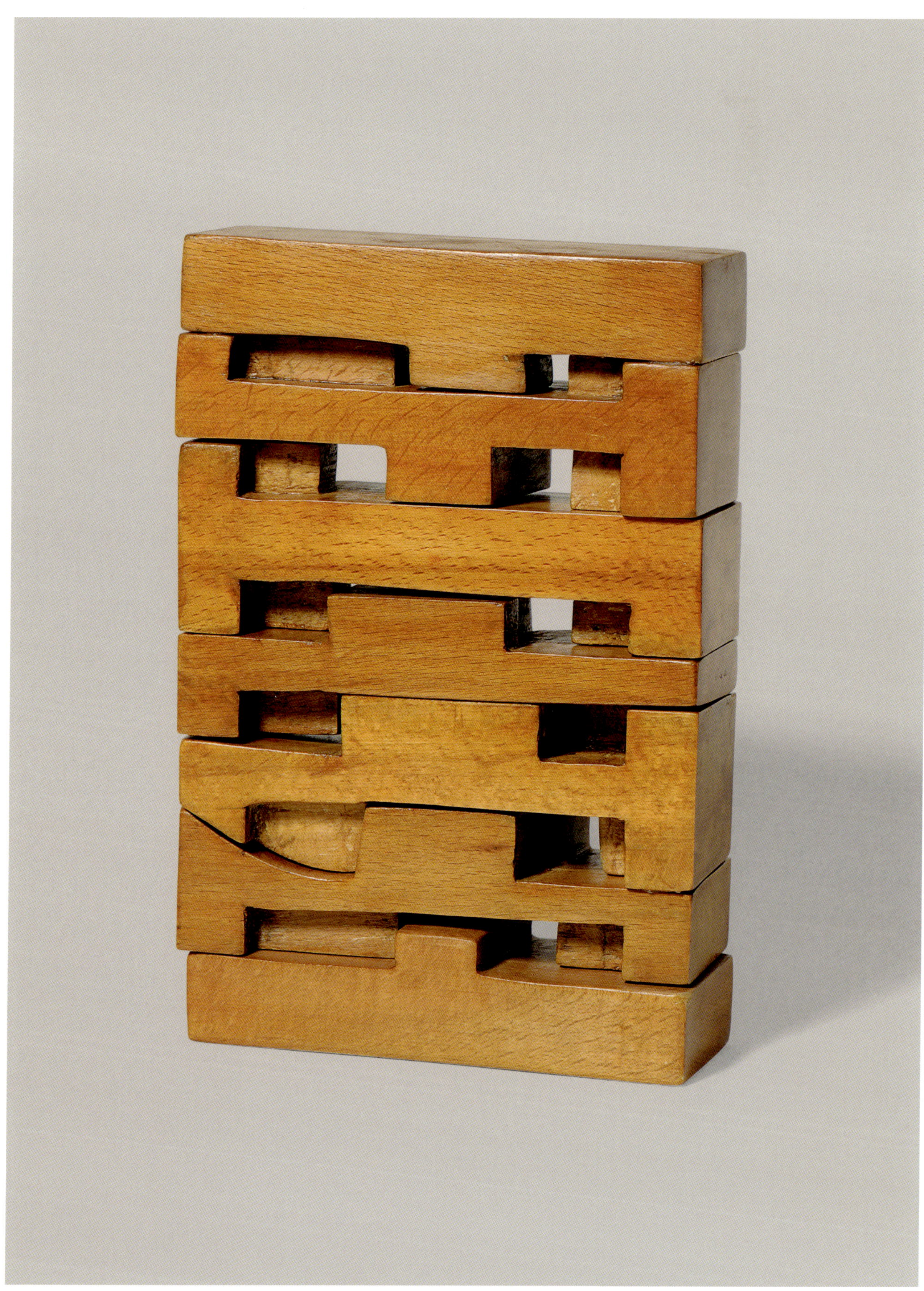

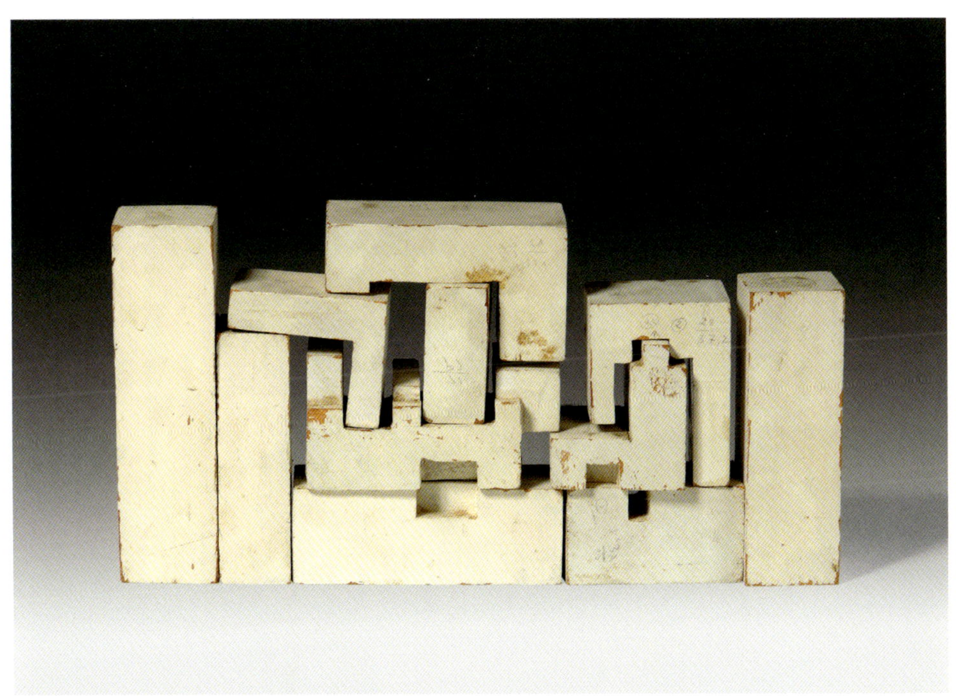

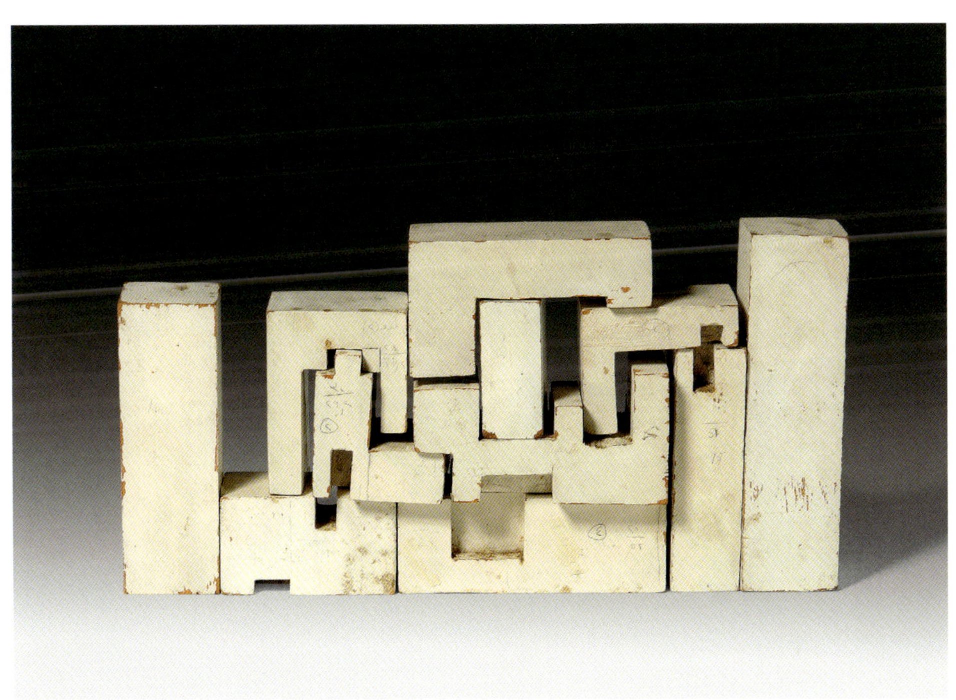

59
Poem 1963–5
Wood
25 × 17 × 5

60
Poem Wall 1963–5
White wood
29 × 35 × 4

61
(overleaf)
Poem of Five Verses
1963–5
White wood
29 × 13.5 × 10.3

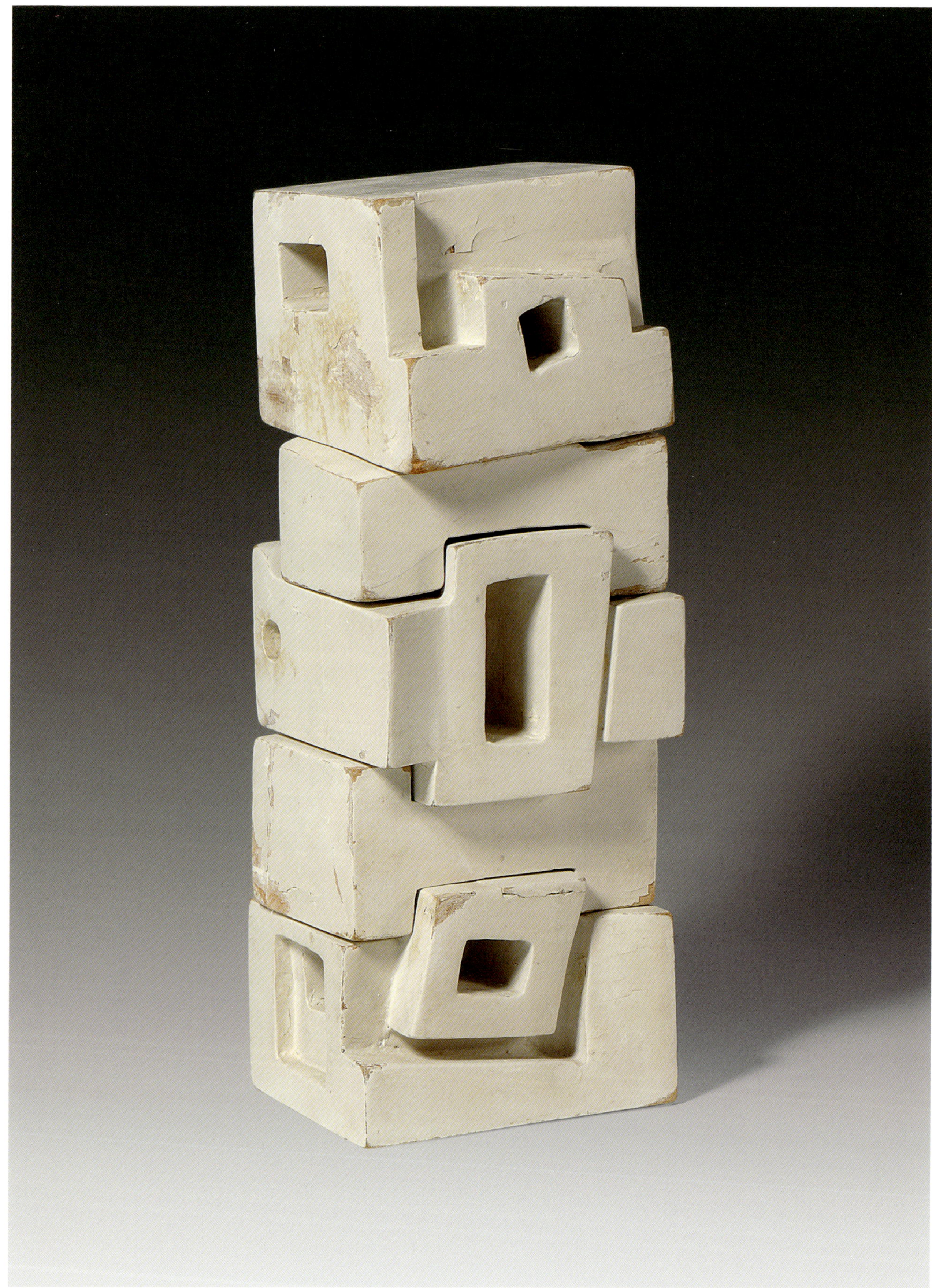

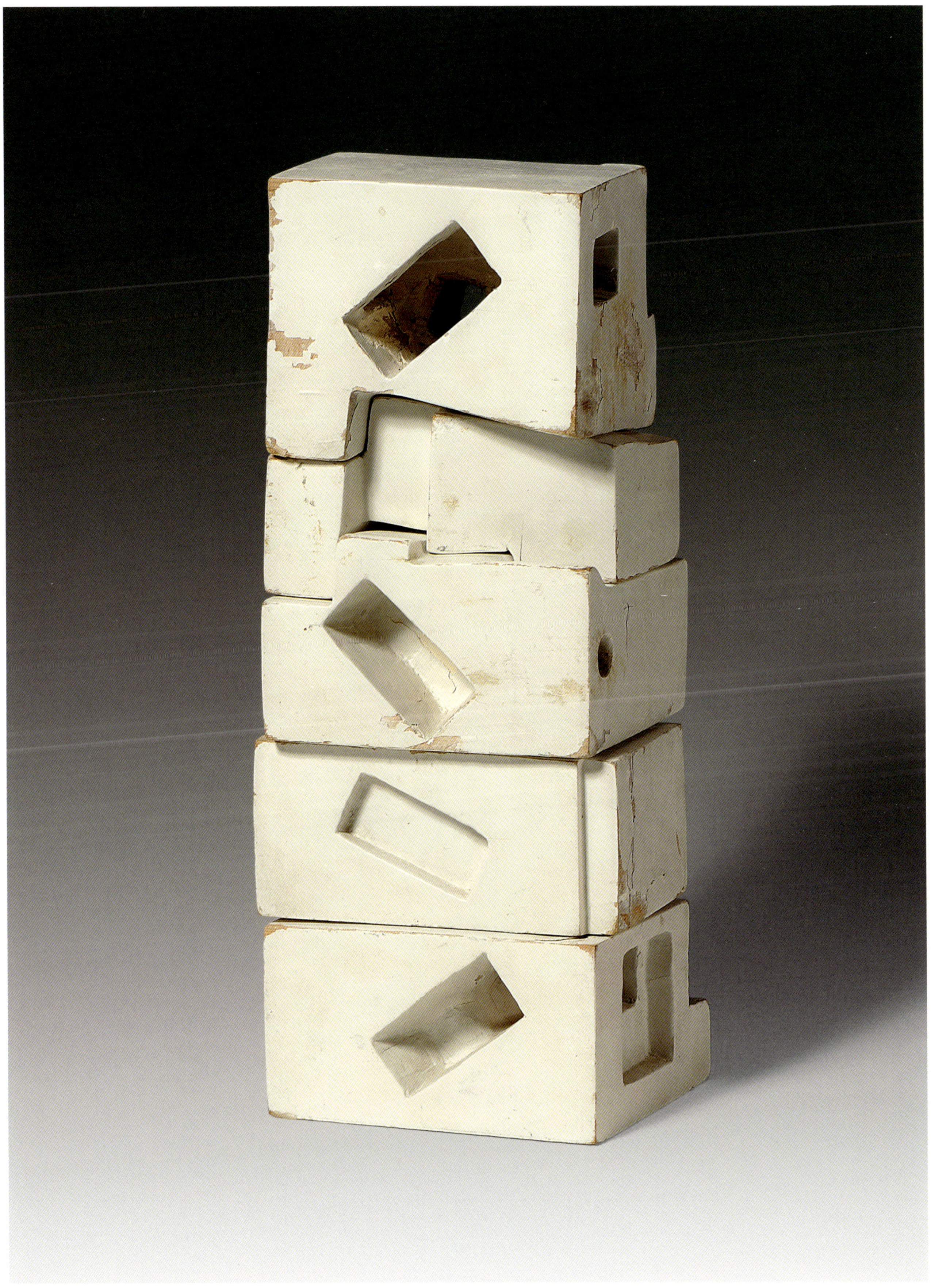

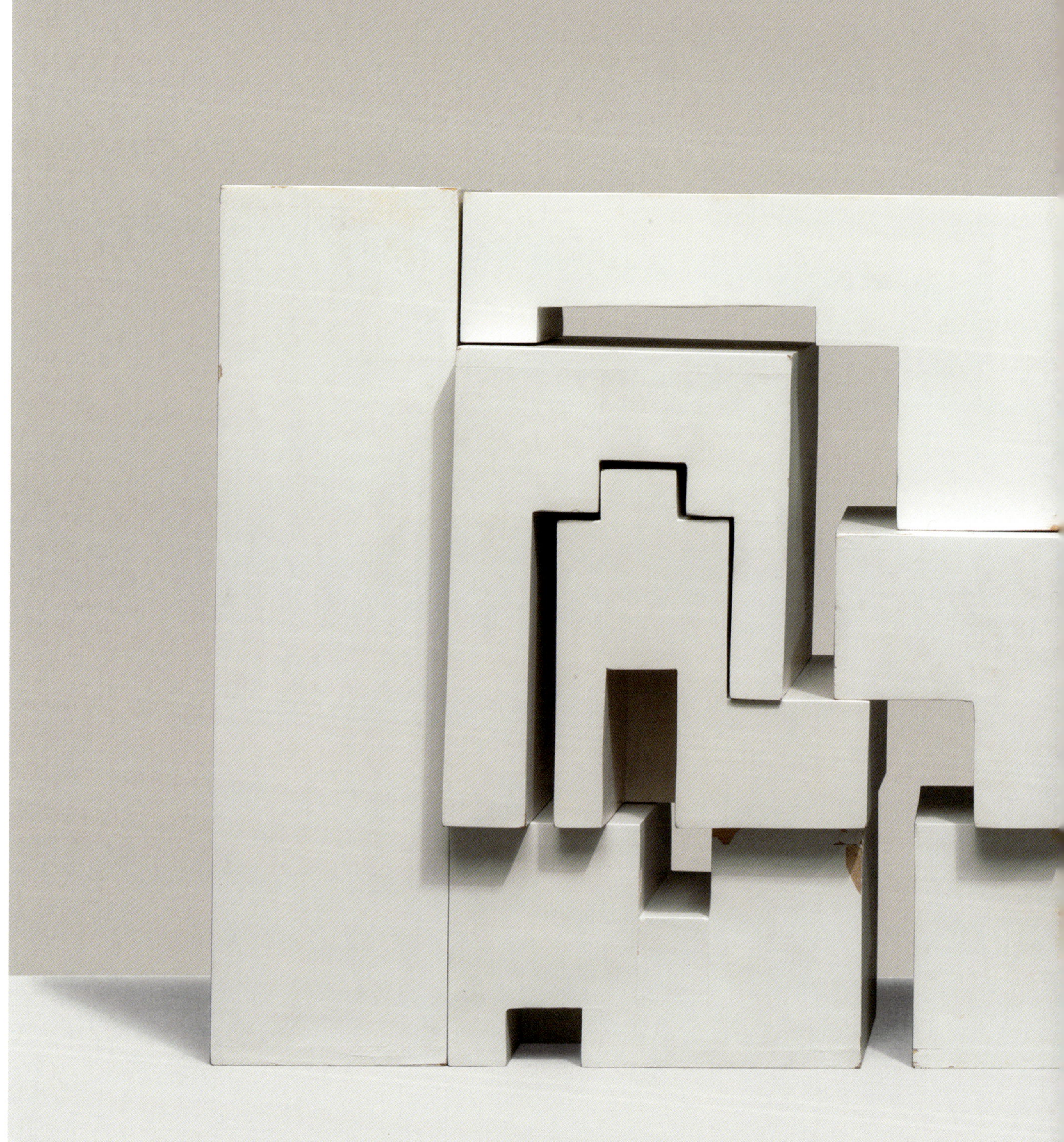

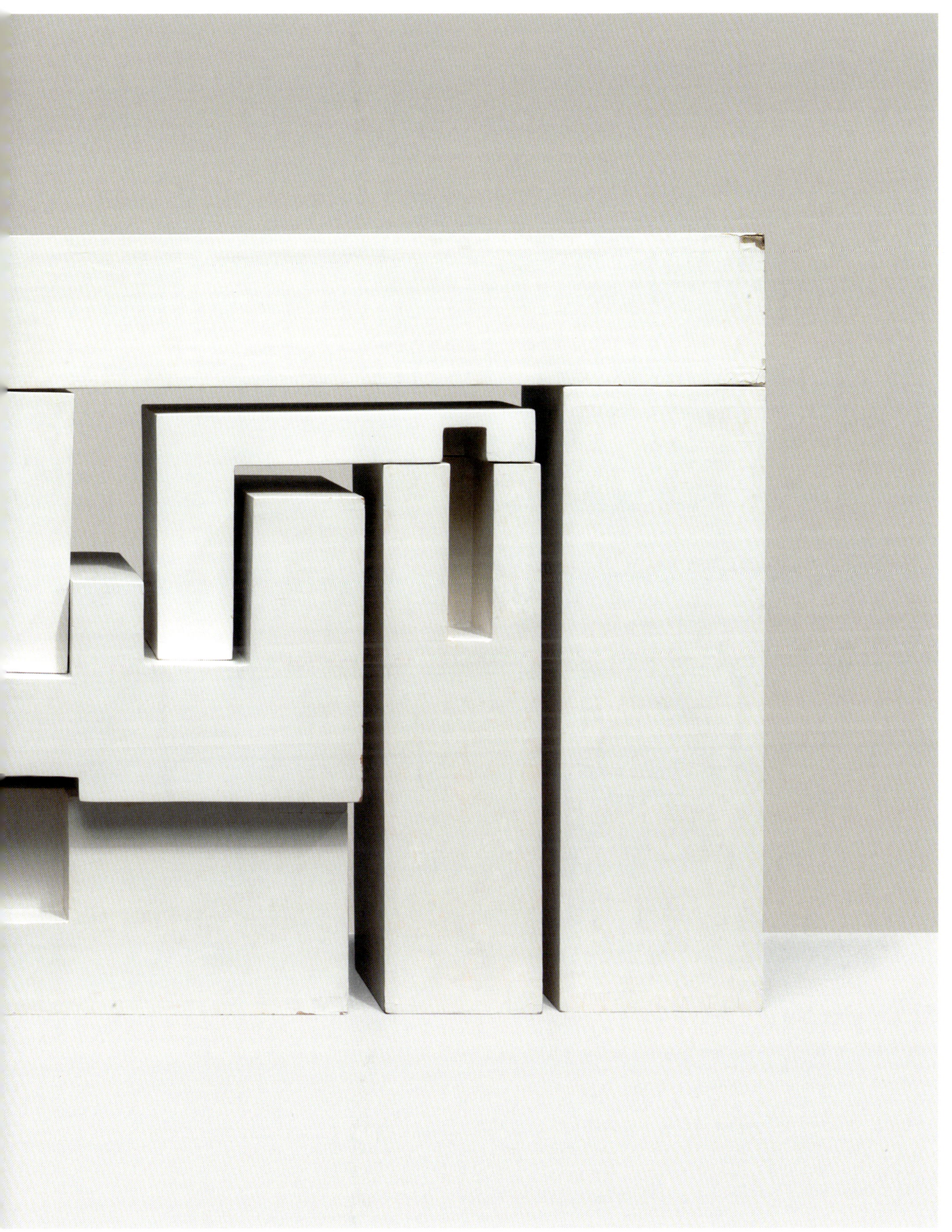

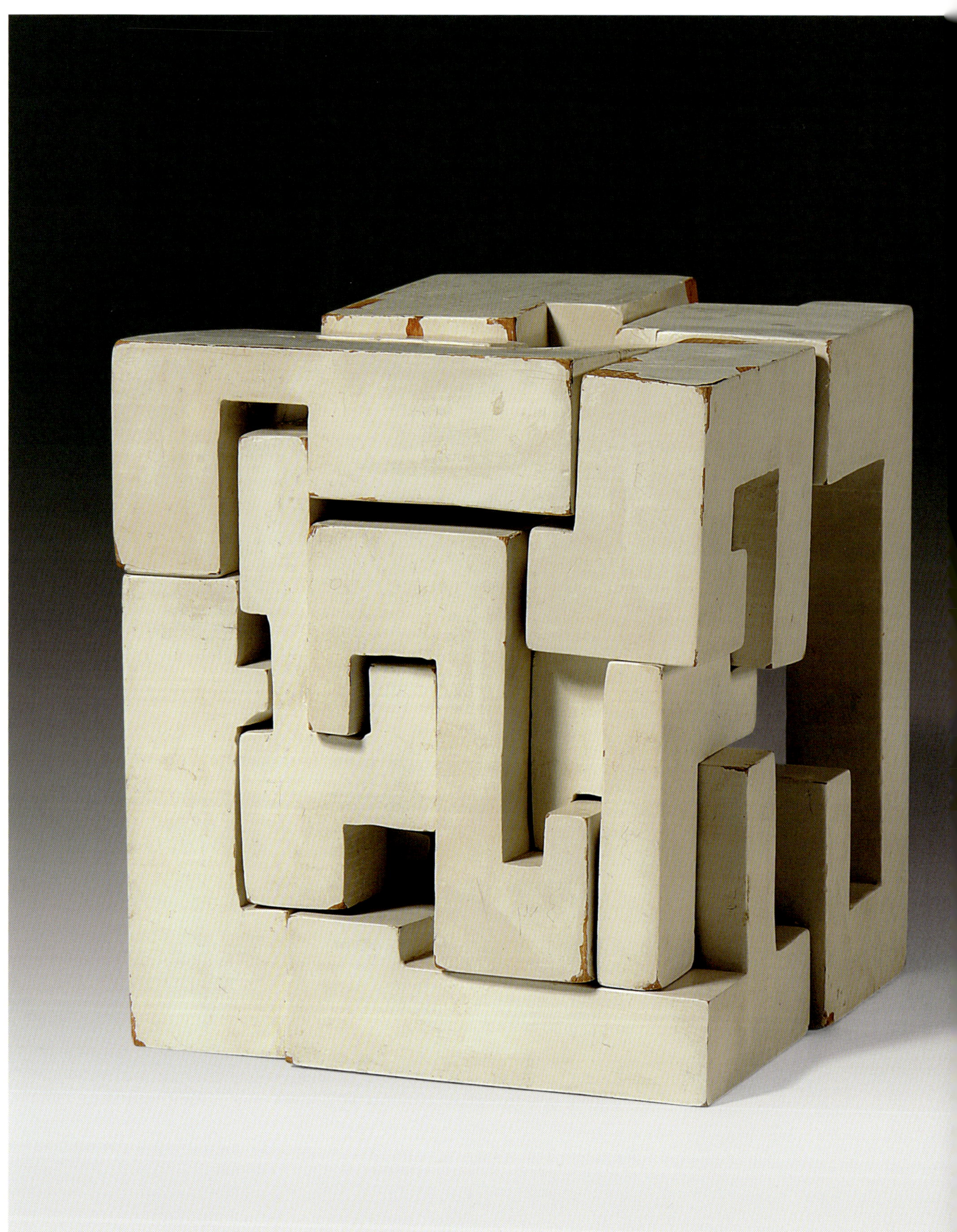

62
(previous pages)
Poem Wall 1963–5
Wood
70 × 160 × 2

63
(this page)
Poem Cube 1963–5
White wood
16 × 16 × 16

64
(overleaf)
Poem 1963–5
Wood
33 × 17 × 17.5

65
(overleaf)
Poem 1963–5
Stone
73 × 33 × 12

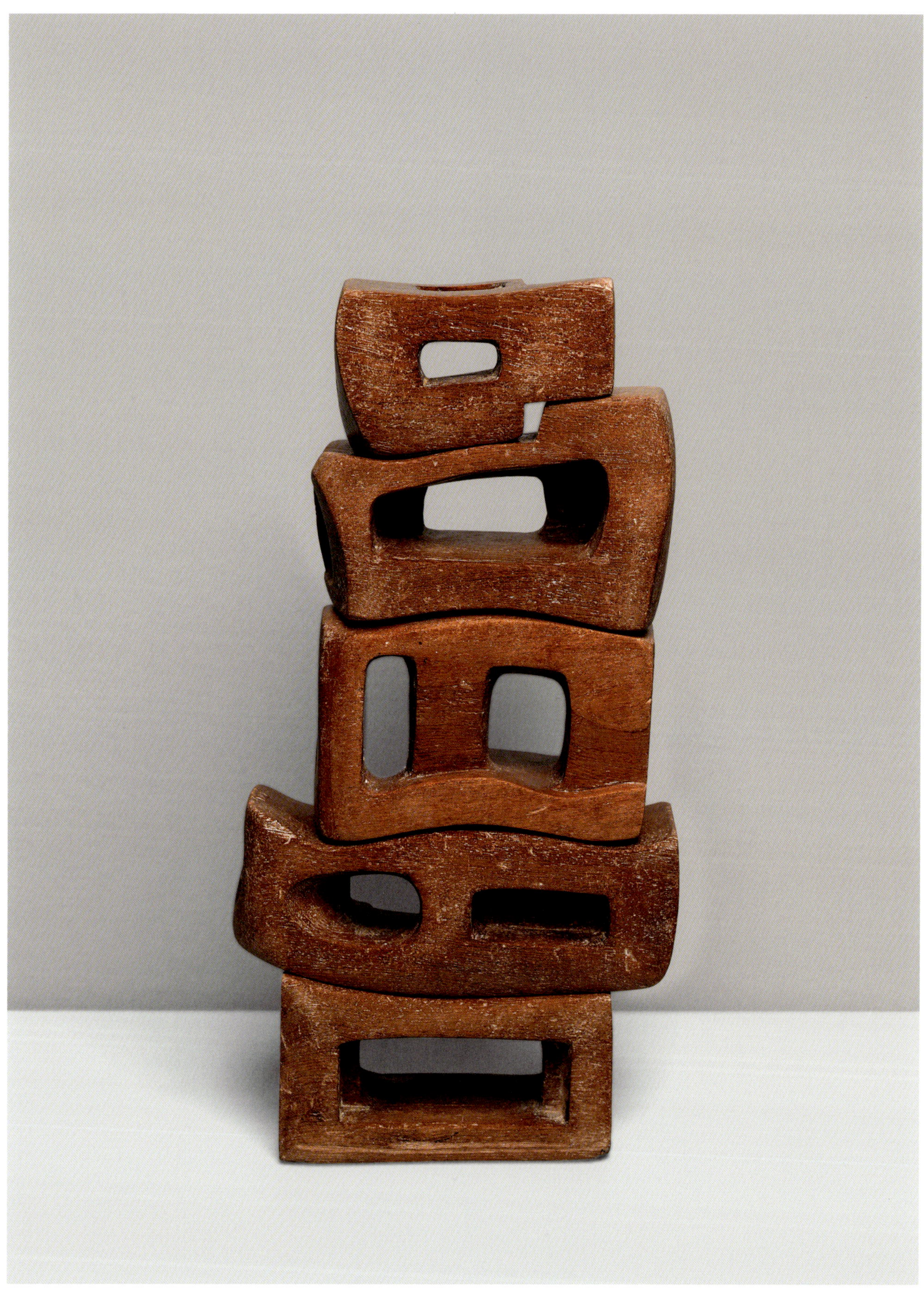

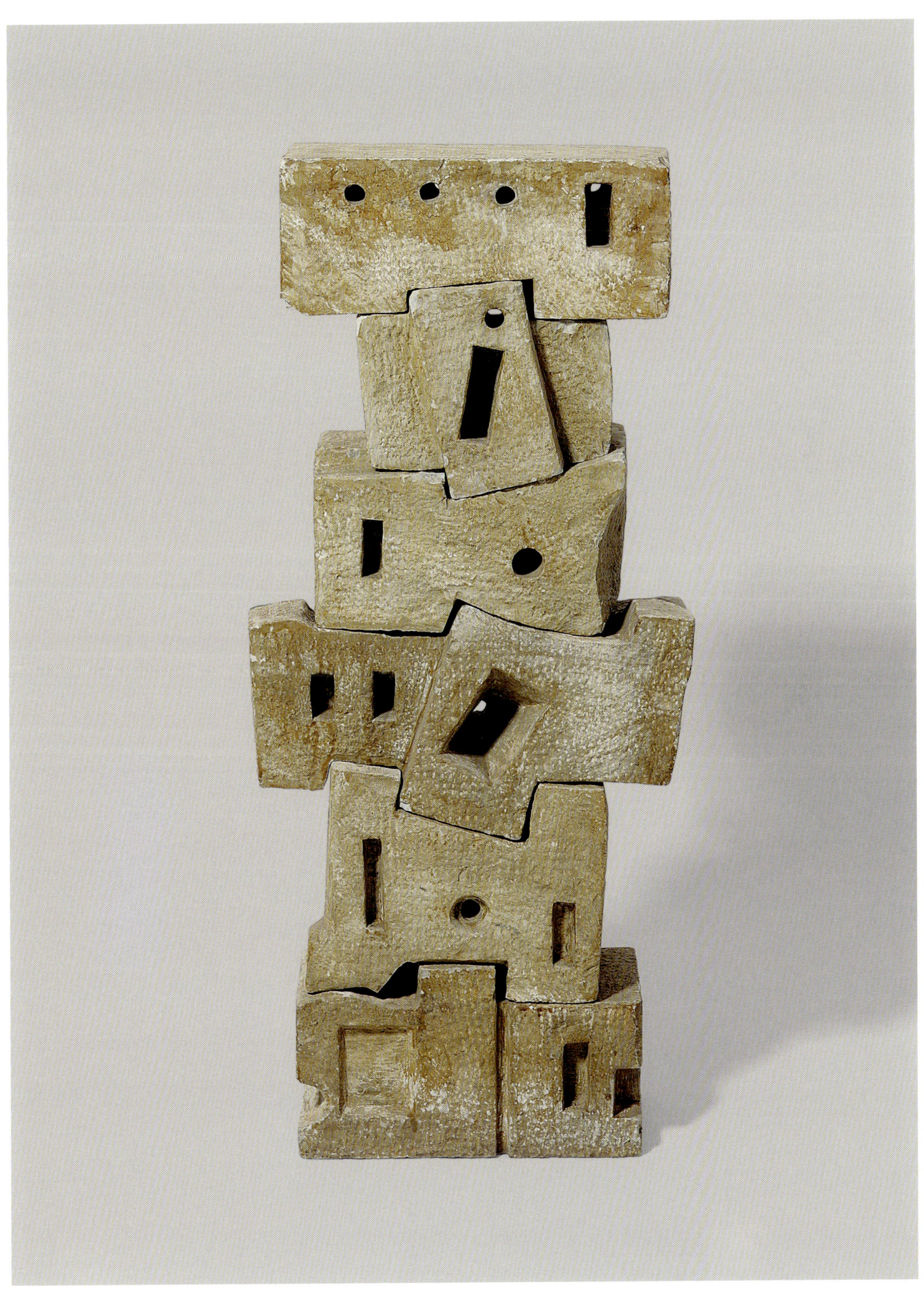

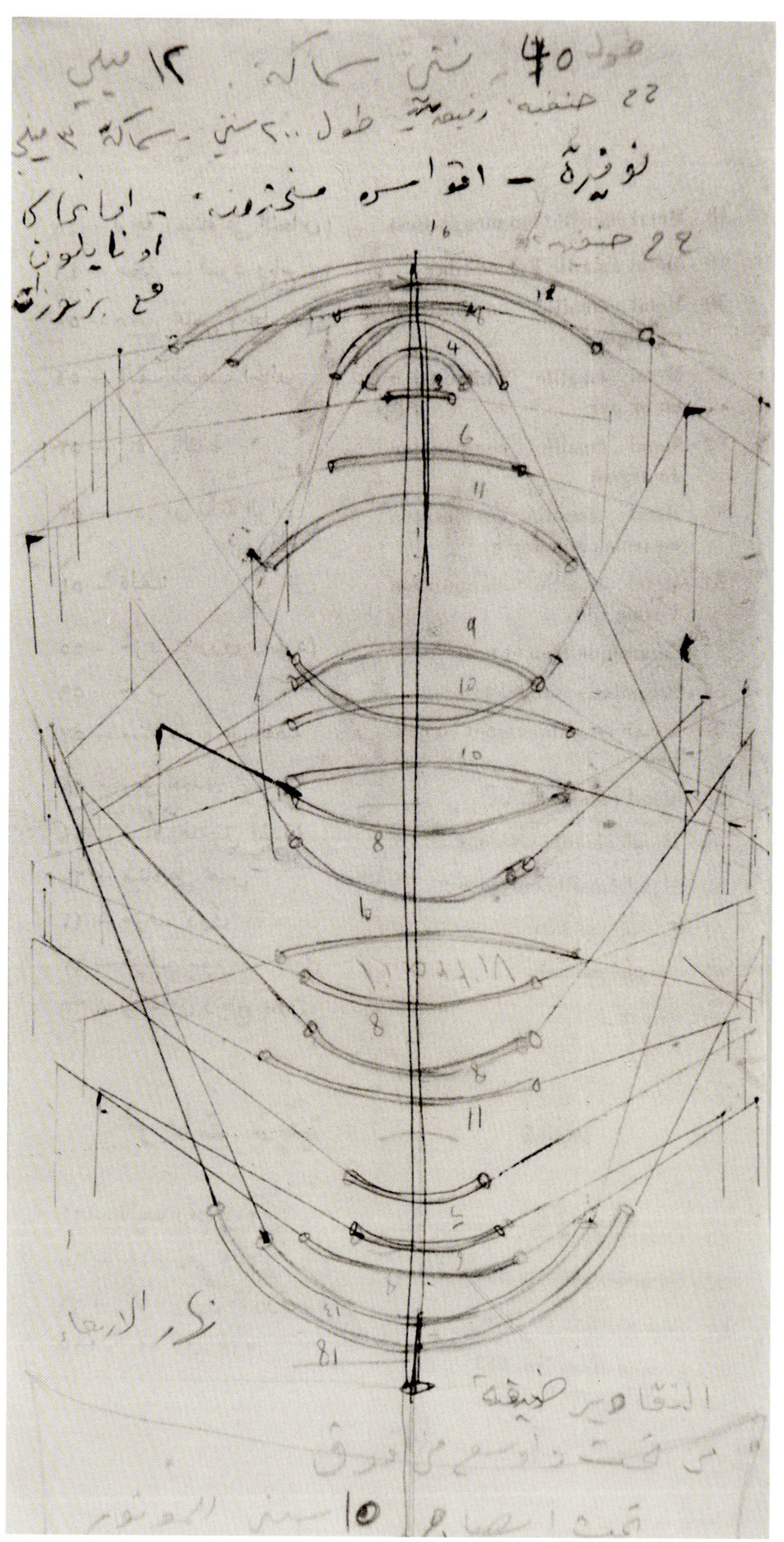

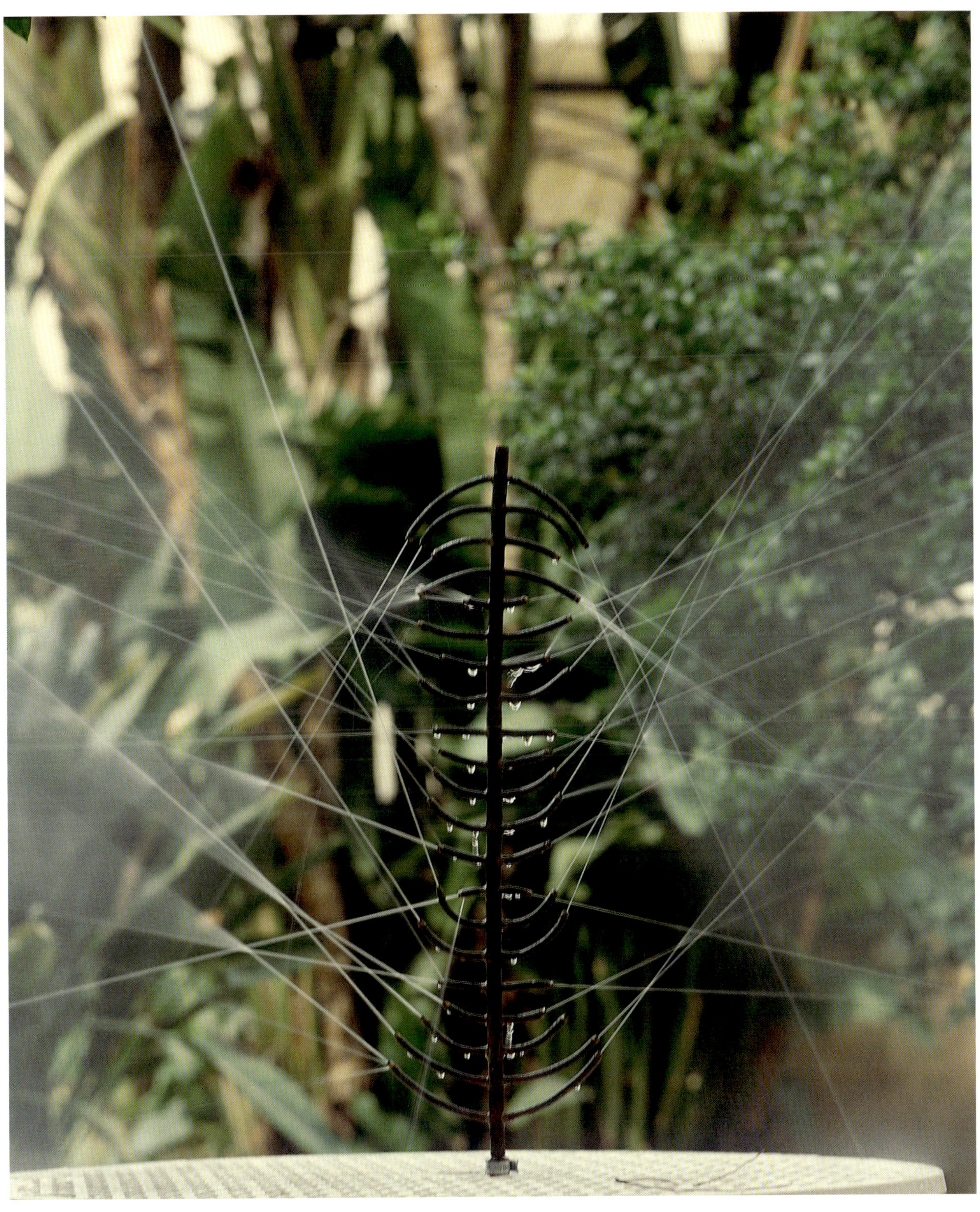

66
Sketch for *Water Project*
1980–3
Pencil on paper
24 × 12

67
Water Project 1980–3
Copper and water
51 × 13.5 × 2

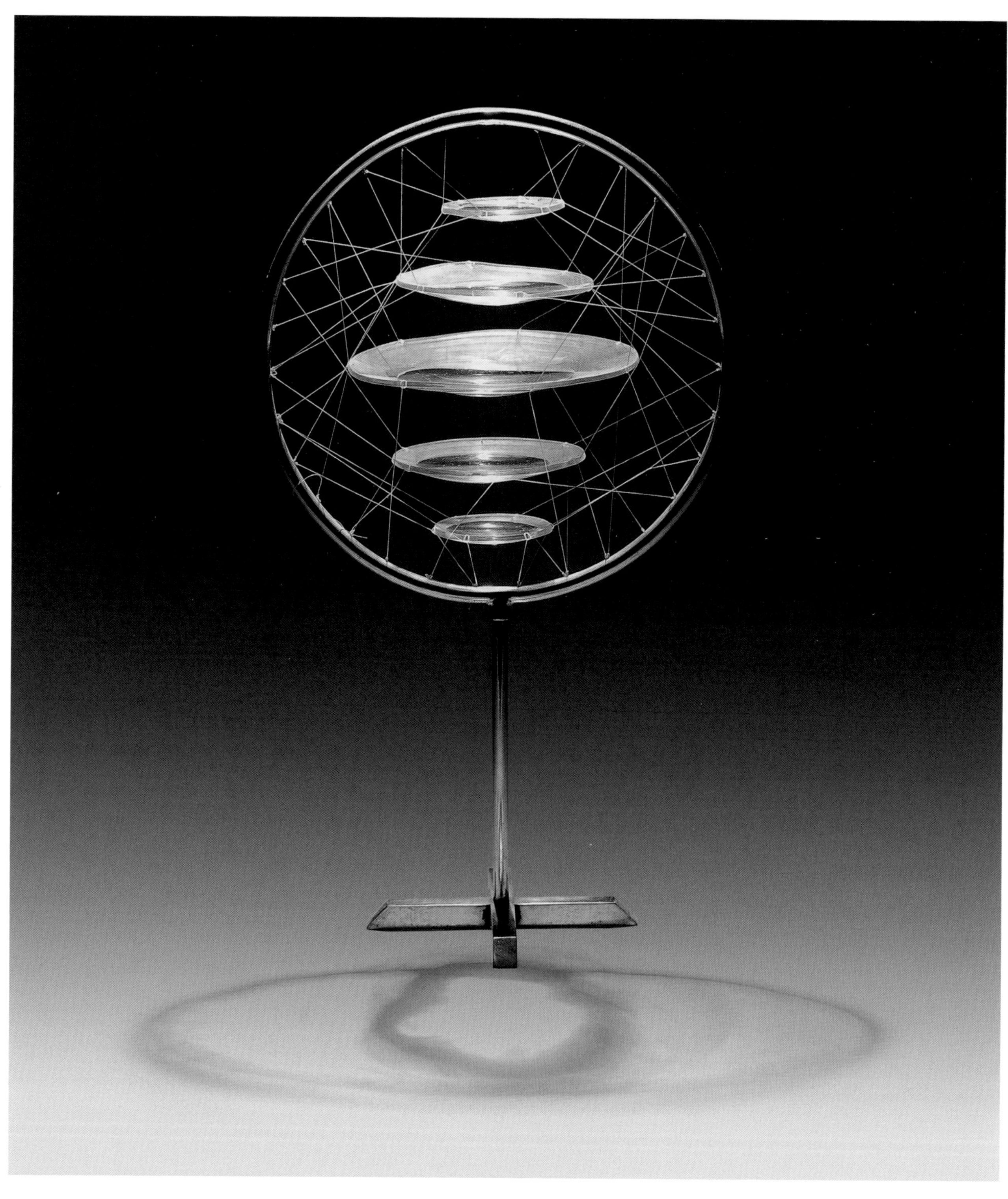

68
Water Lens 1969–71
Plexiglass, stainless
steel and water
87×53×30

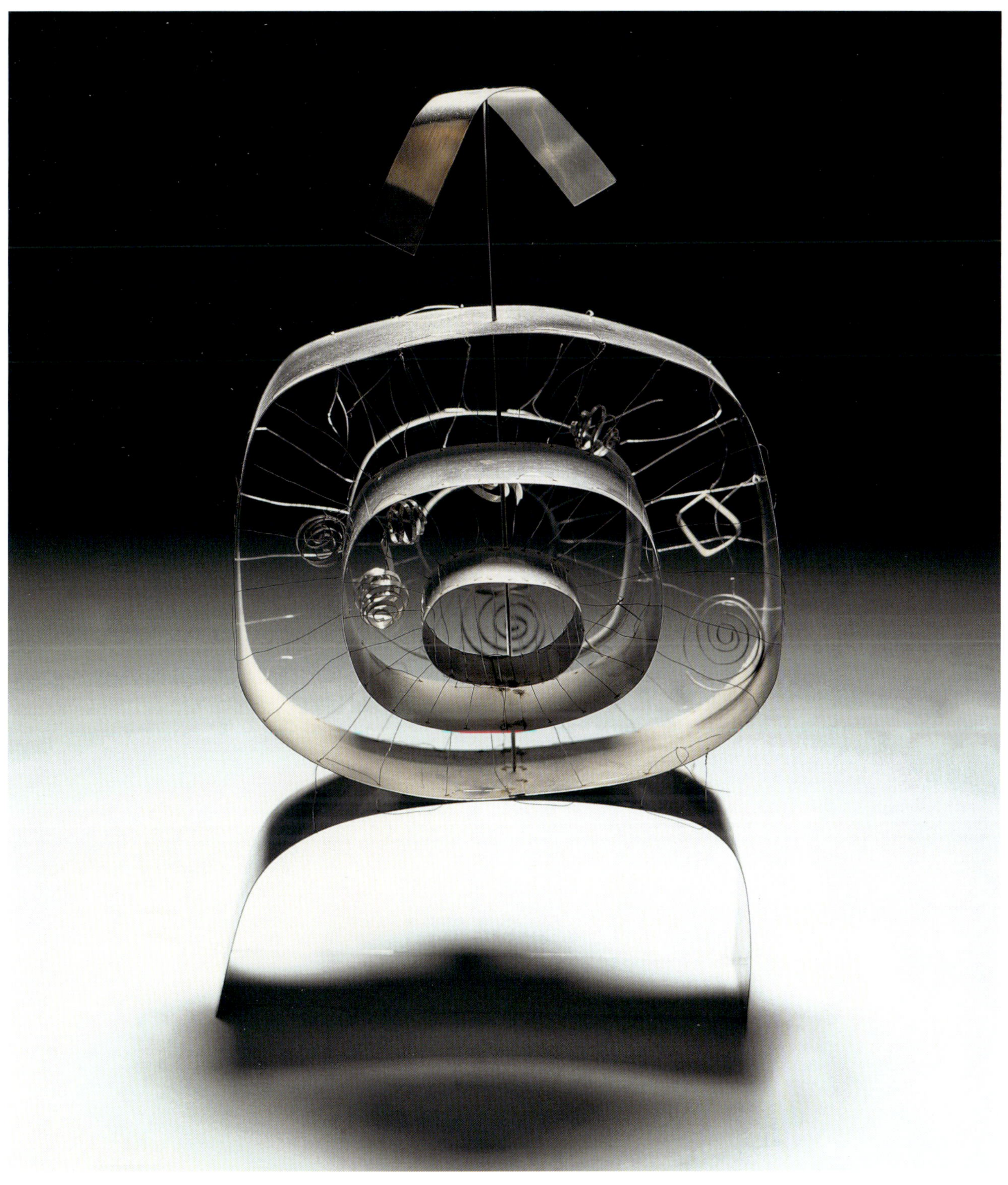

69
Intercircles 1972–4
Stainless steel
and nylon
55×32×10

70
Water Project
1980s
Aluminium
and plastic
150 × 28 × 5

71
Trajectory of the Arc 1972–4
Plexiglass
and nylon
78 × 20 × 20

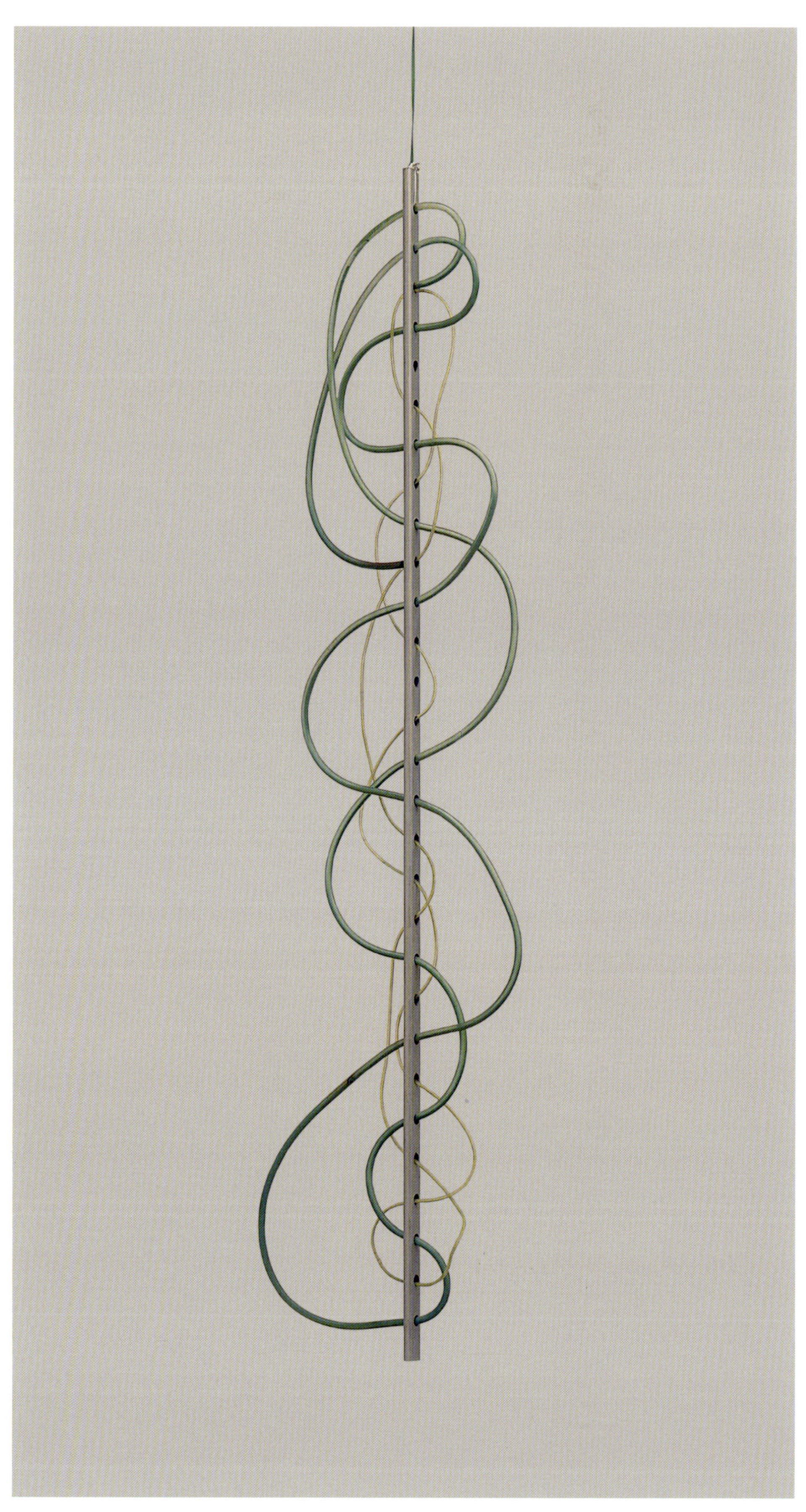

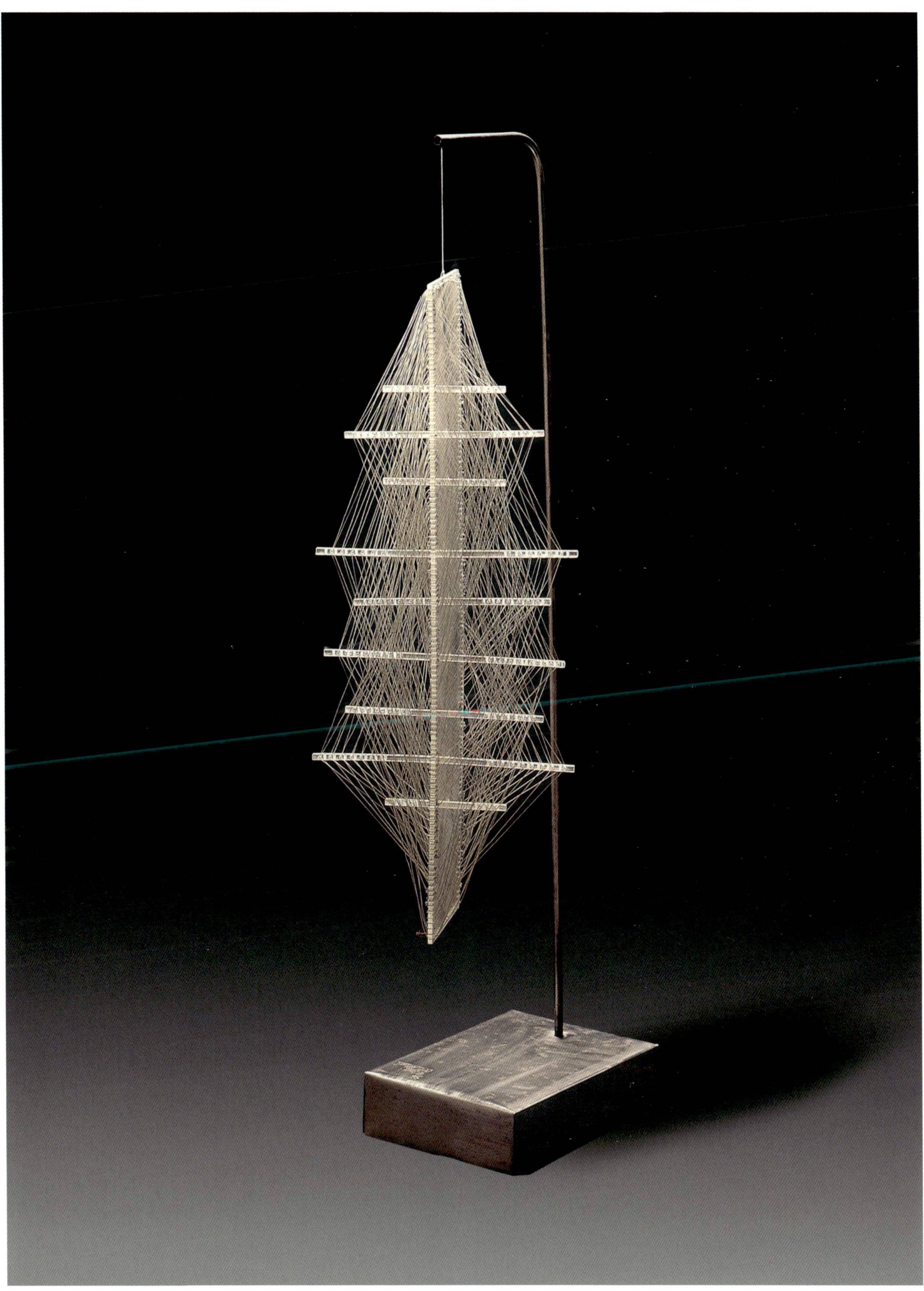

72
Trajectory of One Line 1972–4
Plexiglass and nylon
150 × 50 × 50

73
Untitled (Inter-cube) 1970–2
Plexiglass and nylon
176 × 44 × 44

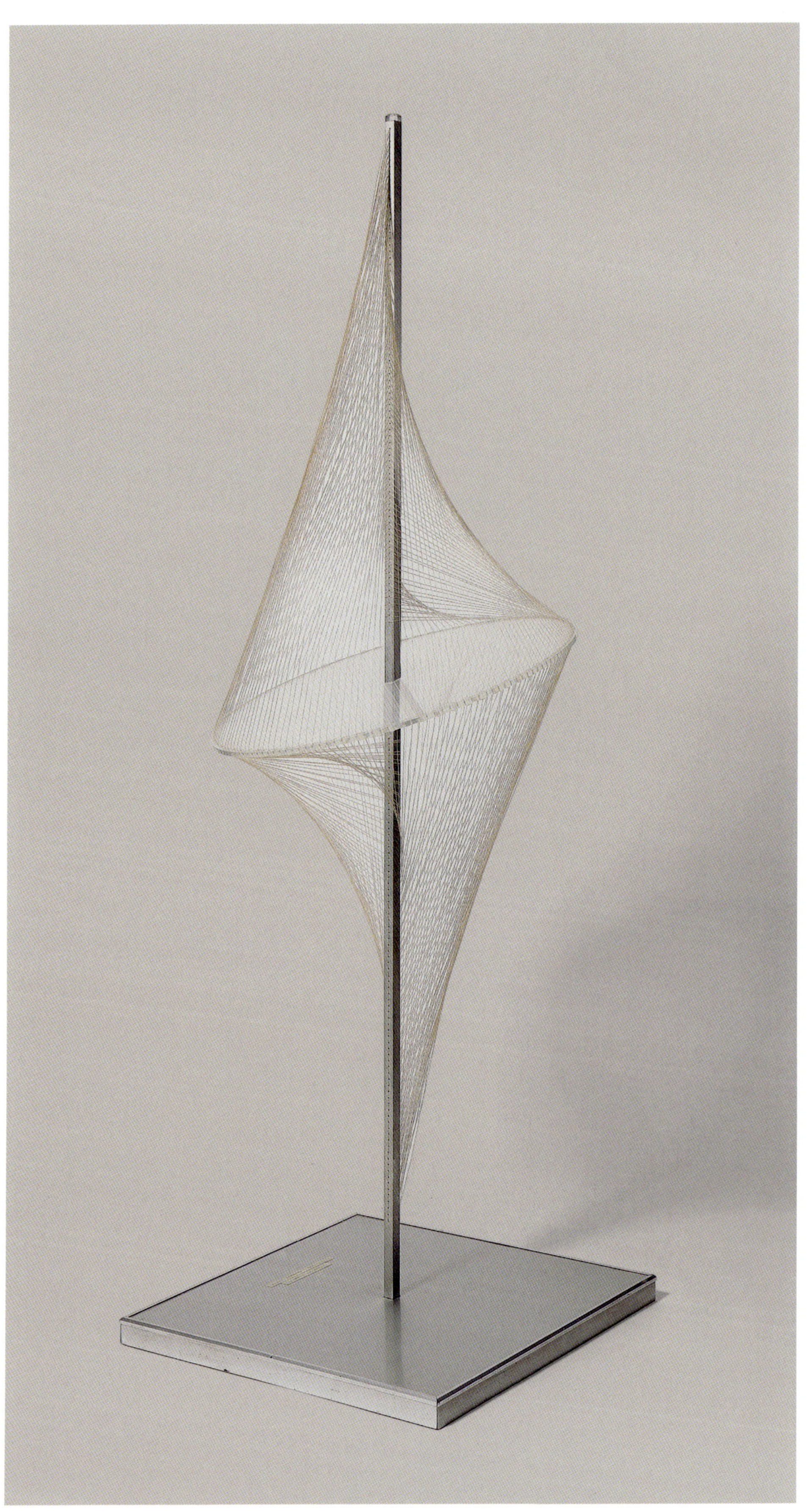

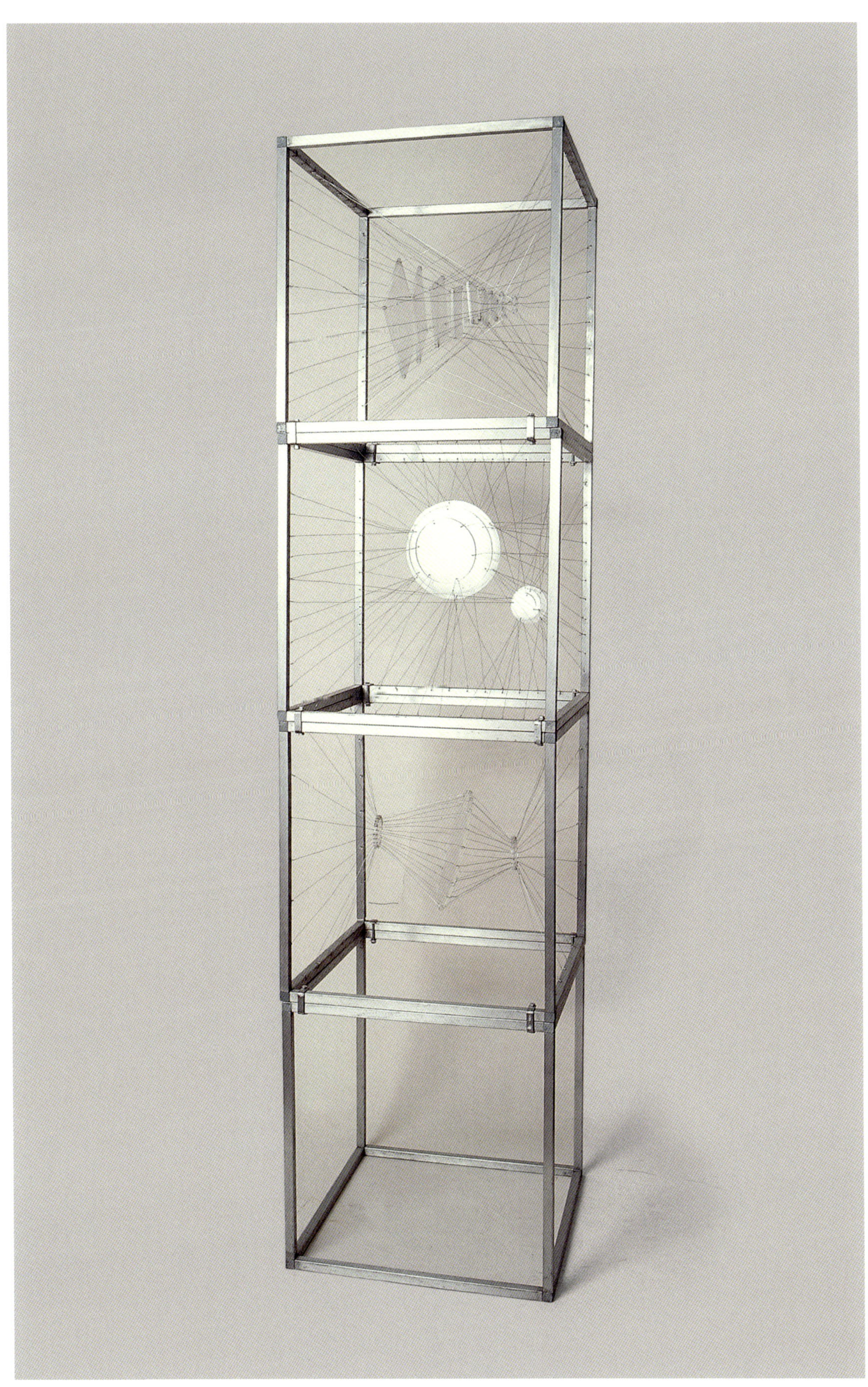

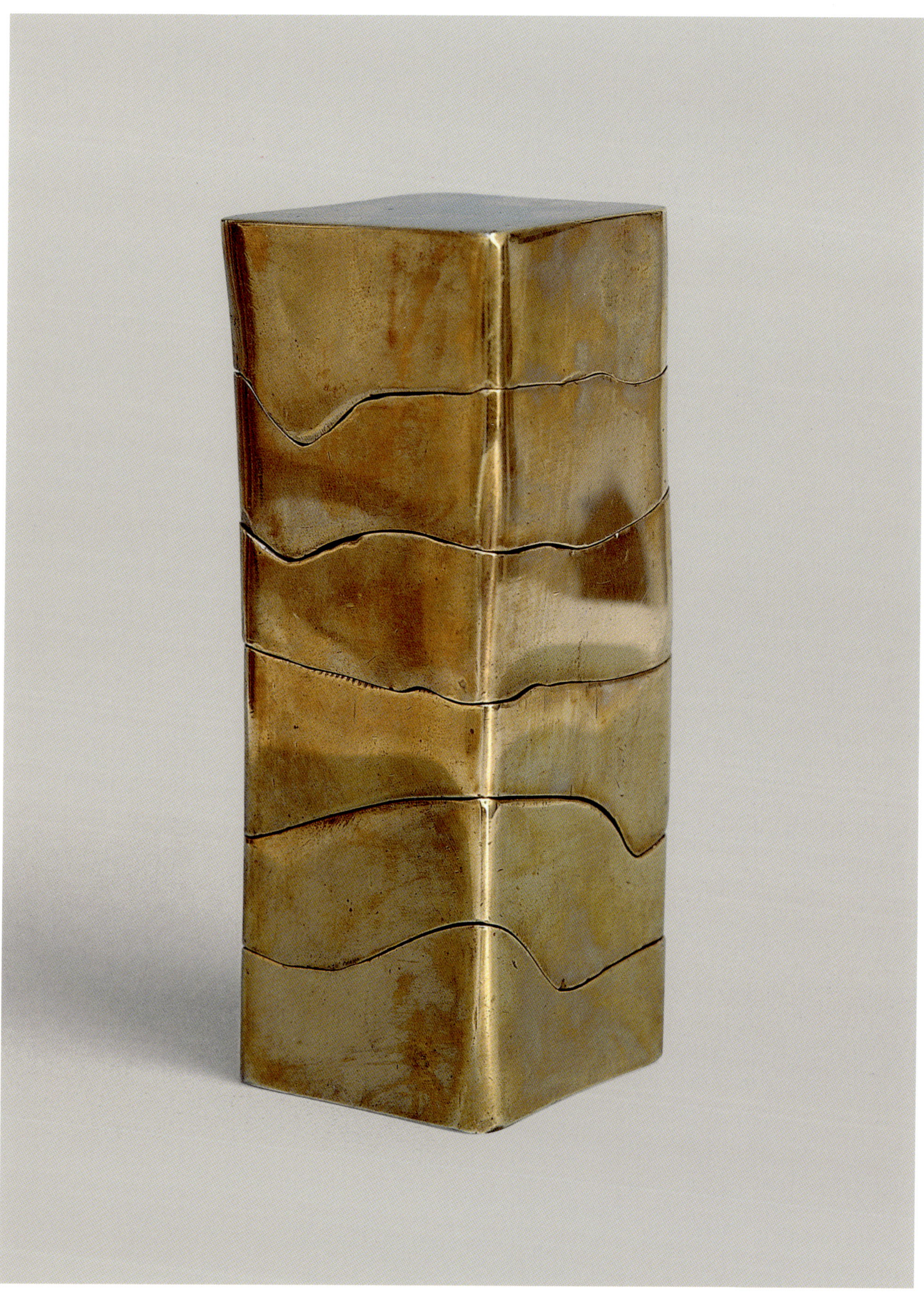

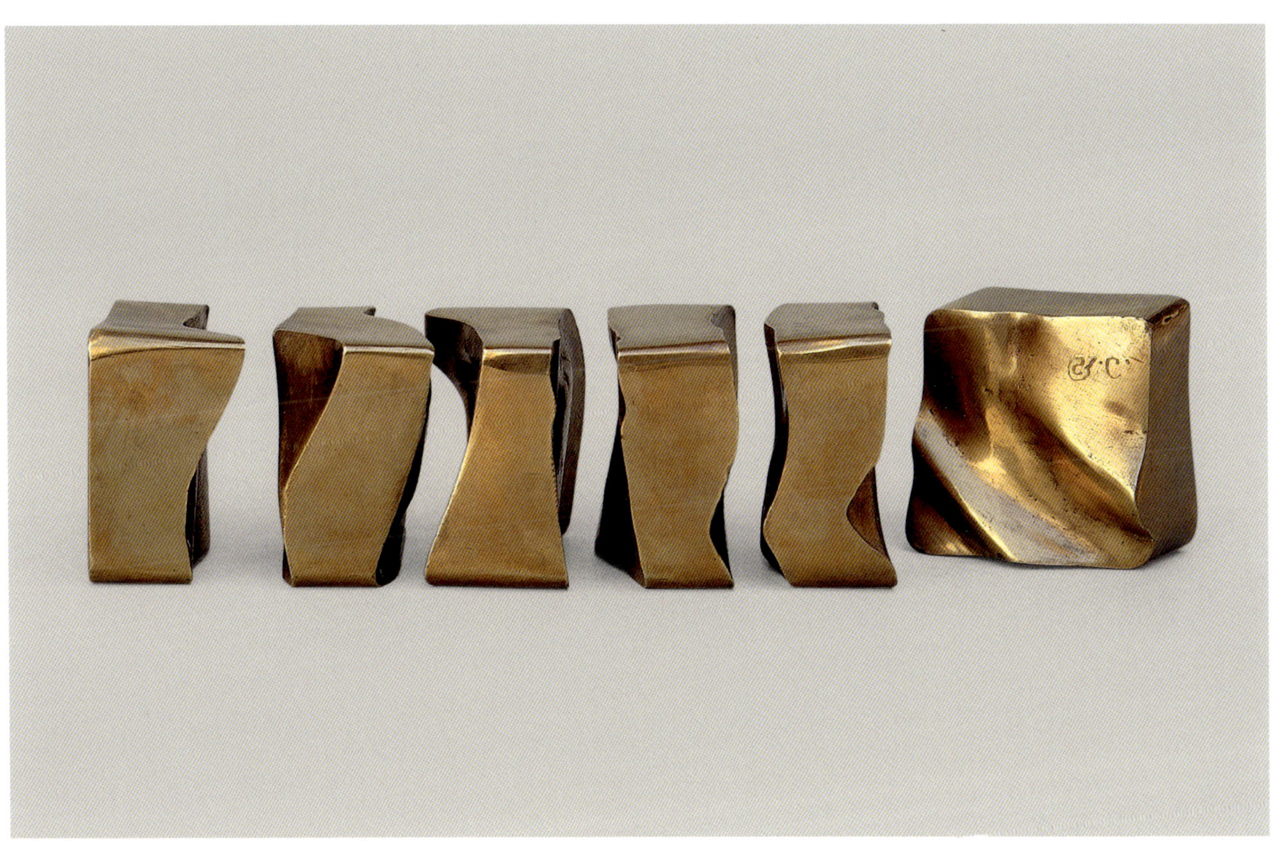

74
Poem 1972–4
Brass
13.5 × 4.5 × 5

75
Trajectory of the Arc 1972–4
Brass
9×13×9

76
(opposite)
Water Project
1972–4
Brass
20×7×7

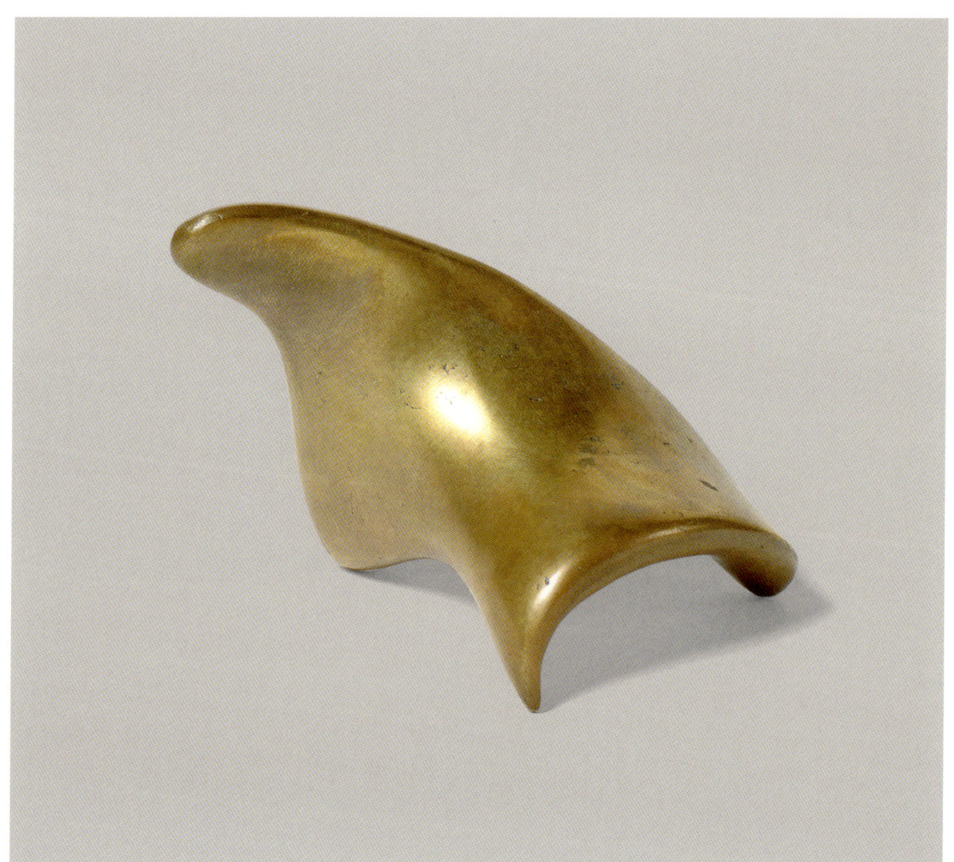

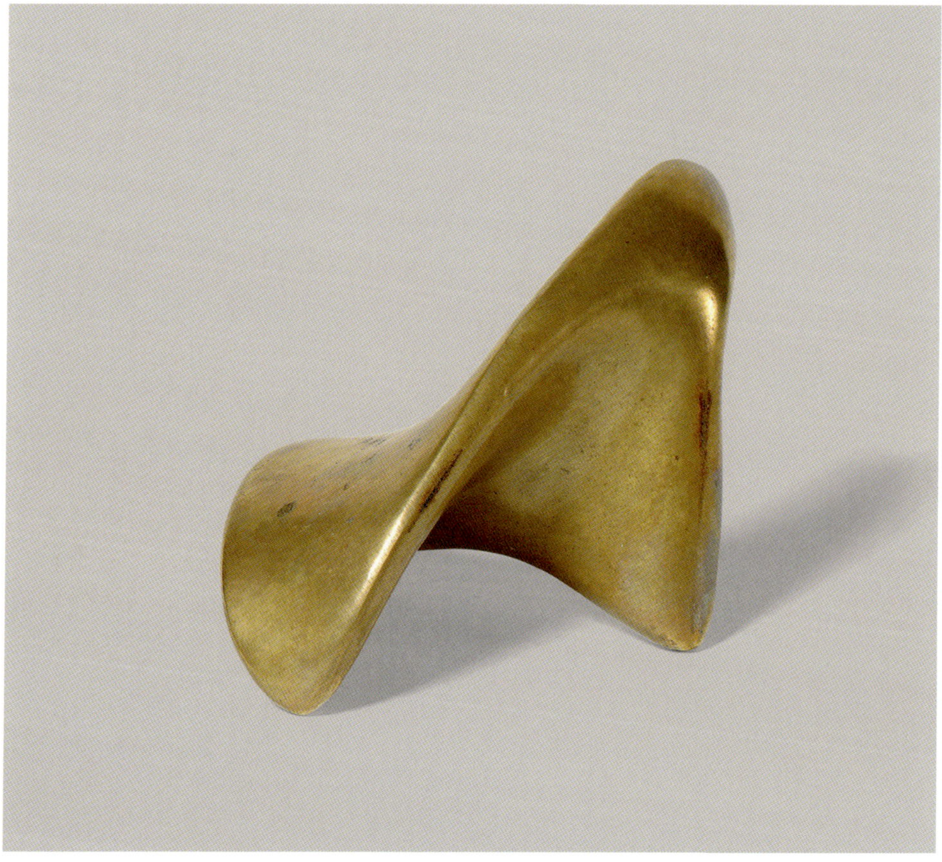

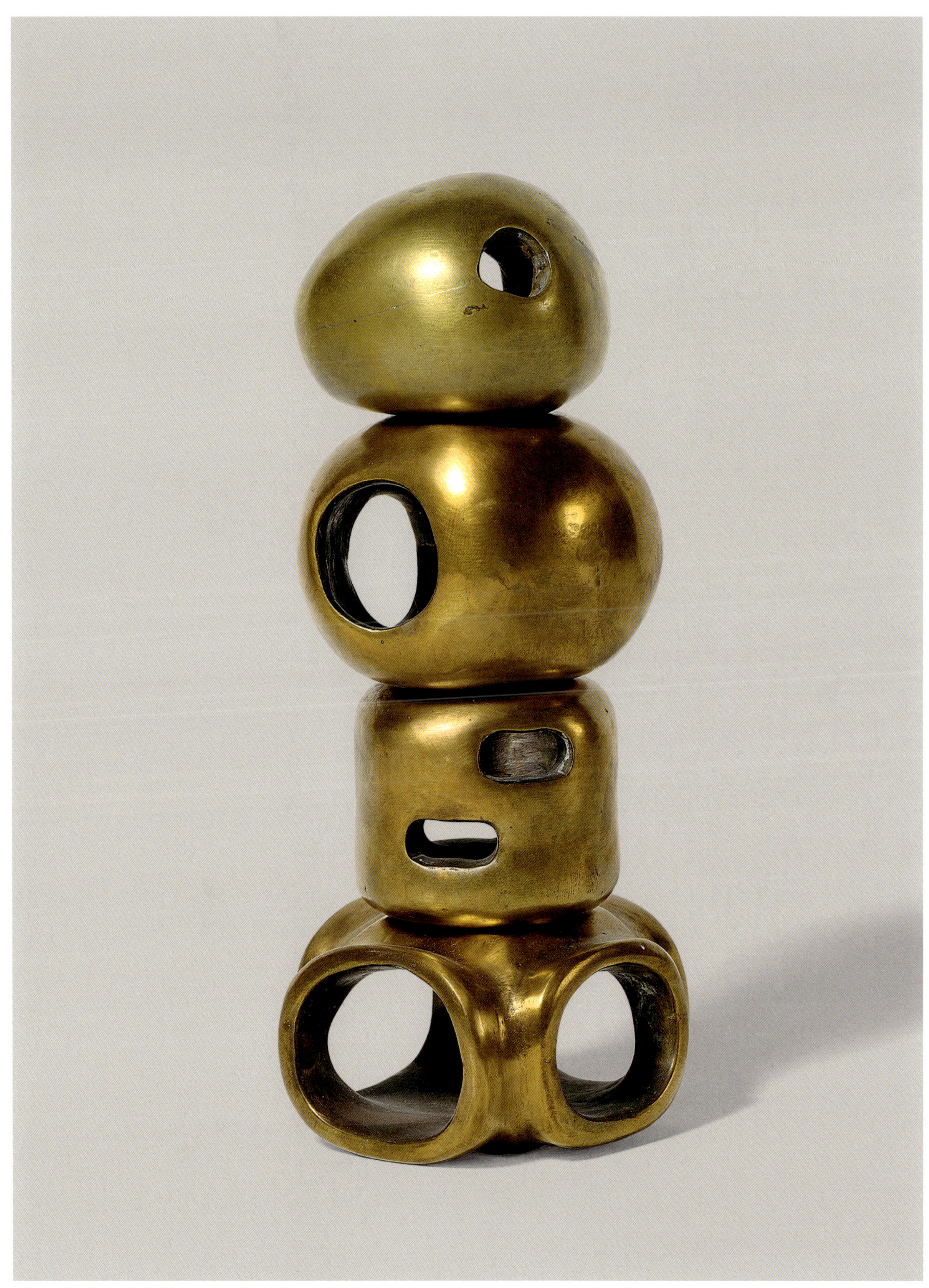

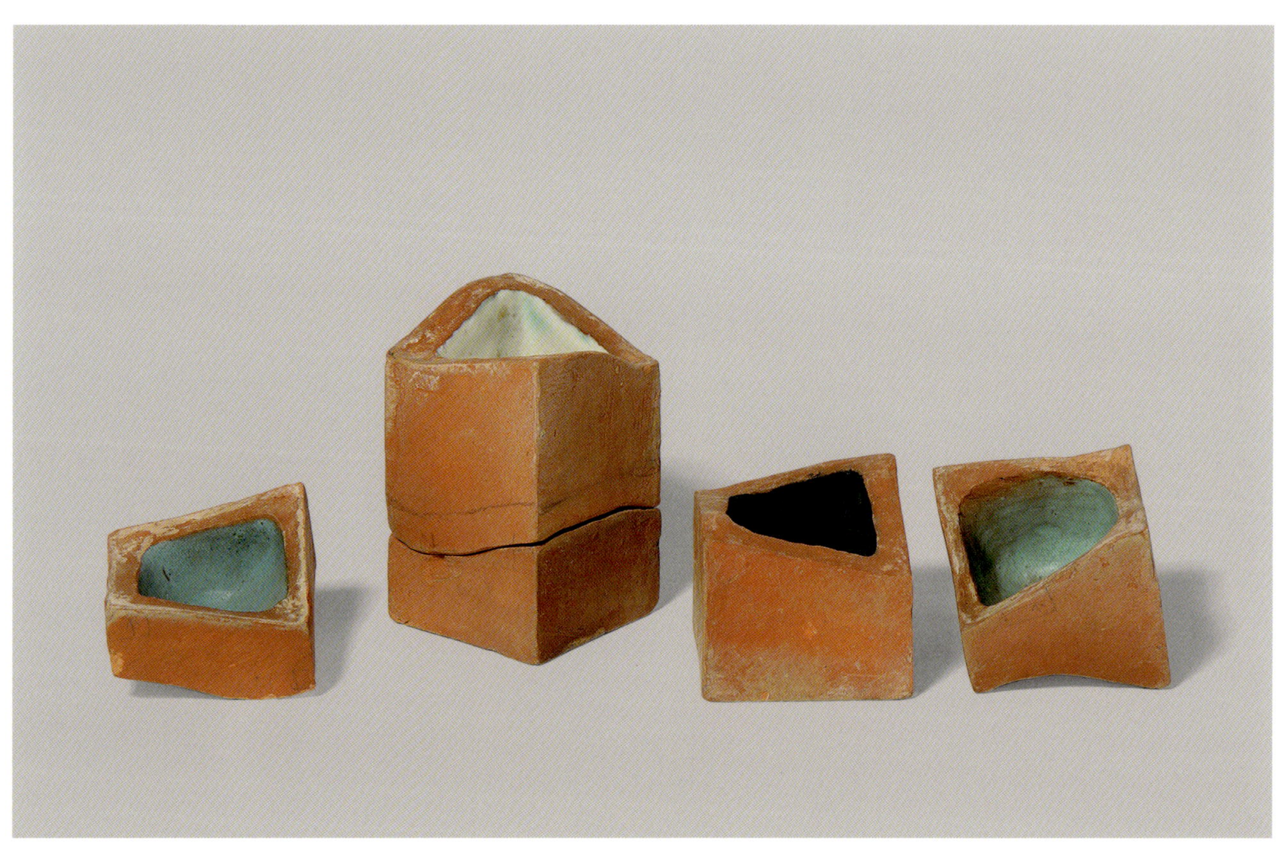

77
Poem Box 1972–4
Enamelled terracotta
19.5 × 5.5 × 5.5

78
(overleaf)
Water Project 1972–4
Terracotta
26 × 6

79
(overleaf)
Water Project 1972–4
Terracotta
19 × 9 × 5

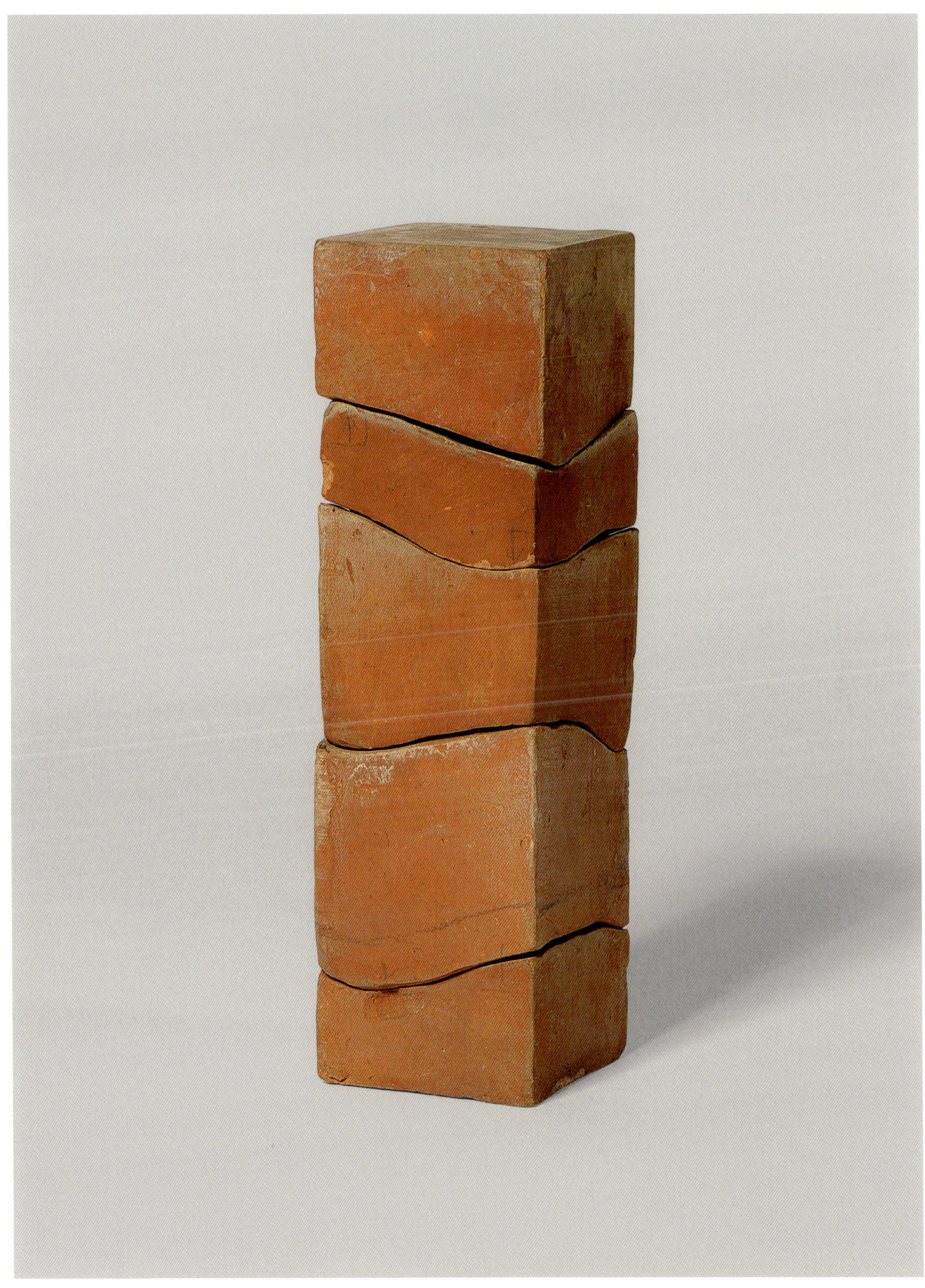

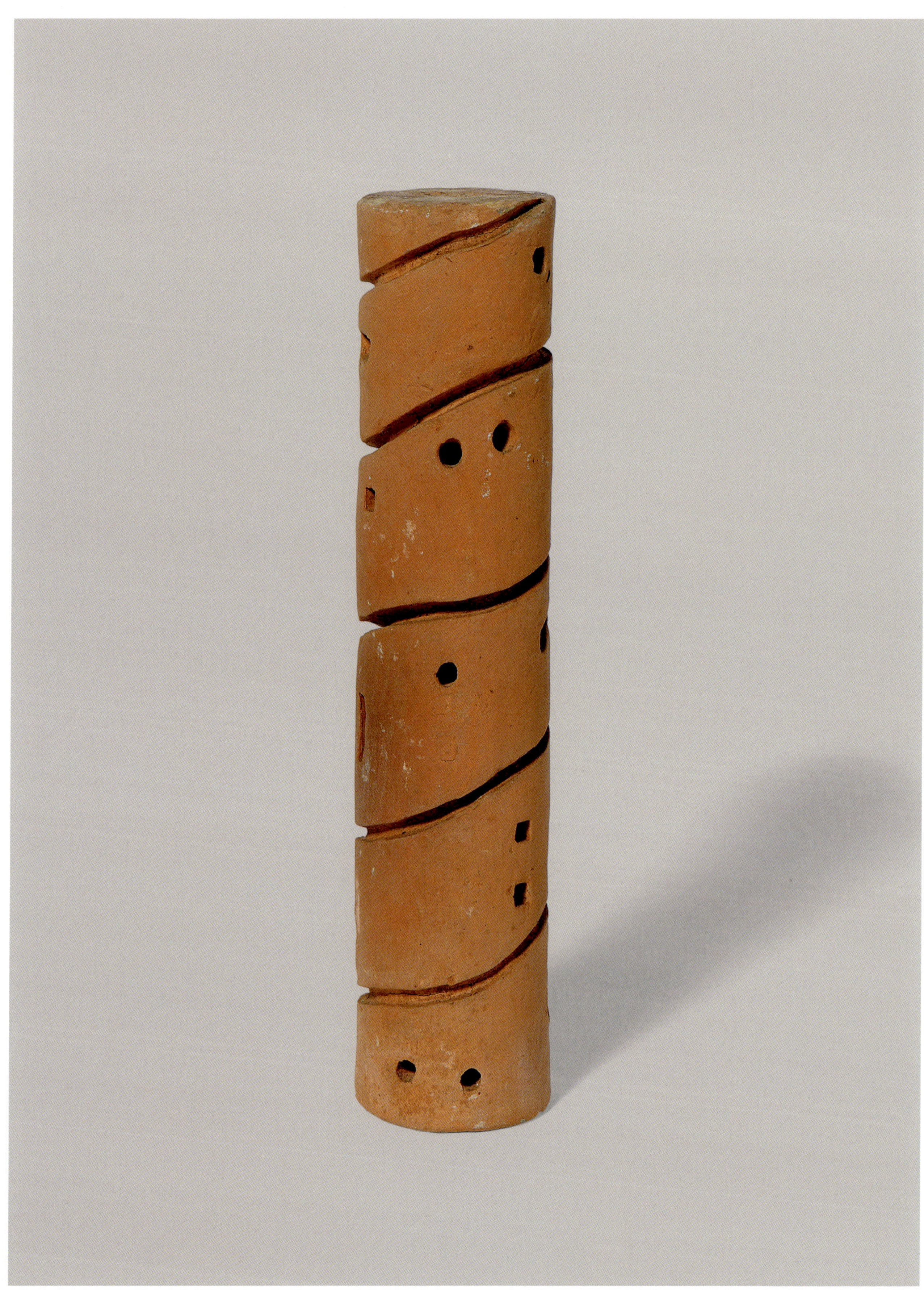

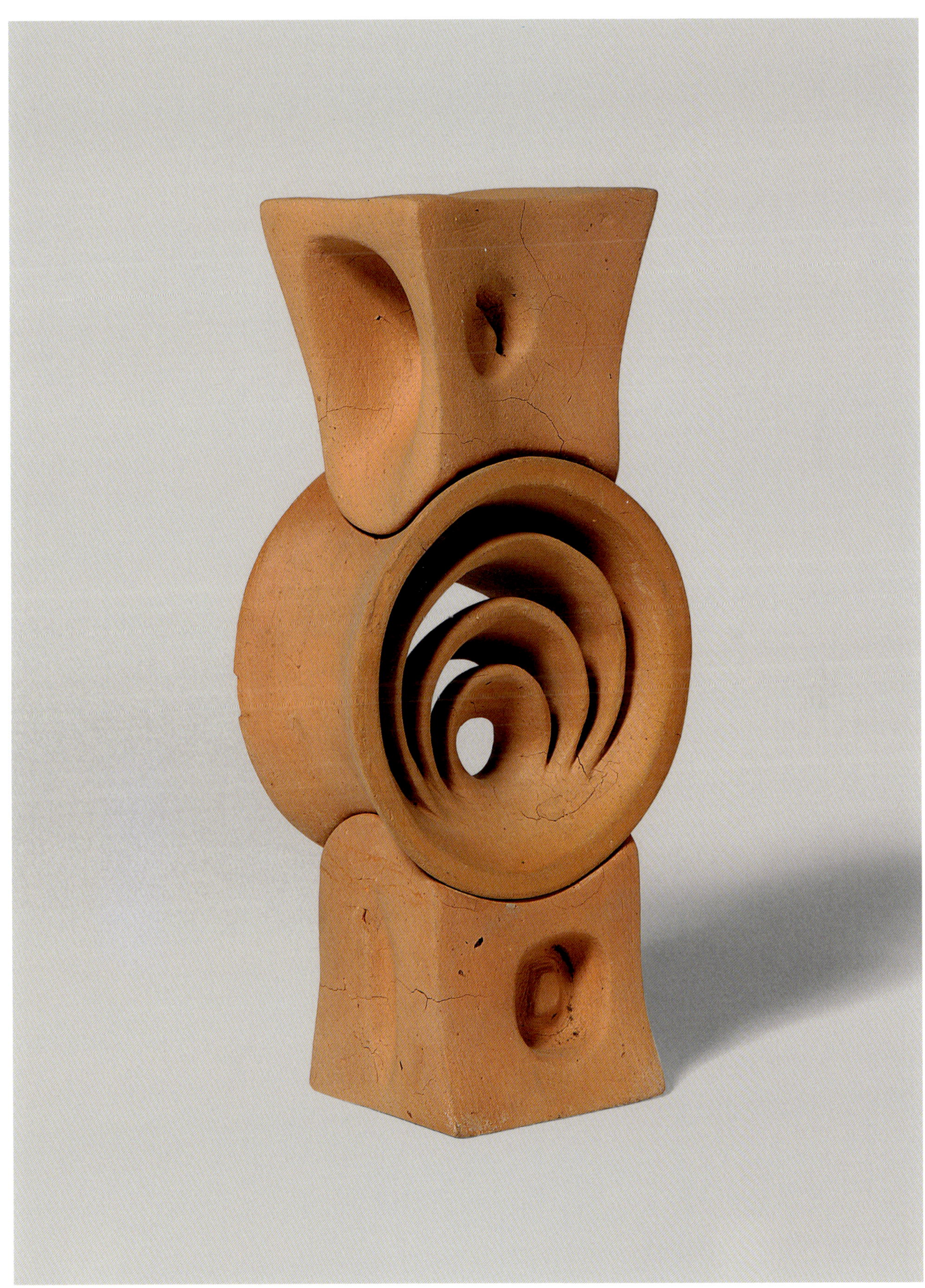

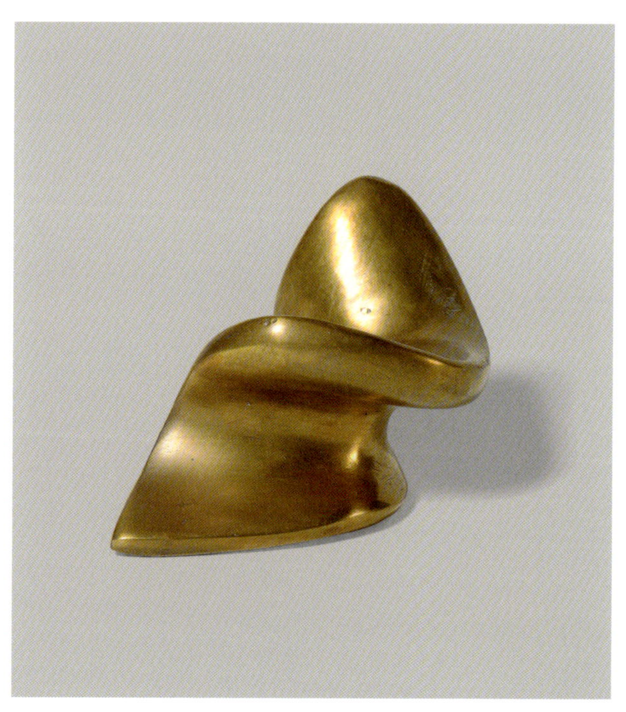

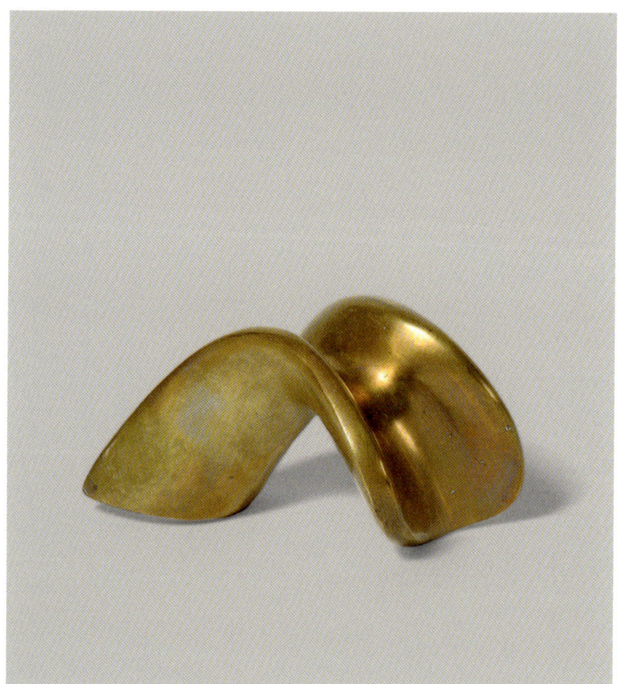

80
Trajectory of the Arc 1972–4
Brass
4×13×5

81
Trajectory of the Arc 1972–4
Brass
9×25×9

82
Poem 1972–4
Aluminium
18×5×6

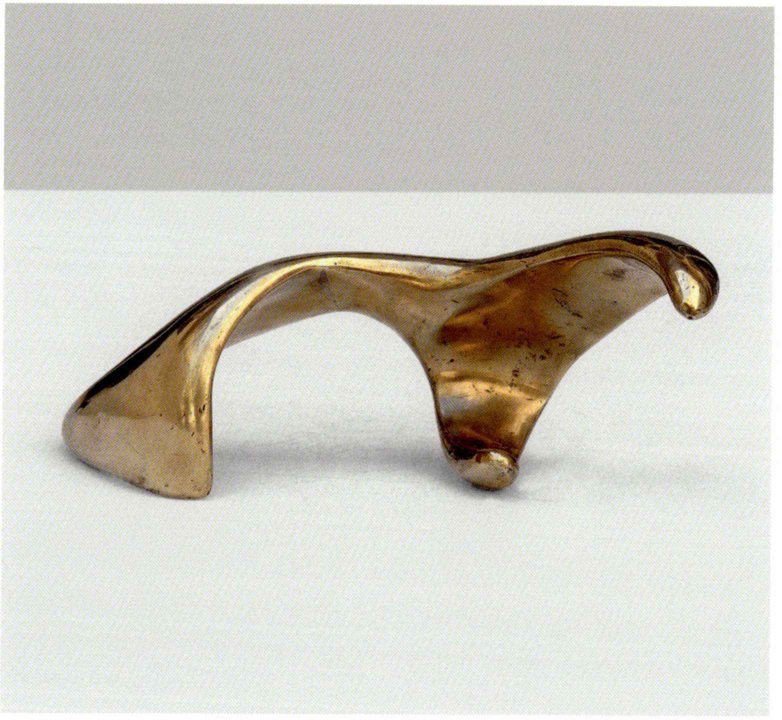

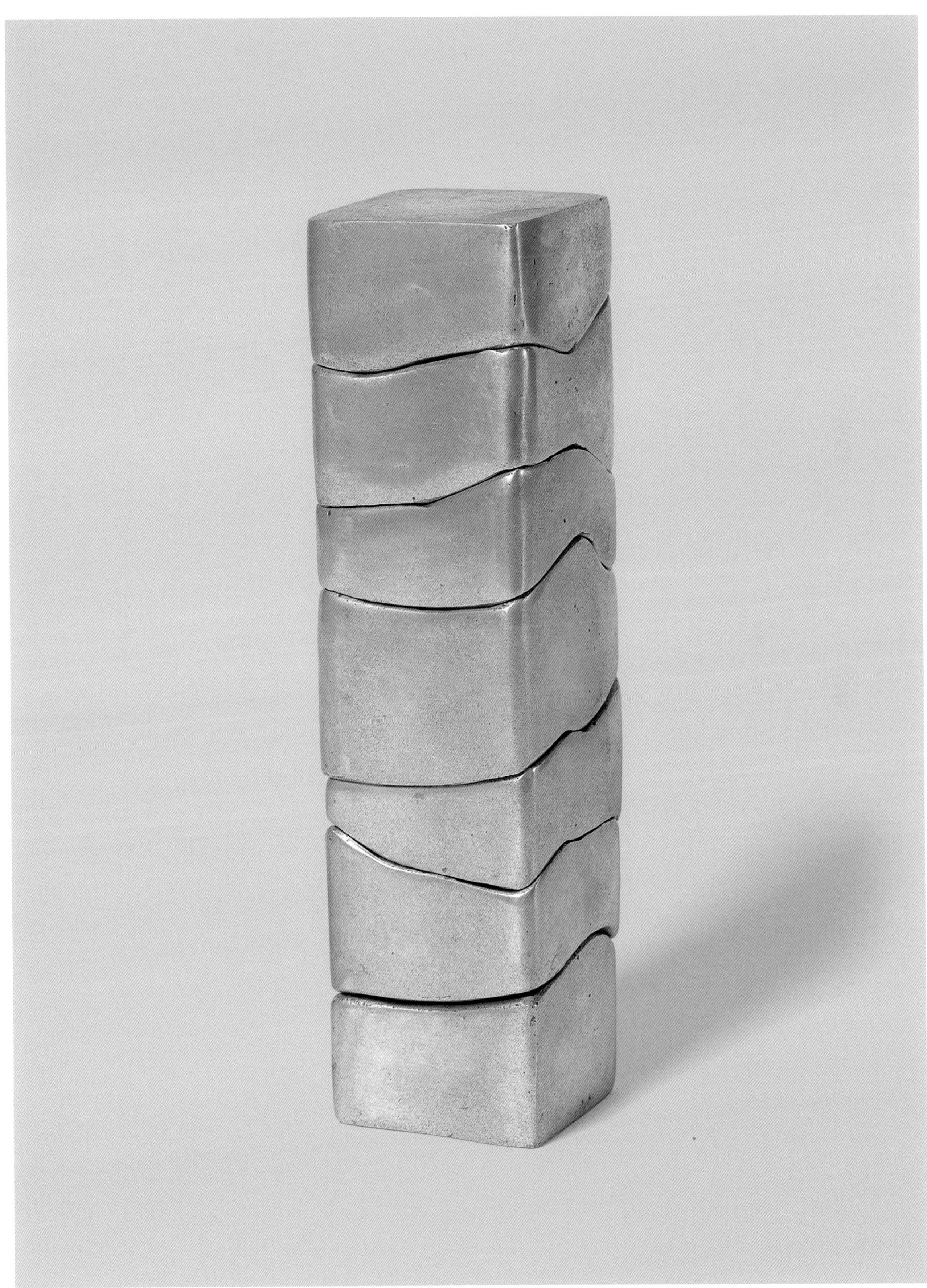

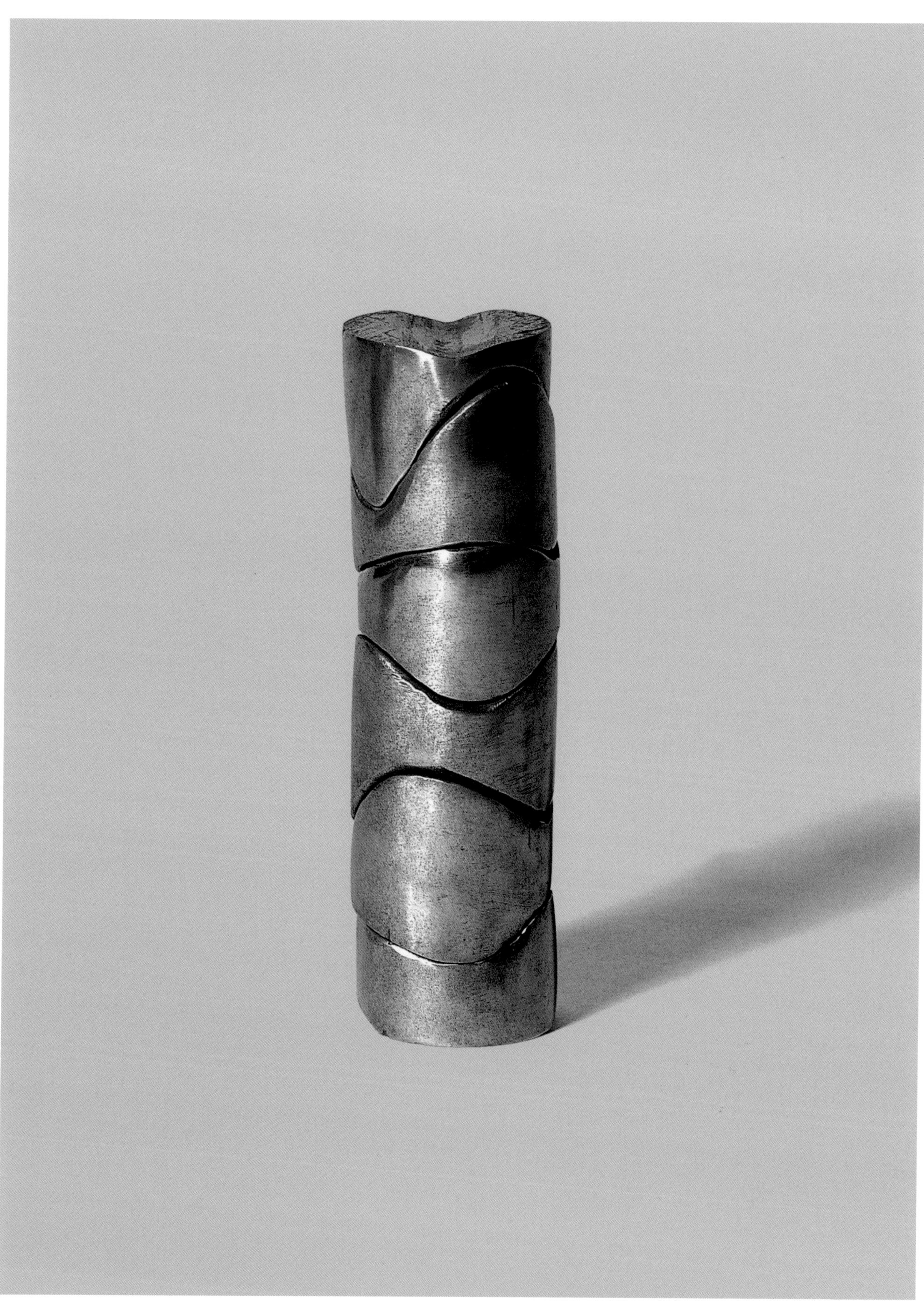

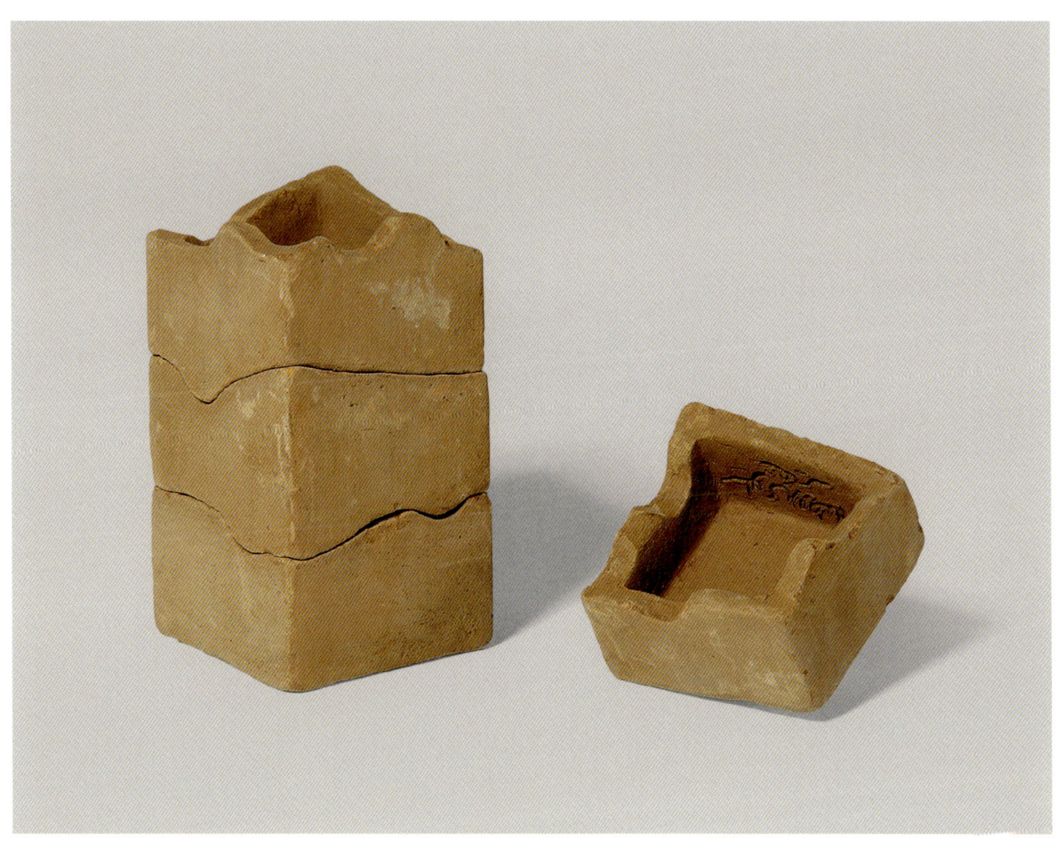

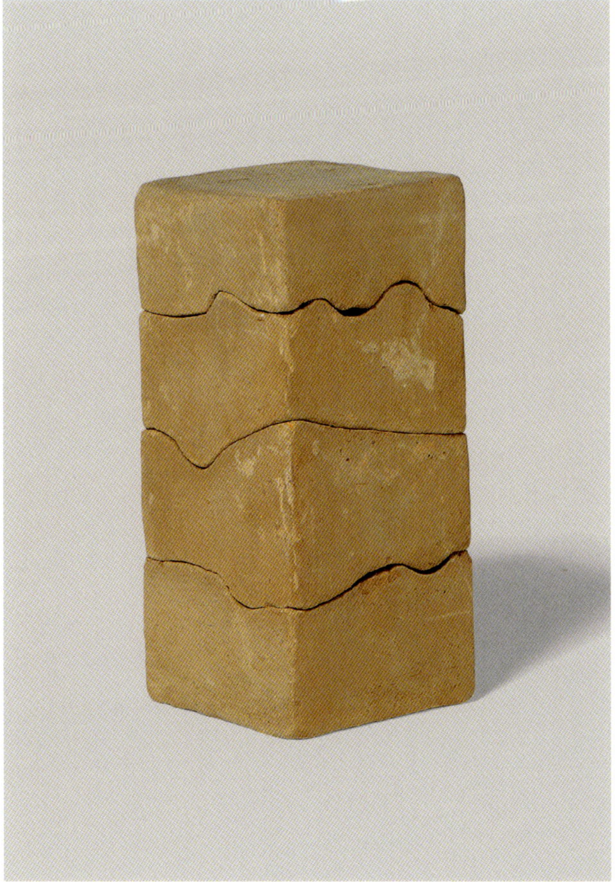

83
Poem Cylinder
1972–4
Aluminium
18 × 5.5

84
Poem 1972–4
Clay
14 × 6.5 × 6.5

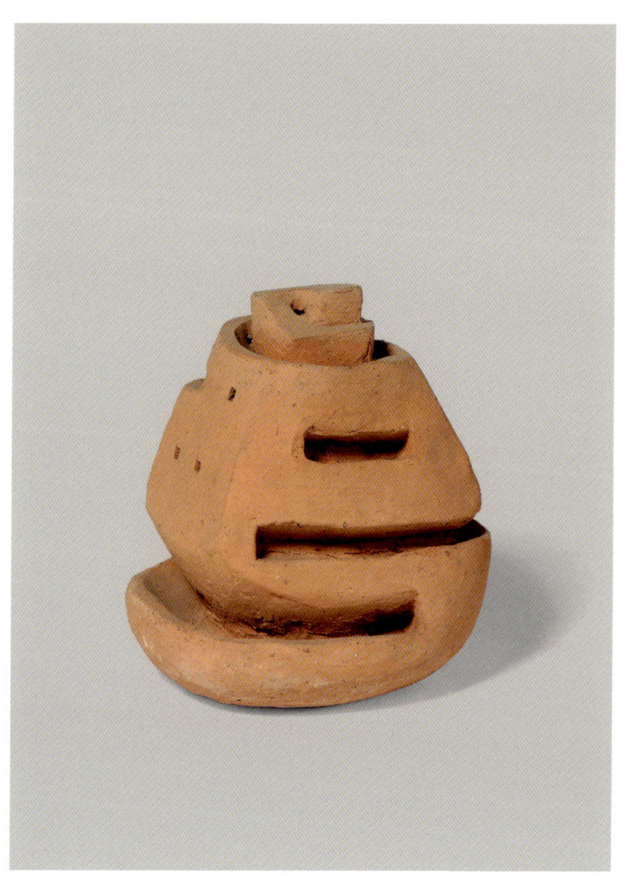

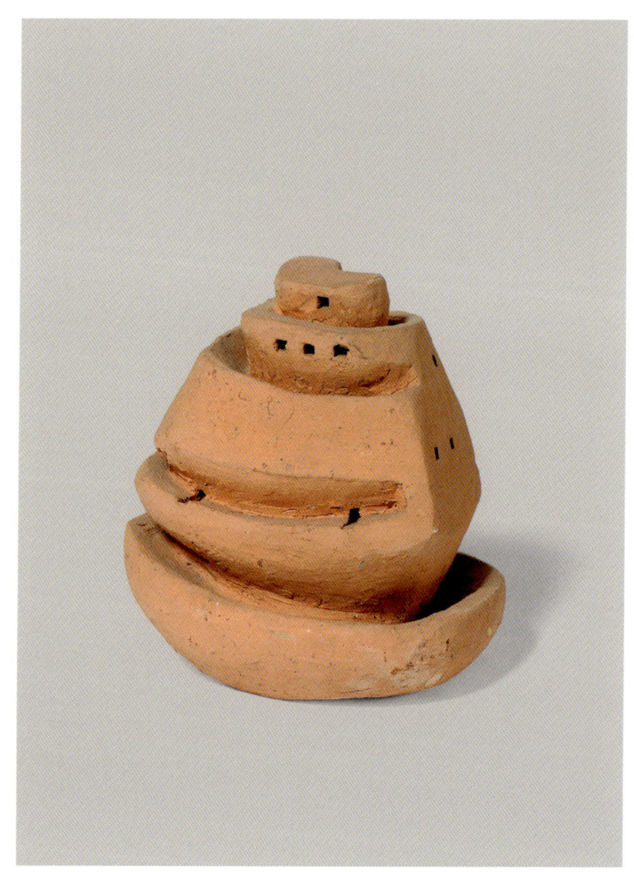

85
Water Project 1972–4
Terracotta
19 × 15 × 12

86
Water Project 1973
Clay and metal
18 × 13 × 13

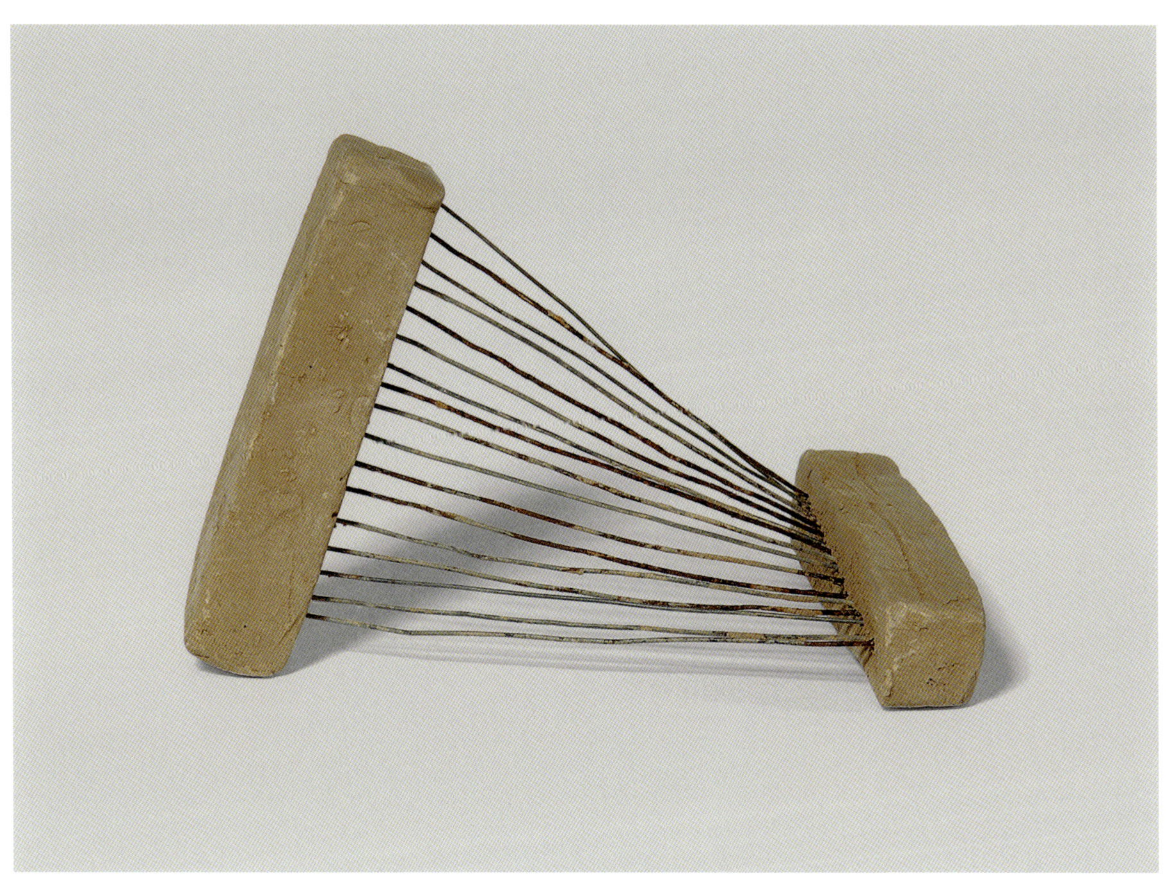

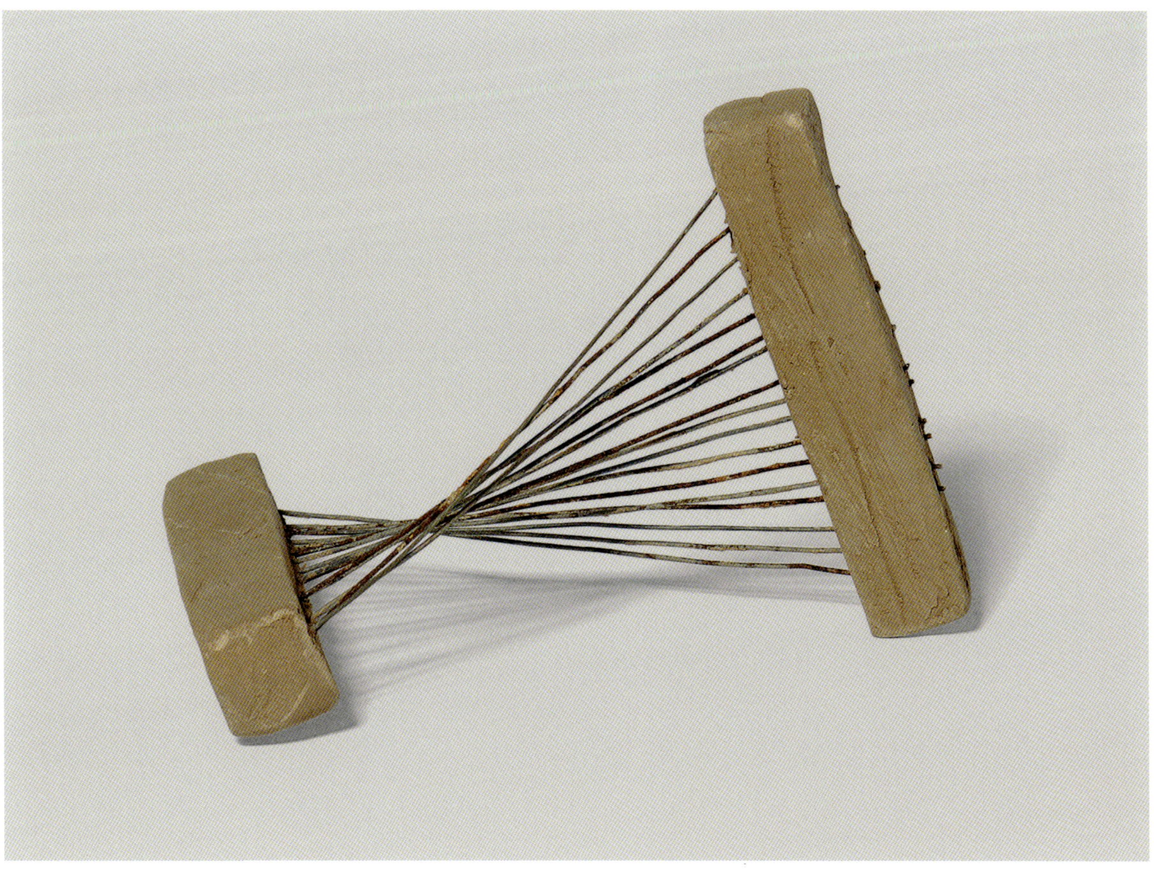

87
Water Project 1973
Clay and plastic
8×12×5

88
Water Project 1973
Clay and plastic
18×10×10

89
(overleaf)
Project for Public Housing 1973
Terracotta
14×19×3

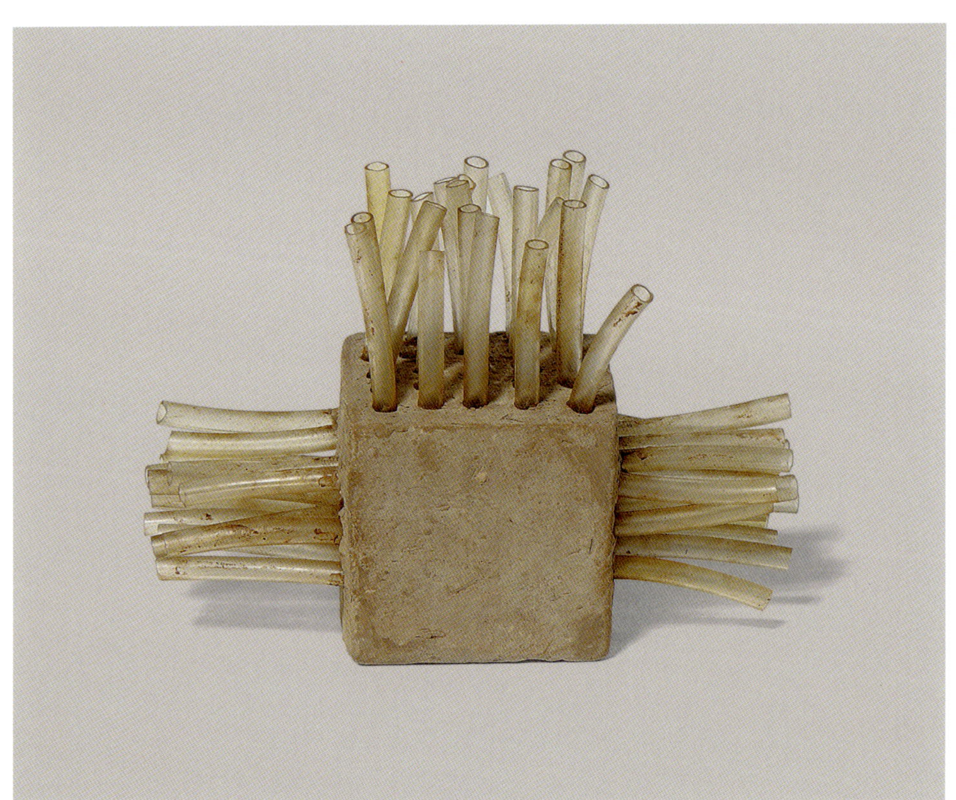

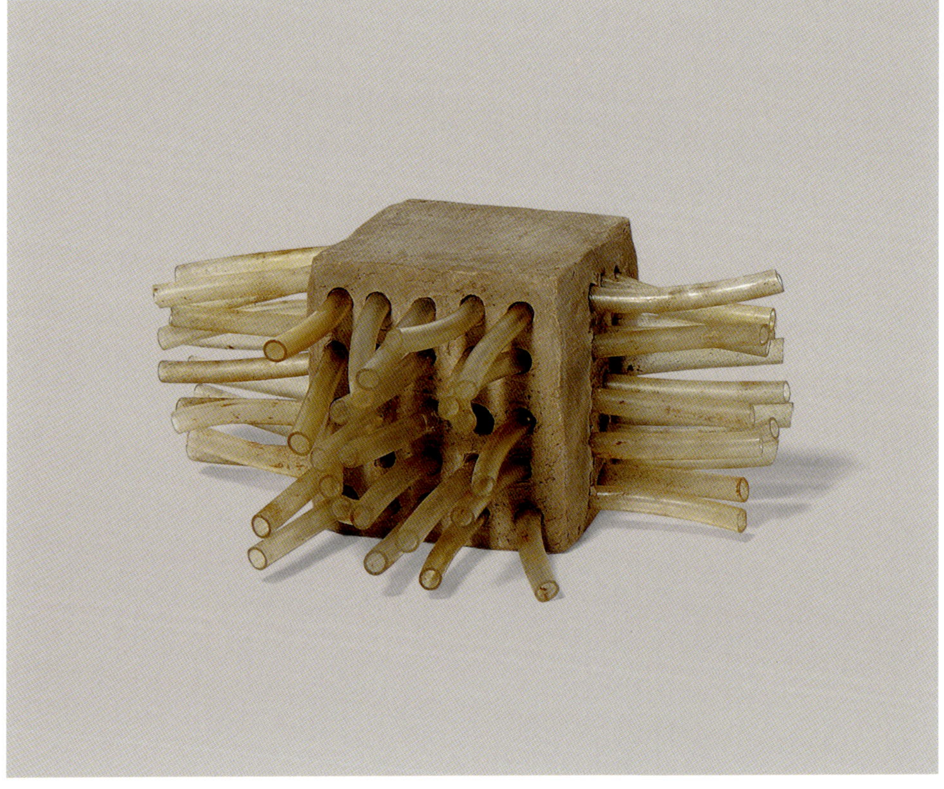

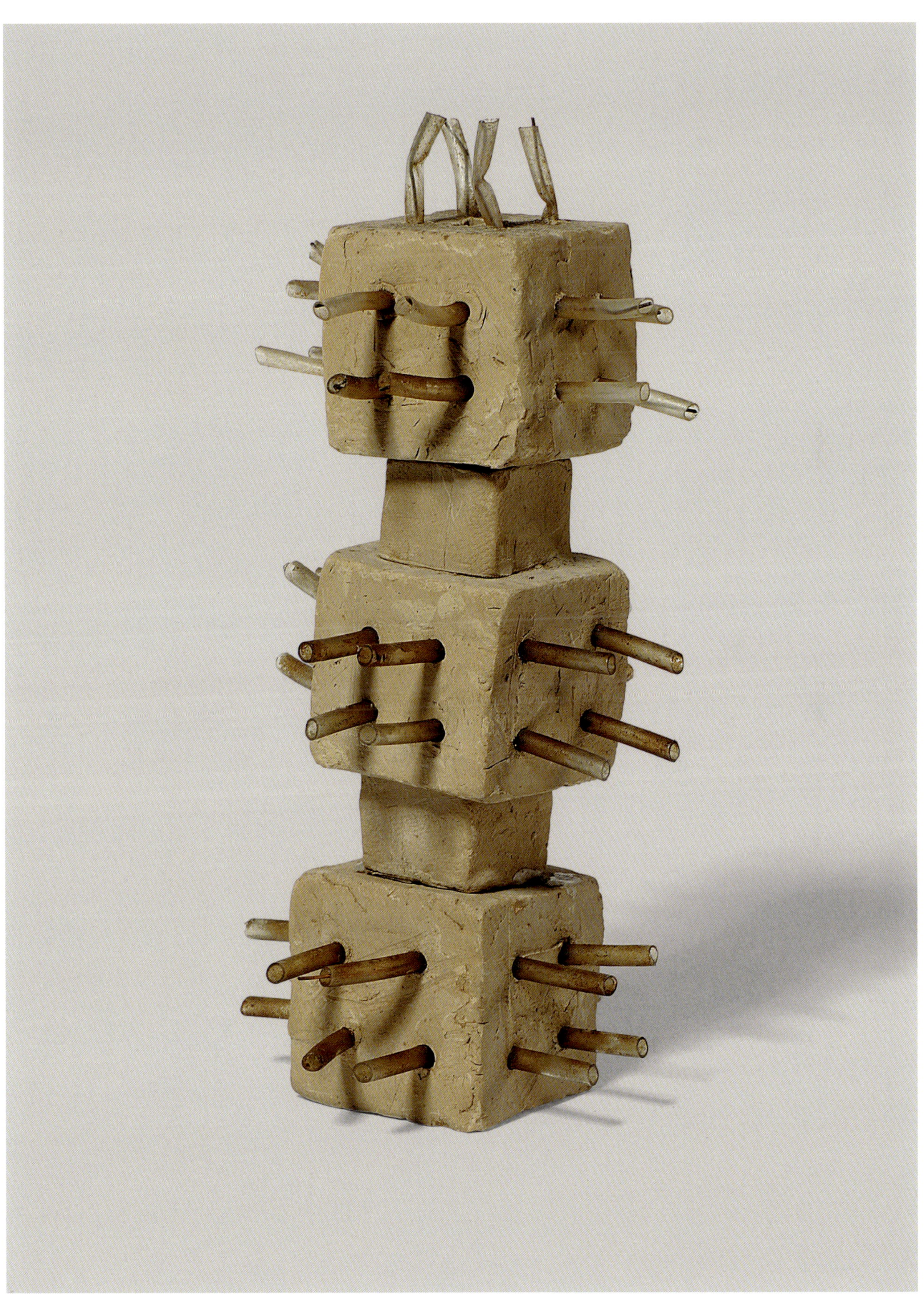

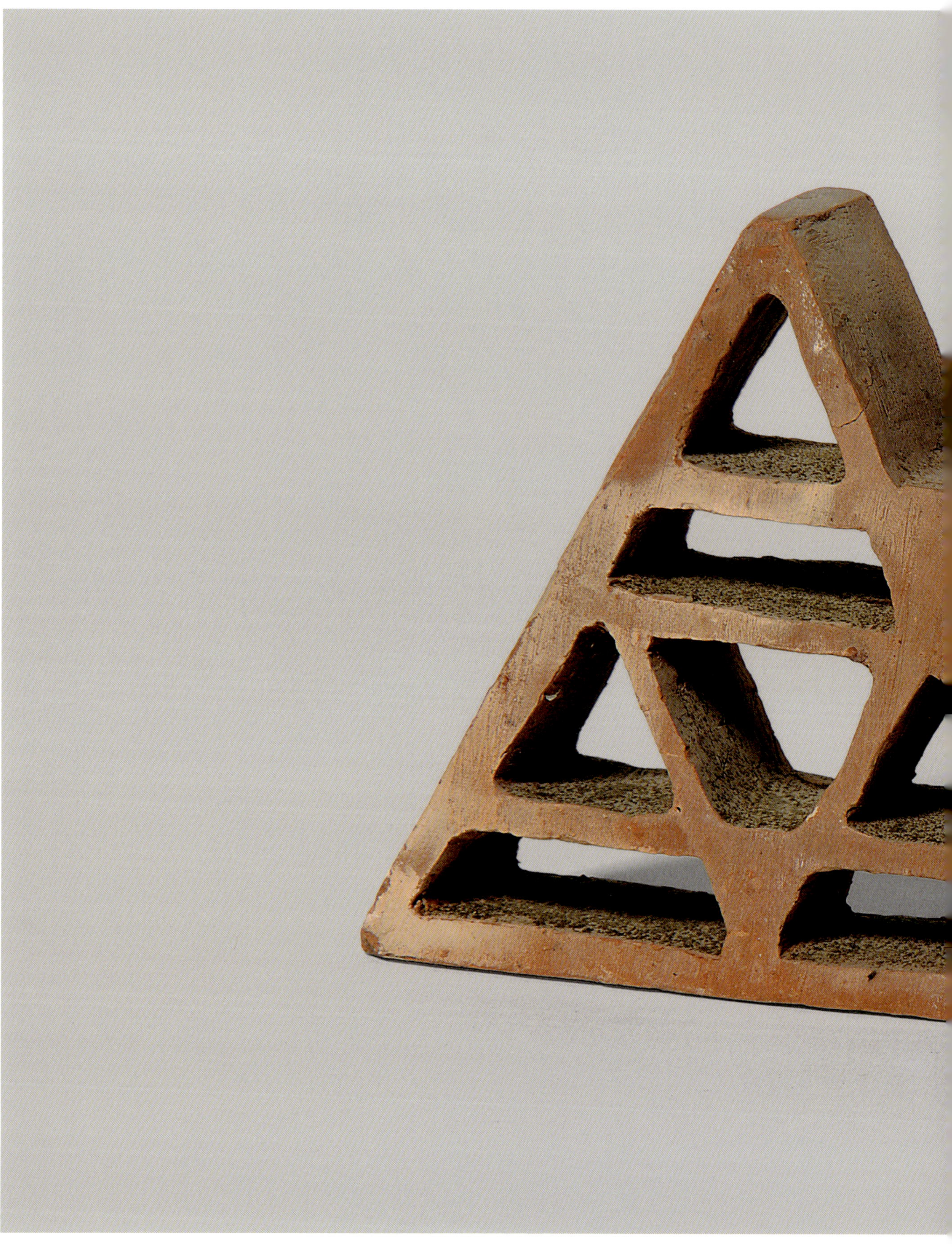

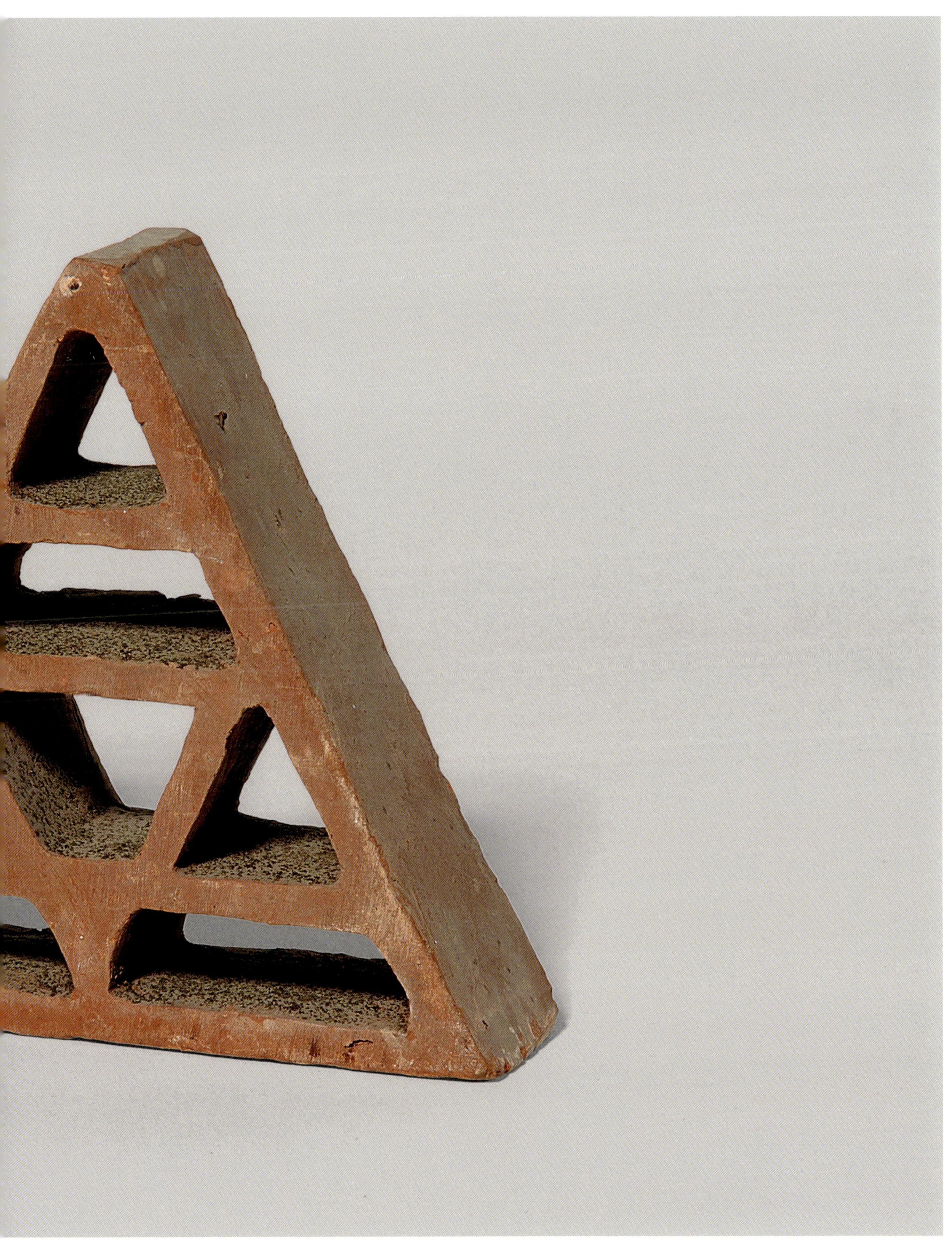

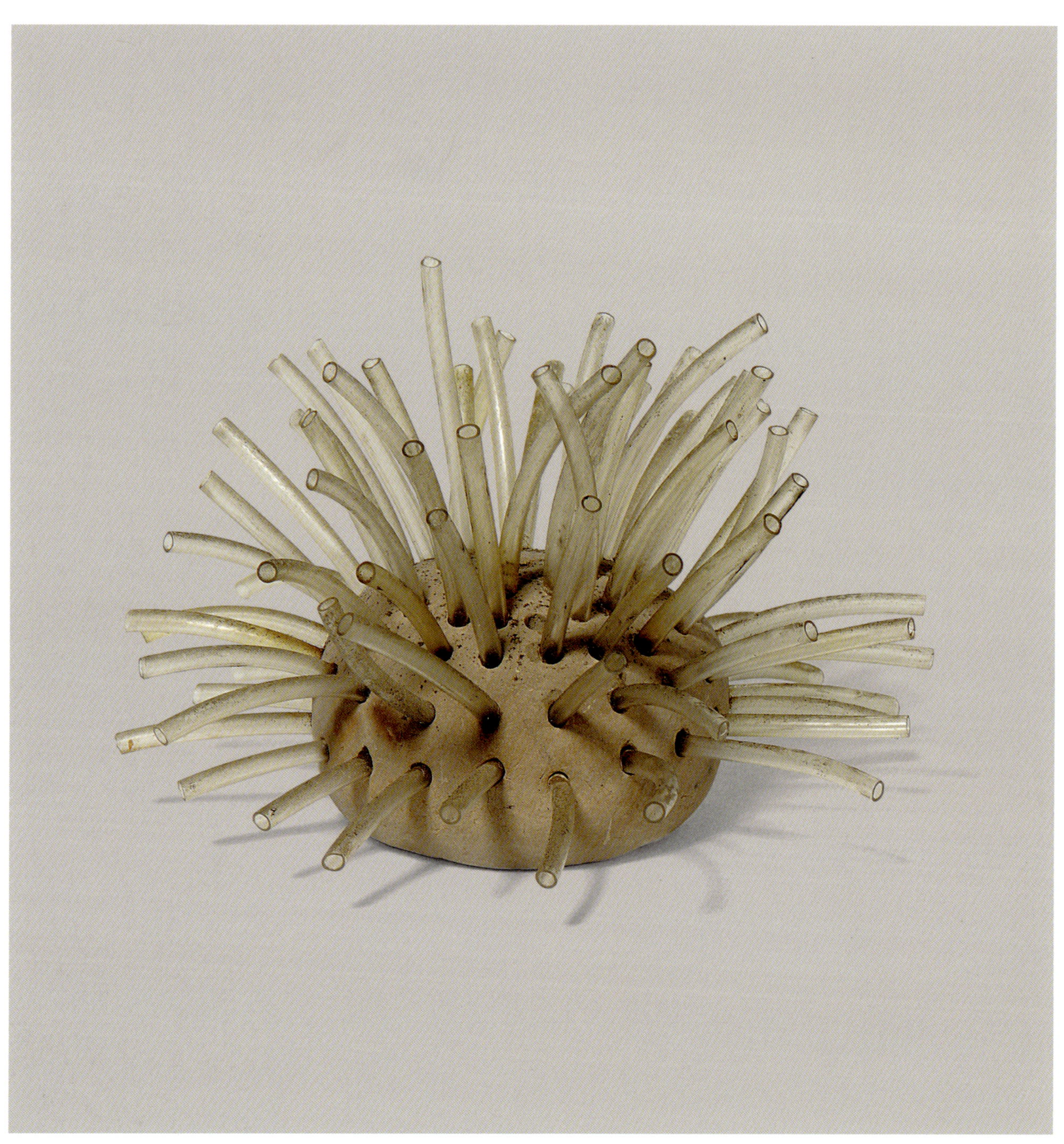

90
Water Project 1973
Clay and plastic
13 × 9 × 9

91
Water Project 1973
Clay
36 × 7 × 7

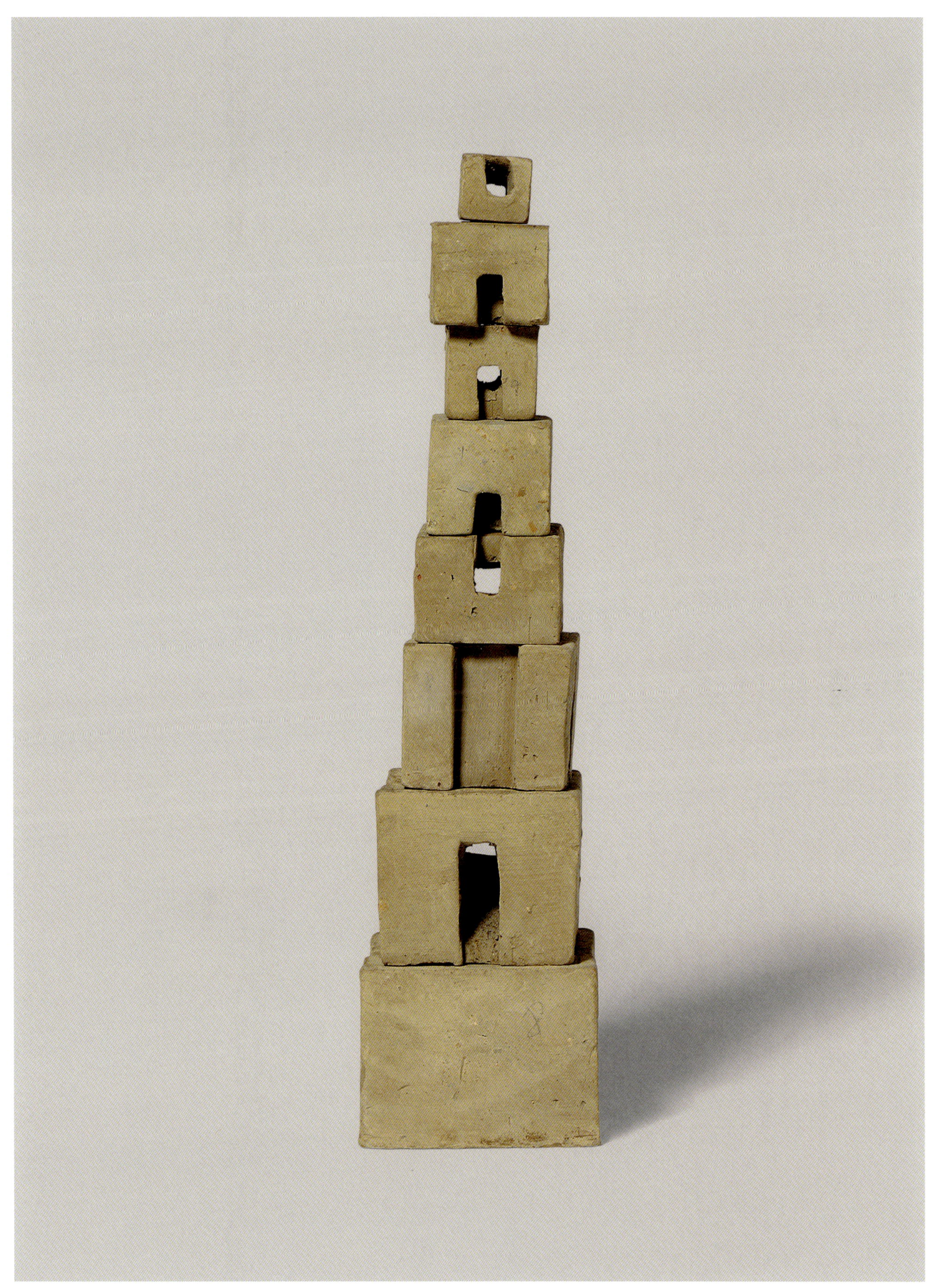

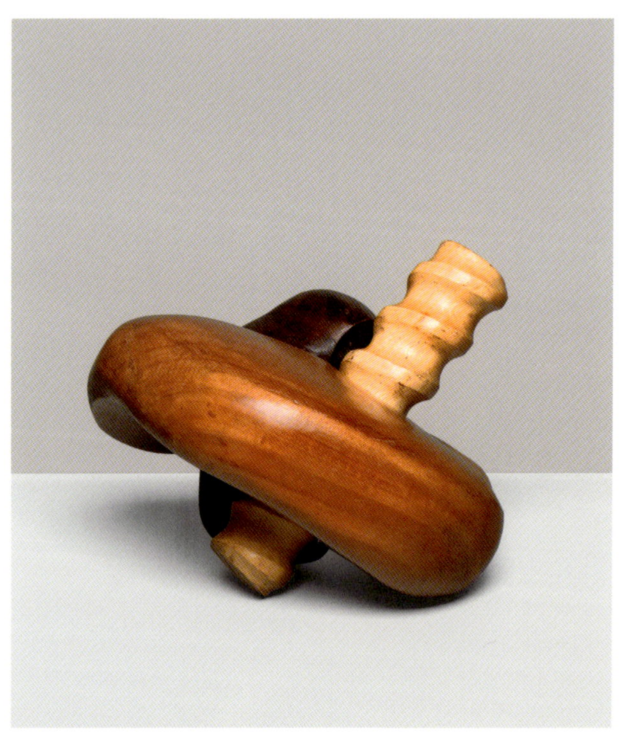

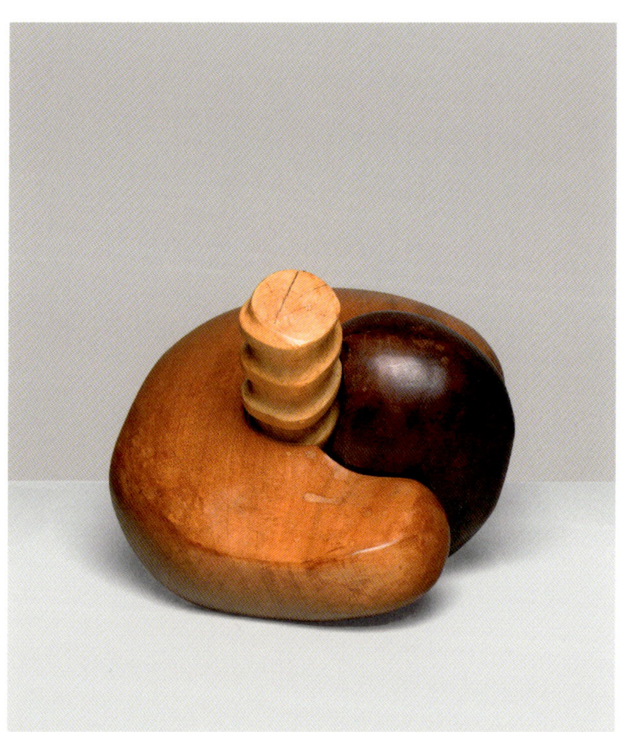

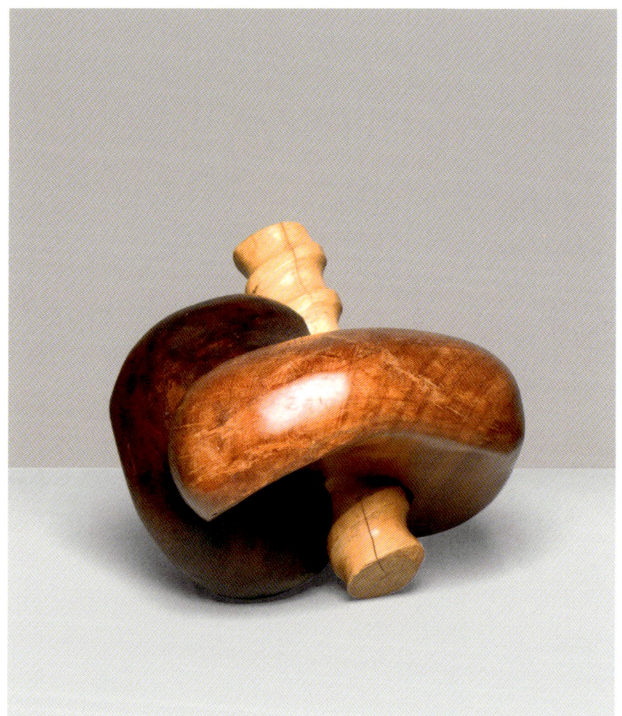

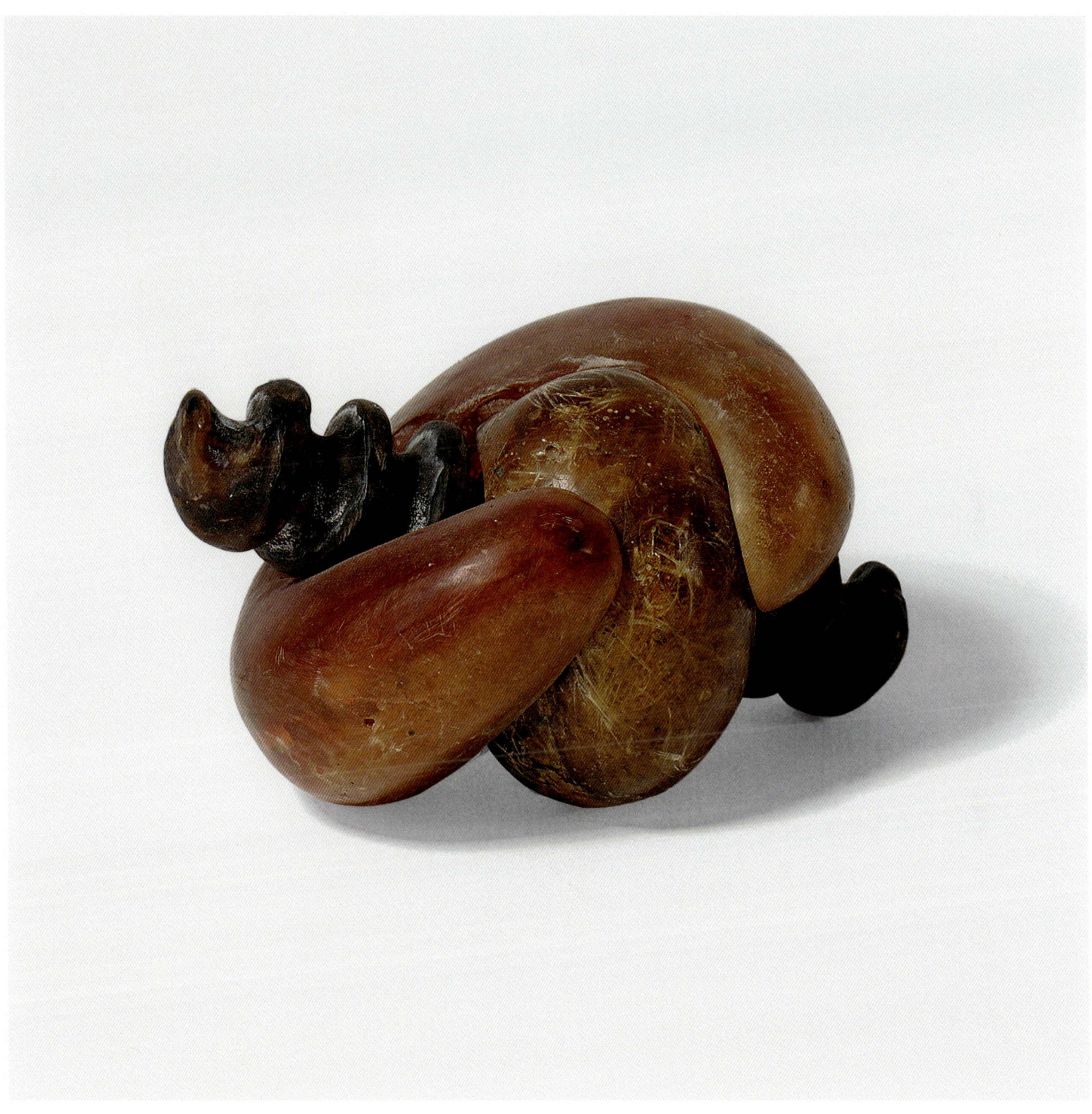

92
The Screw 1975–7
Wood
31 × 31 × 27

93
The Screw 1975–7
Fibreglass
16 × 6 × 9

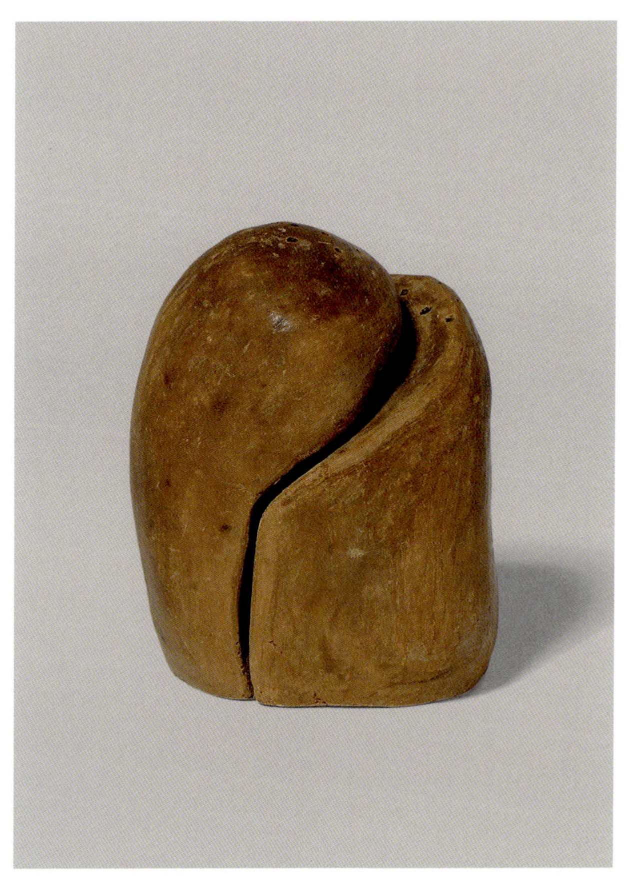

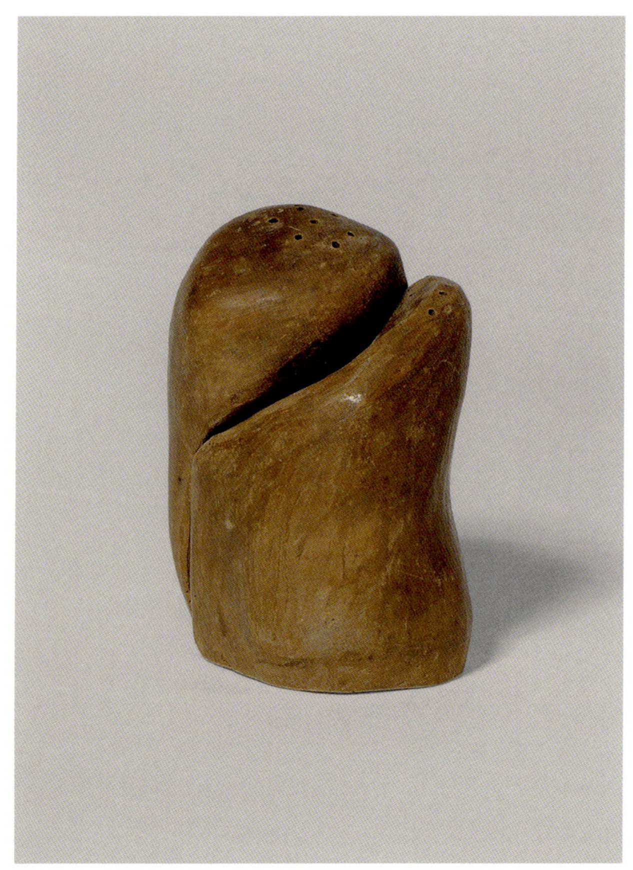

94
Dual, Salt and Pepper 1975–7
Terracotta
Each piece 8 × 6 × 5

95
Ring 1975–7
Silver
3.5 × 1.5 × 1.5
3.5 × 2.5 × 1.5

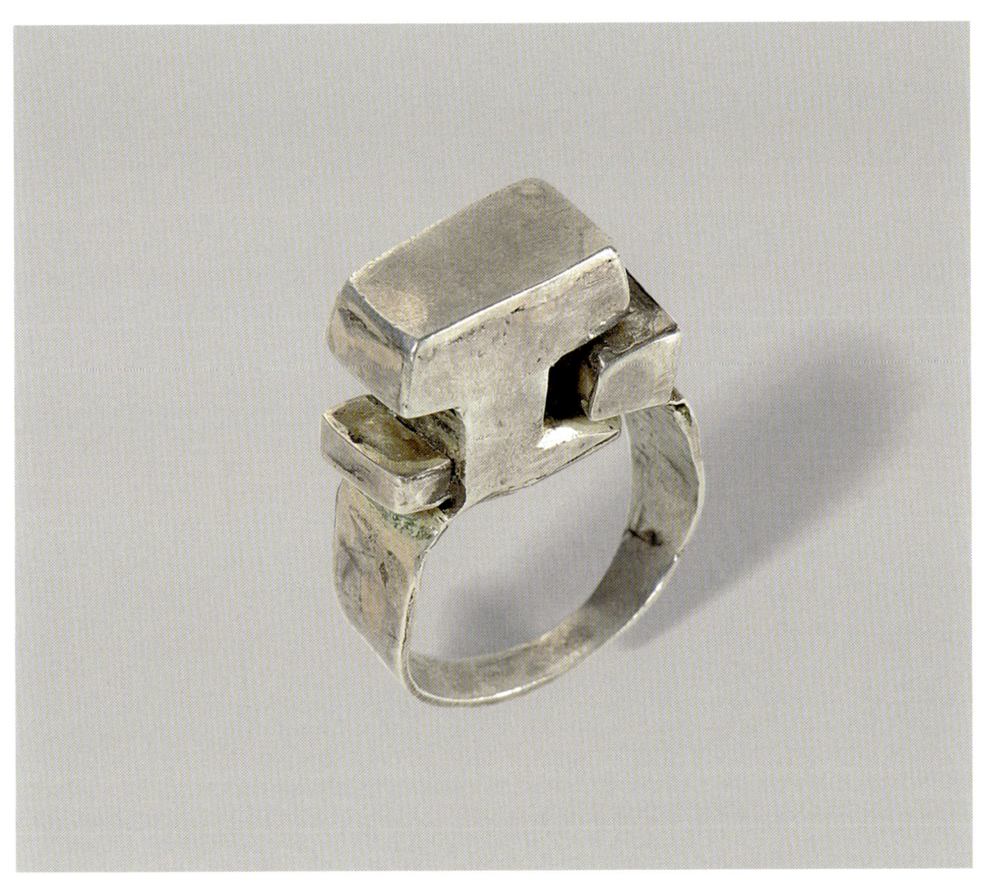

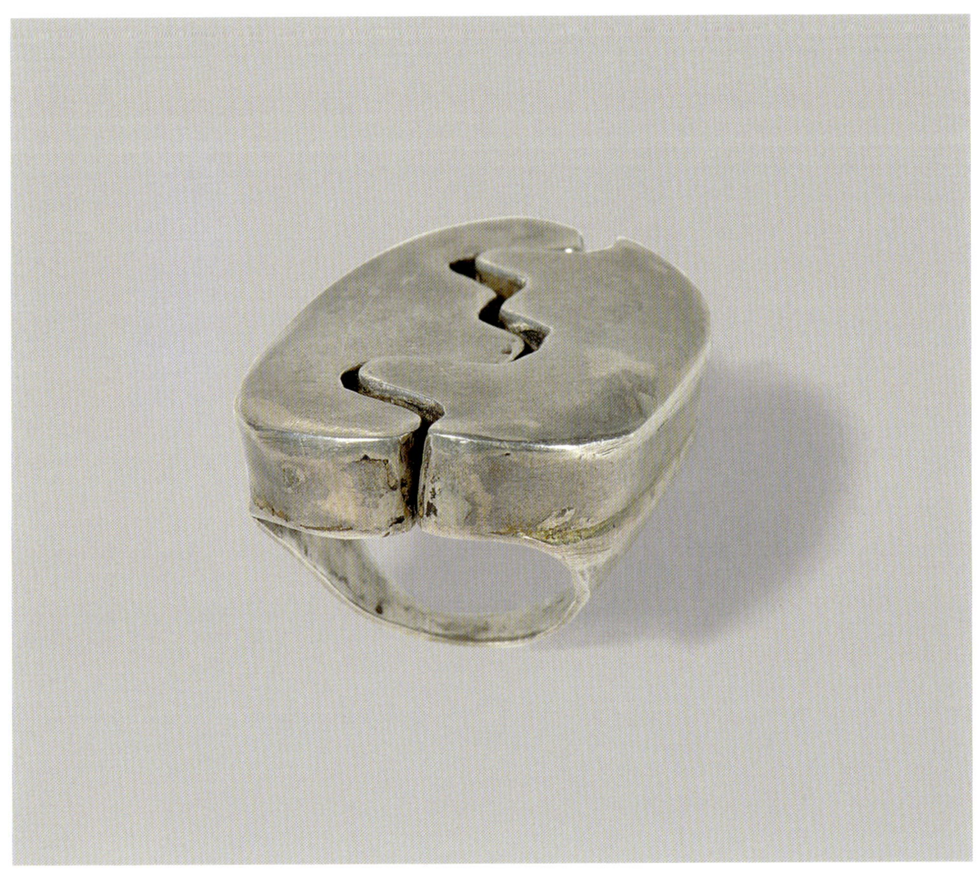

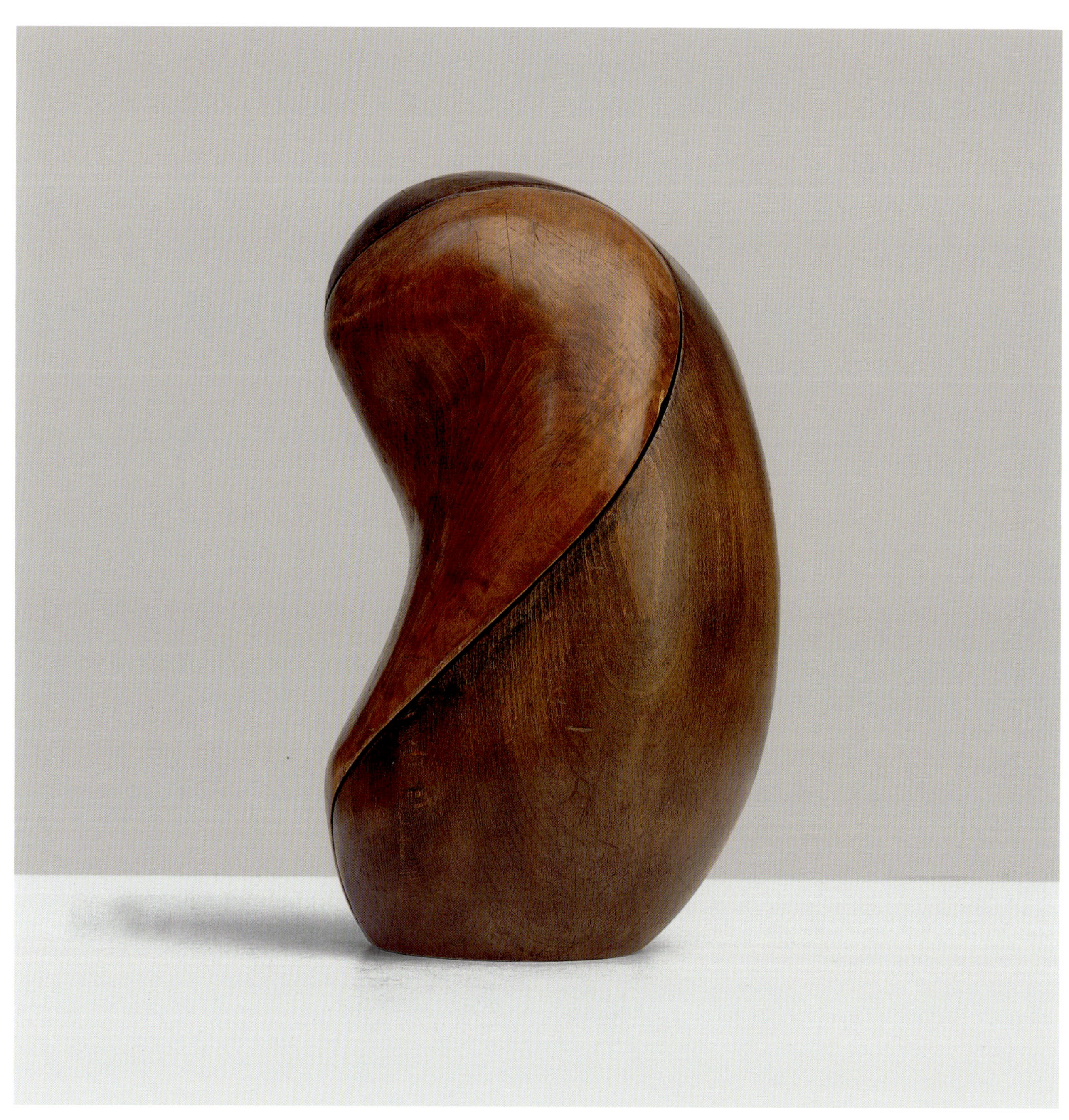

96
Dual 1975–7
Wood
36 × 23 × 23

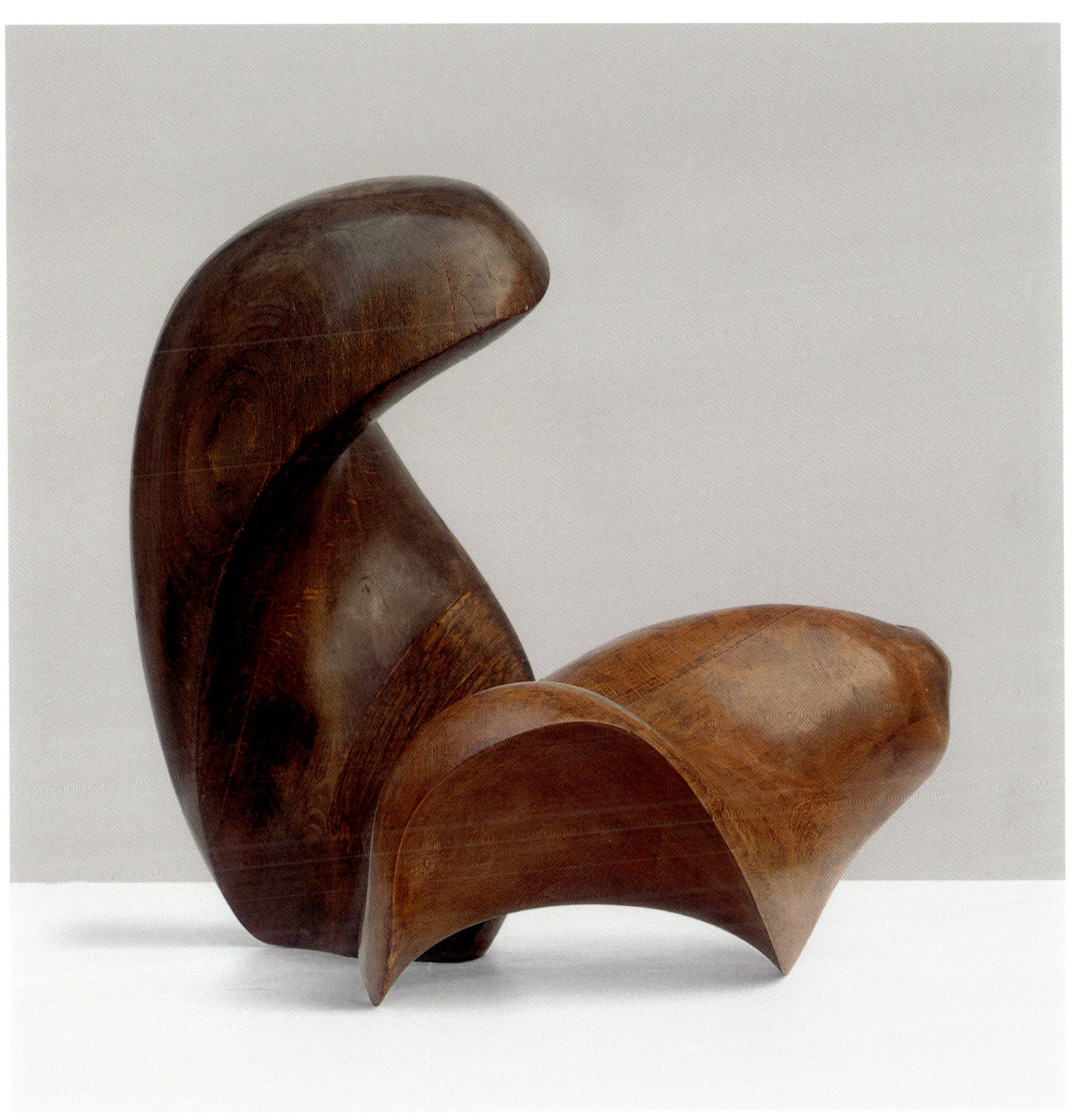

97
Dual 1975–7
Enamelled terracotta
13×13×13

98
Dual 1975–7
Fibreglass
33×32×26.5

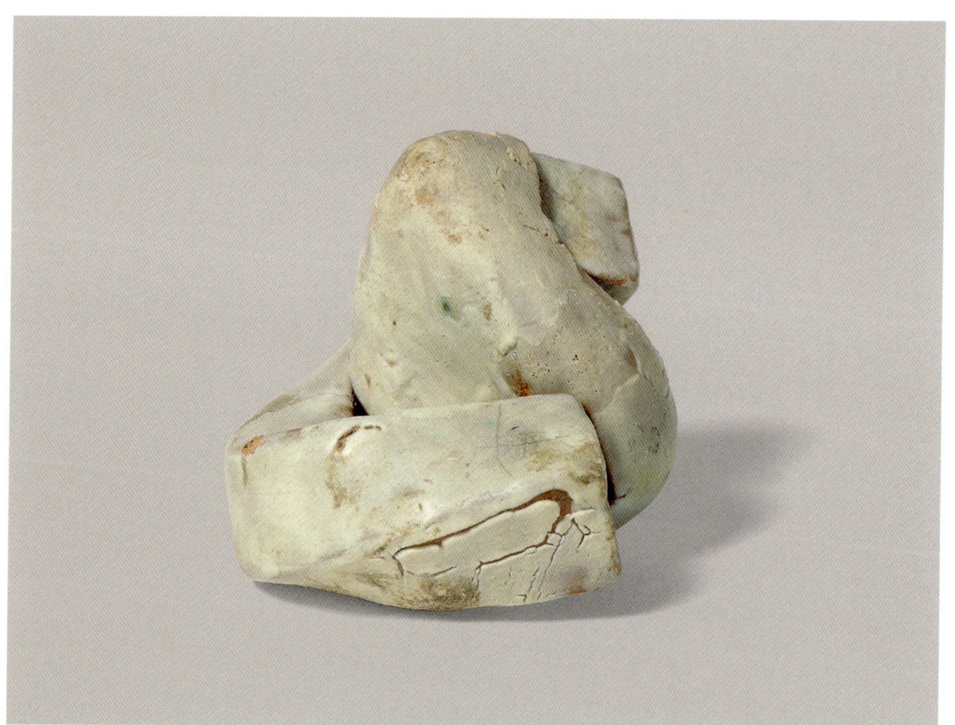

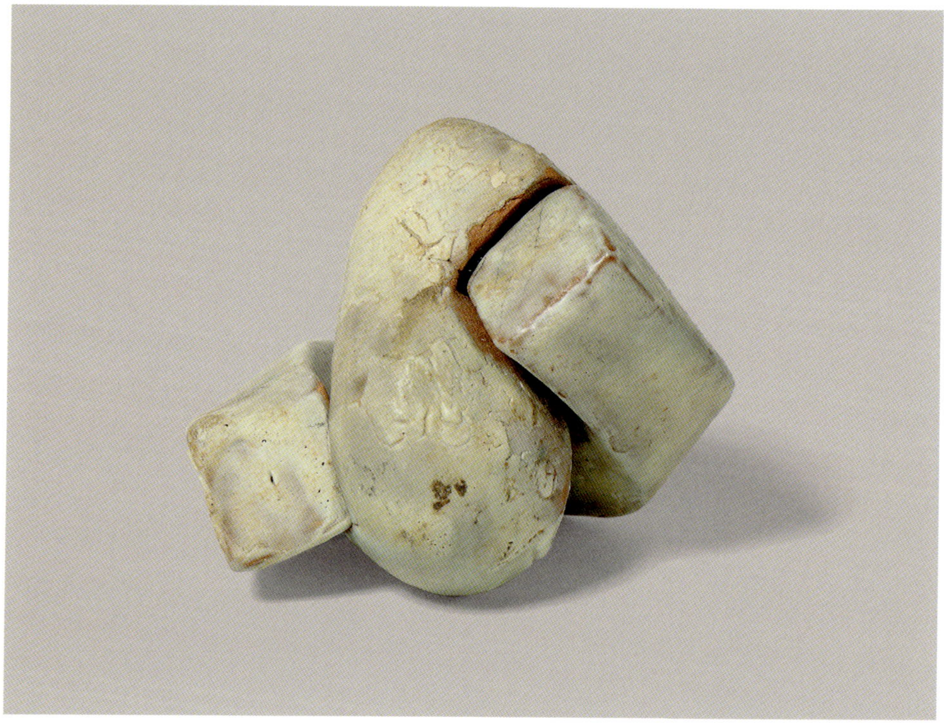

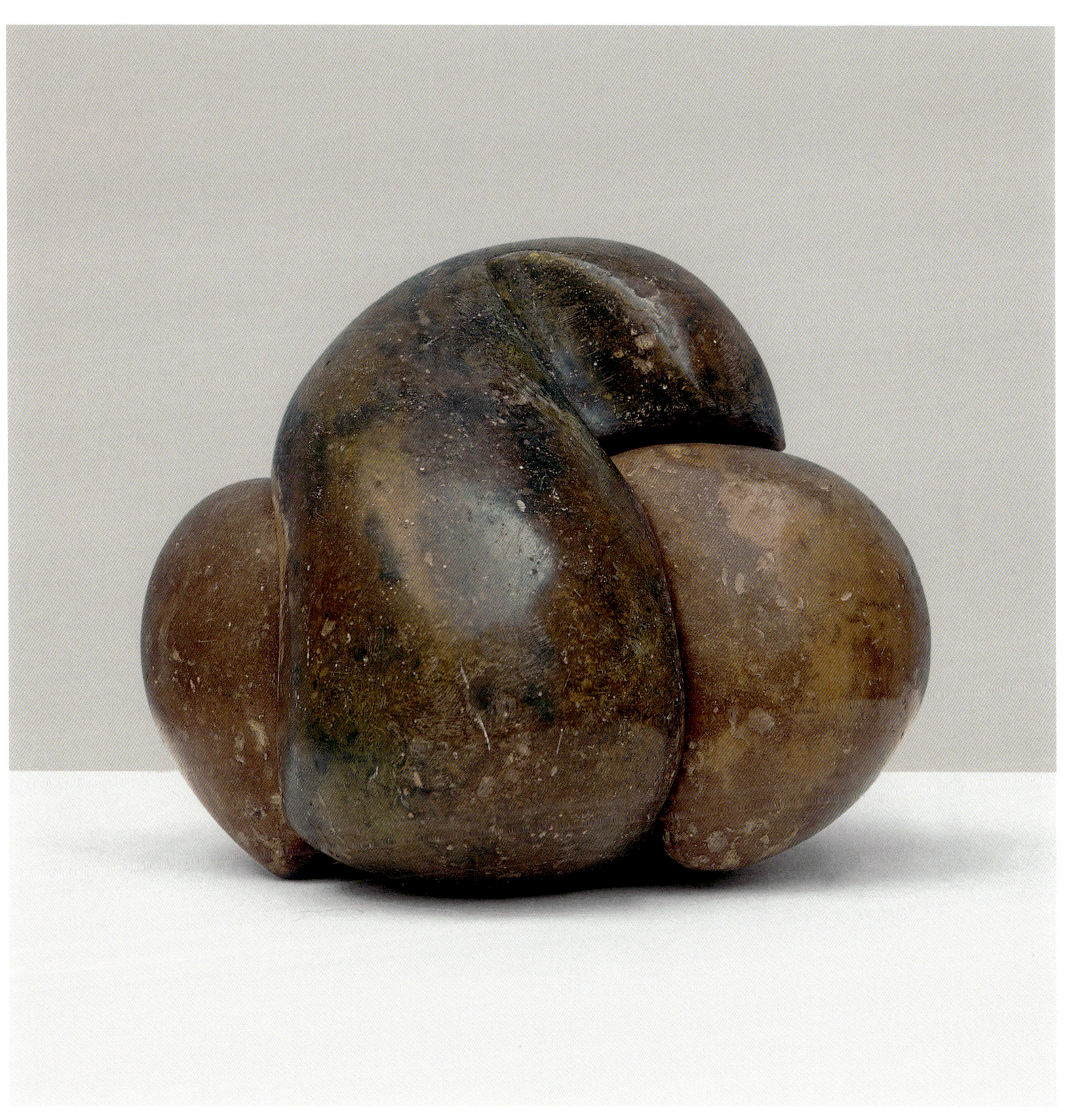

99
Dual 1978–80
Brass and
aluminium
15×6×6

100
Dual 1978–80
Aluminium
8×9×6

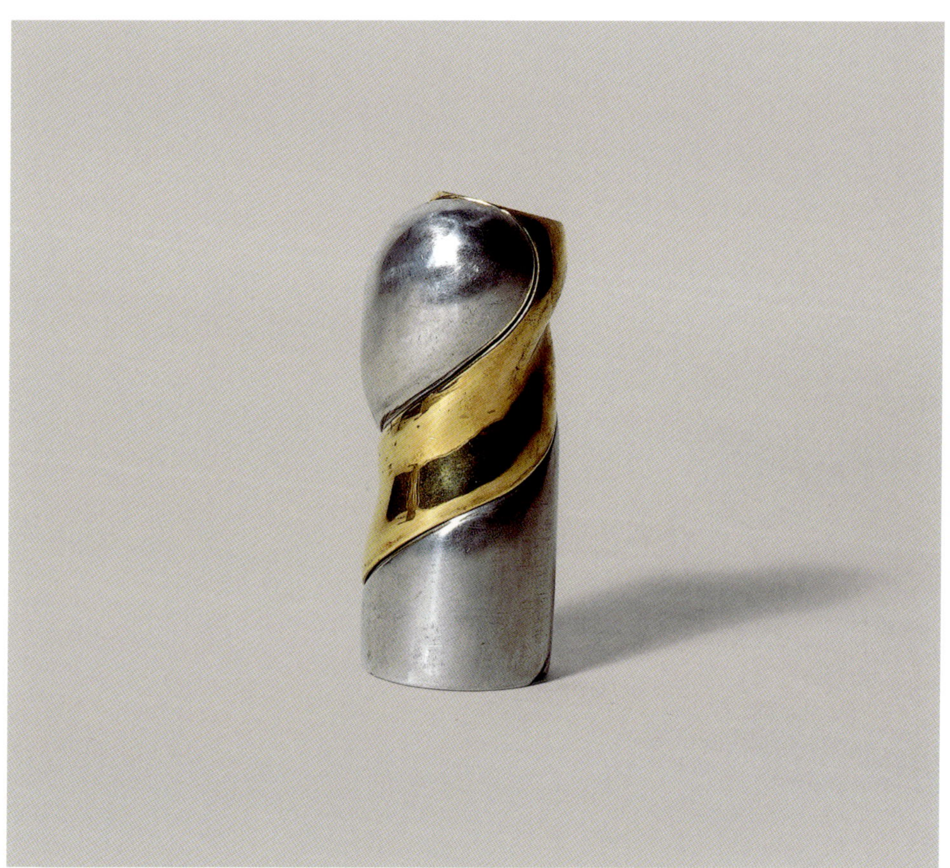

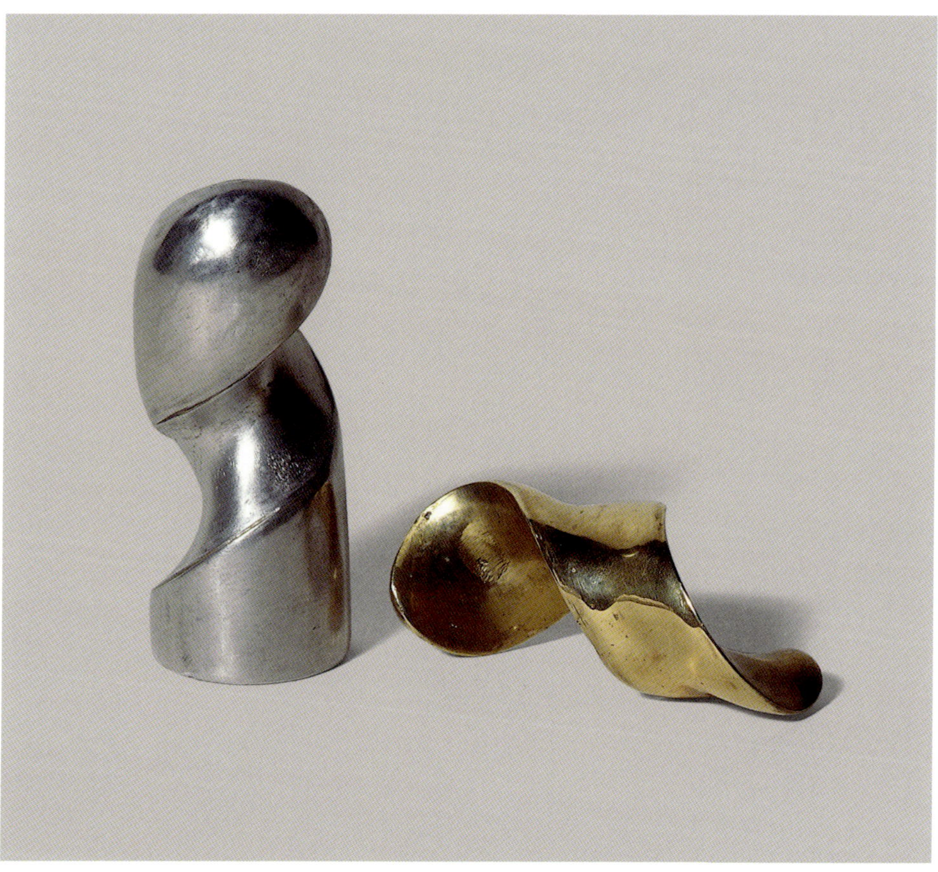

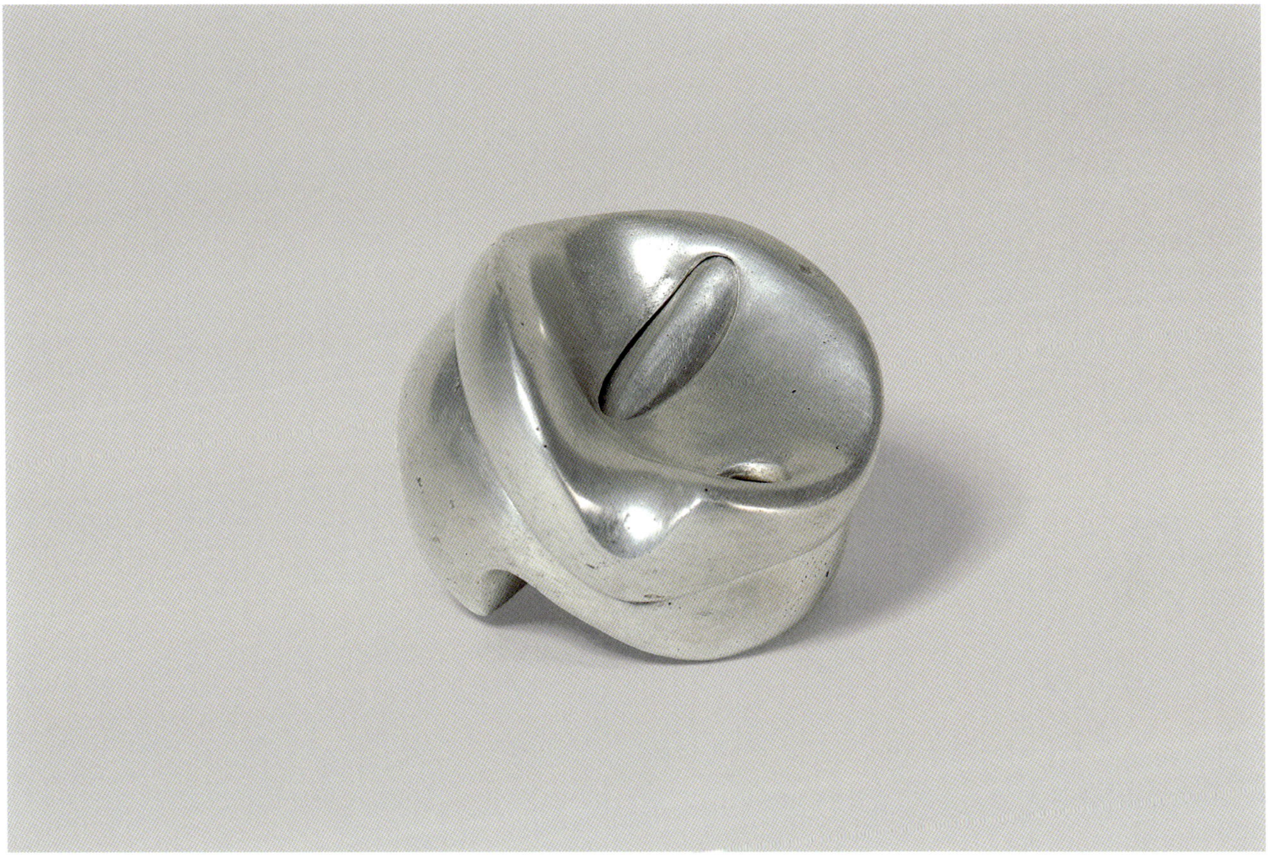

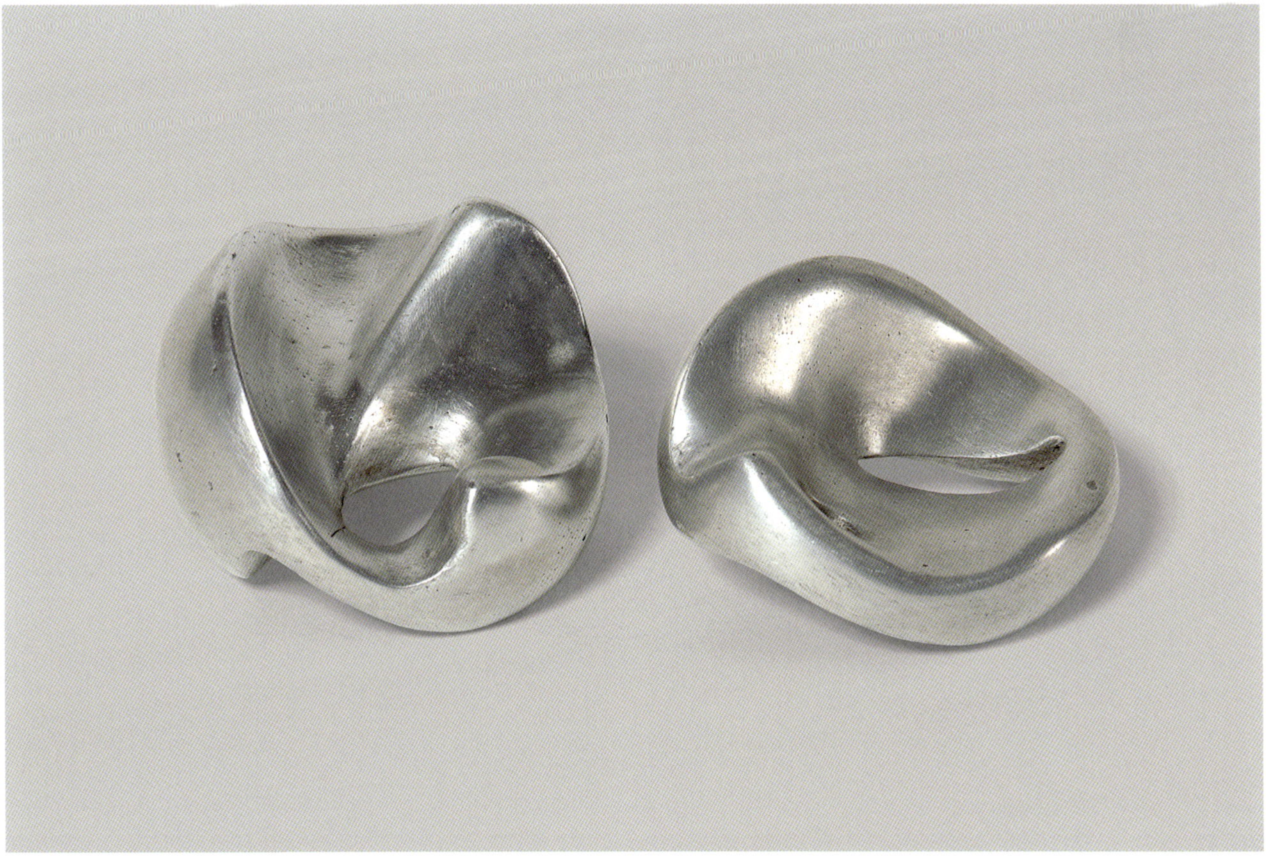

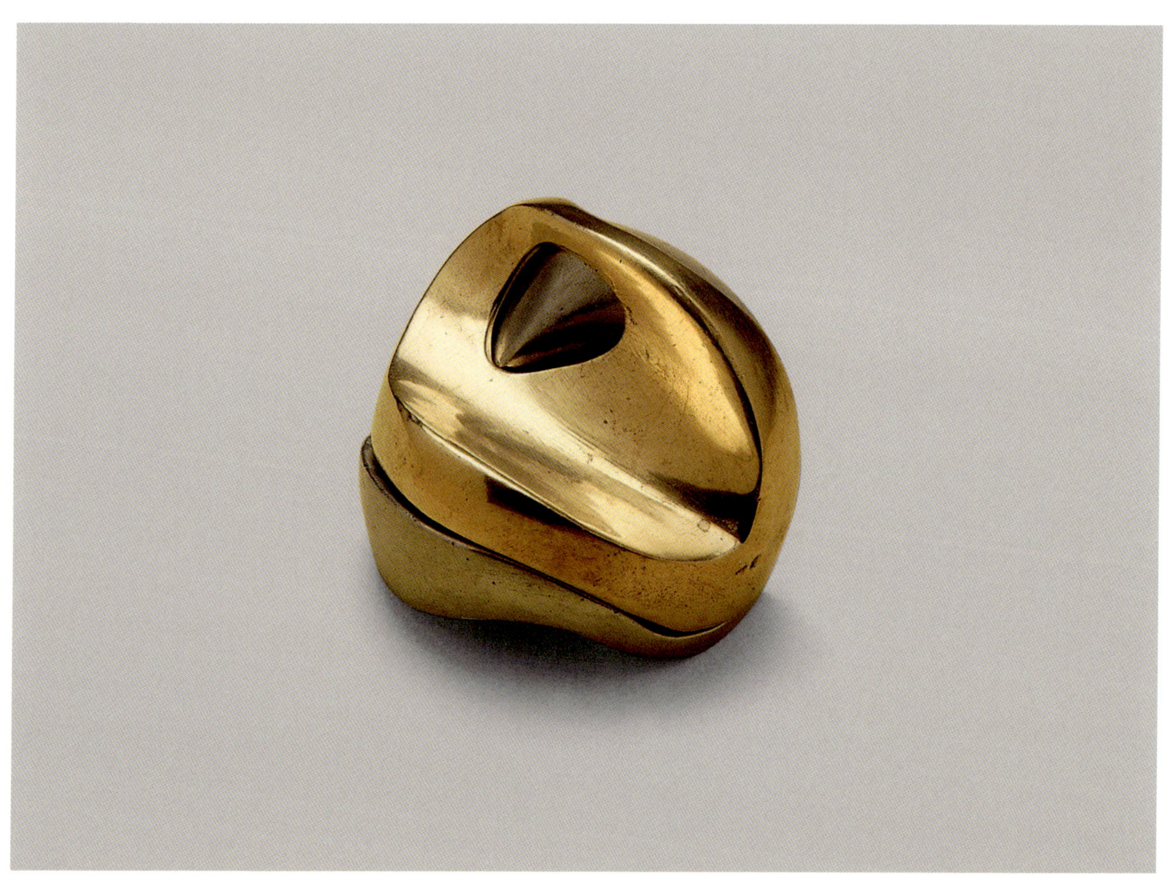

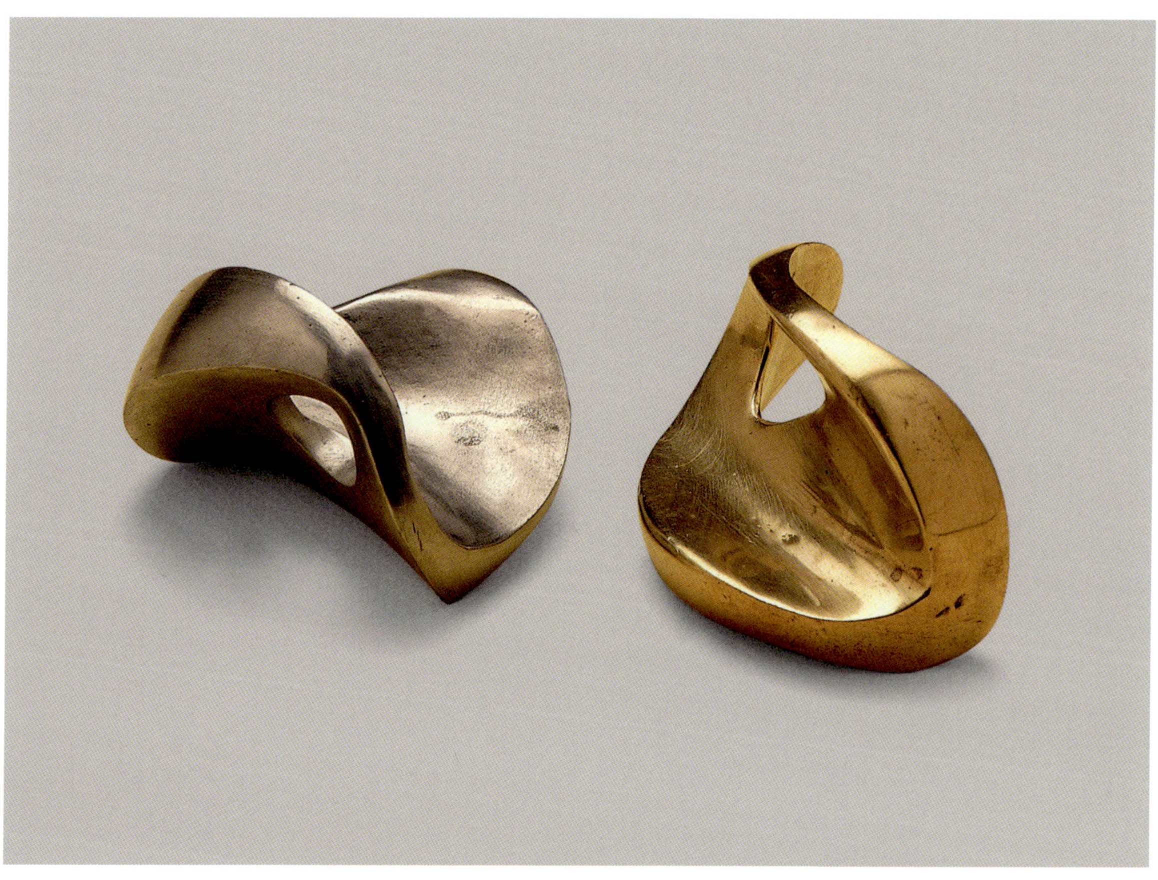

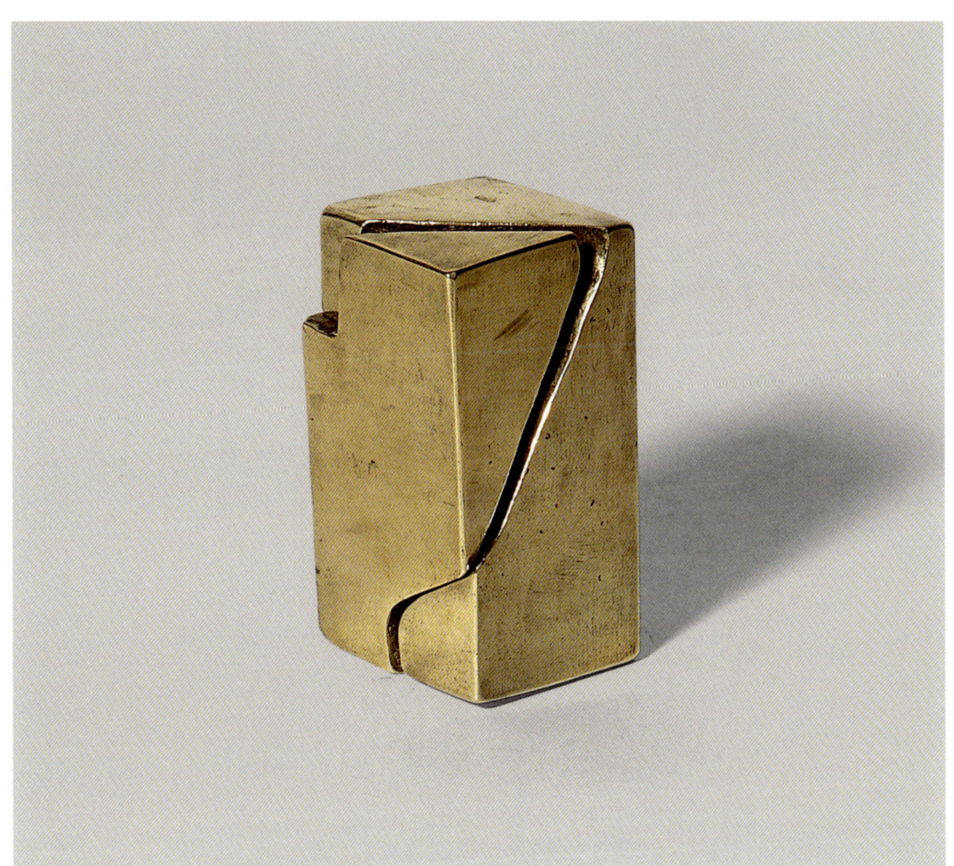

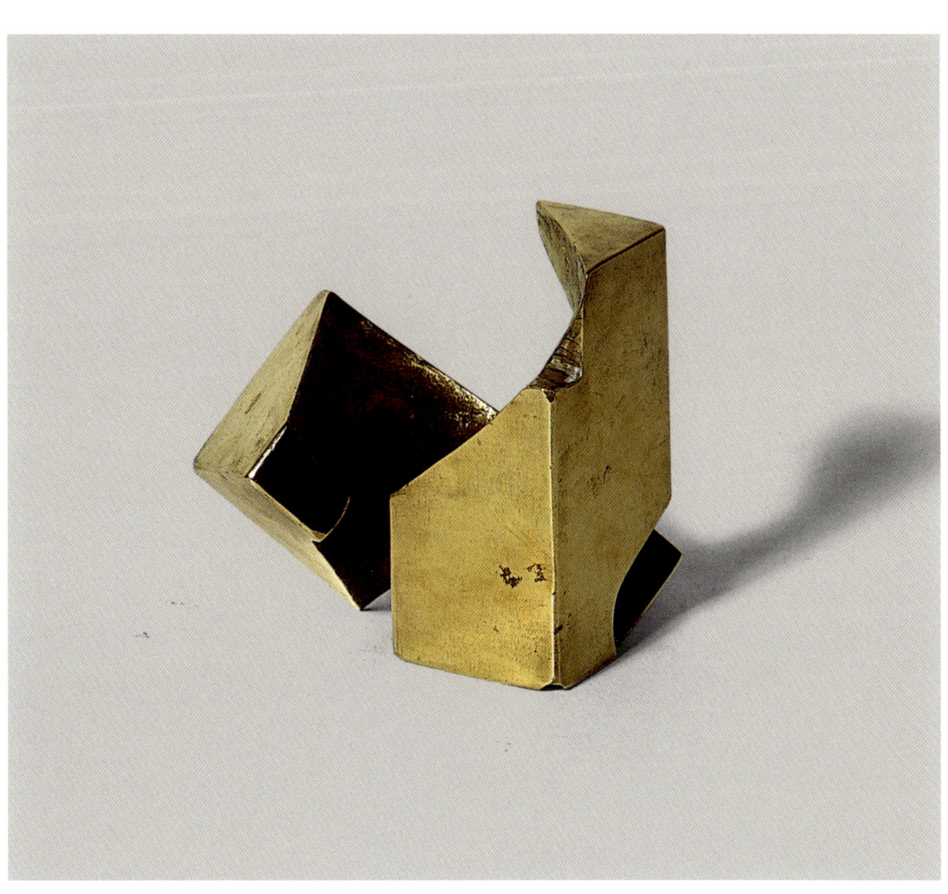

101
Dual 1978–80
Brass
and aluminium
6×6×7

102
Dual 1983–5
Brass
9.5×4.5×5.5

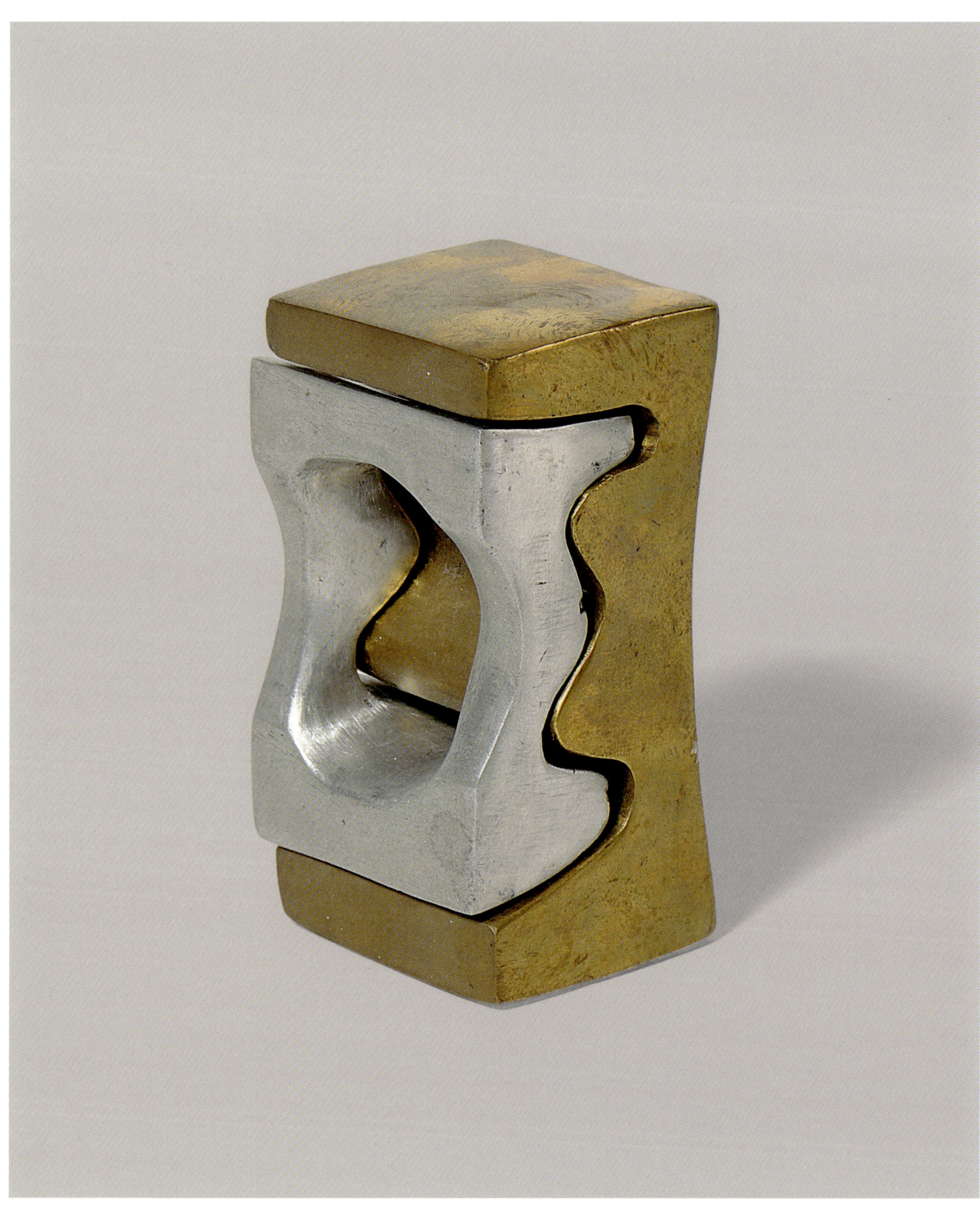

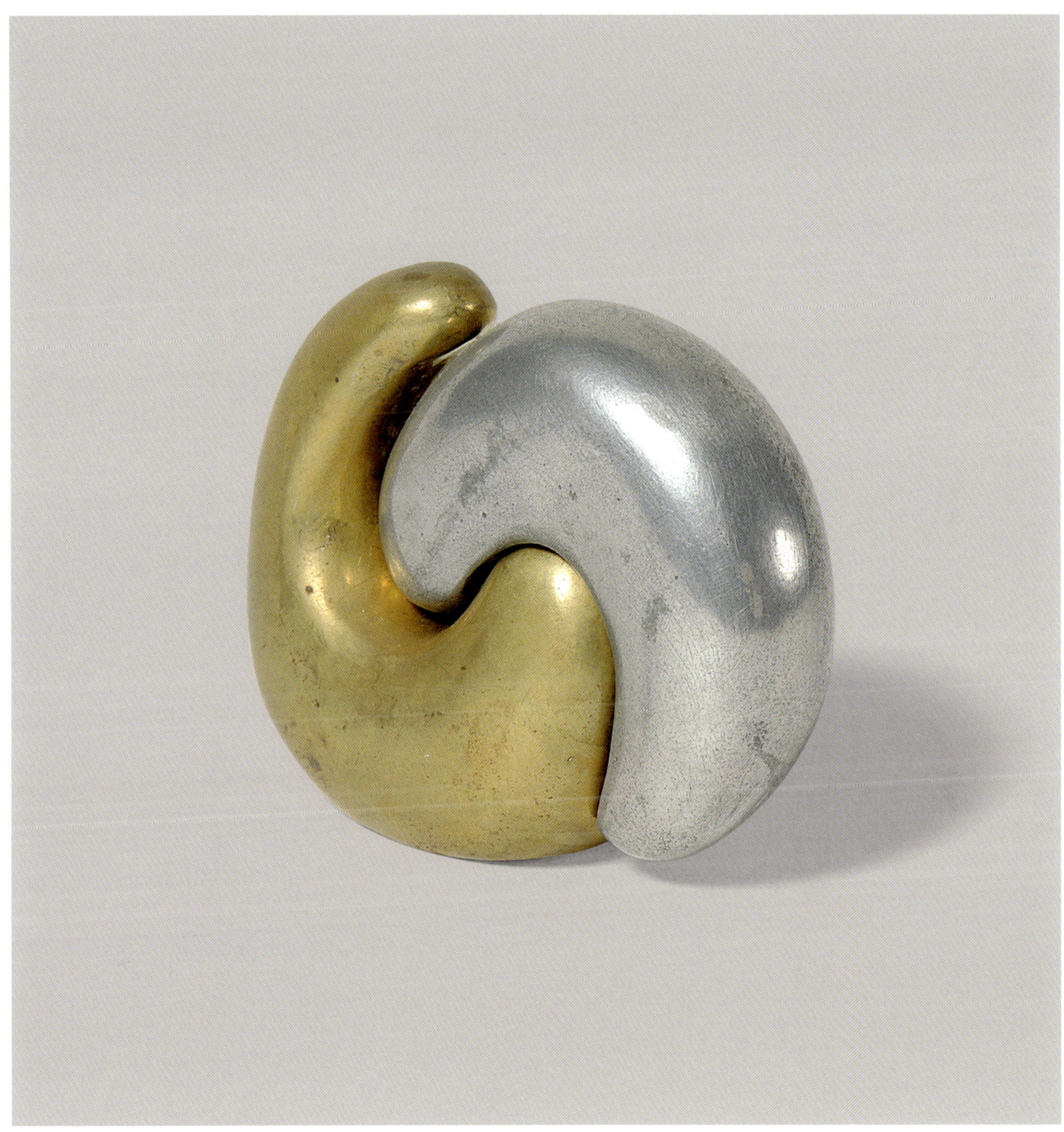

103
Dual 1978–80
Brass
and aluminium
4×4×8

104
Dual 1978–80
Brass
and aluminium
7×3×8

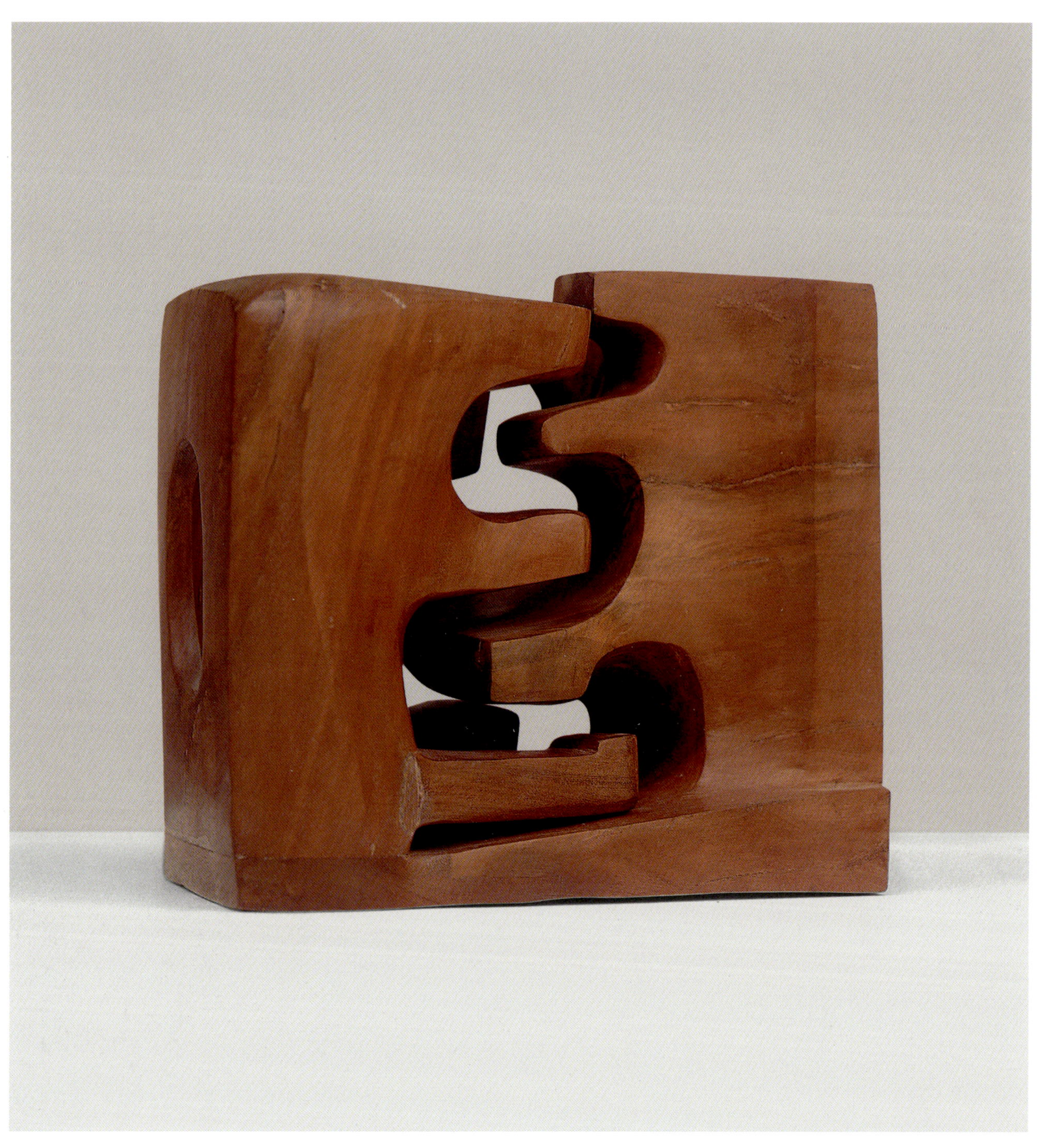

105
Dual 1980s
Wood
16 × 20 × 30

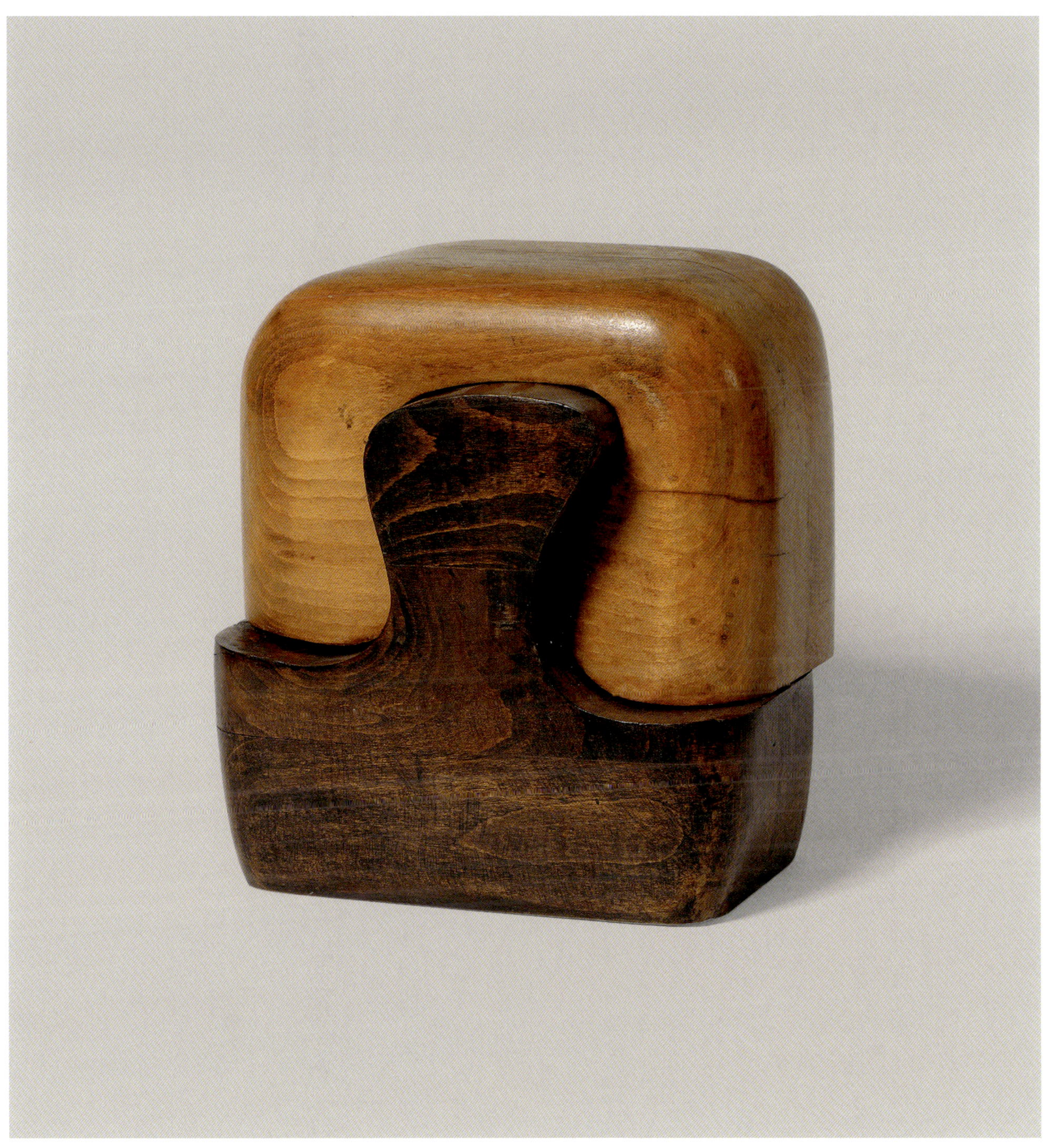

106
Dual 1975–7
Wood
22×19×12
(each piece)

107
(overleaf)
Water Project 1980
Terracotta
26×10×10

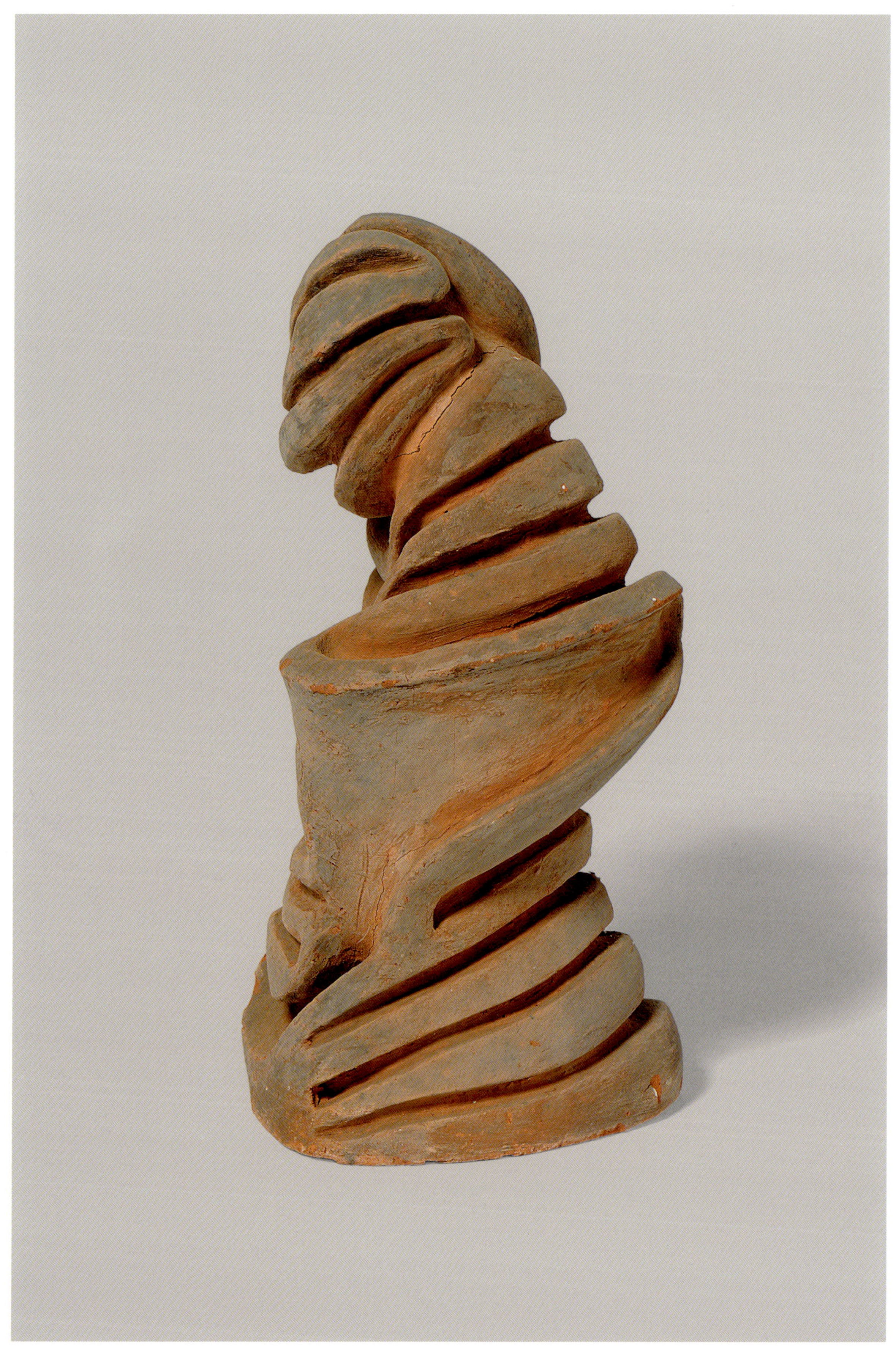

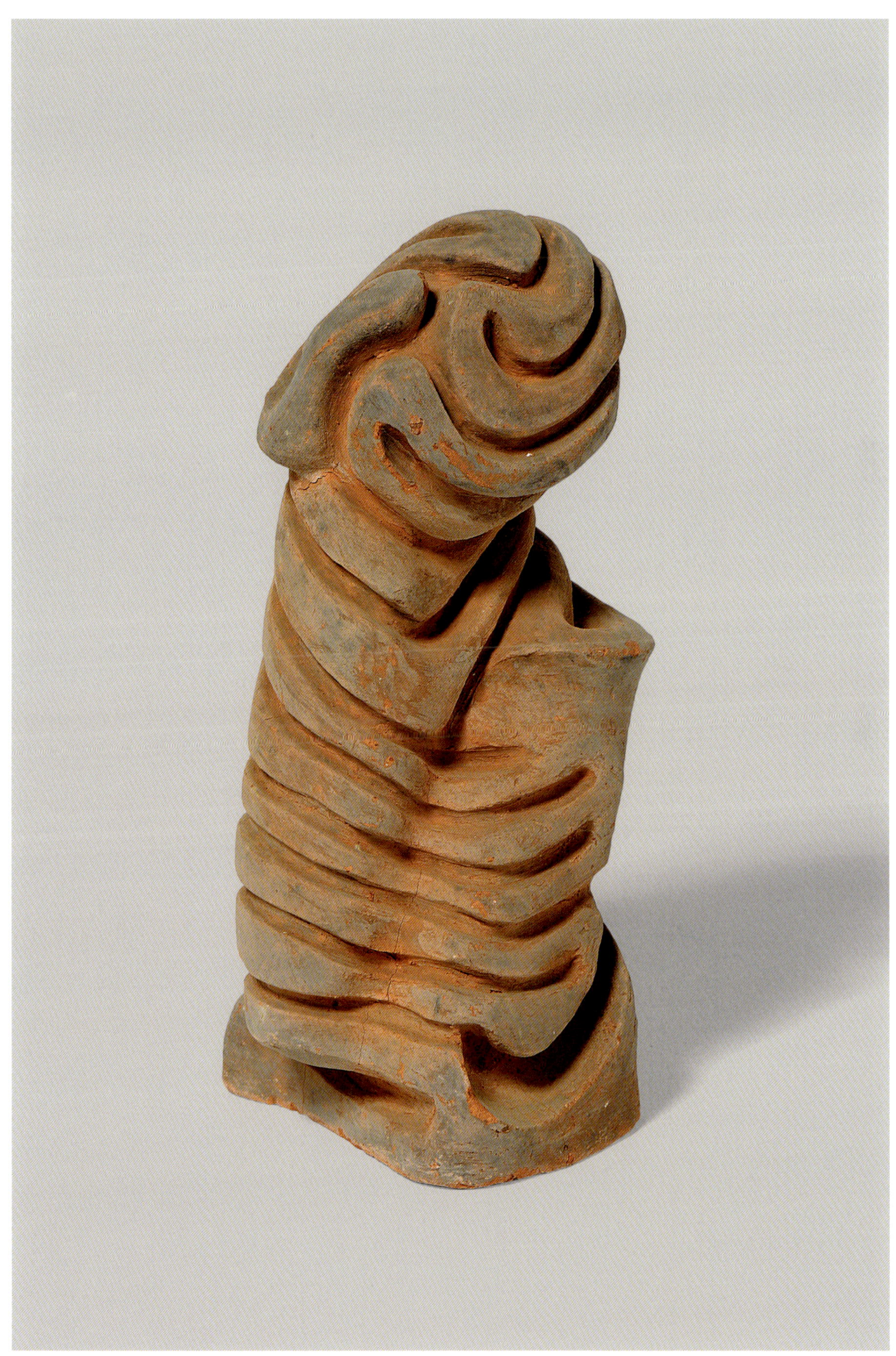

108
DNA Section 1980s
Wood
80 × 14 × 14

109
Dual 1980s
Wood
38 × 17.5 × 16

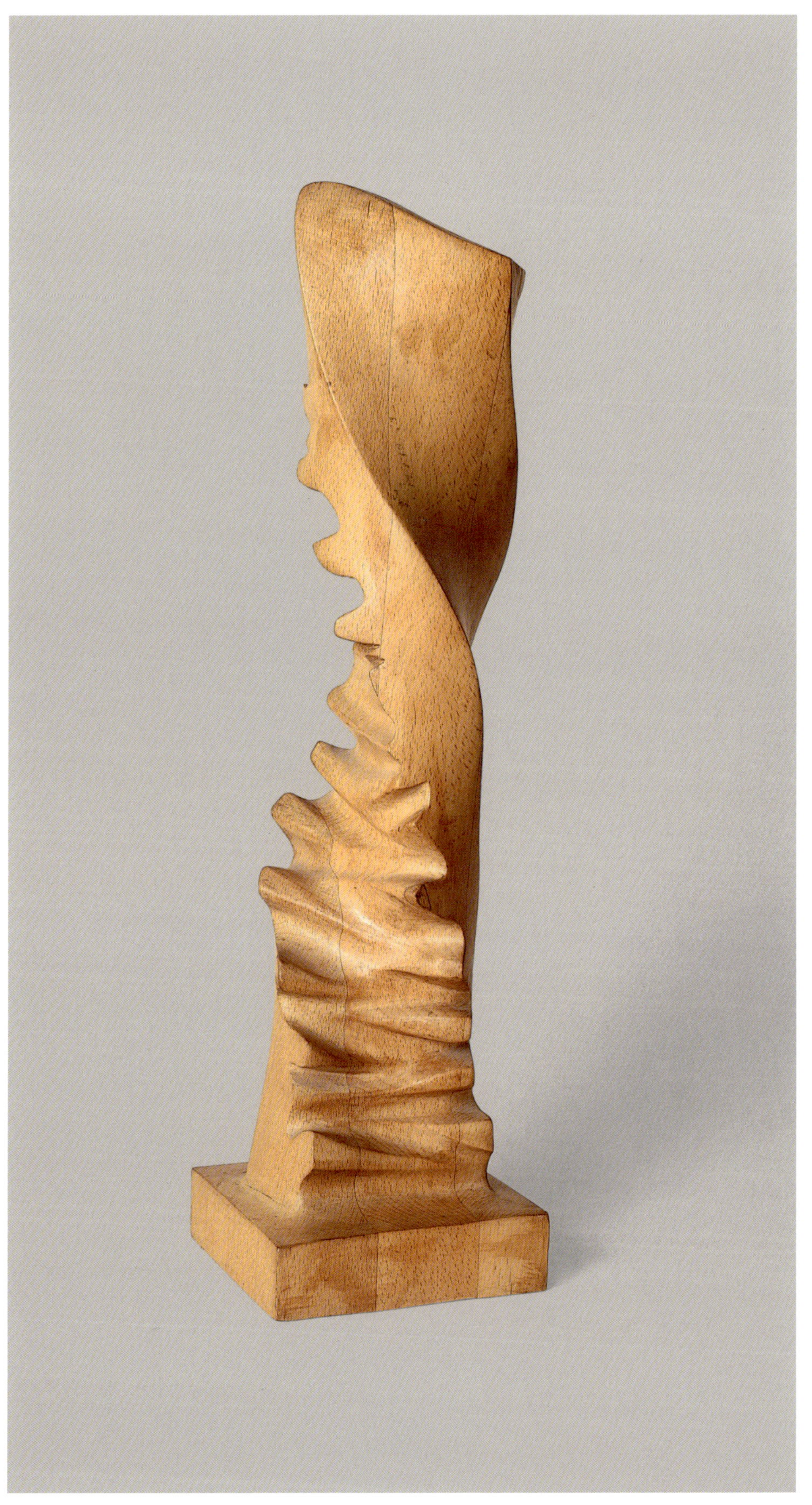

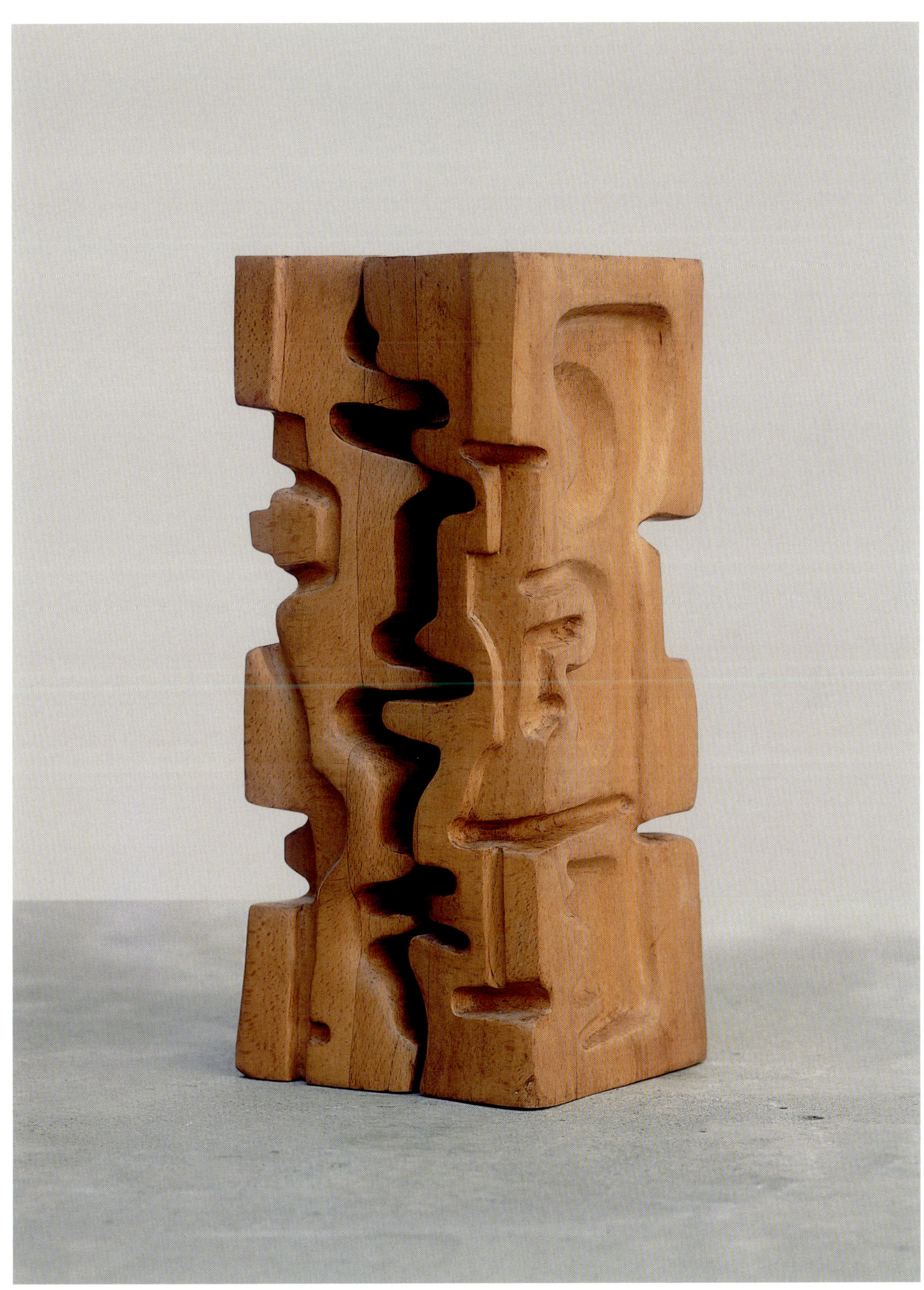

The Potentiality of the Thing
Saloua Raouda Choucair's modular sculpture

> In her comparison of Greeks and Arabs she found that the Greeks excelled in describing and treating knowledge, categorizing entities into human, animal, plant and inert, whereas the Arabs never described things as they exist but rather treated the probability and potentiality of the thing. This is creative, not descriptive ...[1]

There have been many attempts to characterise the art of Saloua Raouda Choucair as a fusion of Arab tradition and Western modernism. The artist's biography lends weight to such interpretations. Born in Beirut in 1916, Choucair was tutored by the Lebanese artists Omar Onsi and Moustafa Farroukh, prominent impressionist and realist painters. At the American University of Beirut she encountered the challenge laid down by a professor who pronounced the cultural superiority of the Greeks over the Arabs and, having discovered her passion for Islamic art and architecture during a trip to Egypt in 1943, she set out to prove her belief in the strength, validity and relevance of non-objective art of Middle Eastern design. Choucair spent three important years in Paris from 1948 to 1951, where she encountered and absorbed the current themes, trends and philosophies of European modernism before returning to her homeland to dedicate the rest of her life to carving out her personal vision. These simple facts alone may be enough to support the claims that she was the first true abstract modern artist in Lebanon (and perhaps the Arab world).[2] However, any attempt to truly understand the complexity of Choucair's ideas and their various sources, as well as her unique contribution to the global art of the twentieth century, must begin with an examination of her work.

Choucair is perhaps most widely recognised and celebrated for her modular sculptures – works which seem to visibly combine her various influences, as though she had literally taken these references apart, played with the combined elements and assembled them anew. Though her biography helps to locate her practice historically, geographically and culturally, the formal logic of her paintings and sculptures is in fact more challenging to place or define. In part this is due to Choucair's belief in a pure, universal art that transcends the boundaries of culture, gender or ethnicity. Striving towards this impossible goal but held back by circumstances, Choucair never fully reached her potential as an artist. Yet the potential of the idea (and the idea of potential) is a constant theme within her work.

Line and curve

In the late 1940s, possibly before she had even visited Paris and encountered the works of the modern European masters in the flesh, Choucair began to make geometric paintings inspired by her studies of Islamic art, architecture and mathematics. Choucair was born into the Druze religion and was not religiously orthodox in any sense, but she was fascinated by the art and philosophy of Islam as communicated through the Arabic language. Employing the two most basic elements of Islamic design, the straight line and the curve, she started with simple shapes formed from angular lines and curves juxtaposed, which were then repeated in various combinations, divisions and differing orientations across the picture plane. These early canvases are given titles such as *Fractional Module*, *Positive and Negative Module*, *Composition in Blue Module* or *Fractional Rectangular Module*. Though it is unclear whether these titles were assigned at a later date, they certainly indicate that Choucair's earliest abstract compositions have at their heart a system based on mathematics and unbound geometric units.

In Paris Choucair found like-minded individuals committed to the pursuit of abstract or non-objective art at the Atelier d'art abstrait, which she frequented in 1950 in her capacity as volunteer assistant to the Directors. The Atelier enabled artists such as Jean Dewasne, Edgard Pillet, Robert Jacobsen and Richard Mortensen to share ideas and inspiration to fuel their work. Choucair prepared slides of works by Kandinsky, Vasarely, Mondrian and Malevich for lectures and discussions. Her studies of the modern masters simply confirmed her belief that certain Arab and Islamic practices had already prepared the ground in reaching 'the purest form' or 'essence' of art centuries earlier. As she noted, 'Kandinsky's studies of the point and the line, which we recently viewed, are studies that the Muslim artist undertook in the first century after the Hijra'.[3] And in her 1951 article titled 'How Arabs Understood Pictorial Art' for *Al-Abhath* magazine, she wrote:

> Arab artists did not care to depict visible, concrete reality as perceived by human beings. Rather, in their quest for beauty, they reached into the essence of the subject, stripping it of all the blemishes associated with art since the time of the Greeks until the end of the nineteenth century. Arab artists didn't employ pictorial illusions of dimension or perspective, nor did they distort reality to underscore a certain concept. They did not exploit pictorial art for the sake of literature, nor did they wish to add to art any spirit that was not in its true nature.[4]

Choucair was impressed by the way in which Islamic art attempted to describe something so vast and complex that it could not be fully comprehended by human beings, but using only very simple means such as the circle and straight line. She was interested in the ability of a line to follow a trajectory that allows it to transform itself into numerous shapes. The line and curve persist as basic elements of a visual language that preoccupied Choucair throughout her career, finding its way into a variety of media and forms and including painting, sculpture, textiles, murals and other domestic designs. She made her first-known sculptures

110
Trajectory of a Line 1957–9
Wood
74×34×25

111
(overleaf)
Interform 1960–2
Wood
110×28×28

112
(overleaf)
Sculpture with One Thousand Pieces
1966–8
Wood
147×36×36

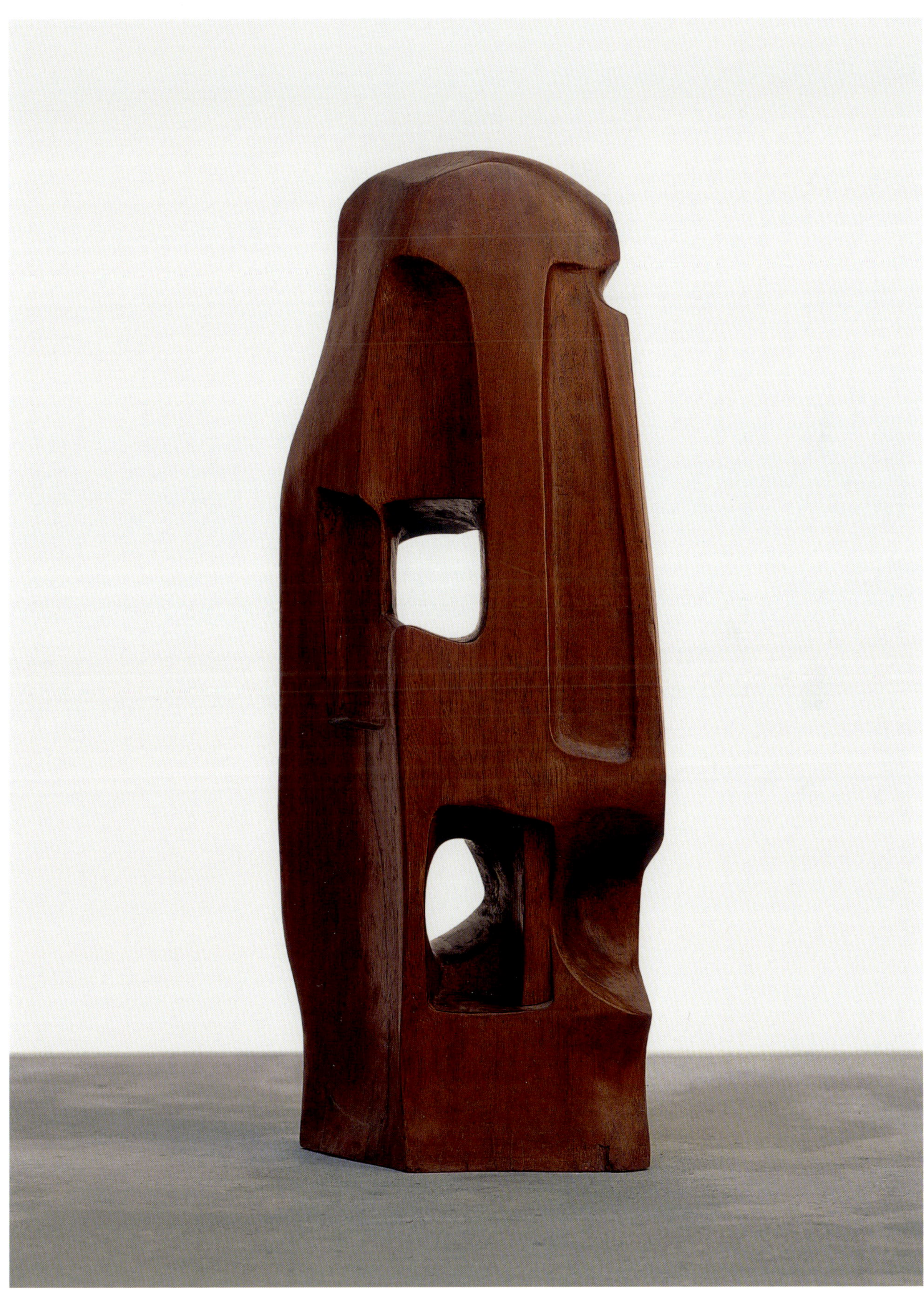

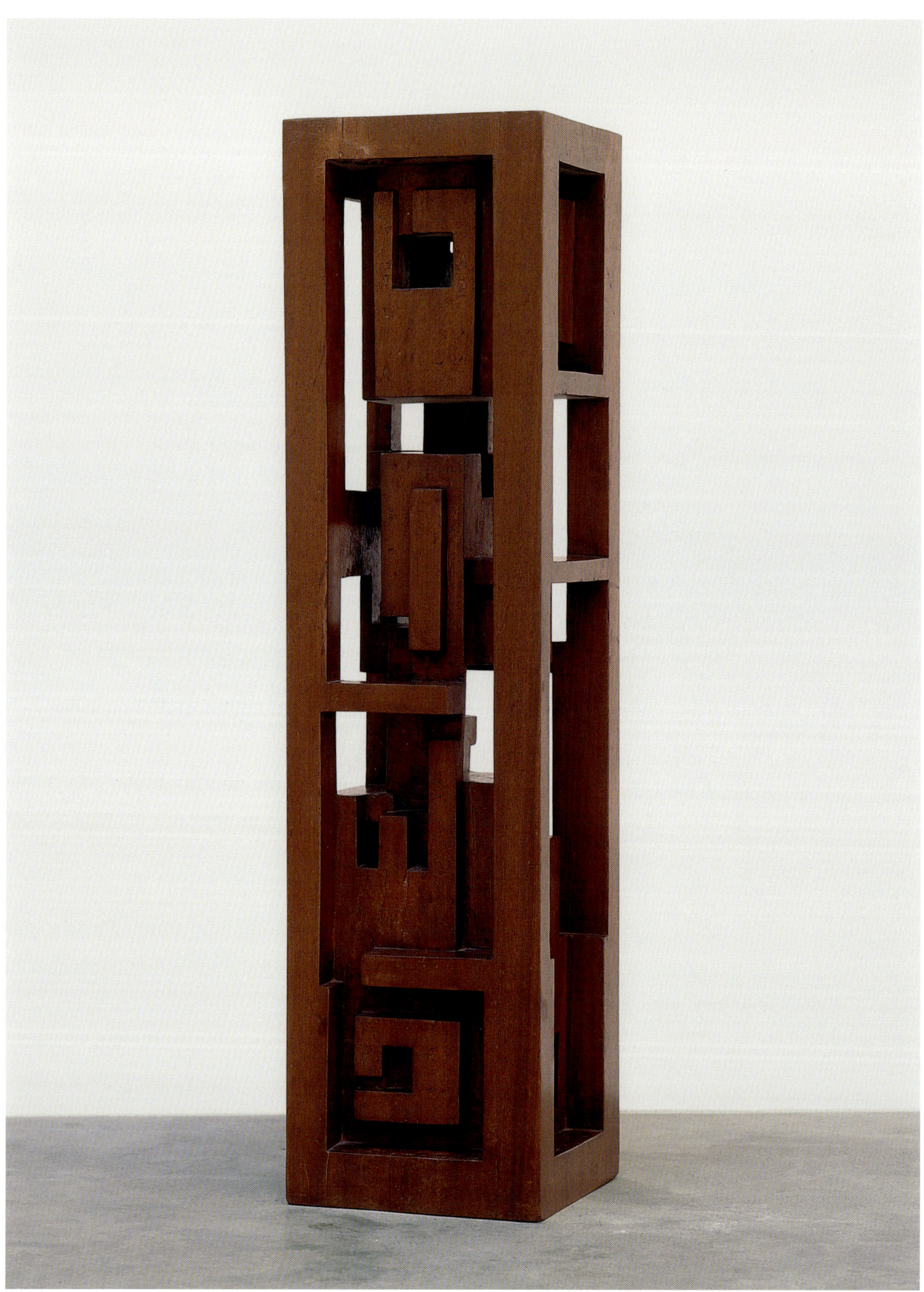

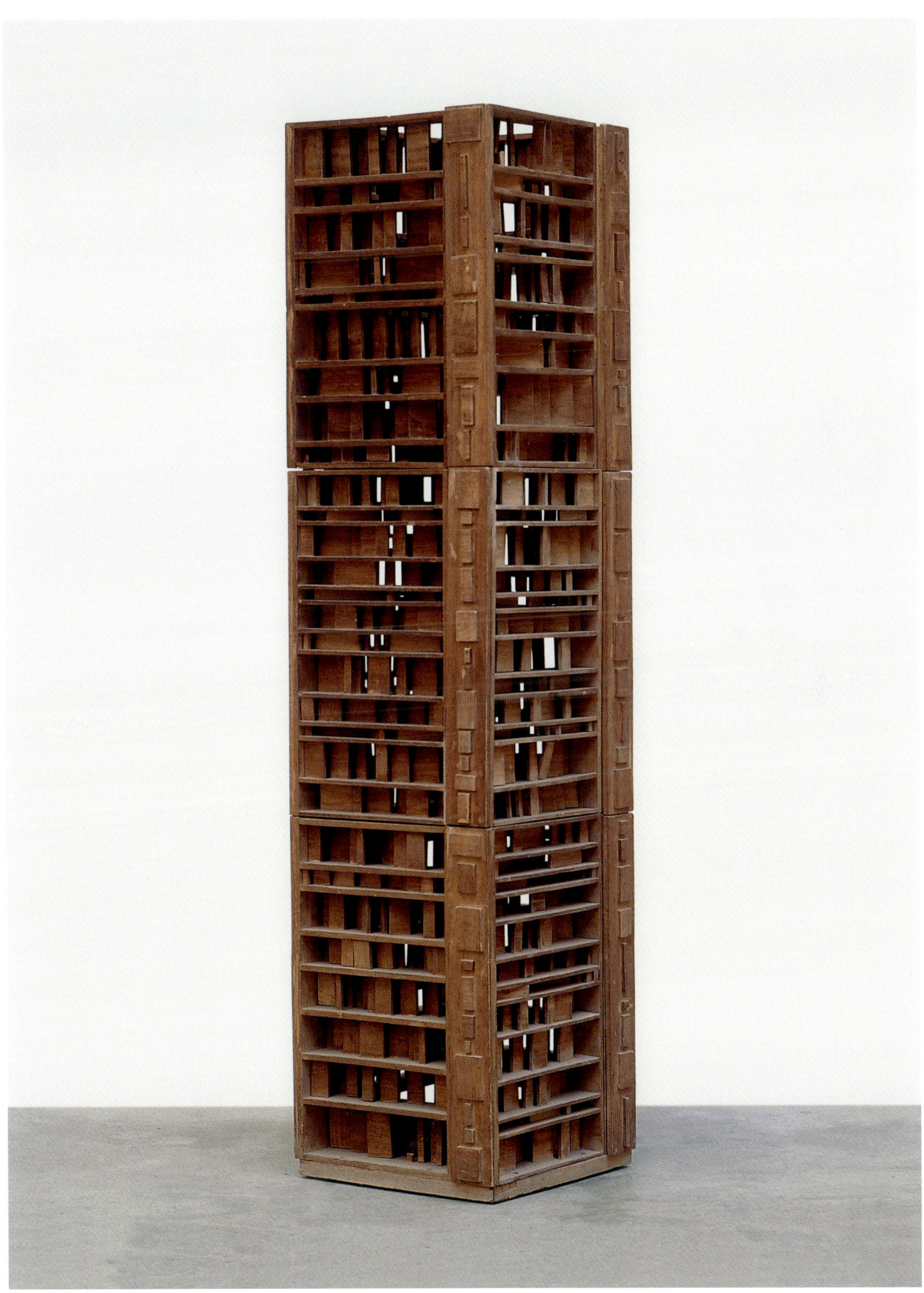

in the late 1950s. In 1957, following a trip to the USA where she had explored the techniques of enamelwork and jewellery making, she began modelling in clay and carving wood. Her first sculptural series, titled *Trajectory of a Line*, clearly incorporates the line and curve in differing combinations carved as niches from solid blocks of wood. The pieces are not large, the tallest being just over a metre high, and as hand-carved objects they have a very human, tactile quality.

In the 1970s Choucair explicitly revisited her study of the curve in a new series of small sculptures modelled in clay and then cast in brass, this time titled *Trajectory of an Arc*. Choucair often used clay as a way of sketching in three dimensions or thinking through her ideas for larger, monumental sculptures. She would make maquettes for pieces that would later be carved in wood or cast in metal. A terracotta piece – roughly the size and shape of a small slipper– curls up at the edges as if quickly shaped in the palm of a hand. This object appears to be at a nascent stage in its development, having an unfinished look. It may have been intended to become a vessel or another object of use such as an ashtray. Other forms are reproduced in various different materials, as though the artist was exploring their physical properties and seeking the most appropriate texture, weight and temperature as well as appearance for a particular idea.

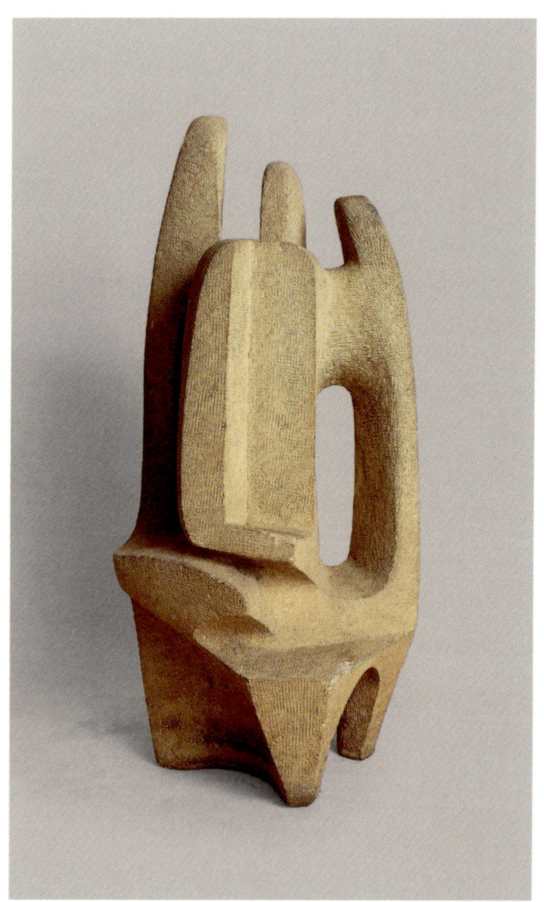

113
(above and opposite)
Trajectory of a Line 1957–9
Stone
82×35×21

Closed form

Choucair's first, tentative experiments with modelling clay perhaps mark the start of her concern with 'closed form' in sculpture, another key element of her practice as identified by writers such as the Lebanese-American artist and critic Helen Khal:

> Closed form is distinguished by the absolute containment of energy of an object or image within a defined inner space, as opposed to the open form characteristic of much Western art, in which the object or image penetrates and is vitalized by the space around it. Closed form is a physical expression of inviolate introspection, of an inner spiritual energy. One sees it manifested in the architecture of Islam – in its domed mosques, its centralized living spaces and walled-off gardens.[5]

Khal's claim about the 'open form characteristic of much Western art' may be a misleading generalisation (one could reference, for example, the British sculptors Henry Moore and Barbara Hepworth, both leading figures in direct carving who explored the tension between interior and exterior forms and open and closed composition) but her description of the 'inner spiritual energy' of an object and reference to the architecture of Islam are useful points to bear in mind when considering Choucair's modular sculptures.

Following the *Trajectory of a Line* series, Choucair produced a number of wood and stone 'Interforms' in which geometric shapes are carved out and constructed within a simple cube or rectangular frame.

Interform 1960–2 (fig.111) is a tower-like structure made of a cherry-coloured wood, standing over a metre high. Its complex, multifaceted interior is made up entirely of angular shapes – cubes and L-shaped corner pieces that appear to be stacked within an outer frame. The piece has an architectural quality, reminiscent of geometric designs found in the mid-century modernist buildings constructed in Beirut following Lebanese Independence. *Sculpture with One Thousand Pieces* 1966–8 (fig.112), perhaps the most complex of Choucair's modular wooden towers, resembles a high-rise apartment block with a dense network of exterior and interior windows and doors. Though the resemblance may be more coincidental or intuitive than intentional, Choucair did have a strong interest in architecture, having once stated that given another life she would choose to be an architect rather than an artist.

In contrast to the carefully constructed labyrinthine *Sculpture with One Thousand Pieces*, *The Tower* 1960–2 (fig.114) is a simple, flat slab of white stone with irregularly shaped circles and ovals roughly carved into its surface. It tapers towards the top like an Egyptian obelisk or even a simplified Islamic minaret. In both these pieces light passes through the hollowed-out interiors, the negative spaces being an important part of the design. In fact, Choucair installed a light inside *Sculpture with One Thousand Pieces*, using it as a lamp within her home. This simple gesture speaks volumes about the paradoxical quality of her art, which is at once something practical, liveable, a body of work that has remained with the artist for most of her life and has quite literally become part of the furniture, yet still radiates the energy she believed to be contained at the core.

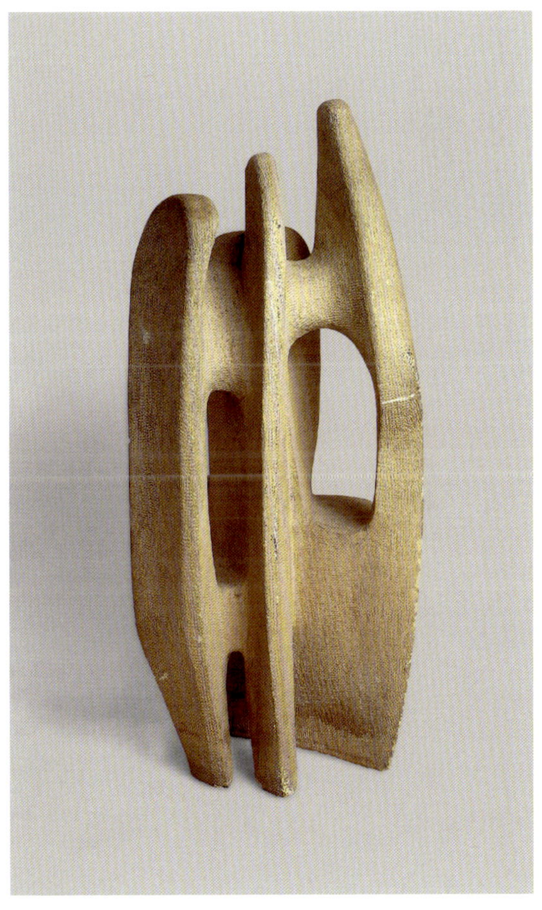

Modules

Choucair adopted the French term 'module' to refer to those basic elements she had been working with since 1947. By the mid-1960s she was making modular sculptures grouped under the title *Emboîtement*. Each sculpture was made up of separate but interlocking pieces of carved stone, wood or metal. The pieces are arranged in a set sequence, slotting together like vertical jigsaw puzzles, though they may be separated into smaller sculptures. Derived from the French *emboîter* (to box in or encase), emboitement is also the name of an outmoded biological theory suggesting that an egg contains the germs of all its future descendants, each germ being encased within another germ. Choucair was interested in scientific theories and would probably have been aware of this definition and was doubtless drawn to the idea of the biological potential contained within all living things. Like the British Constructionists Victor Pasmore, Kenneth Martin and Mary Martin, who drew upon the theories of biologist and mathematician D'Arcy Wentworth Thompson as material from which to source ideas and designs in the 1950s, or the American artist Jay Hambidge, who formulated the idea of 'dynamic symmetry' in art and design in the 1920s, Choucair was also fascinated by the geometry of nature, naturally occurring proportional systems and rhythms. In her eighties she

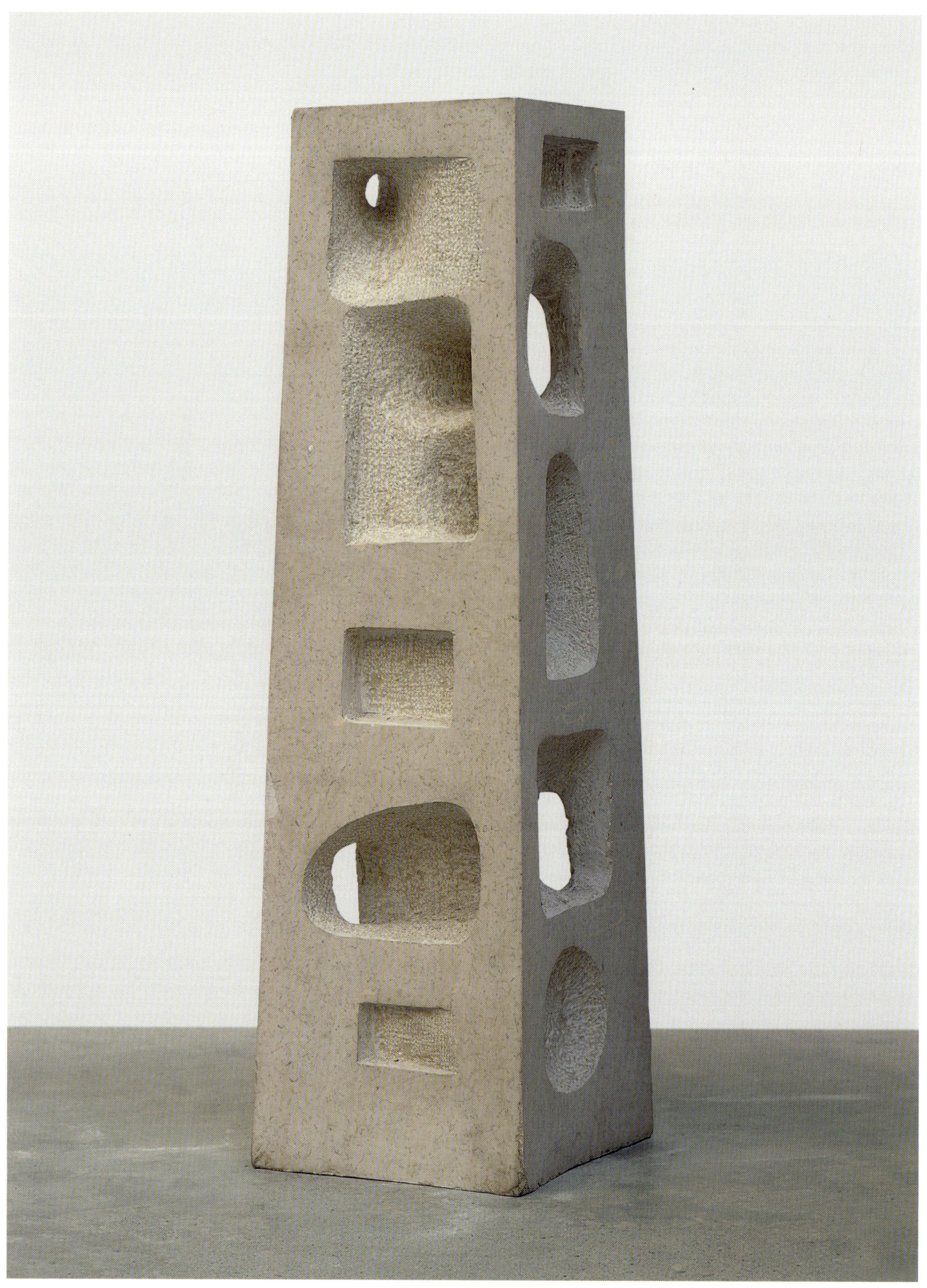

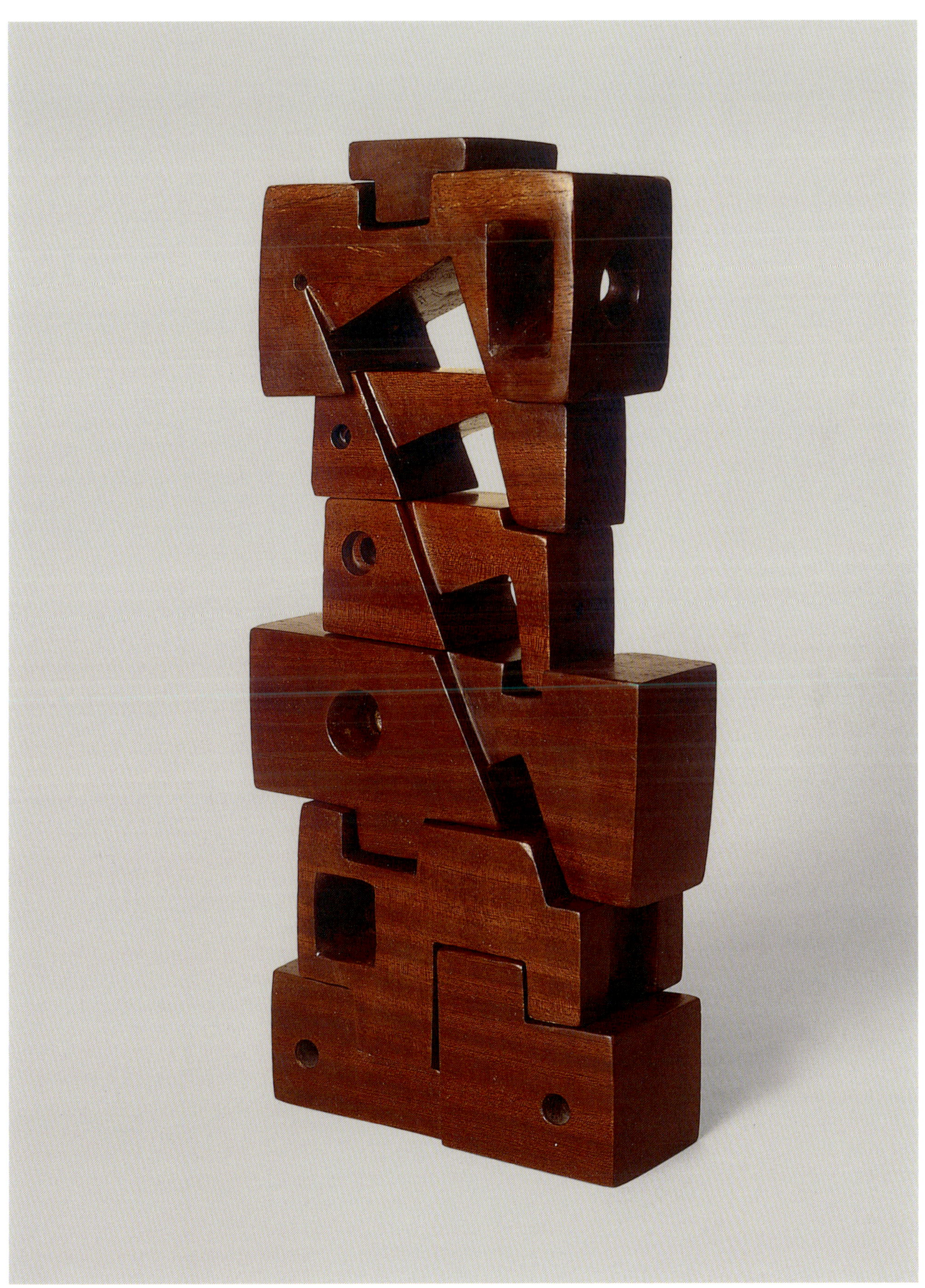

114
(previous pages)
The Tower 1960–2
White stone
100×40×24

115
(previous pages)
Poem 1963–5
Wood
38×18.5×5

produced a series of *Visual Meters* as a result of her interest in the double helix structure of DNA. As she stated,

> Like every artist, I look for a new conception of beauty, of how I see the world in terms of the many different forms and materials it contains. In everything around me I find this beauty of form, this perfect order of shape, proportion, and design sequence. I try to make others see it too. I look upon my work as the mirror of our age.[6]

Following the *Emboîtement* pieces, Choucair began to experiment more freely with stacked, modular towers made of carved Ramleh stone. Initially titled 'Elements Additionels', these towers could be made of any number of segments which, unlike those in the *Emboîtements*, are interchangeable or subtractable. The whole may be divided into separate, smaller sculptures. *Infinite Structure* 1963–5 (fig.8) is a surviving example, standing at nearly 2.5m when stacked vertically. Each segment or module is carved from a brick-like block of the same proportions, though the pattern of carved rectangles or circles differs. The suggestion, therefore, is of a potentially infinite number of permutations given the position or orientation of each module.

Choucair revisited the idea of infinity with a new series of modules she created in the 1980s. *Movement of the Angle* 1983–5 (fig.116), a polished stone modular tower, brings to mind Brancusi's *Endless Column* with its concertina-like appearance. Choucair would doubtless have been introduced to Brancusi's work during her time in Paris and, like him, she was interested in traditional crafts founded on a belief in the integration of art and life or design for living. Unlike Brancusi's column, *Movement of the Angle* is not a static structure. When individual modules are twisted or stacked upside down, the movement of the line that runs from top to bottom alters, changing the shape of the whole tower.

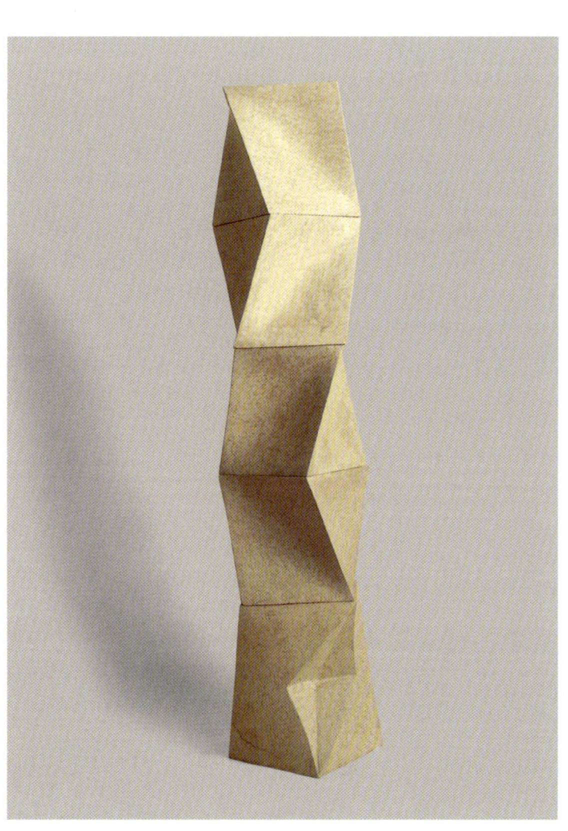

116
Movement of the Angle 1983–5
Stone
177×15×15

Considering her work alongside the modular sculpture that was a phenomenon within European and North American art of the 1960s, and that continued certain constructivist principles in sculpture, would be a way to locate Choucair's practice from this period within a global context. The paradox of potentially infinite sequences of highly contained elements is at play within much of the minimalist sculpture of the 1960s and 1970s. Donald Judd and Carl Andre famously made stacked pieces with repeated modular units. Unlike Choucair, they employed industrial materials and methods to explore physical facts and rational concepts, abandoning the hand-carved or crafted aspects of sculptural practice. But Choucair does share with the minimalists a desire to escape the idea of Romantic expression, or personal, subjective statement in favour of the objective and rational. She also shares with them an interest in the potential of a sculpture to be re-made or re-thought through interaction.

Separation and unity

In later years Choucair grouped the modular sculptures created in the 1960s and originally known as 'Emboîtement', 'Artist's Formula' or 'Joined Units' under the new title 'Kasa'id' or 'Poems', following her interest in the structure of Arabic poetry, in which a verse or stanza may stand alone as well as being part of a complete poem. *Poem of Nine Verses* 1966–8 (fig.117) is made up of nine interlocking carved wood pieces. The illustrations overleaf show the sculpture stacked in two ways. On the left the pieces are carefully placed at the same orientation, giving the structure a fairly regular, rectangular, box-like shape. On the right the top six pieces are turned at a 90-degree angle to the bottom three, giving the sculpture the shape of an inverted 'T' from the photographer's viewpoint.

With a number of works titled *Additionnels* Choucair invited visitors to take the structure apart and stack the pieces in any number, order and combination they chose. The artist's playful spirit and her love of puzzles and equations certainly found an outlet in this aspect of her practice. Later pieces, such as the *Sliding Structures* from the 1980s, resemble beautifully crafted wooden toys designed to be handled and played with. Choucair's lively, inventive mind and creative spirit do seem to be most clearly embodied in this aspect of her practice, but in order to do justice to her ideas it is necessary to look beyond her personal qualities and to consider her belief in the potentiality of all things, a belief that stems from her research into Arab and Islamic concepts of creativity. Samir Sayigh has described Choucair's modular sculpture as follows:

> For her, sculpture is formed beginning from the repetition or accumulation of a formulaic, quasi-geometric unit that constitutes the essential element, indeed the only element, which then accumulates and multiplies to eventually form the single statue – it will repeat, break off, overlap, run adjacent or touching, thus composing the single artistic work. Thus sculpture, if we wanted to define it from a purely aesthetic perspective, defines itself by the absence of sculpture, meaning that what will give this sculpture its spirit is not the form or the volume or the formulaic or geometric unit; rather, it is the movement that this form or geometric unit undertakes in its accumulation, growth and repetition. That is, it is this empty space, this invisible, absolute abstraction. For the movement here is intangible and disembodied, even illusory, hypothetical, potential, and will not materialize or be seen unless the eye bring it to life, the eye that knows how to return the sculpture to its original state, that is, to its beginning as a unit, then follow along with it step by step.[7]

Sayigh indicates that it is the responsibility of the viewer, the 'eye that knows…', to see the potential within the work. Other critics have argued that it is not necessary to fully understand Choucair's methods – based as they often are on geometric, mathematical calculations – in order to appreciate the harmonious, sequential and tactile effects.

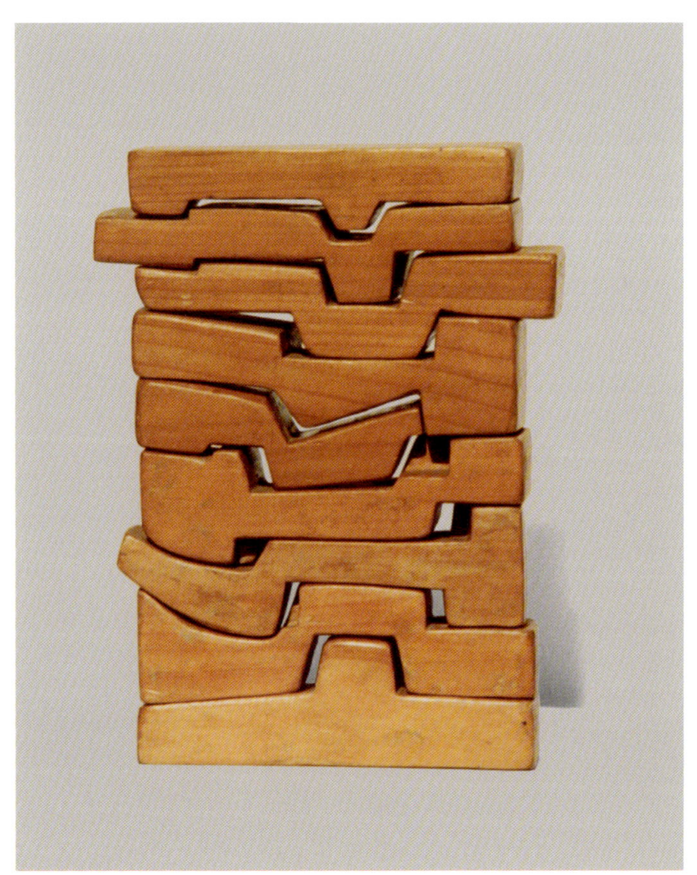

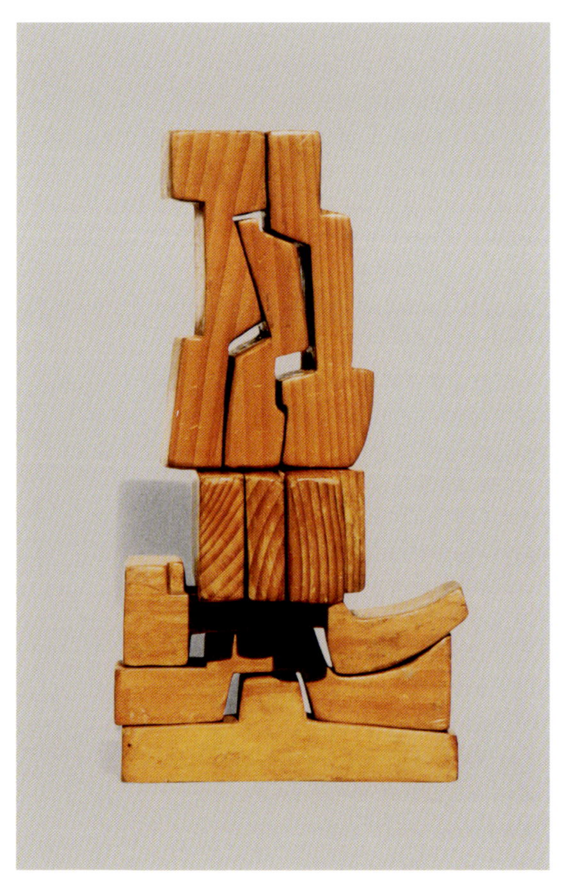

117
Poem of Nine Verses
1966–8
Wood
29 × 22 × 7

In the mid-1970s – a time of pre-war turmoil in Lebanon – Choucair began to make a series of works that essentially focused on the separation and unity of existence. Titled *Duals*, these small sculptures made in wood, bronze, fibreglass or aluminium have been described as both 'a synthesis of the search for unity and separateness that forms the core of her creative purpose' and 'symbols of her yearning for the unity of her city as Beirut entered the Civil War'.[8] They have also been called 'mathanawis' or poetic couplets. Though it may not have been the artist's intention to create erotic or psychoanalytically charged work, these pieces bring to mind surrealist traditions in sculpture, *The Screw* 1975–7 (fig.119) being perhaps her most obviously phallic piece in the series. Some of the taller wooden pieces are cut in half by a rhythmic, wavy line which recalls Choucair's interest in the trajectory of the line. Other *Duals* are squat, coiled objects with a more organic quality, made of materials such as fibreglass as well as painted clay.

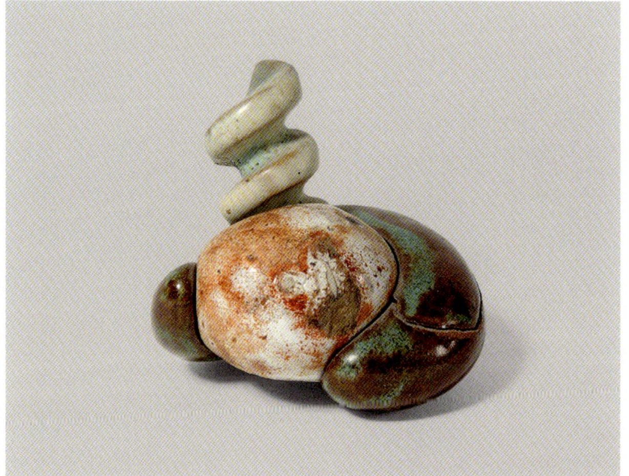

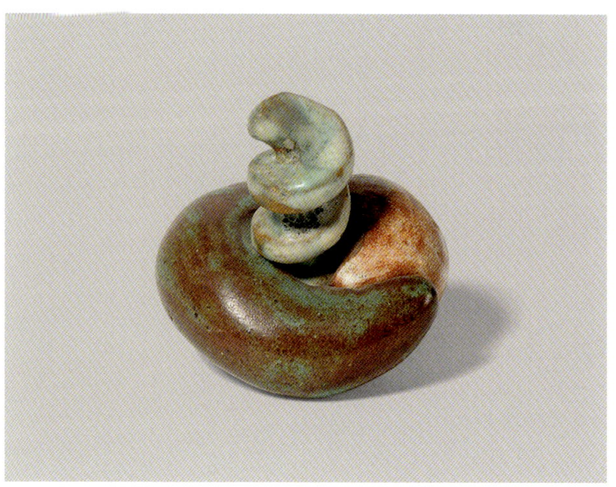

118
The Screw 1975–7
Enamelled terracotta
9×9×9

Movement

Choucair's experiments with relatively new materials such as fibreglass led her towards a more blatant consideration of liquidity and movement. In the early 1970s she was invited to exhibit at the Salon de Mai in Paris and needed to make a light sculpture to travel. She was fascinated by tension which she explored in works such as *Static Dynamism* 1972–4 (fig.118) and *Trajectory of the Arc* 1972–4 (fig.71), both of which were constructed using metal – aluminium or stainless steel – and nylon thread. The movement in these pieces is mostly potential, or at least subtle, as they are not 'kinetic' sculptures, as such. Nevertheless, Choucair was shocked when a visitor commented on the resemblance of her works with plexi and nylon thread to the kinetic experiments of the Russian Constructivist Naum Gabo. Believing herself to be truly original, she abandoned this method of working, but aspects of her earlier experiments re-surface when she later became interested in sculpting with water, designing fountain heads that force fine jets of water to take on the 'trajectory of the line' or the appearance of a complex woven thread.

In the majority of Choucair's sculptural output, movement is potential rather than literal. Jack Aswad has provided a useful reference to the Arabic verb *tanmit* to describe the 'modulation' of Choucair's work, semantically linking 'movement' with 'module' in order to describe the relationship between the two:

> From 'al-nammat' (pattern) that is the method, manner, variety, category, or type, the Arabs of yore had a denominative verb: ('tanmit') to pattern. They used to say, 'nammata lahu

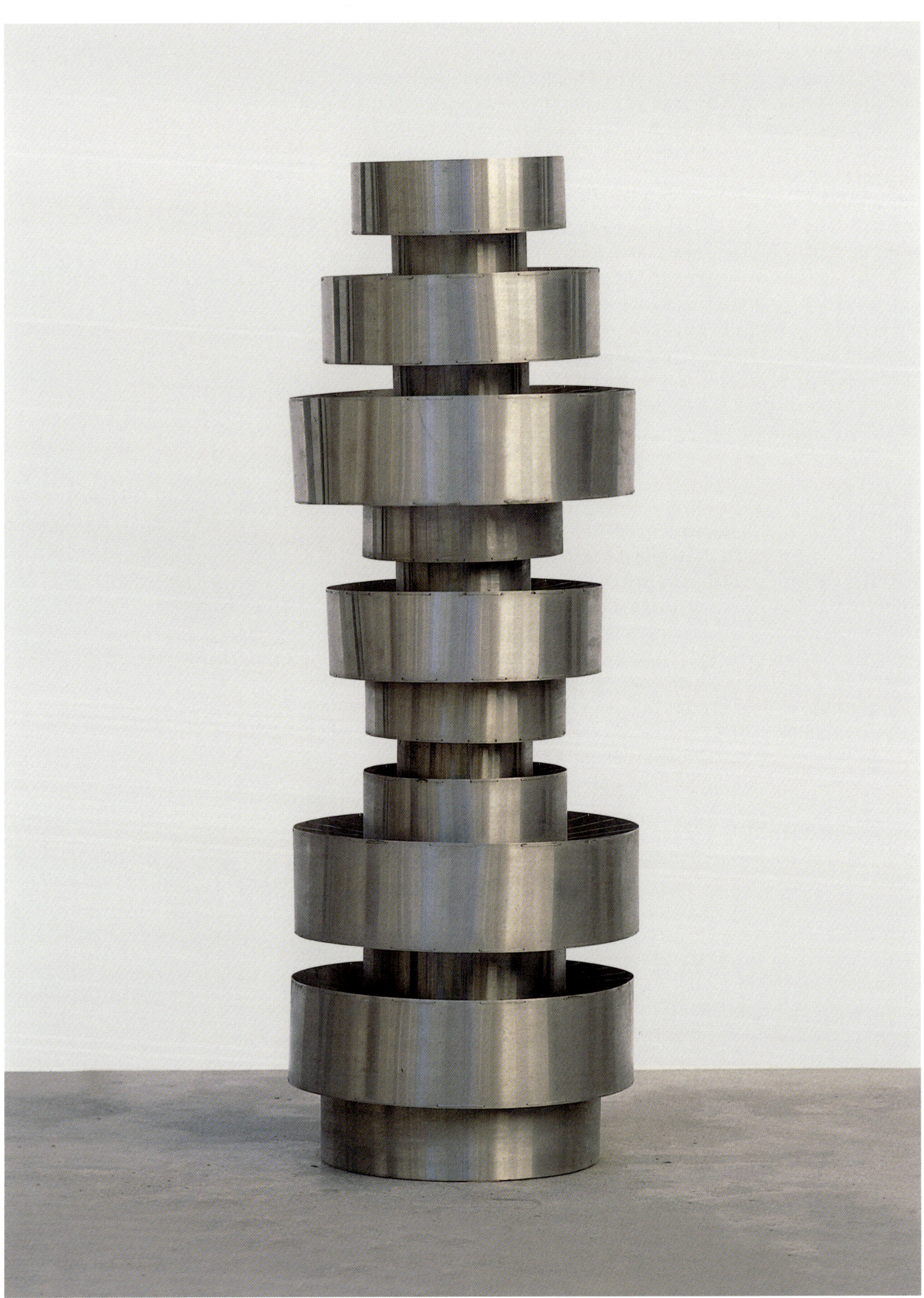

> 'ala al-shi' (he patterned for him toward something) which meant 'he guided him to it'. If we were to make this verb transitive, then al-namat (the pattern) would be preferable to 'al-qaalib al-taswiri [pictorial mold] for what Choucair called in French 'module', for it would allow us to see the 'tanmit' (modulation) in the work, in other words the commutating, adjusting, and 'inflecting' of the field, that is at once its hodological orientation.[9]

This definition brings us closer to an understanding of the movement and potential inherent in the modules Choucair used to make up her rich, varied and complex body of work. It is perhaps appropriate that her last major retrospective exhibition in Beirut to date, organised by her daughter Hala Schoukair in 2011, was titled *A Project in the Making*. In her introductory text to the exhibition, Schoukair writes: 'The art of Saloua Raouda Choucair has the ability to grow and transform. This hallmark keeps her art alive; by definition and design, Choucair's art is a project that is always, "in the making".'[10]

Ann Coxon

119
Static Dynamism 1972–4
Stainless steel
124×46

120
(overleaf)
Flat Vase 1980–2
Enamelled terracotta
11×9×3

Flat Vase 1980–2
Enamelled terracotta
8×10×1

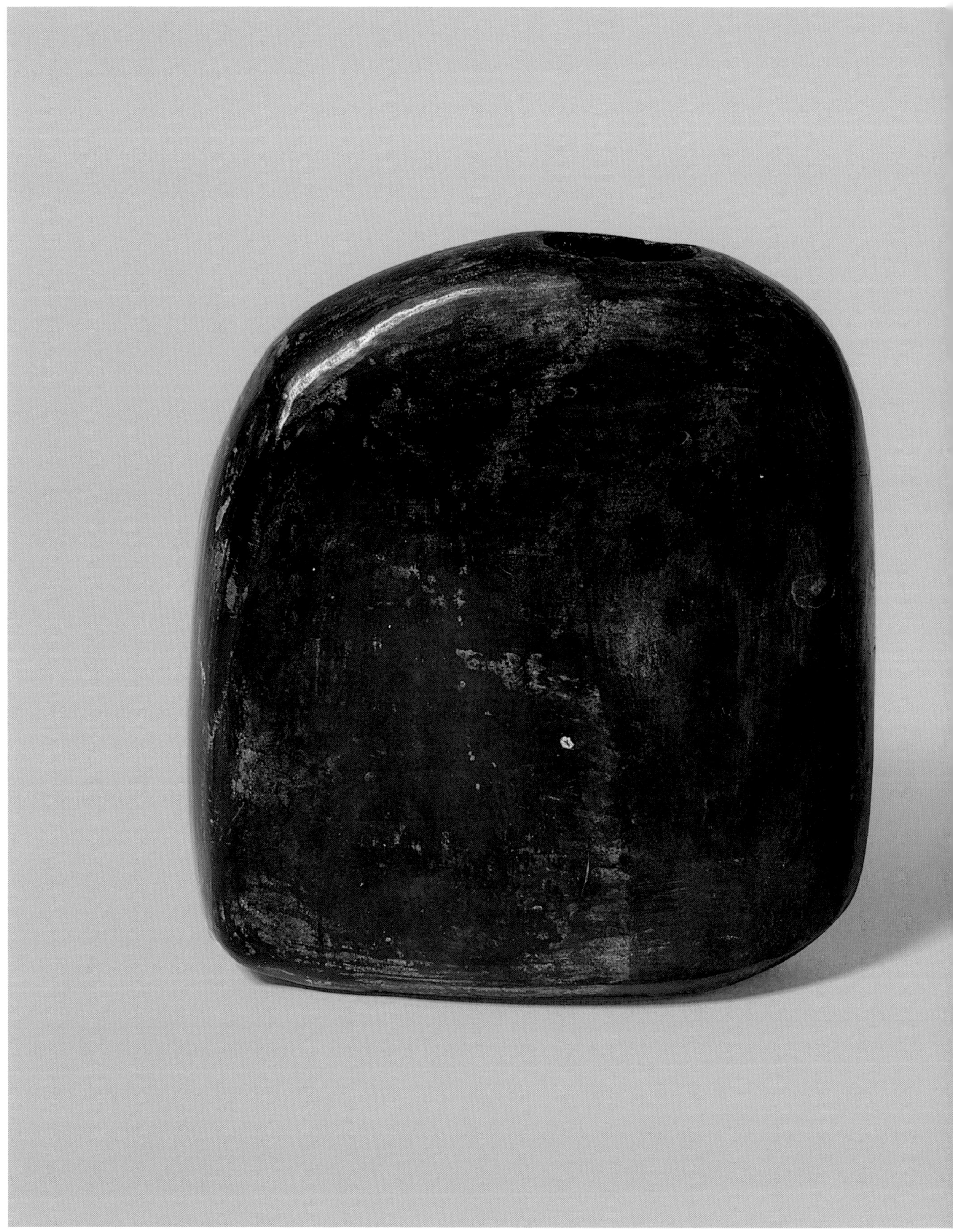

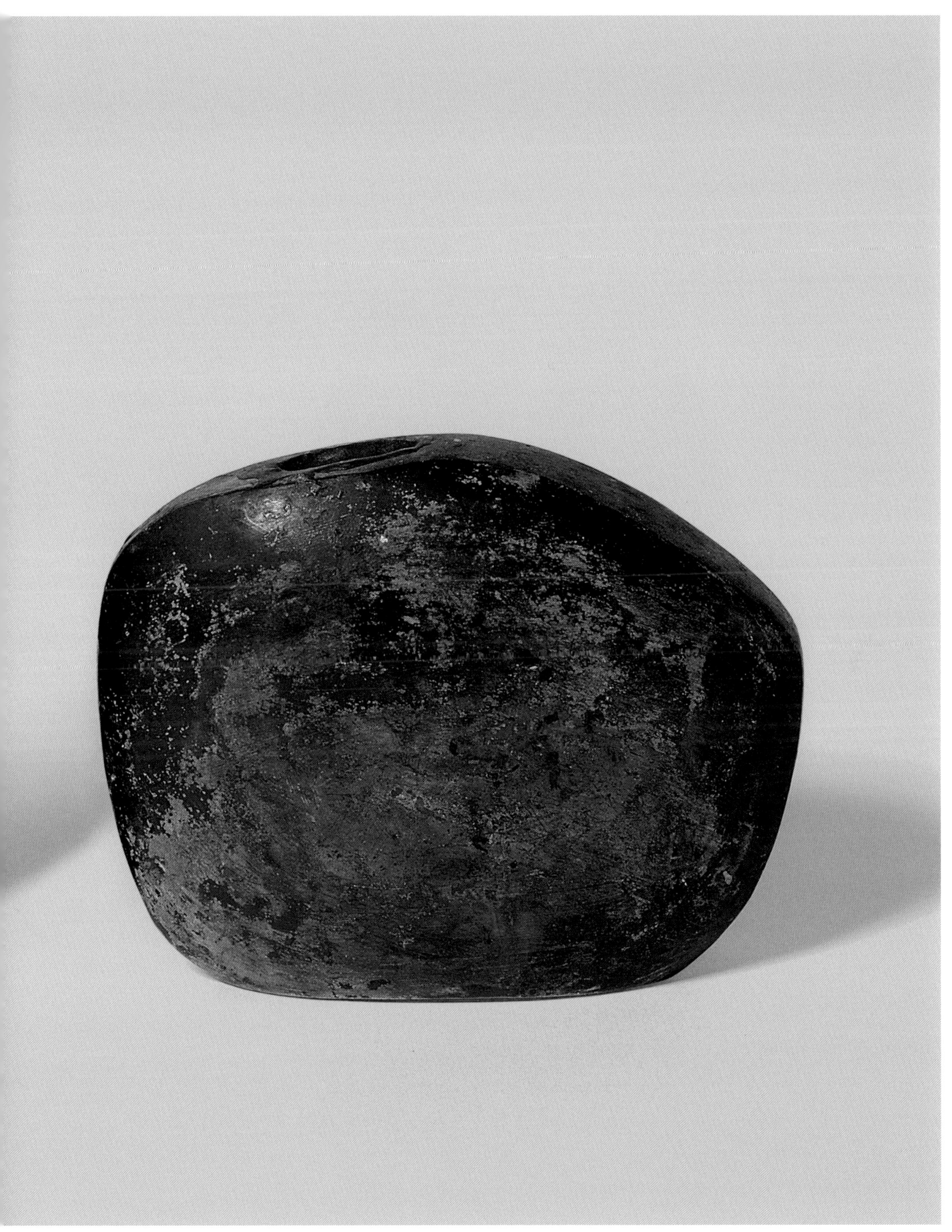

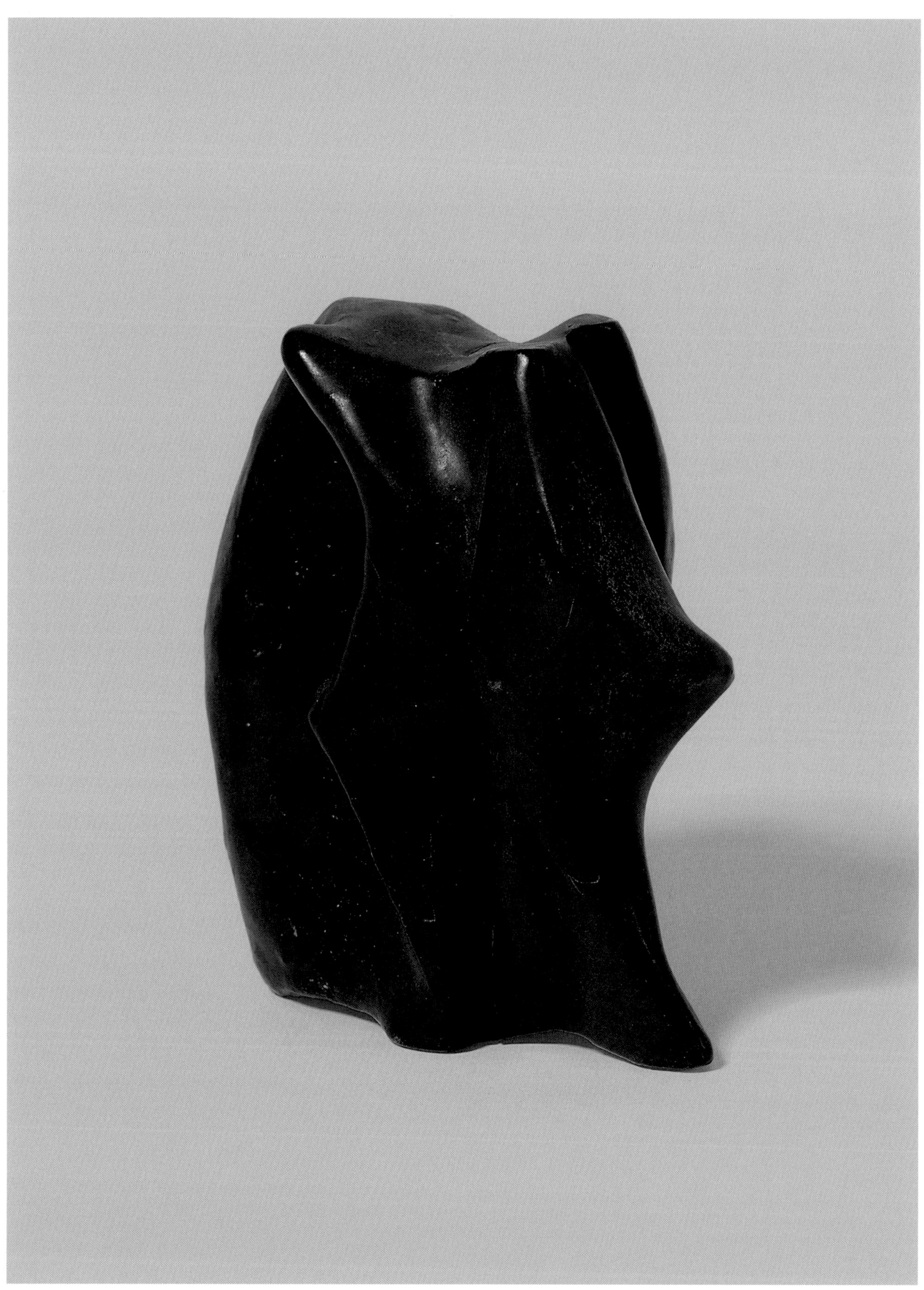

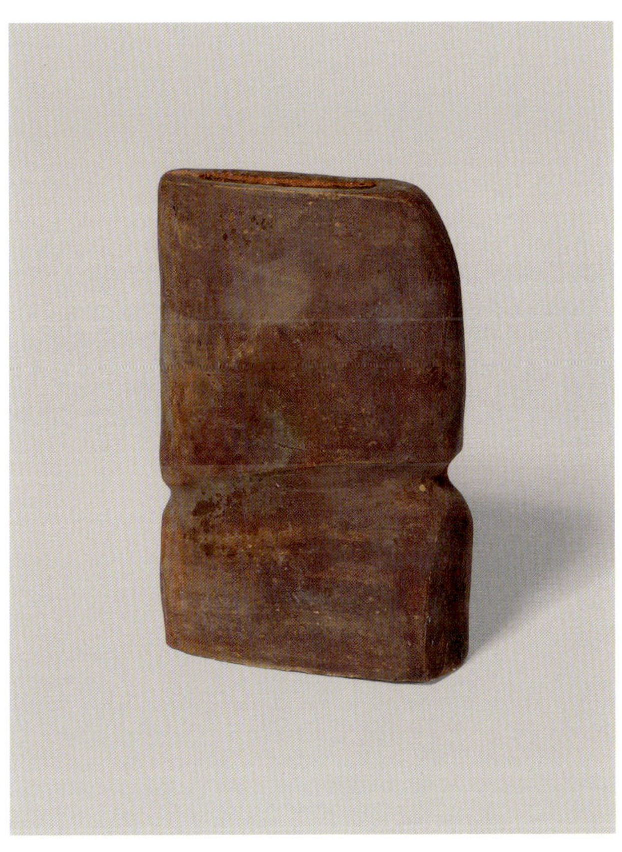

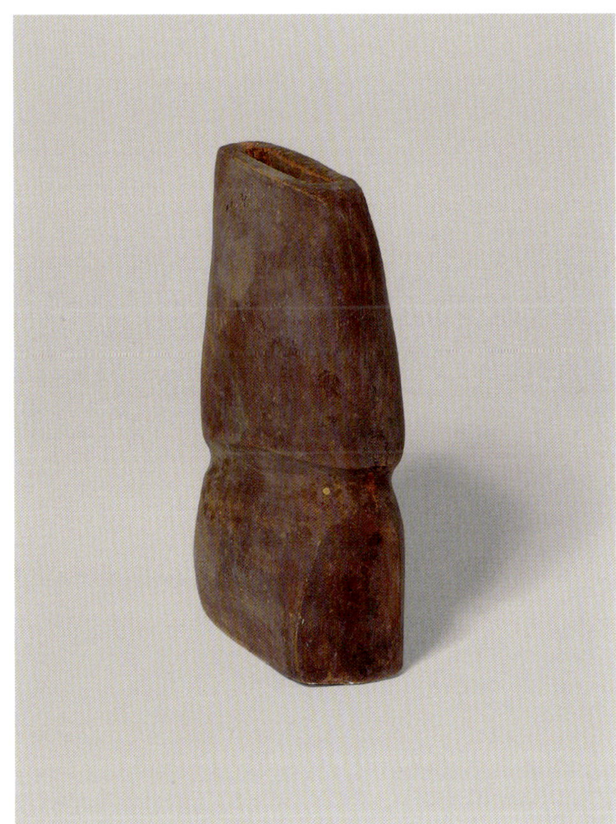

121
Module 1980–3
Enamelled terracotta
13 × 11 × 6

122
Flat Vase 1980–2
Terracotta
13.5 × 8 × 3

123
(overleaf)
Module 1980–3
Wood
75 × 46 × 25

124
(overleaf)
Module 1980–3
Wood
28 × 40 × 19

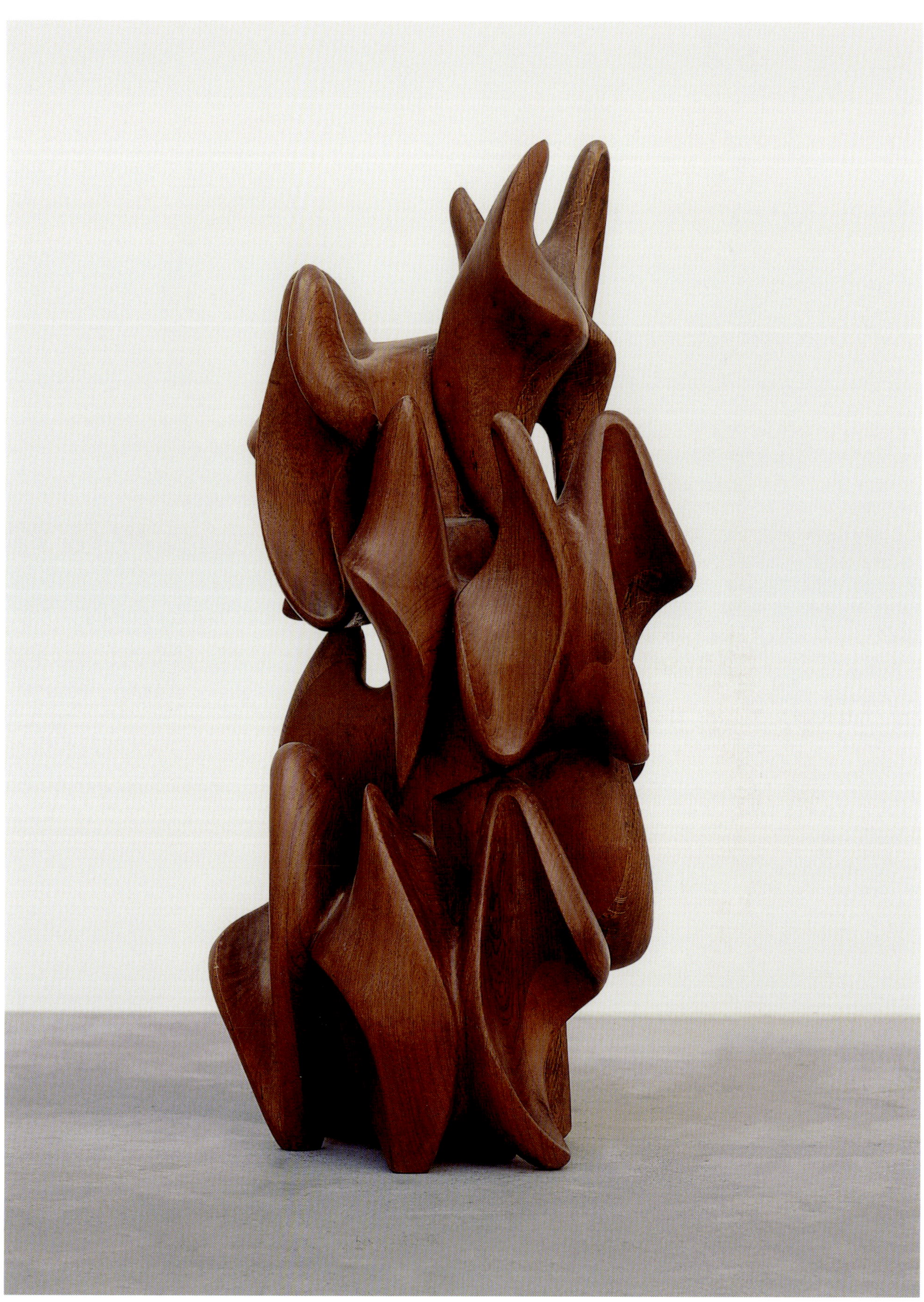

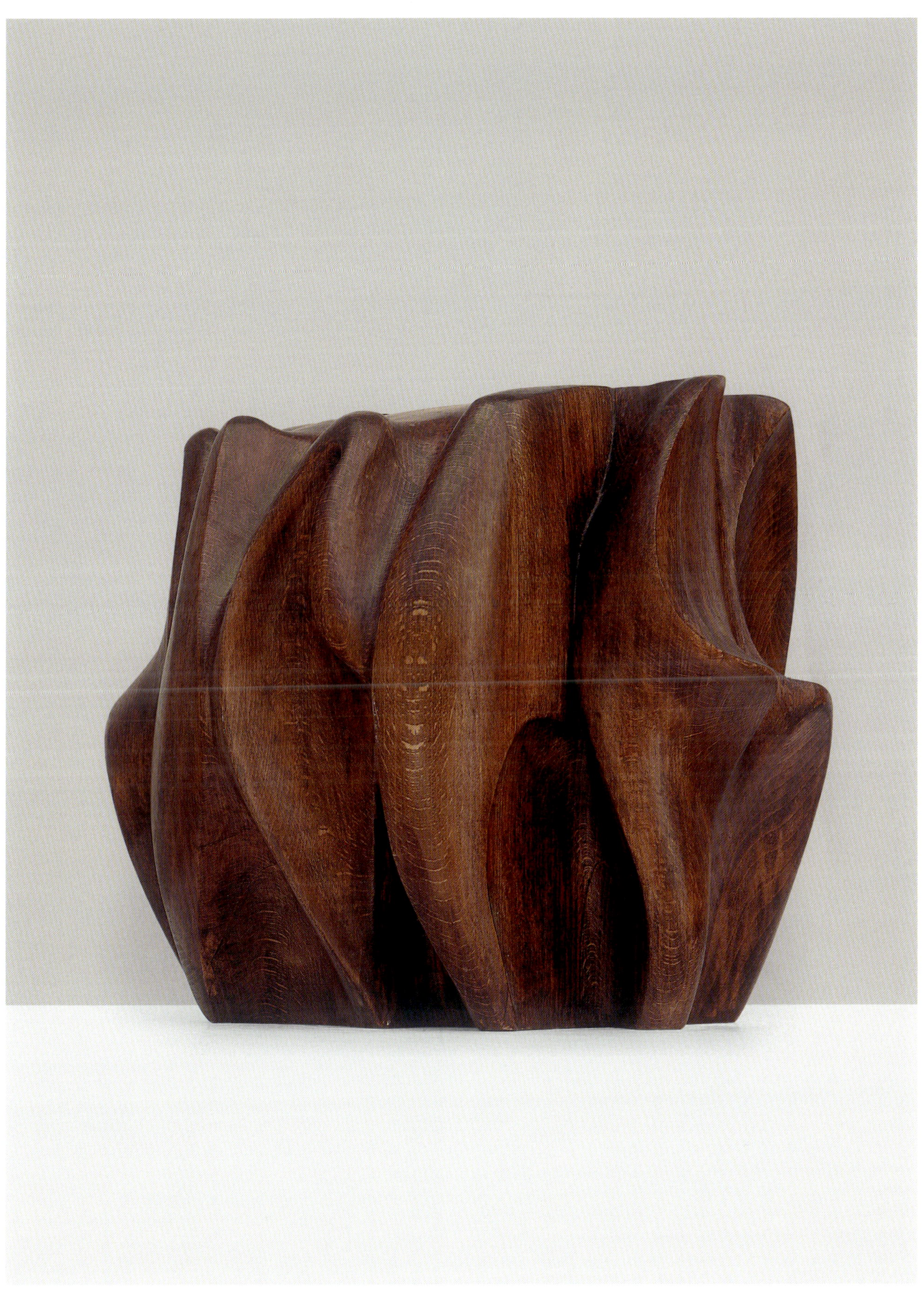

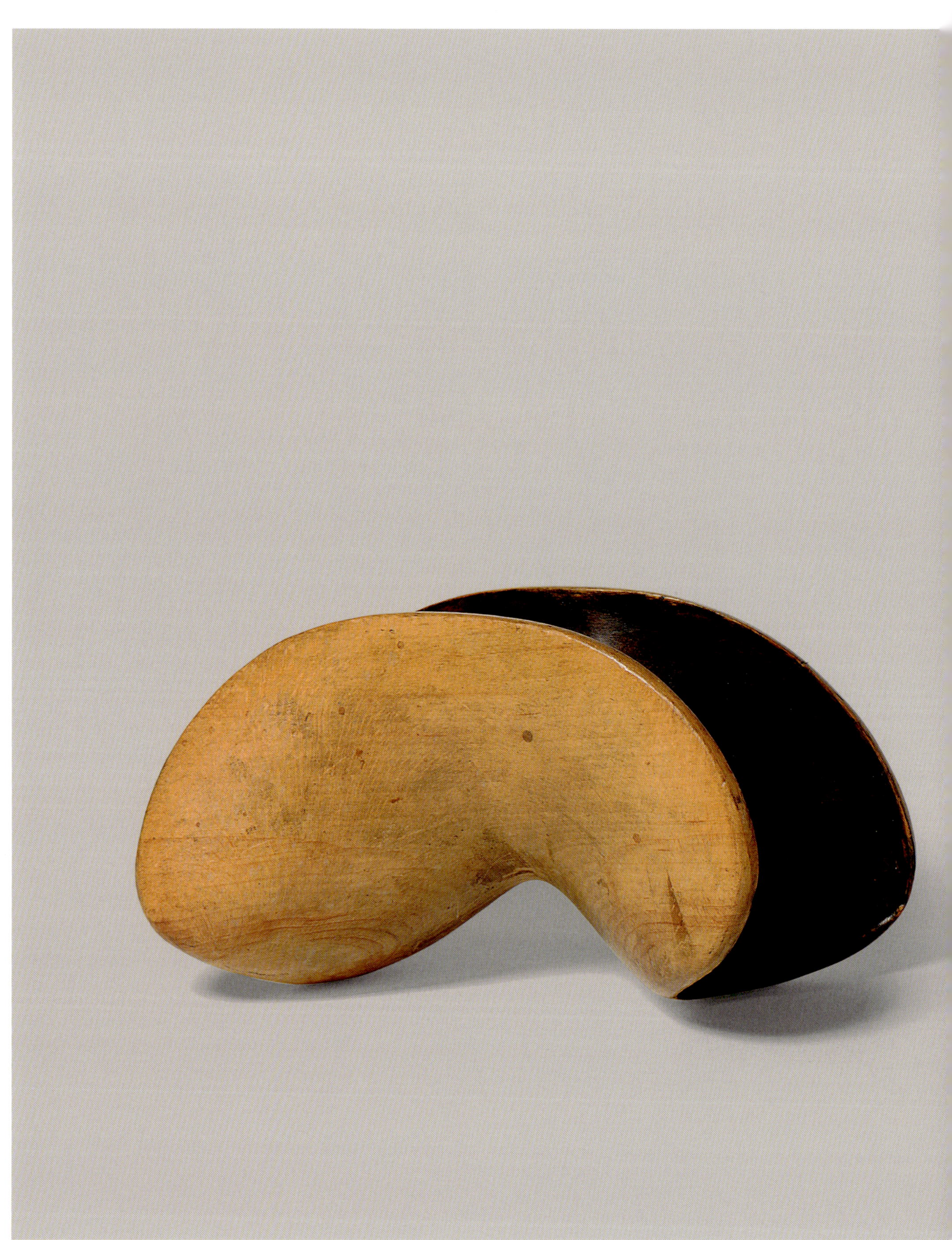

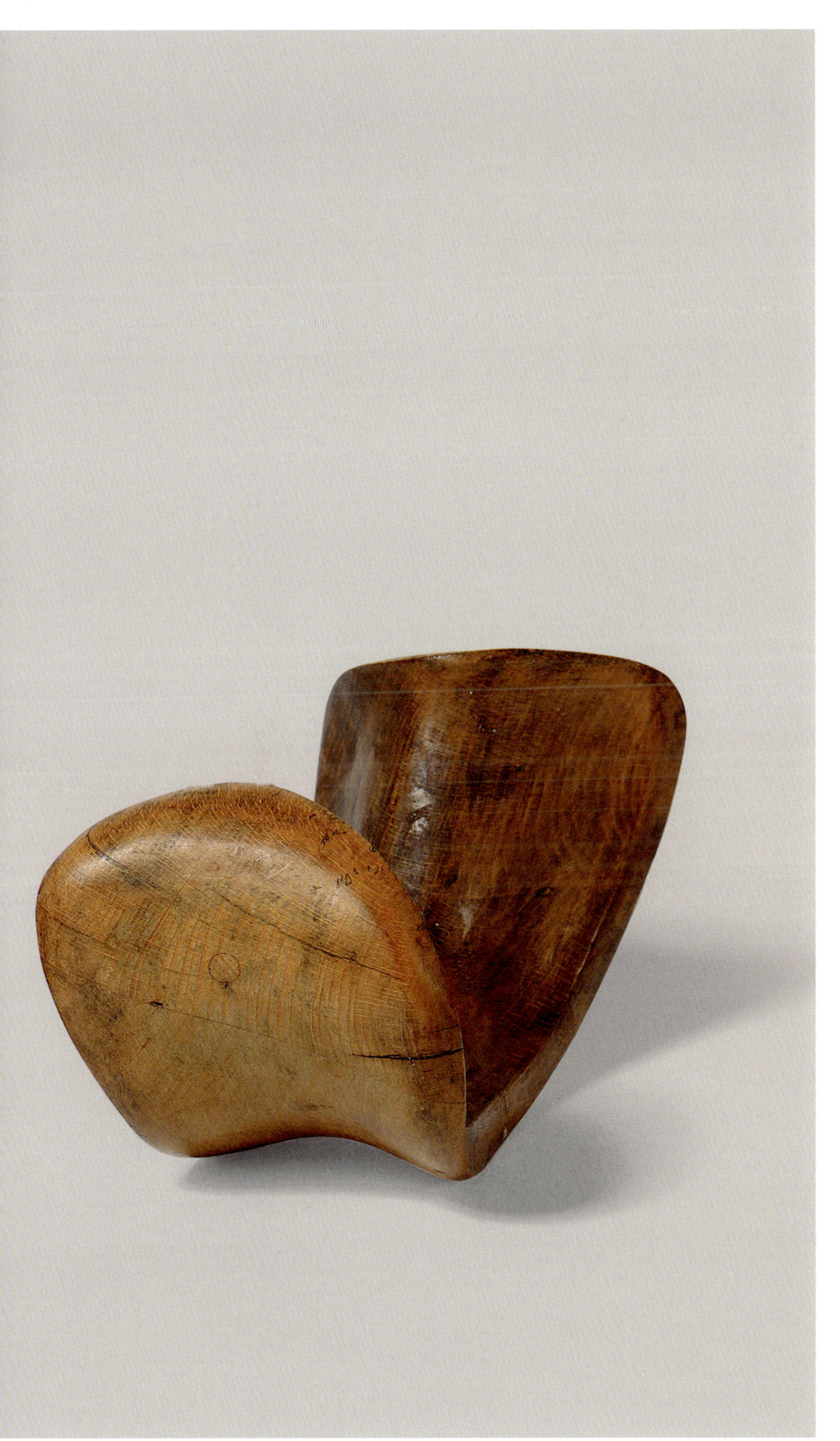

125
Module 1980–3
Wood
10 × 20 × 10
(each piece)

126
Infinite Structure 1983–5
Terracotta
3 × 6 × 4 (each piece)

127
Poem of Nine Verses 1966–8
Aluminium
27 × 21 × 7

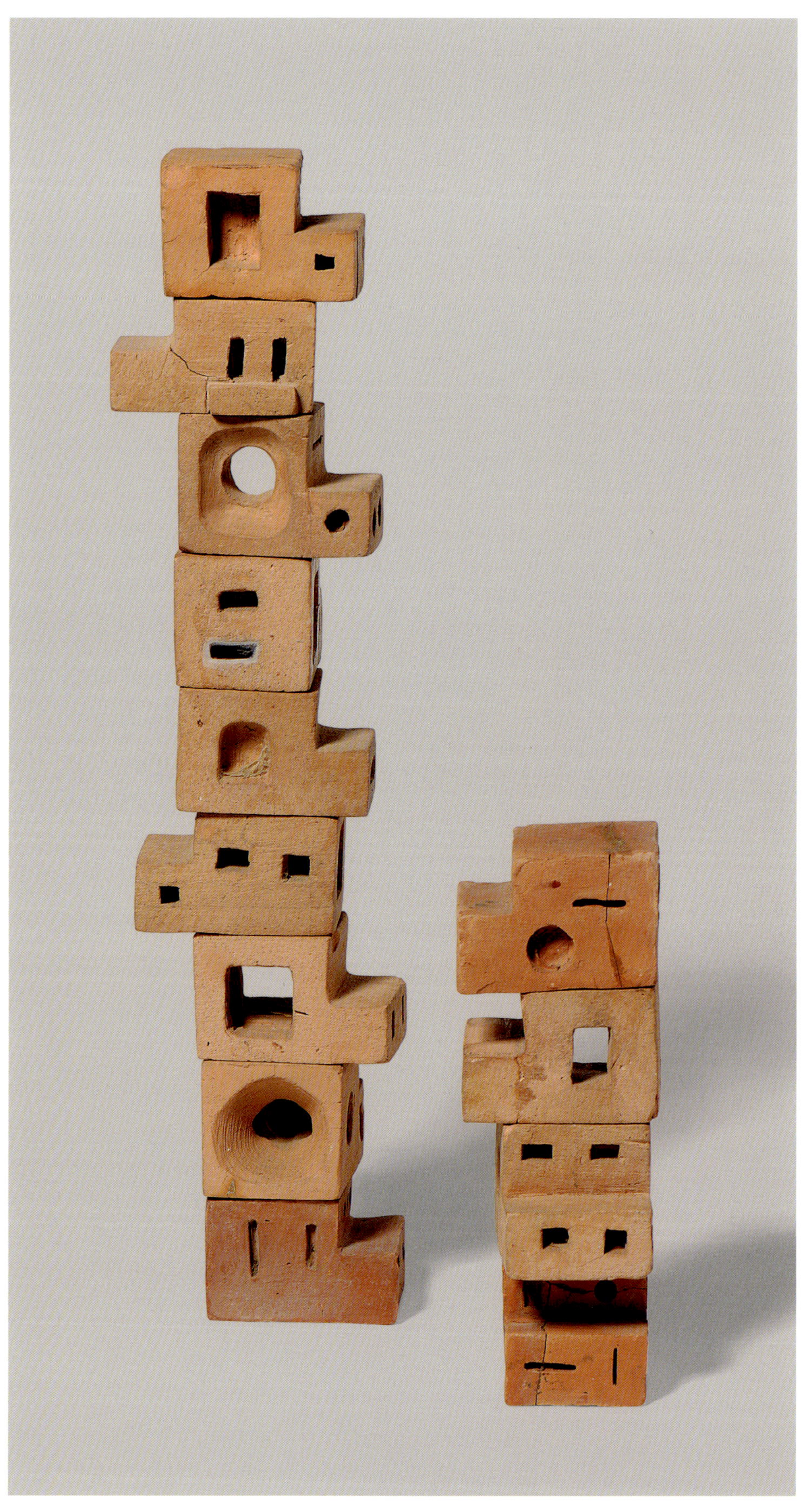

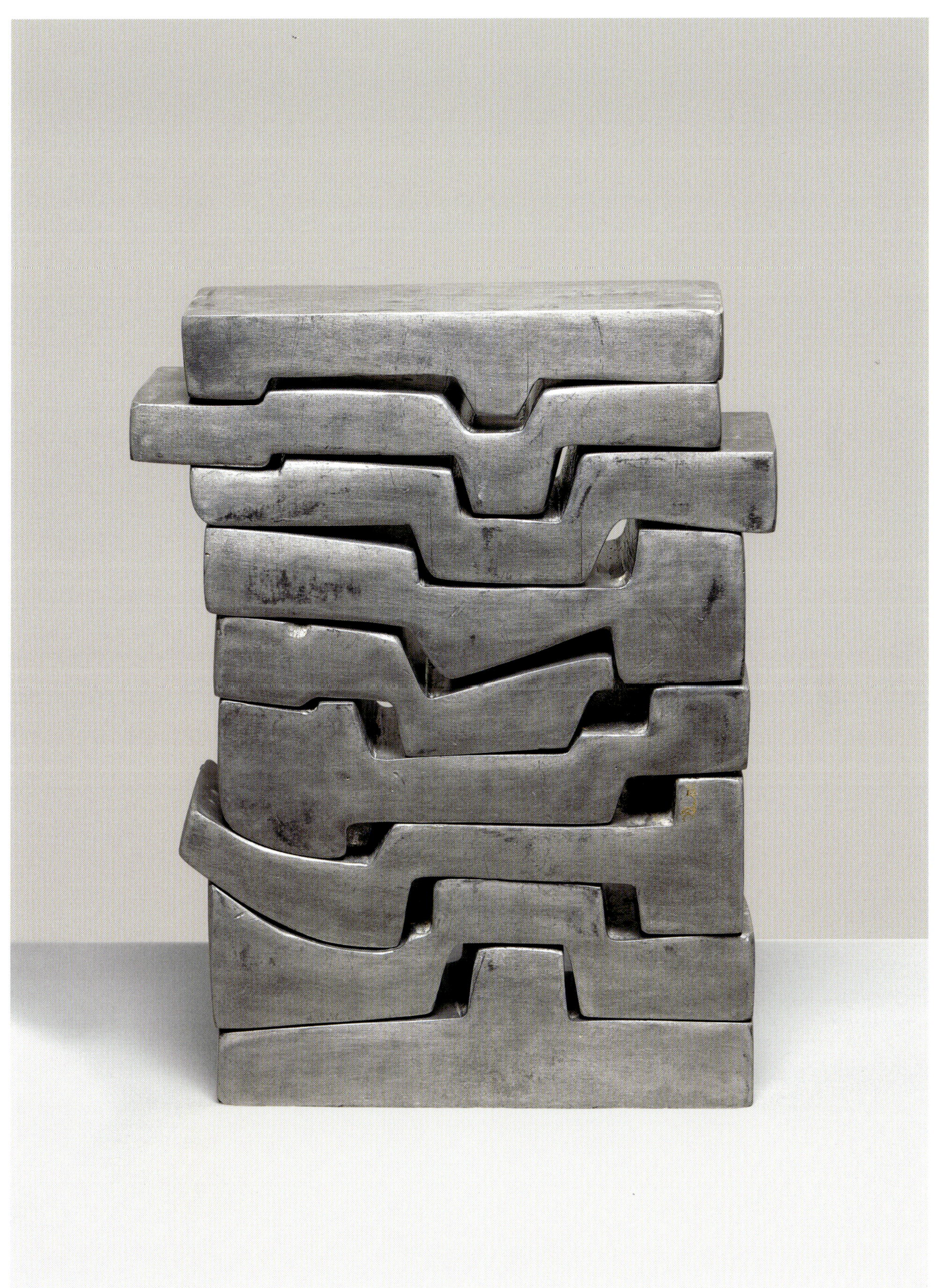

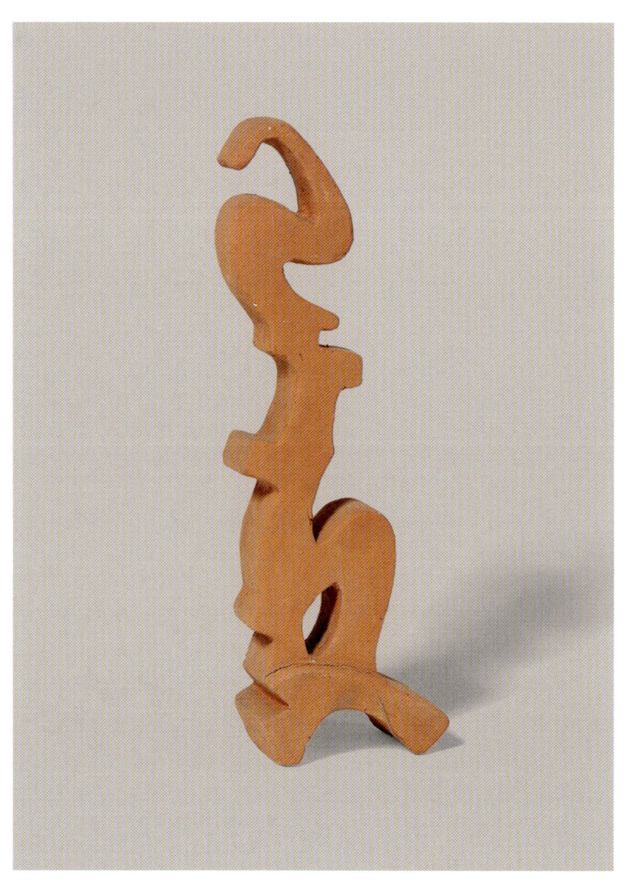

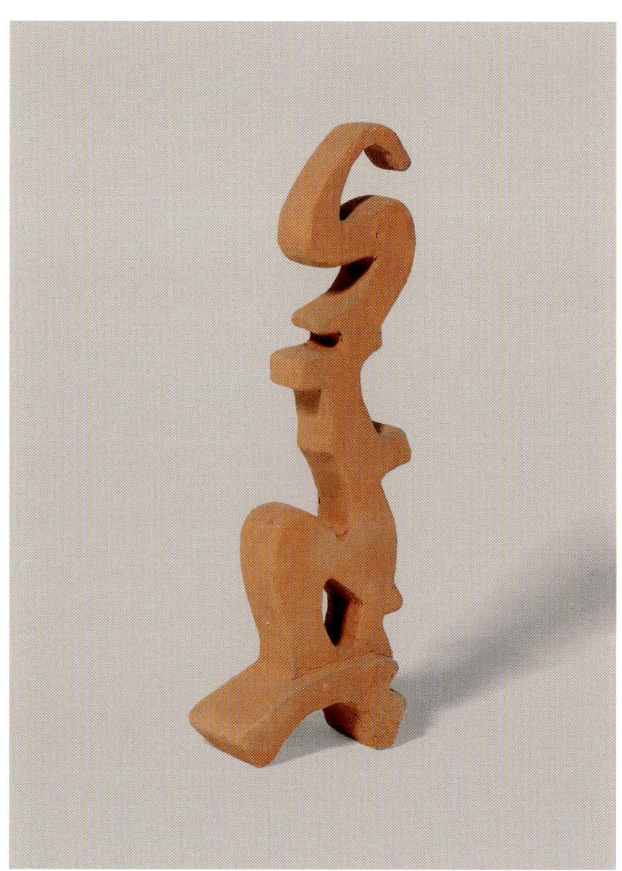

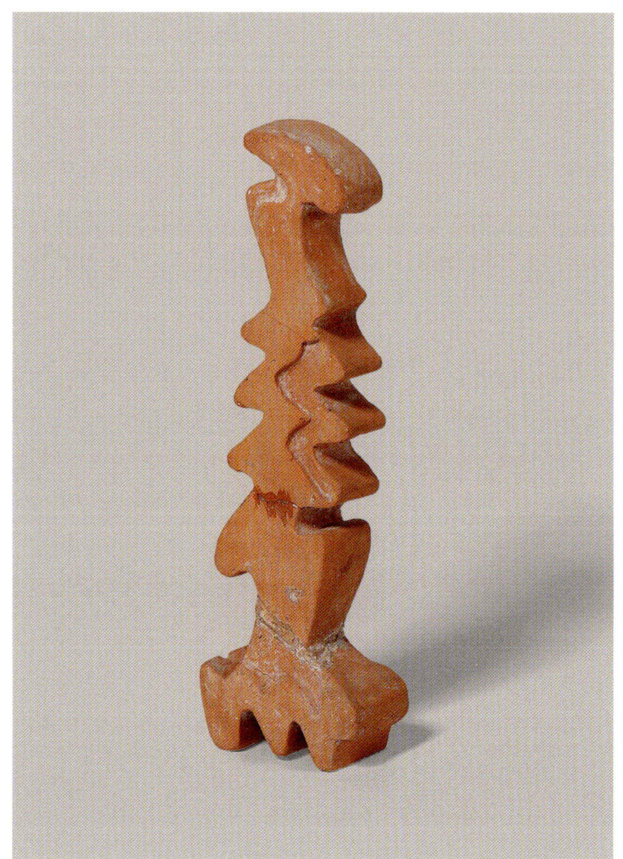

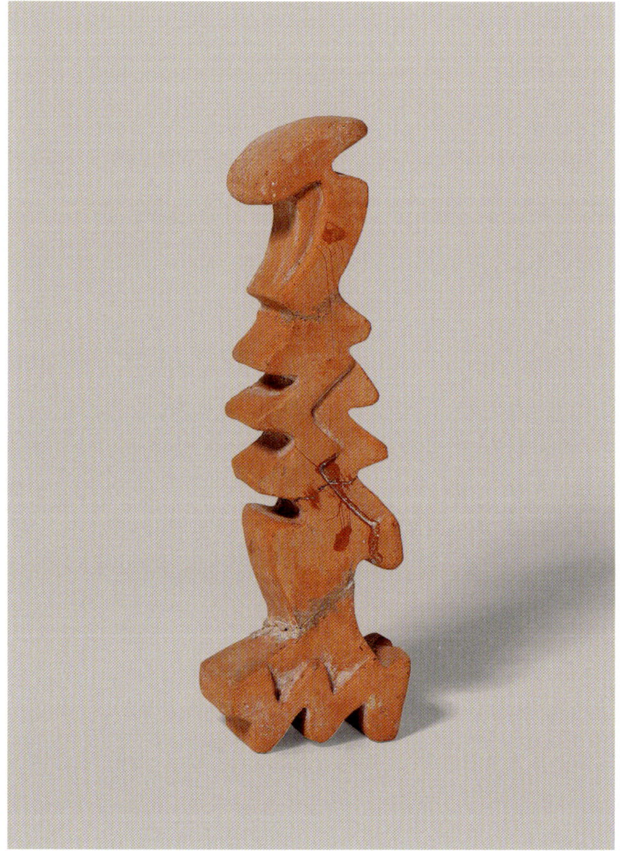

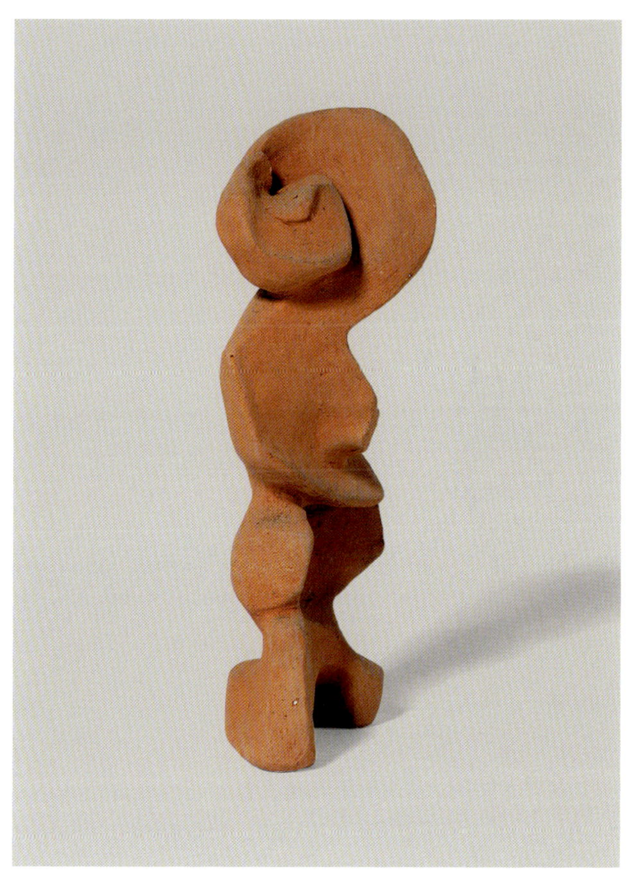

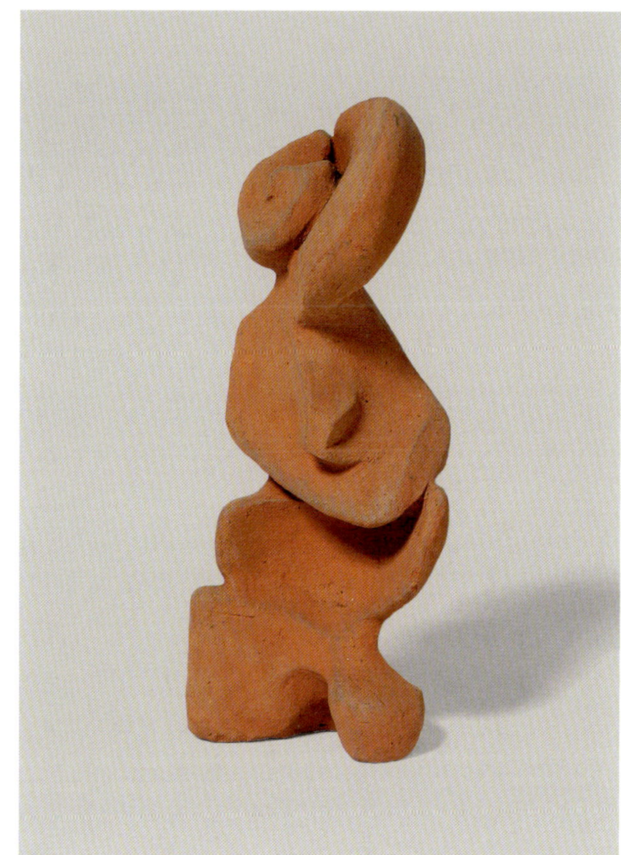

128
From
The Rhyme Series
1994–6
Terracotta
30 × 9 × 5

129
From
The Rhyme Series
1994–6
Terracotta
23 × 7 × 4

130
From
The Rhyme Series
1994–6
Terracotta
22 × 8 × 4

131
(overleaf)
Ode 1966–8
Terracotta
12 × 6 × 6

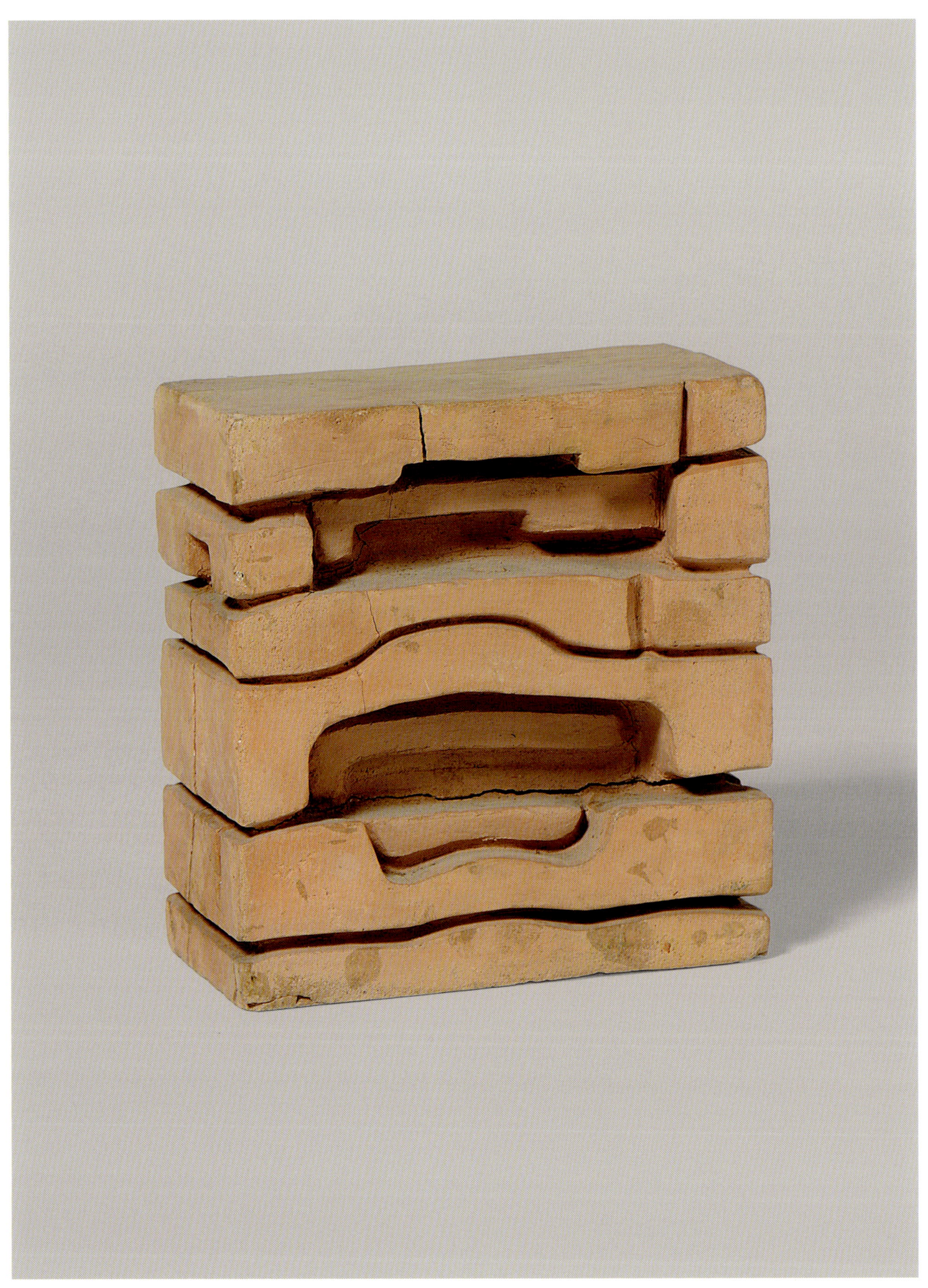

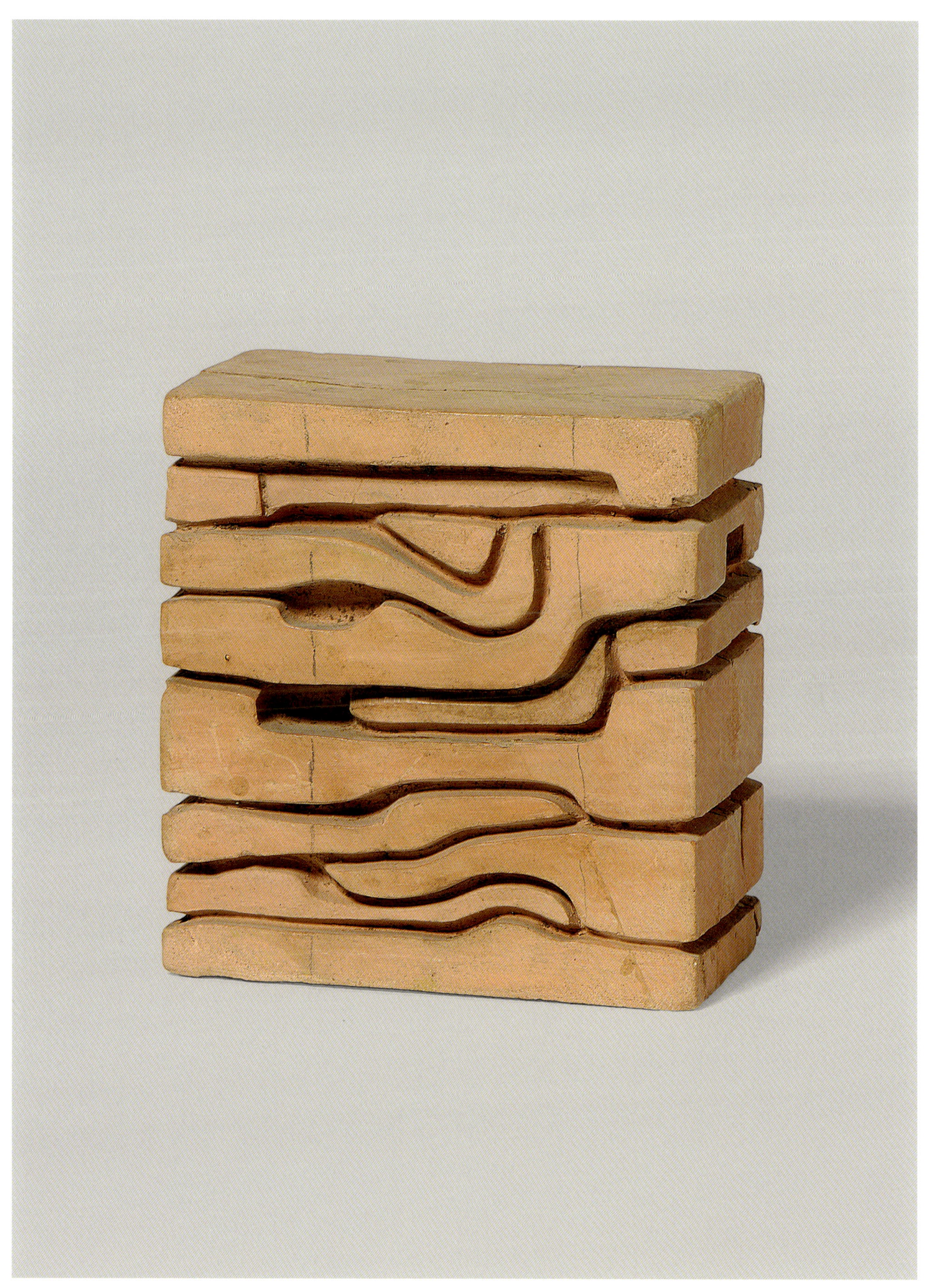

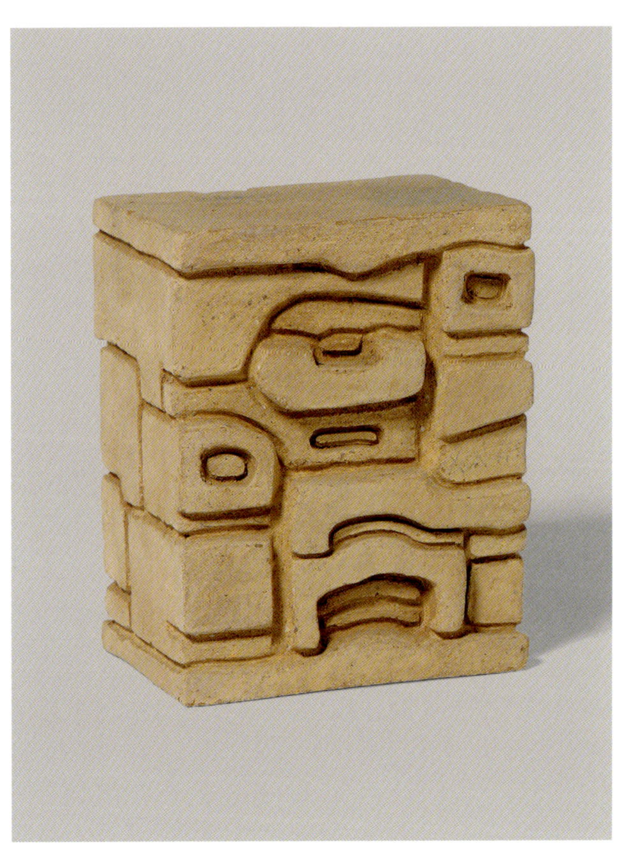

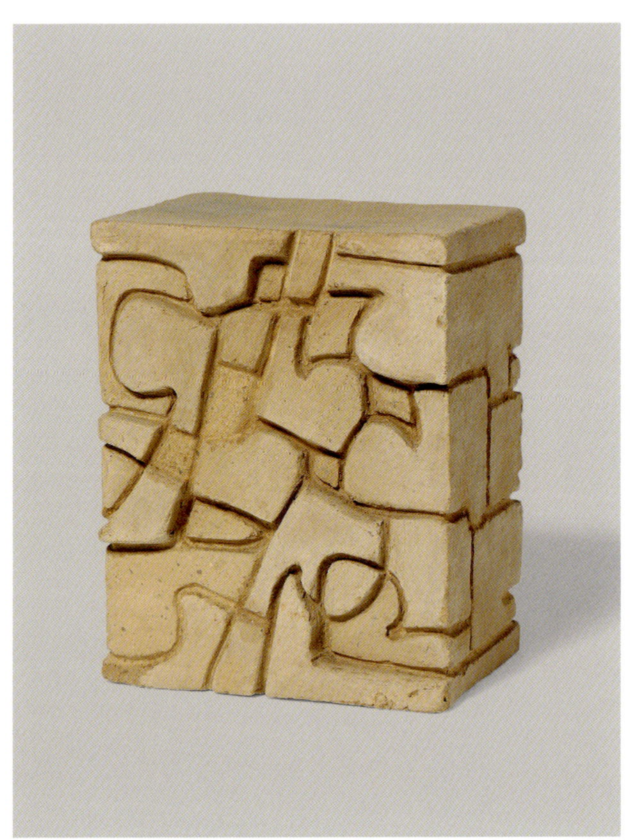

132
(above)
Ode 1983–5
Terracotta
15 × 12 × 8

133
(right)
Poem of Three Verses 1963–5
Wood
55 × 33 × 20

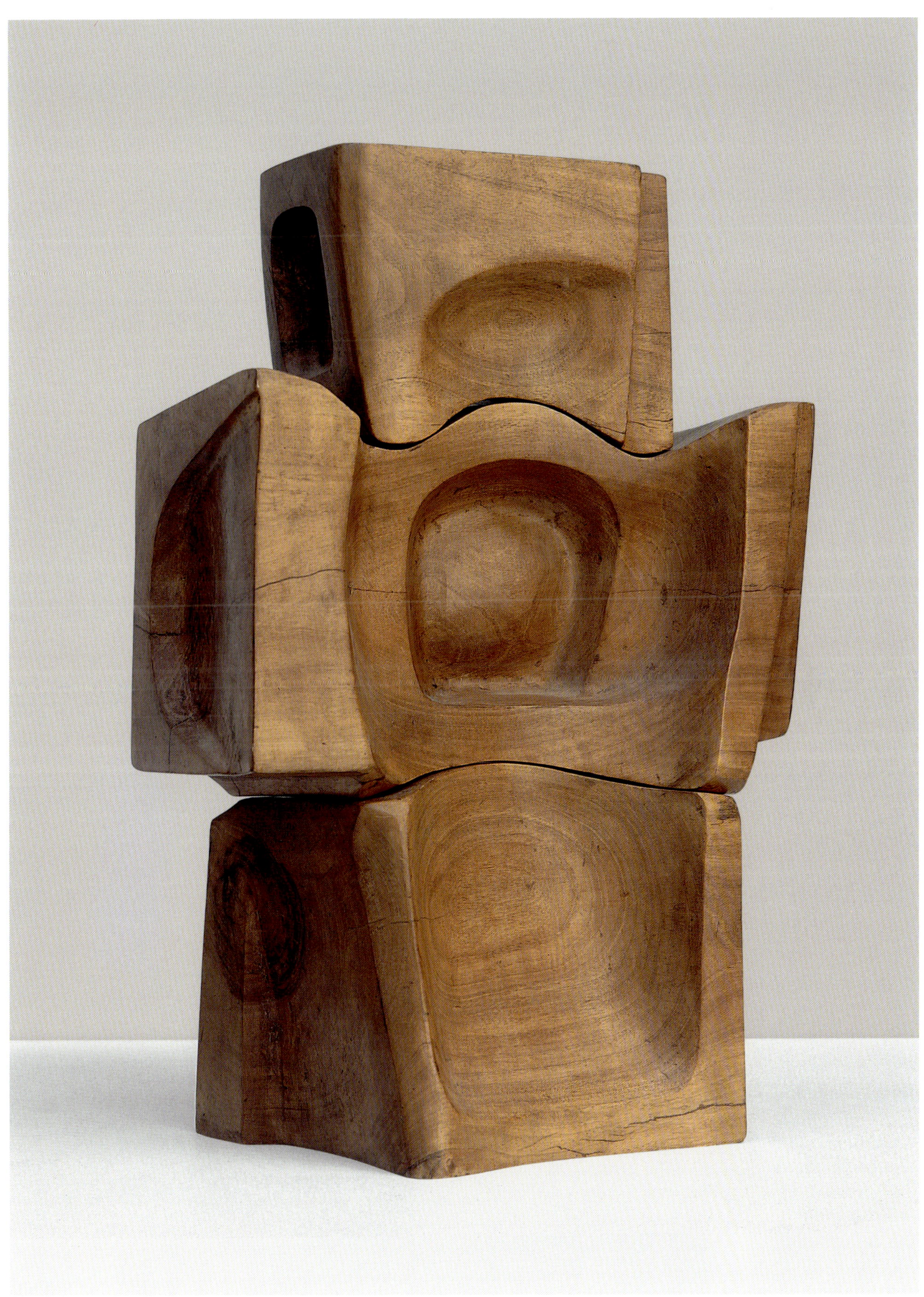

Two Lovers in a Park at Midday
The urban imagination of Saloua Raouda Choucair

Beirut is famous for a great many things, but green space, public parks and civic plazas have never been high on the list. The tiny, unmarked, tree-lined square that is tucked into the southern seam of the downtown district, where it hosts one of just two public sculptures by the pioneering abstract artist Saloua Raouda Choucair in the city where she was born, is therefore something of a strange and unexpected secret. Now surrounded by parking lots on three sides, the square is splayed out around the gnarled trunk of an ancient ficus tree. It is edged with purple flowers and adorned with a sizeable reflecting pool, which for reasons unknown has been left to dry. The whole thing sits rather awkwardly below the elevated high-speed ring road that runs parallel to the coast and whisks traffic between East and West Beirut. The ring road defines the economic exclusivity of the city centre and sets it apart from the poorer, more popular district of Basta, which eventually gives way to Mazraa and then to the southern suburbs that lie between here and the airport out of Beirut. As such it cuts off pedestrian traffic, both physically and psychologically, which has had the effect of drastically reducing the number of people who might otherwise gather in the square and encounter Choucair's work.

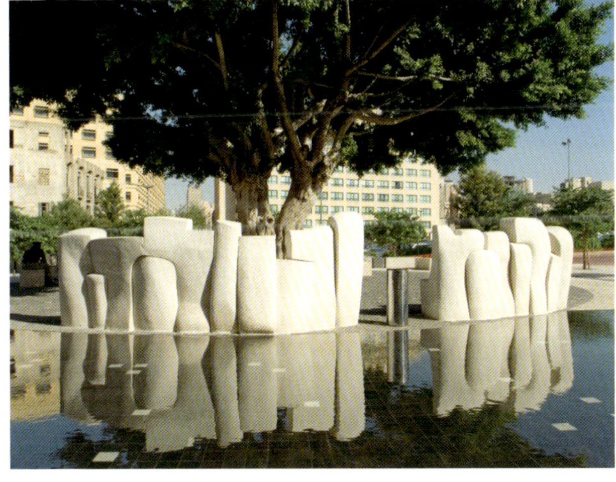

134
Bench 1998
Stone
170 × 570 × 70
Photographed in Mir Amin Garden, Beirut, in 2006, courtesy of Solidere

A hundred years ago the area around the square was a suburb. Fifty years ago it was a slum. During Lebanon's fifteen years of civil war it was abandoned and afterwards it was destroyed. The private real-estate company Solidere, which was established in 1994 to carry out the urban renewal of Beirut's city centre, flattened almost everything in this neighbourhood (like so many others) except for the skeleton of the Grande Theatre, a cultural and architectural relic, and a pink house with white trim that dates back to the French Mandate and looks like a birthday cake (previously the address of several foreign embassies, the building now stands totally vacant). The neighbourhood is identified on contemporary maps of Beirut as Bashoura, though many a historian and urban sociologist will tell you this name is fake, a fabrication made up to mask the fact that, however bland and businesslike it may be today, the area is best known for its close proximity to Beirut's former red-light district.

For a while, some five or six years ago, the square and its surroundings were always empty, particularly in the aftermath of the eighteen-month-long occupation of downtown Beirut by Hezbollah and its affiliated parties, who were Lebanon's political opposition at the time. During that period, there was never anyone around except for a single

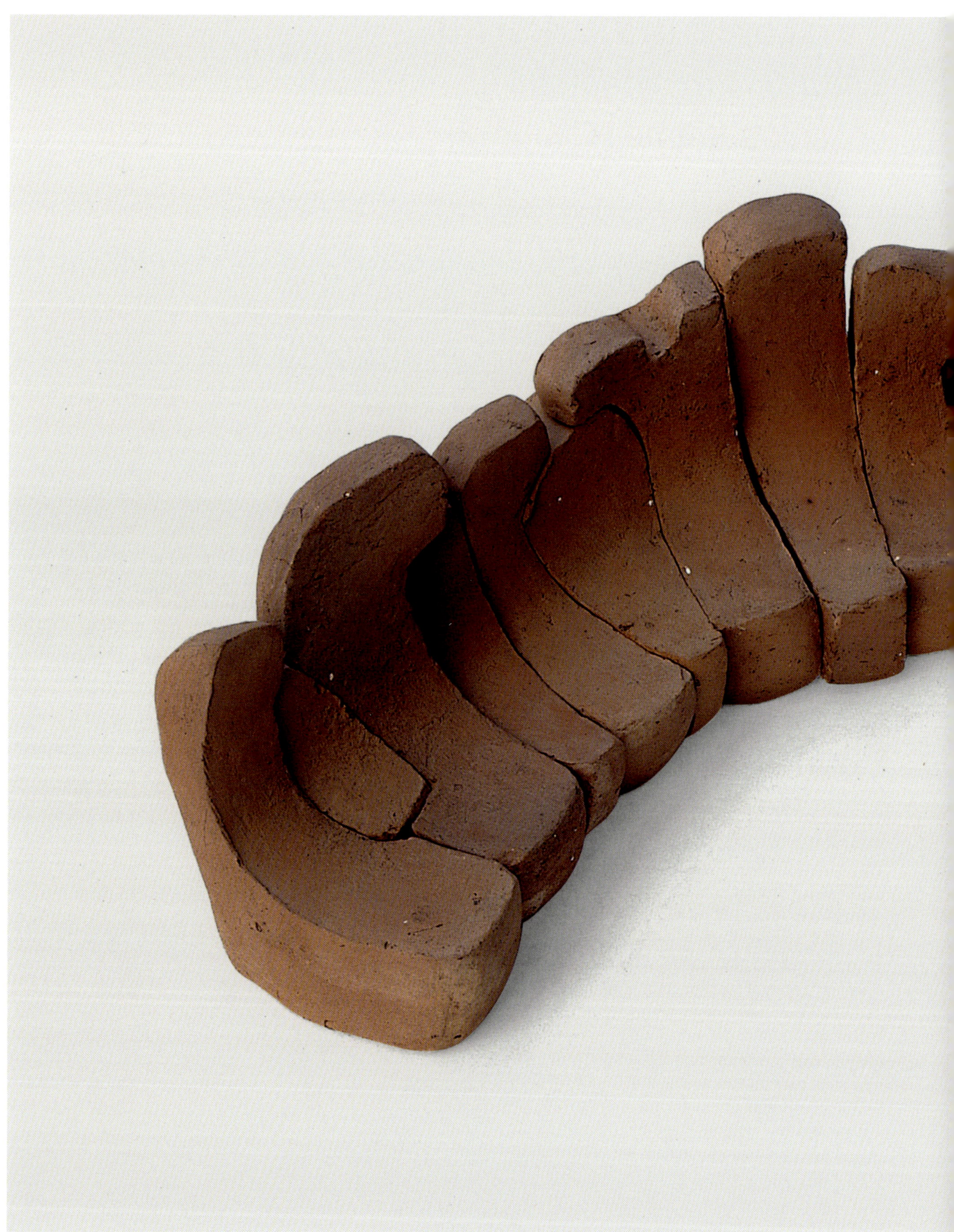

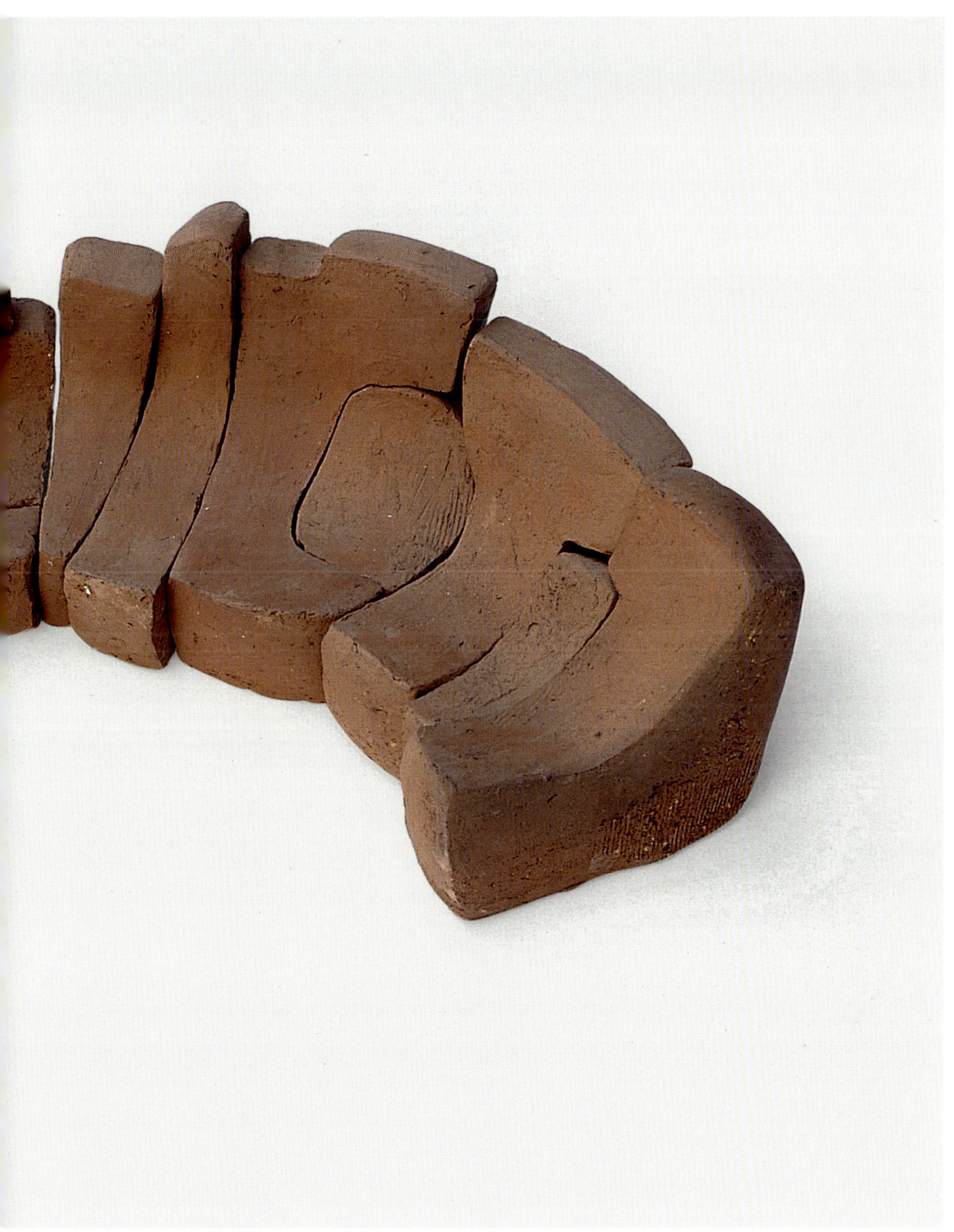

135
(previous pages)
Project for a Bench
1969–71
Terracotta
9 × 45 × 8

uniformed guard from a private security firm, one of many in Solidere's small army of enforcers, who habitually stashed his newspaper, his lunch, spare coffee cups and a change of clothes in the folds of the square's ficus tree. Choucair's sculpture back then was covered in black marker graffiti – mostly of the kind scrawled by love-struck teenagers, with a few more pointed political critiques of Syria following the demonstrations of 2005, when Lebanon's former prime minister, Rafik Hariri, also Solidere's founder, was killed in a massive car bomb blast just a few kilometres away, precipitating Syria's withdrawal from the country after thirty years of de facto occupation.

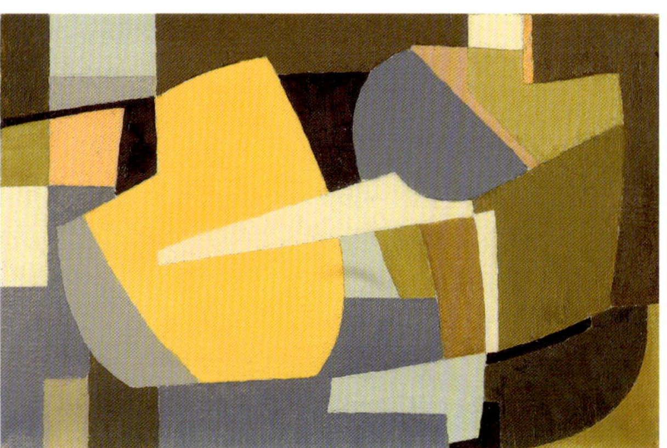

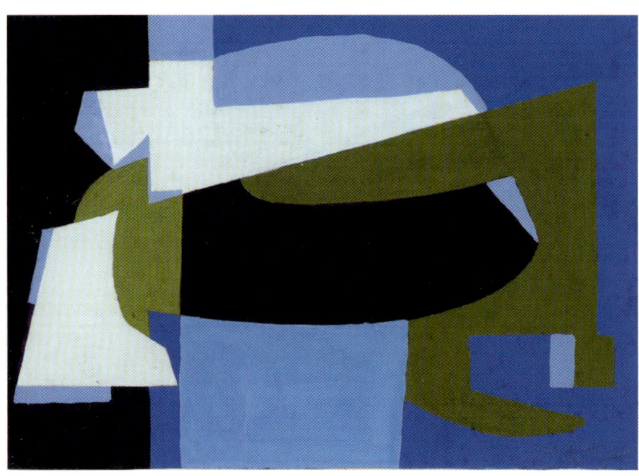

136
Narrow Rhythmical Composition 1953
Gouache on paper
26.5 × 40

137
Rhythmical Composition 1951
Gouache on paper
24.2 × 35

On a weekday afternoon in the summer of 2012, however, Choucair's work had been mostly scrubbed clean. The square showed signs of life. Two security guards, one with a bandaged forearm, kept lackadaisical watch as office workers zipped around the surrounding side streets on scooters. A father with his wife and child on the back of a single motorbike swerved around an erratically moving taxi. The father gesticulated angrily and called the driver an animal. In other words, the area had begun to look and sound more like the rest of Beirut, less like an abandoned theme park or a forgotten stage set.

A young couple came to share a coffee and a juice and what appeared to be a very serious conversation. After glancing around the square they perched themselves next to each other on the edge of Choucair's sculpture. It is, after all, an artwork doubling as a fully functional piece of street furniture – a semicircular bench made of seventeen stone pieces, all earthy curves and fine lines hinting at the mystery of how they slot together. Look quickly and the pieces resemble the members of a large family pressed into a compact space, or a puzzle that has been beautifully resolved, or a faint notion of union that has been suggested but not spelled out. The couple's chaste but no less public displays of affection, of intimacies turned inside out, were somehow perfectly suited to the mood of the piece, their actions as conceptually flawless as the physical configuration of the sculpture's parts is flawed.

Anyone reasonably familiar with Choucair's work – who has been to her studio and seen her shelves upon shelves of diminutive models and maquettes made of clay, wood, brass, fibreglass and stone, which span more than half a century – surely knows that her bench is meant to be arranged with those seventeen pieces flush together in the shape of a half moon. A tiny version of the piece in rough terracotta (fig.135) makes the point clearly enough, as does a slightly larger version rendered in smooth white stone. Solidere, which bought three of Choucair's sculptures in 1998, split the bench in two, thus breaking the curve and disrupting the play of lines that are formed by the pieces coming together. Initially this was done to make room for a walkway of stone slabs that ran through an expanse of grass and into the centre of the square, though most of those design elements have since been removed. The results of dividing the bench are dubious at best, and they speak to the limitations of entrusting an artwork to a private corporation in the absence of a public, civic-minded museum.

This matters first of all because this particular sculpture is important enough in the context of Choucair's view of her own oeuvre for a photograph of the full-sized piece to be wrapped round the front and back covers of her only published monograph to date, *Saloua Raouda Choucair: Her Life and Art*, edited by her daughter, Hala Schoukair. Second, and perhaps more importantly, it matters because this is the piece that comes closest to fulfilling Choucair's wishes and achieving her ambitions – and still it falls short.

Choucair, who is now in her nineties and no longer producing work, has played with the scale of her sculptures for decades. Even the gouaches and paintings she made in the 1940s, 1950s and 1960s can be read as anticipatory gestures, as studies for the kind of movements evoked by her three-dimensional pieces. More specifically, Choucair seems to have imagined, again and again, that her sculptures would be enlarged and made monumental, that a shift would occur from a model small enough to be placed in a viewer's hands to an object large enough to envelop that viewer's body. She seems not only to have imagined, but to have meticulously planned for that to happen in the pages and pages of notes she kept in her studio, listing materials, machines and craftsmen with whom she wanted to work and detailing tens, hundreds and thousands of mathematical equations and ratios for scaling up.

That shift from intimate to monumental, private to public, individual encounter to collective experience has been mostly mental throughout the history of Choucair's practice. The bench for downtown Beirut was one of the very few instances where it was tried. The fact that it was never quite right and remains so to this day exemplifies one of the more painful ways in which Beirut – the city that so obviously challenged, shaped and informed Choucair's work – has repeatedly let her down. But at the same time it illuminates the vastness and depth of her civic imagination – of her commitment to art's function in society and her belief in its place as part of the day-to-day lived experience of the city – in a country that has given her very few viable reasons to believe in such things.

Of course, it should be noted that when Choucair was born, in 1916, Lebanon was not a country at all, but an outlying territory of the Ottoman Empire. Beirut was a tiny city with a tortuous past, destroyed several times by earthquake and fire before it was shaped by the wars of the modern era. Little more than a provincial backwater until the nineteenth century, Beirut was utterly transformed when a consortium of imperial administrators and French financiers had the foresight to expand its port and extend its railways just as middle-class travel, mass-market trade and economic migration began to take off. Choucair grew up against the backdrop of tremendous change that followed, starting with the First World War, which saw that same port blockaded, the population diminished by plague and famine, and her father conscripted into the Ottoman army. He died of typhoid fever in Damascus within a year of Choucair's birth. Her mother struggled heroically to support the family and remain independent of her in-laws.

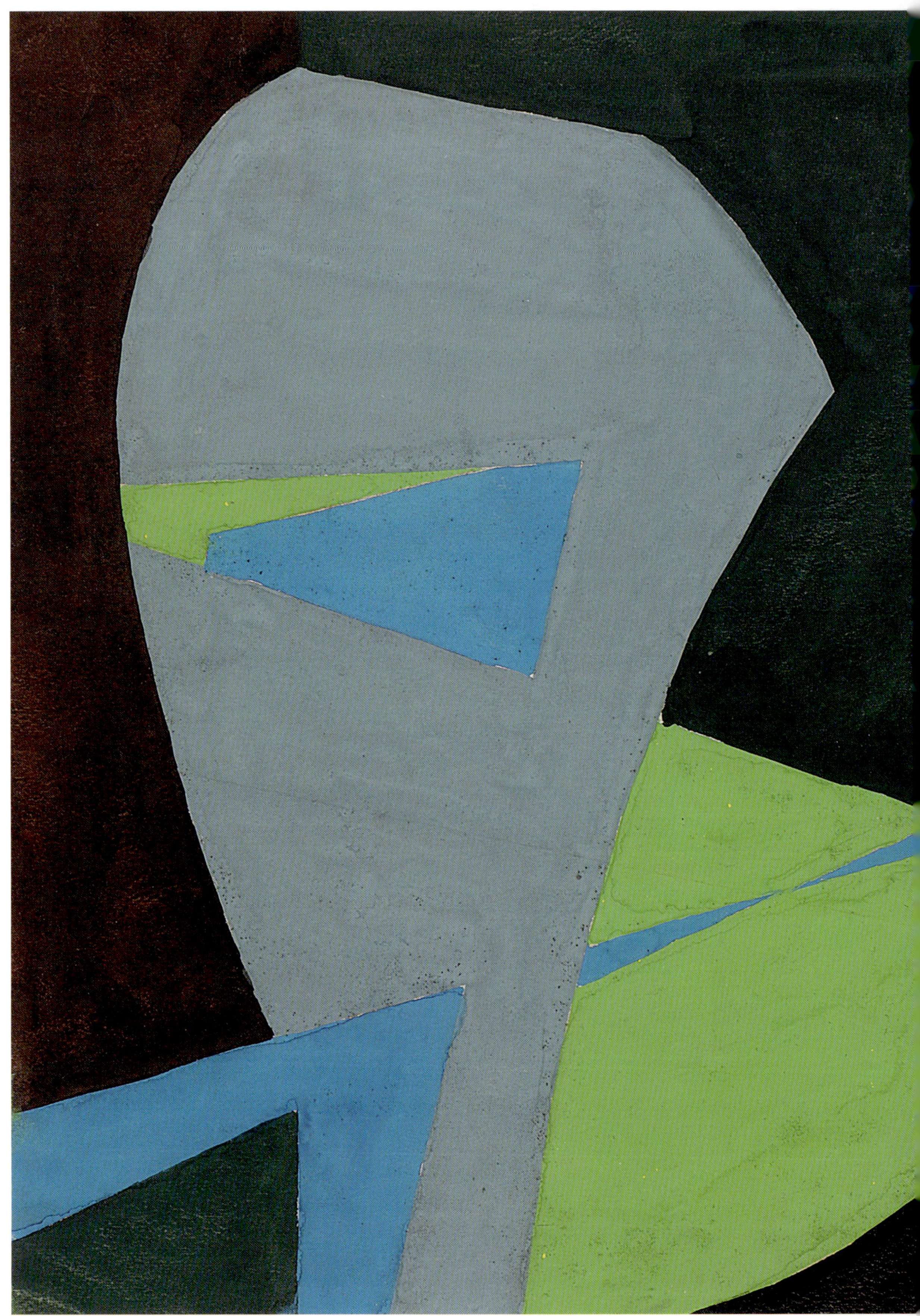

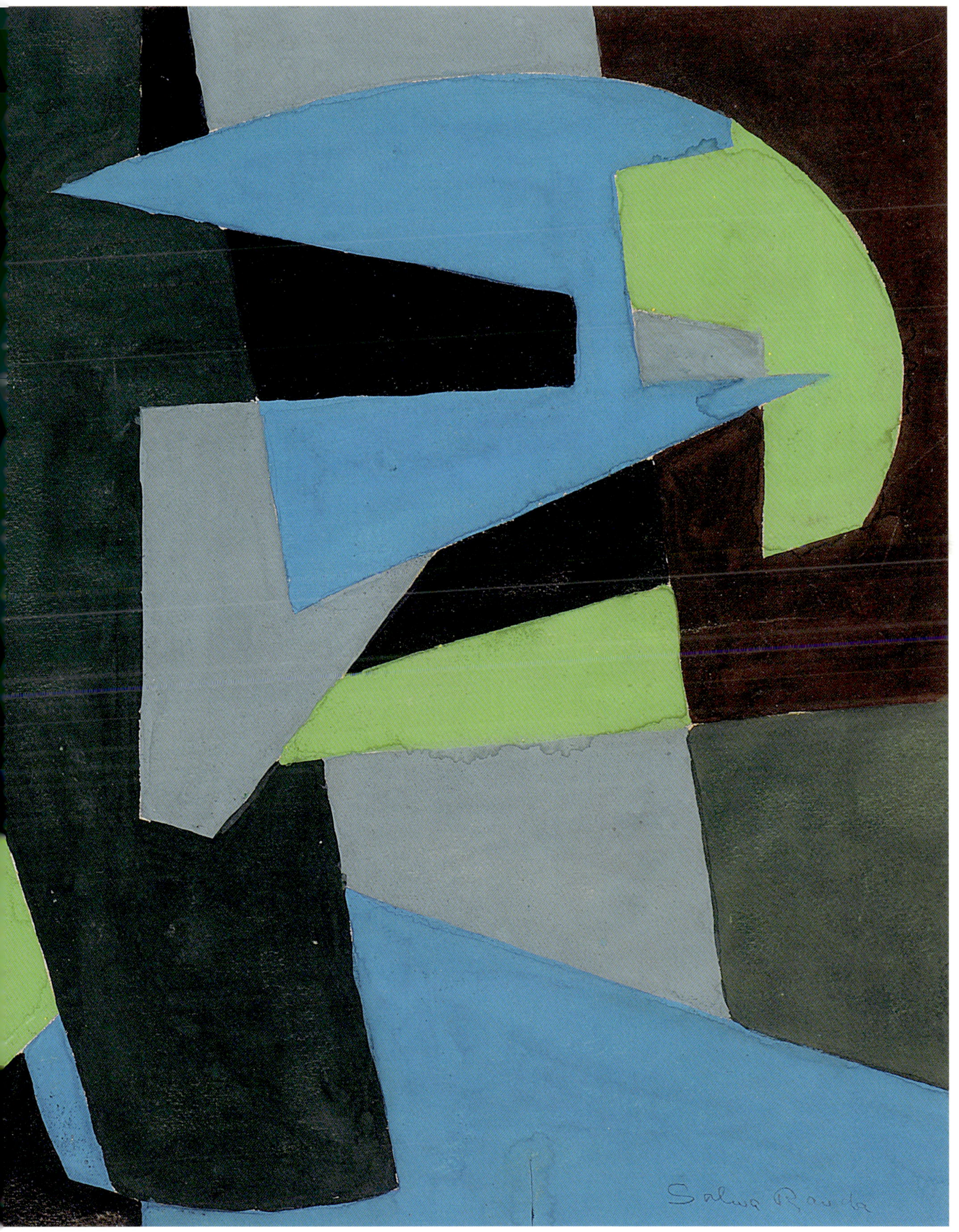

138
(previous pages)
Rhythmical Composition 1952
Gouache on paper
27.3 × 42

Choucair's education was far less tragic than her early family life. She was sent to a progressive new school for girls whose aim was to train the bold citizens of a new nation rather than the competent wives of a conservative culture. Choucair was a tomboy and an old-school Beiruti, who lived in the beachside neighbourhood of Ain al-Mreisseh and would run down to the shore with her sister, day or night, and hurl herself off of the rocks and into the sea for a swim. She learned to draw and was apprenticed to two of Lebanon's most renowned painters, Omar Onsi and Moustafa Farroukh. She then travelled to Paris where she attended the atelier of Fernand Léger. But she was a confident and rebellious student. The art historian and anthropologist Kirsten Scheid describes how she was expelled by a drawing teacher and sketched on the floor outside the classroom door. According to the critic and fellow painter Helen Khal, Choucair was deeply insulted by one of her professors at the American University of Beirut, who called Arab civilisation inferior to Greek; her angry riposte was to give him a long and precocious history lesson.

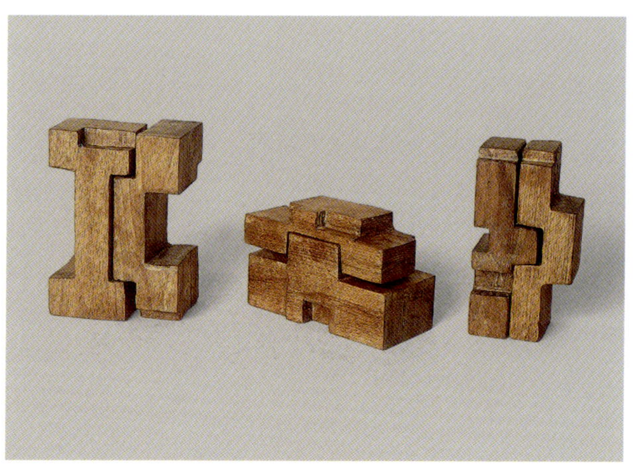

139
Poem 1966–8
Wood
29 × 17.5 × 6.5
(stacked)

As Choucair matured as an artist, Lebanon embarked on one of the few episodes in its modern history marked by the ambitions of a serious state-building programme. This was the era of President Fouad Chehab, a far-sighted reformer who instituted development projects and chipped away at social welfare problems. He later became so disgusted with the stubbornness of feudal politics and resistance to change that he refused to run for office again in 1970, even though he surely would have won the support of Lebanon's Parliament. Choucair, meanwhile, may have been derided by the Lebanese ambassador to France, who asked her, in effect, why she did not make nicer, more authentic artworks; she may also have been consistently misunderstood by the local press. But she was certainly of her time, of her history and of her constantly cross-referencing culture – influenced on one hand by the Egyptian architect Hassan Fathy and his concept of an architecture for the people, his housing for the poor and his earthbound, pared-down approach to modernism, and on the other by the risky, visionary urbanism of Le Corbusier, whose Unité d'habitation in Marseille she visited like a pilgrimage site, taking copious photographs and notes (figs.5–7).

What direction would Choucair's work have taken if Lebanon had not collapsed in the 1970s? In the mid-twentieth century Beirut enjoyed a brief but potent interlude as a cosmopolitan capital of glamour and intrigue, all of it heartily mythologised in the half-century since as the city's so-called 'golden age'. In many ways that was Choucair's time, the formative years of her practice. But Beirut is better remembered as the place that ran itself into the ground through fifteen years of chaotic, depraved, cynical and confusing civil war. In those years Choucair retreated to her studio. What else could she do? Yet even then she continued to imagine her sculptures on an urban scale, big enough to live in. Beirut has always been a testing-ground for notions of radical democracy, rapacious capitalism, political dissidence, resistance and modernity in the Arab world, but at the same time it continues to provide

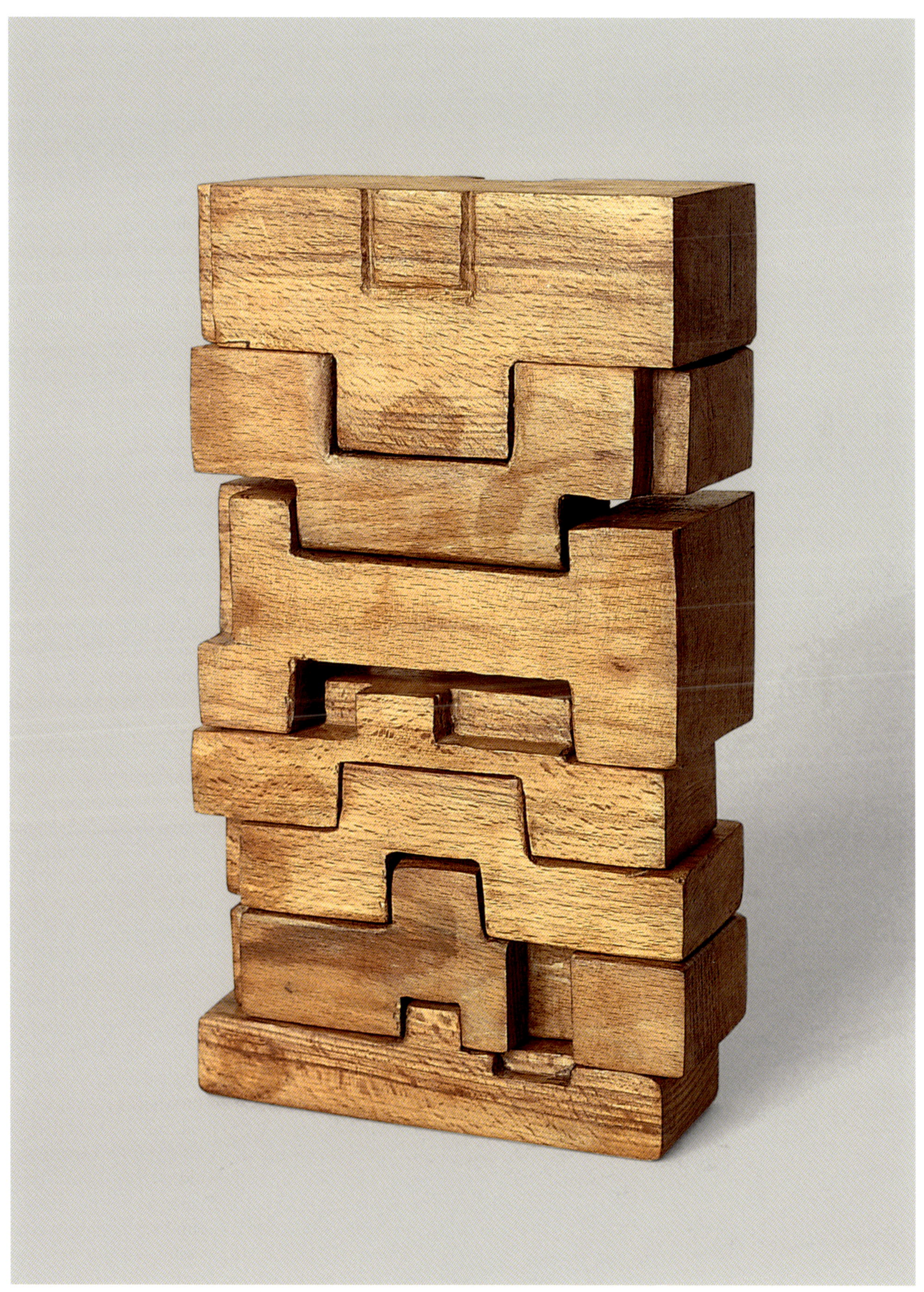

terribly apt examples of how spectacularly all of those things can fail in the absence of a coherent or accountable public, to say nothing of a credible citizenry. And yet despite or perhaps even because of that, Beirut since the 1990s has come to wield an influence wildly disproportionate to its size. This is largely because it has, against all efforts and expectations, gathered a critical mass of tough-minded, stylistically sophisticated, conceptually inclined artists who have over the past two decades actively reconfigured what experiments with documents, archives, memory, history, trauma, photography, video, and performance could mean, not only in Lebanon but also for the world at large. Now that the contemporary art scene has established itself in Lebanon and generates steady international interest, artists, curators and historians have begun peeling back the layers of art production to the modernist era, without nostalgia or sorrow. Here the most consequential discovery – for the arc of Lebanon's art history and for the story of international modernism and abstract art – is Choucair's oeuvre.

Choucair mainly stopped painting in the 1960s. Her mesmerising 'modules' – paintings and luminous gouaches made by a mathematical process of repeating, halving and quartering a shape in a given composition to create rhythm, depth and a sense of movement – gave way to the typologies of sculptures she called 'interforms', 'trajectories', 'odes', 'poems' and 'duals'. Running through the (still lamentably thin) body of knowledge that has accumulated around Choucair's oeuvre is the insistence that critical interpretations of her work must be one and the same with her artistic will. And according to everyone who knew her in the years when she was most active, her work contains no symbolic, representational or emotional content. But of course there are meanings and traces and evocations beyond the artist's own intentions. Moreover, for all her love of science and rational thought, her notes on the nature of consciousness and her palpable interest in the forms and rituals of Sufism (where, among other things, the intimacy of ecstasy is publically performed) suggest that there is room for more sentient and philosophical responses to her work. She once laughed when her sculptures were read as erotic, but she did not contradict the account.

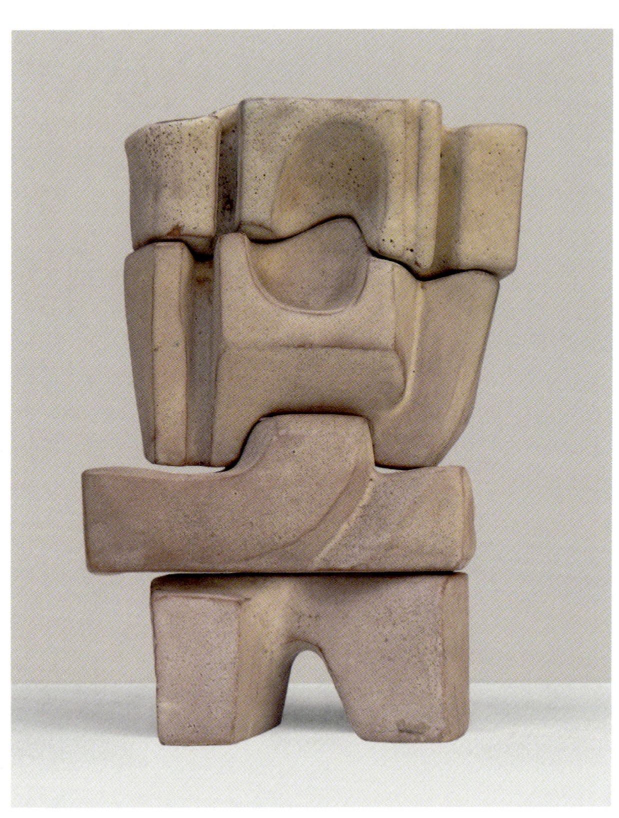

140
Poem 1963–5
Enamelled terracotta
16×10×7

It was a friend of Choucair's who first floated the theory that her 'duals' were about division in the context of Lebanon's civil war and Beirut being torn apart. Each piece consists of two halves that pull apart or fit together, leaving a thin space between them like a scar. Choucair's daughter, Hala, has likened them to embodiments of a Sufi principle seeking the end of all dualisms (such that the practitioner and the divine are one). And in many ways Choucair is close to the poet Adonis's conception of Arab modernity and Arab poetics. For one thing, Adonis dates Arab modernity to the eighth century, with the Sufi mystics who were the first to compose poetry as urbanites rather than nomads. For another, Adonis and Choucair share a commitment to the notion of giving form to thought. The scar that runs through each of Choucair's 'duals' is similar to the gap Adonis describes in *An Introduction to Arab Poetics* (1985):

> If Arab poetic modernity is partly based on the liberation of what has been suppressed – that is, on the expression of desire – and on everything that undermines the existing repressive norms and values, and transcends them, then ideological concepts like 'authenticity,' 'roots,' 'heritage,' 'renaissance' and 'identity' take on different meanings. Traditional notions of the continuous, the coherent, the one, the complete, are replaced by the interrupted, the confused, the plural, the incomplete, implying that the relationship between words and things is constantly changing: that is, there is always a gap between them which saying or writing the words cannot fill. This unbridgeable gap means that the questions 'What is knowledge?,' 'What is truth?,' 'What is poetry?' remain open, that knowledge is never complete and that truth is a continuing search.[1]

Beirut may one day learn to honour Choucair's work and legacy, when it discovers how to bring her bench back together so the gaps between those seventeen pieces make sense and are able to teach us a thing or two about ourselves. In the meantime, we can try, and we can continue to search.

Kaelen Wilson-Goldie

Notes

Kirsten Scheid
Distinctions That Could be Drawn, pp.41–55

1. Unfortunately it has not been possible to track the timing of this professionalisation. Journalists Karam Milhim Karam, Yusif Ghussub, Fu'ad Sulaiman and Khalil Taqi al-Din critiqued their society in many ways, art exhibitions being one facet of their intellectualisation of their engagement in society. Some of those who began writing in the 1940s, for example Thuraya Malhas, Rose Ghurayib and Victor Hakim, studied aesthetics or literature formally and wrote articles without appearing to have any contracted employment. The hiring of professional art writers by local newspapers seems to have begun in the 1960s, long after the papers had allocated sections to reporting on *thaqafiyya* (cultural) events and ideas. Today many of Beirut's newspapers and magazines either give the job of art writing to an artist, such as Gaby Ma'mari who wrote for *Al-Diyar* in the 1990s, or they may assign it to a reporter who works on another beat, such as Ahmad Bazzun who has written for *Al-Safir* since the mid-1990s. Some prominent papers have long-term contracts with people who have undergone training accrediting their opinions, such as Nazih Khatir, who studied at the Louvre in the 1950s and has for decades written for *Al-Nahar* (interview 21 June 2000), or Maha Sultan, who studied art history in France and wrote a masters thesis on Habib Srur at the Université de la Sainte Esprit, and has been writing for *Al-Hayat* since the 1980s (interview 17 November 1996).
2. Becker 1982, p.112.
3. Lederman 1989, p.230.
4. Ibid.
5. See Nochlin 1988, p.42.
6. Fawaz 1983; Gates 1998.
7. *Outlook*, vol.4, no.10, 26 May 1951, p.4.
8. Beaulieu 1962.
9. S.H. 1952.
10. Andraus 1962.
11. 'Akrawi 1962.
12. Ghurayib 1962.
13. Malhas 1962.
14. Muysati 1952.
15. *Al-Adib* 1952.
16. Koenig 1995, p.3.
17. Guilbaut 1995.
18. Ibid., p.33.
19. From the early 1940s, growing numbers of practising and aspiring artists headed for New York, where artistic production was eagerly promoted, in a bid to claim American cultural superiority – and with it economic and political superiority. According to Serge Guilbaut, 'It had to be seen that America was in fact defending the same complex and cherished civilizations as the Europeans' (Guilbaut 1995, p.33). Even Paris was infected by the lure of New York. Though on the US home front abstract expressionism, exemplified by Jackson Pollock, was scorned and feared as subversive – indeed, potentially pro-Communist – painters associated with the style were promoted abroad by the US government, and specifically by the CIA, as an expression of American individualism and liberty (Monahan 1995; Cockcroft 1974). While the CIA connection was not publicly known, many Paris-based artists were antagonised by the apparently anti-ideological stance of abstract expressionism. Abstract and representational styles were 'in violent conflict', according to a contemporary commentator, and were conflicted within themselves (Descargues 1950, p.170). In their quest to be the most forward-looking heirs of Picasso and Matisse, French artists faced several choices: perpetuating figurative art (the wider French public was generally unwilling to accept anything more modern than post-Impressionism and surrealism); embracing social realism (the official style of the French Communist Party after 1947); or formulating an engaged abstraction that rivalled Pollock aesthetically but embraced specific visions for modern society. These choices were debated throughout the late 1940s and early 1950s in publications such as, *Combat*, *Arts de France*, *Art d'aujourd'hui* and *XXe Siècle*, the latter two of which frequently featured American abstract artists. Across the Atlantic the *Magazine of Art* commissioned critiques of the various French trends for its April 1950 issue.
20. See Shaybub 1951.
21. Najla Tannus 'Akrawi, interview 11 November 2004.
22. Koenig 1995, p.5.
23. Ibid.
24. During the autumn of 1949 Léger's painting was included in a highly celebrated solo exhibition at the Musée d'Art Moderne in Paris (*Art d'aujourd'hui*, vol.1, no.4, back cover).
25. In the preparatory sketch at the Minnesota Institute of Art it is a damascene-worked table with two-tone decoration and arabesque curves; in the final canvas this has been simplified into squares and trimmed with three small white circles, perhaps suggesting mother-of-pearl inlay.
26. Shone 1997. The furniture is a divan with sumptuous pillows of damascene red and gold design tossed across it; the floor covering consists of harlequin patterning and bold stripes in a contrasting colour; and the wall behind is a jumble of rectangular patterning.
27. Allsen 2004.
28. Baxandall 1972; Panofsky 1991, pp.63–6.
29. The only feature jarring that space is a long, thin, tubular shape, perhaps a reference to Léger's idiosyncratic 'tubism'.
30. Clark 1956, p.106. Interestingly, when in November 2004 I showed copies of the pictures to Choucair, who was by then suffering from Alzheimer's, her immediate response was to see them as a version of the Three Graces, except for the numerical difference.
31. I am inspired in my interpretation of this by Linda Nochlin's (1999) discussion of George Seurat's *Poseuses* 1887–8 (Art Institute of Chicago).
32. The artists who worked at L'Atelier d'art abstrait were primarily from a group that had been showing together since 1946 at Denise René's Paris gallery (Koenig 1995, p.8).
33. *Art d'aujourd'hui*, vol.2, no.1, back cover.
34. Koenig 1995, p.8.
35. *Art d'Aujourd'hui*, vol.2, no.1, back cover.
36. These debates were on such topics as 'What is Painting?', 'What is

Figurative Painting?', 'What is Abstract Painting?', 'Science and Beauty', 'Mondrian and Neo-plasticism', 'Constructivism', 'Paradoxes of Decorative Art', 'Colour', 'Kandinsky's Theoretical Writings' and 'The Technology of Painting' (*Art d'aujourd'hui*, vol.2, no.3, p.30; vol.2, no.5, p.31; vol.2, no.7, p.30; vol. 2, no.8, p.30).

37. Jack al-Aswad notes that Pillet called the pattern he turned and traced 'patrons', but he asserts that the technique of composing the picture was essentially the same (Aswad 2002).

38. For Magnelli see the retrospective essay by Léon Degand in *XXe Siècle*, vol.1, no.1, pp.39–42. For Deyrolle and Dewasne, see *Art d'aujourd'hui*, vol.1, no.3, p.29 and *XXe Siècle*, vol.1, no.1, p.58. See also Charles Estienne's long essay on Deyrolle in *Art d'aujourd'hui*, vol.2, no.5, pp.18–21. For Pillet, see Léon Degand's review and accompanying illustration in *Art d'aujourd'hui*, vol.2, no.2, p.31. For Mortensen, see Degand's review of his show at Galerie Denise René, in *Art d'aujourd'hui*, vol.2, no.1, p.30. For Vasarely, see the painting reproduced for the critique of the Salon de Mai in *Art d'aujourd'hui*, vol.2, no.6, p.28, and *XXe Siècle*, vol.1, no.1, p.58.

39. Seuphor 1950, cited in Aswad 2002.

40. The artist who came closest to Choucair's approach is perhaps Edgar Pillet, although his work confined itself to the basic geometric trio of circle, square and triangle and he did not allow his forms to 'wander'. Choucair's other great experimental collaborator was Alberto Magnelli, who generated compositions from the accumulation of a few repeated shapes, with complex layers of overlapping indicated by tonal shifts. Yet his work was also distinctly different from Choucair's: whereas her stencilled shapes strictly echo each other, Magnelli's become compressed, stretched or otherwise distorted by unseen external forces. In other words, Magnelli's compositions suggest forces other than repetition, whereas Choucair's explore the variety that can result from endless but strict reiteration. A review of the impact of mathematical studies on art can be found in Mankiewicz 2000.

41. Guilbaut 1995

42. Degand 1951, p.32.

43. Malhas 1962.

44. Degand 1951, p.32.

45. Serge Guilbaut (1995, p.63) wrote of this period: 'What is complicated and fascinating in this duel is that, at this exact same time, some French artists and critics in Paris were also trying to define a new type of art in opposition to the traditional school of Paris and were using some of the same arguments as the American critics.'

46. This statement appears in the inaugural issue of *Art d'Aujourd'hui* (vol.1, no.1, p.3). Other 'Eastern' artists whose sojourn in Paris was celebrated by the magazine were Najed, Fahr-el-Nissa Zeid, Olive Tamari, Schalhoub and Jamil Hamoudi.

47. Al-Ghurayib attended a French Catholic elementary school and then the Sidon American High School (the American Junior College in Beirut), where she studied Sufism, and the American University of Beirut, where she specialised in Arabic literature (Rose al-Ghurayib, interview 2 October 2000). Regrettably, I do not have similar background information for Fu'ad Muysati or 'S.H.'.

48. The story varies: sometimes it refers to *'amal* (works) and at others to *'alam* (flags) or *al-'alam al-lubnani* (the Lebanese flag). See Zughaib 1979, and Faisal Sultan, 'Salwa Rawda Shuqair ... lahma wa hiwar wa shahadat' ('Saloua Raouda Choucair ... an overview, a dialogue, and testimonies'), Al-Safir, vol.7, no.2289 (1980) p.11. Archived material, Saloua Raouda Choucair Archives Beirut.

49. Najla Tannus 'Akrawi, interview 11 November 2004.

50. Sulh 1994.

51. Nadim Dimashqiyya, interview 11 November 2004

Ann Coxon
The Potentiality of the Thing, pp.119–33

1. Zughaib 1979.

2. As proclaimed by Helen Khal (Khal 1987, pp.57–8).

3. Quoted in Aswad 2002.

4. Quoted by Helen Khal, 'Embodying the Spirit', in Choucair 2002.

5. Ibid.

6. Quoted in Khal 1987.

7. Samir Sayigh, 'Saloua Raouda Choucair: Distinctiveness of Style and Individuality of Vision', *Al-Kifah Al-'Arabi*, 25–31 July 1983, pp.70–1. Archived material from the Saloua Raouda Choucair Archives, Beirut, Lebanon.

8. Helen Khal, 'Embodying the Spirit', in Choucair 2002.

9. Aswad 2002.

10. Schoukair 2001.

Wilson-Goldie
Two Lovers in a Park at Midday, pp.151–61

1. Adonis 1990, p.101.

Bibliography

Adonis, *An Introduction to Arab Poetics*, trans. Catherine Cobham, London 1990.

ʿAkrawi 1962
Najla Tannus ʿAkrawi, 'Salwa Rawda Holds Exhibition', *Alumnae Bulletin*, vol.9, no.2, 1962 (Saloua Raouda Choucair Archives, Beirut).

***Al-Adib* 1952**
'Barqiat' (Telegraphs), *Al-Adib*, vol.11, no.4, p.70.

Allsen 2004
J.M. Allsen, 'World of the Arts', electronic document, http://facstaff.uwww.edu/allsenjm/WOTA/IMAGES/leger.htm, accessed 10 October 2004.

Andraus 1962
Farid Andraus, 'Salwa Rawda: une imagination sans limites', *Magazine*, 8 March 1962, p.61 (Saloua Raouda Choucair Archives, Beirut).

Aswad 2002
Jack Aswad, 'Muʿadalat hassiyya [Sensory Equations]', in Choucair 2002, pp.17–35, trans. K. Scheid.

Baxandall 1972
Michael Baxandall, *Painting and Experience in Fifteenth-Century Italy*, Oxford 1972.

Beaulieu 1962
Simone Aubrey Beaulieu, 'Les Quatres royaumes de Saloua Raouda', *L'Orient*, 24 February 1962 (Saloua Raouda Choucair Archives, Beirut).

Becker 1982
Howard Becker, *Art Worlds*, Berkeley 1982.

Berggren 1985
J.L. Berggren, 'History of Mathematics in the Islamic World: The Present State of the Art', *Middle Eastern Studies Association*, vol.19, no.1, pp.9–29.

Choucair 2002
Saloua Raouda Choucair: Her Life and Art, Beirut 2002. Translation by K. Scheid available at http://www.srchoucair.com.

Clark 1956
Kenneth Clark, *The Nude: A Study in Ideal Form*, Princeton 1956.

Cockcroft 1974
Eva Cockcroft, 'Abstract Expressionism: Weapon of the Cold War', *Artforum*, vol.12, no.2, pp.39–41.

Degand 1951
Léon Degand, 'L'Épouvantail de l'académisme abstrait' ('The Bogeyman of Abstract Art'), *Art d'Aujourd'hui* vol.2 no.4 pp.32–3.

Descargues 1950
Pierre Descargues, 'Painting in Paris', *Magazine of Art*, vol.43, no.4, pp.169–81.

Fawaz 1983
Leila Fawaz, *Merchants and Migrants in Nineteenth-century Beirut*, Cambridge, MA, 1983.

Garb 1999
Tamar Garb, '"Men of Genius, Women of Taste": The Gendering of Art Education in Late Nineteenth-Century Paris', in *Overcoming All Odds: The Women of the Académie Julian*, New York 1999, pp.115–33.

Gates 1998
Carolyn L. Gates, *The Merchant Republic of Lebanon: Rise of an Open Economy*, London 1998.

Ghurayib 1962
Thérèse Ghurayib, 'Sajjad, lawhat, siramik, wa nahat', *Al-Nahar*, 4 March 1962 (Saloua Raouda Choucair Archives, Beirut).

Guilbaut 1995
Serge Guilbaut (ed.), 'Postwar Painting Games: The Rough and the Slick', in *Reconstructing Modernism: Art in New York, Paris, and Montreal 1945–1964*, Cambridge, MA, 1995, pp.30–79.

Khal 1987
Helen Khal, *The Woman Artist in Lebanon*, Institute for Women's Studies in the Arab World, Beirut 1987.

Koenig 1995
John-Franklin Koenig, 'Abstraction chaude in Paris in the 1950s', in *Reconstructing Modernism: Art in New York, Paris, and Montreal 1945–1964*, ed. Serge Guilbaut, Cambridge, MA, 1995 [1992], pp.1–16.

Lederman 1989
Rena Lederman, 'Contested Order: Gender and Society in the Southern New Guinea Highlands', *American Ethnologist*, vol.16, no.2, pp.230–47.

Malhas 1962
Thuraya Malhas, 'Salwa Rawda tidf'a rishataha fi rukab al-ʿalamiyya', *Baryut*, vol.16, no.4315, p.3.

Mankiewicz 2000
Richard Mankiewicz, *The Story of Mathematics*, London 2000.

Monahan 1995
Laura Monahan, 'Cultural Cartography: American Designs at the 1964 Venice Biennale', in *Reconstructing Modernism: Art in New York, Paris, and Montreal 1945–1964*, ed. Serge Guilbaut, Cambridge, MA, 1995, pp.369–416.

Muysati 1952
Fuʾad Muysati, 'Fann al-tajrid wa fann-al-taʿbir fi al-rasim', *Al-Hayat*, vol.7, no.1789, p.4.

Nochlin 1988
Linda Nochlin, 'Why Have There Been No Great Women Artists?', in *Women, Art, and Power, and Other Essays*, New York 1988 [1971], pp.145–78.

Nochlin 1999
Linda Nochlin, 'Body Politics: Seurat's *Poseuses*', in *Representing Women*, London 1988 [1971], pp.216–37.

Panofsky 1991
Erwin Panofsky, *Perspective as Symbolic Form*, trans. Christopher Wood, New York 1991

Salomon 1996
Nannette Salomon, 'The Venus Pudica: Uncovering Art History's "Hidden Agendas" and Pernicious Pedigrees', in *Generations and Geographies in the Visual Arts: Feminist Readings*, ed. Griselda Pollock, London 1996, pp.69–87.

Schoukair 2001
Hala Schoukair, *A Project in the Making*, exh. leaflet (Beirut Exhibition Center), Beirut 2001.

Seuphor 1950
Michel Seuphor, 'Painting in Paris', *Magazine of Art*, vol.4, no.43, p.180.

S.H. 1952
'Maʿrad li al-rasim al-tajridi fi Bayrut', *Al-Nahar*, vol.19, no.5022, p.4.

Shaybub 1951
Edvick Shaybub, 'Maʿa al-fannana Salwa Rawda', *Sawt al-mar'a*, vol.7, no.12, p.36.

Shone 1997
Richard Shone, 'Fernand Léger', *Artforum*, vol.36, no.3, pp.105–6.

Sulh 1994
Munah Sulh, 'Shihada li ustath Munah al-Sulh', in *Masira al-khamsin ʿam: al-Nadi al-Thaqafi al-ʿArabi, 1944–1994*, Beirut 1994, pp.25–8.

Zughaib 1979
Henri Zughaib, 'Salwa Rawda Shuqair tahtaraf fann al-nahat bi fil ʿibara sadamatha min Charles Malik', *Al-Hawadith*, 16 March 1979, pp.70–1. (Saloua Raouda Choucair Archives, Beirut).

Exhibited Works

Except where specified otherwise, works have been lent by the Saloua Raouda Choucair Foundation, Beirut.

Measurements are given in centimetres, height before width and depth.

For works that are illustrated, figure numbers are given at the end of entries.

Self-Portrait 1943
Oil paint on canvas
45.5 × 42
1

Experiment with Calligraphy 1947–50
Gouache on paper
48 × 31
15

Experiment with Calligraphy 1947–50
Gouache on paper
48 × 31
16

Fractional Module 1947–51
Oil paint on canvas
49 × 59.5
14

Fractional Module 1947–51
Oil paint on canvas
50 × 59
13

Fractional Module (Sphinx) 1947–51
Gouache on paper
16 × 140
21

Two=one 1947–51
Oil paint on canvas
62 × 82
3

Composition in Blue Module 1947–51
Oil paint on canvas
59.5 × 80
Tate. Purchased with funds provided by the Middle East North Africa Acquisitions Committee 2011
17

Paris-Beirut 1948
Gouache on paper
32 × 23.5
12

Les Trois Graces 1948
Gouache on paper
35.5 × 25
44

Nude with a Tree 1948–9
Gouache on paper
36 × 25
43

Untitled 1948–9
Gouache on paper
36 × 25
47

Les Peintres Célèbres 1 1948–9
Gouache on paper
25 × 36
51

Nude with Iris 1948–9
Gouache on paper
36 × 25
48

Subhan 1950
Gouache on paper
32 × 25
11

Visual Meter 1950s
Gouache on paper
25 × 50
20

Visual Meter 1950s
Gouache on paper
20 × 29
19

Visual Meter 1950s
Gouache on paper
20.5 × 29.5
22

Rhythmical Composition with Red 1951
Oil paint on canvas
24 × 31
18

Composition 1951
Oil paint on canvas
90 × 60

Rhythmical Composition 1952–3
23 × 30
28

Rhythmical Composition with Yellow 1952–5
Oil paint on canvas
100 × 124
19

Composition in Brown 1952–5
Gouache on paper
23 × 31
25

Composition, Two Ovals 1952–5
Gouache on paper
19 × 29.5
35

Rhythmical Composition 1952–5
Gouache on paper
17 × 25
26

Composition with Verticals 1952–5
Gouache on paper
10 × 13.8
24

Composition with a Circle 1956–8
Gouache on paper
25 × 32
27

Rhythmical Composition with Blue 1956–8
Gouache on paper
33 × 24
31

Composition for Tapestry 1956–8
Gouache on paper
11.5 × 30.5

Composition for Tapestry 1956–8
Gouache on paper
20.5 × 49
29

Untitled 1956–8
Oil paint on canvas
30 × 43

Composition for Tapestry 1956–8
Gouache on paper
12 × 30.5
30

Trajectory of a Line, Tripod 1957–9
Fibreglass
41 × 21 × 17
55

Vessel 1957–9
Terracotta
13 × 21 × 4

Trajectory of a Line 1957–9
Stone
82 × 35 × 21
113

Trajectory of a Line 1957–9
Wood
74 × 34 × 25
110

Trajectory of a Line 1957–9
Brass
19 × 7 × 7
56

Trajectory of a Line, The Cave 1957–9
Fibreglass
37 × 24 × 22
54

Fractional Module 1959–60
Oil paint on wood
60 × 45
33

Gradual Rhythmical Composition 1959–60
Gouache on paper
23 × 48

Gradual Rhythmical Composition 1959–60
Gouache on paper
22 × 50
23

Secret of a Cube 1960–2
Wood
28 × 19 × 19
58

Interform 1960–2
Wood
110 × 28 × 28
111

Interform 1960–2
Wood
49 × 12 × 12
57

Composition with Arcs 1962–5
Gouache on paper
32 × 47
37

Composition in Yellow 1962–5
Oil paint on canvas
50 × 79.5
32

Composition with Arcs 1962–5
Gouache on paper
25 × 48
36

Composition with Arcs 1962–5
Gouache on paper
24 × 32.5
40

Composition with Arcs 1962–5
Gouache on paper
24 × 33
38

Composition with Arcs 1962–5
Gouache on paper
24 × 33
39

Poem Cube 1963–5
White wood
16 × 16 × 16
63

Poem 1963–5
Stone
73 × 33 × 12
65

Poem of Three Verses 1963–5
Wood
53 × 33 × 20
133

Poem 1963–5
Wood
38 × 18.5 × 5
115

Poem 1963–5
Wood
25 × 17 × 5
59

Poem Wall 1963–5
White wood
29 × 35 × 4
60

Poem of Five Verses 1963–5
White wood
29 × 13.5 × 10.3
61

Poem Wall 1963–5
Wood
70 × 160 × 20
Tate. Presented anonymously 2011
62

Infinite Structure 1963–5
Tufa stone
240 × 48 × 30
Tate. Purchased with funds provided by the Middle East North Africa Acquisitions Committee 2011
8

Poem 1963–5
Wood
33 × 17 × 7.5
Tate. Presented anonymously 2011
64

Ode 1966–8
Terracotta
12 × 6 × 6
131

Sculpture with One Thousand Pieces 1966–8
Wood
147 × 36 × 36
112

Poem of Nine Verses 1966–8
Aluminium
27 × 21 × 7
Tate. Purchased with funds provided by the Middle East North Africa Acquisitions Committee 2012
127

Water Lens 1969–71
Plexiglass, stainless steel and water
87 × 53 × 30
68

Project for a Bench 1969–71
Terracotta
9 × 45 × 8
135

Untitled (Inter-cube) 1970–2
Plexiglass and nylon
176 × 44 × 44
73

Trajectory of One Line 1972–4
Plexiglass and nylon
150 × 50 × 50
72

Intercircles 1972–4
Stainless steel and nylon
55 × 32 × 10
69

Trajectory of the Arc 1972–4
Plexiglass and nylon
78 × 20 × 20
71

Static Dynamism 1972–4
Stainless steel
124 × 46
118

Trajectory of the Arc 1972–4
9 × 13 × 9
75

Trajectory of the Arc 1972–4
9 × 25 × 9
81

Trajectory of the Arc 1972–4
Brass
4 × 13 × 5
80

Water Project 1972–4
Terracotta
19 × 15 × 12
85

Water Project 1972–4
Brass
Four pieces
20 × 7 × 7 overall
76

Poem 1972–4
Clay
14 × 6.5 × 6.5
84

Water Project 1972–4
Terracotta
22 × 8 × 8

Water Project 1972–4
Terracotta
19 × 9 × 5
79

Poem Cylinder 1972–4
Aluminium
18 × 5.5
83

Poem 1972–4
Brass
13.5 × 4.5 × 5
74

Poem 1972–4
Aluminium
18 × 5 × 6
82

Poem Box 1972–4
Enamelled terracotta
19.5 × 5.5 × 5.5
77

Project for Public Housing 1973
Terracotta
14 × 19 × 3
89

Water Project 1973
Clay and plastic
13 × 9 × 9
90

Water Project 1973
Terracotta and metal
13 × 9

Water project 1973
Clay and metal
18 × 13 × 13
86

Water Project 1973
Clay and plastic
18 × 10 × 10
88

Water Project 1973
Clay and plastic
8 × 12 × 5
87

Water Project 1973
Clay
Eight pieces
36 × 7 × 7 overall
91

Dual 1975–7
Fibreglass
33 × 32 × 26.5
98

Dual 1975–7
Wood
36 × 23 × 23
96

Dual 1975–7
Wood
Two pieces
22 × 19 × 12 each
106

Dual 1975–7
Enamelled terracotta
13 × 13 × 13
97

Ring 1975–7
Silver
Two pieces
3.5 × 1.5 × 1.5
3.5 × 2.5 × 1.5
95

Dual 1975–7
Enamelled terracotta
11 × 8 × 6

The Screw 1975–7
Enamelled terracotta
9 × 9 × 9
119

The Screw 1975–7
Fibreglass
16 × 6 × 9
93

Dual, Salt and Pepper 1975–7
Terracotta
Two pieces
8 × 6 × 5 each
94

The Screw 1975–7
Wood
31 × 31 × 27
Tate. Presented by the Saloua Raouda Choucair Foundation Beirut Lebanon 2011
92

Dual 1978–80
Brass and aluminium
6 × 6 × 7
101

Dual 1978–80
Brass and aluminium
7 × 3 × 8
104

Dual 1978–80
Brass and aluminium
4 × 4 × 8
103

Dual 1978–80
Brass and aluminium
12 × 9 × 6

Dual 1978–80
Brass and aluminium
15 × 6
99

Dual 1978–80
Aluminium
8 × 9 × 6
100

Salt and Pepper 1980
Terracotta
Two pieces
8 × 8 × 3 each

Flat Vase 1980–2
Terracotta
13.5 × 8 × 3
122

Flat Vase 1980–2
Enamelled terracotta
11 × 9 × 3
120 (left)

Flat Vase 1980–2
Enamelled terracotta
8 × 10 × 1
120 (right)

Module 1980–3
Wood
10 × 20 × 11 each
125

Module 1980–3
Wood
28 × 40 × 19
124

Module 1980–3
Wood
75 × 46 × 25
123

Module 1980–3
Enamelled terracotta
13 × 11 × 6
121

DNA Section 1980s
Wood
80 × 14 × 14
108

Dual 1980s
Wood
16 × 20 × 30
105

Dual 1980s
Wood
39 × 17.5 × 16
109

Dual 1983–5
Brass
9.5 × 4.5 × 5.5
102

Infinite Structure 1983–5
Terracotta
Three pieces
3 × 6 × 4 each
126

Ode 1983–5
Terracotta
15 × 12 × 8
132

From *The Rhyme Series*
1994–6
Terracotta
23 × 7 × 4
129

From *The Rhyme Series*
1994–6
Terracotta
30 × 9 × 5
128

From *The Rhyme Series*
1994–6
Terracotta
22 × 8 × 4
130

Les Peintres Célèbres
1948–9
Gouache on paper
25 × 36
50

Nude with Roses 1948–9
Gouache on paper
25 × 36
46

Les Peintres Célèbres 2
1948–9
Gouache on paper
35 × 24
52

Composition with Two Ovals 1951
Oil paint on canvas
50 × 185

Untitled 1948–9
Gouache on paper
32 × 22.5

Untitled 1948–9
Gouache on paper
37 × 26
45

Plan for a Pool 1959–60
Gouache on paper
12 × 34

Chores 1948–9
Gouache on paper
25 × 35.5
49

Lenders and Credits

Lenders

All works in the exhibition have been lent by the artist, apart from those from the Tate Collection.

Photo Credits

All images courtesy Saleh Barakat and the Saloua Raouda Choucair Foundation

© Agop Kanledjian figs.3, 15, 16, 18, 19, 20, 21, 22, 23, 24, 25, 27, 28, 29, 30, 31, 38, 39, 40, 43, 45, 46, 49, 51, 56, 59, 61, 63, 64, 65, 72, 75–9, 80, 82, 84, 86, 87, 88, 89, 90, 91, 92, 93, 94, 95, 97, 100, 101, 103, 104, 106, 107, 119, 120, 121, 122, 125, v6, 129, 128, 130, 131, 132

© Solidere fig.134

© Tate Photography figs.8, 36, 62, 64, 66, 92, 127

Copyright

Index

Supporting Tate

Tate relies on a large number of supporters – individuals, foundations, companies and public funders – to enable it to deliver its programme of activities, both on and off its gallery sites. This support is essential in order for Tate to acquire works of art for the Collection, run education, outreach and exhibition programmes, care for the Collection in storage and enable art to be displayed, both digitally and physically, inside and outside Tate. Donations, no matter the size, are gratefully received, either to support particular areas of interest, or to contribute to general activity costs.

Development Office
Tate
Millbank
London SWIP 4RG
Tel: 020 7887 4900
Fax: 020 7887 8098

American Patrons of Tate
520 West 27 Street Unit 404 New York, NY 10001 USA

Tel: 001 212 643 2818
Fax: 001 212 643 1001

Donors to The Tate Modern Project
We remain grateful to all those individuals and organisations who supported the creation of Tate Modern in 2000 as founding donors and sponsors. As we embark on the next stage of Tate Modern's development, we would like to pay particular thanks to the following donors who have supported the current Tate Modern Project.

The Blavatnik Family Foundation
Lauren and Mark Booth
The Deborah Loeb Brice Foundation
The Lord Browne of Madingley, FRS, FREng
John and Christina Chandris
James Chanos
Paul Cooke
Ago Demirdjian and Tiqui Atencio Demirdjian
George Economou
Mala Gaonkar
Thomas Gibson in memory of Anthea Gibson
Lydia and Manfred Gorvy
Noam Gottesman
Maja Hoffmann/LUMA Foundation
Maxine Isaacs
Peter and Maria Kellner
Madeleine Kleinwort
Catherine Lagrange
Pierre Lagrange
Allison and Howard W. Lutnick
Donald B. Marron
Anthony and Deirdre Montagu
Elisabeth Murdoch
Maureen Paley
Daniel and Elizabeth Peltz
Catherine and Franck Petitgas
Barrie and Emmanuel Roman
The Dr Mortimer and Theresa Sackler Foundation
Mr John Studzinski, CBE
Tate Members
Nina and Graham Williams
and those donors who wish to remain anonymous

Tate Modern Benefactors and Major Donors
We would like to acknowledge and thank the following benefactors who have supported Tate Modern prior to 31 October 2012.

29th May 1961 Charitable Trust
Carolyn Alexander
Basil Alkazzi
American Patrons of Tate
Annenberg Foundation
The Fagus Anstruther Memorial Trust
Mehves and Dalinc Ariburnu
The Kenneth Armitage Foundation
The Art Fund
Art Mentor Foundation Lucerne
The Arts & Humanities Research Council
Arts Council England
The Company of Arts Scholars, Dealers and Collectors' Charitable Fund
Charles Asprey
Marwan T Assaf
averda
Miroslaw Balka
Fay Ballard
Lionel Barber
Pedro Barbosa
The Estate of Peter and Caroline Barker-Mill
Trevor Bell
Mr John Bellany
Barbara Bertozzi Castelli
Anne Best
Big Lottery Fund
Mr and Mrs Oliver Bolitho
The Charlotte Bonham-Carter Charitable Trust
Pontus Bonnier
John Botts
Louise Bourgeois
Frances Bowes

Dr Luther Brady
Pierre Brahm
The Estate of Dr Marcella Louis Brenner
British Council
The Broad Art Foundation
Mr and Mrs Ben Brown
Armando Cabral
Pedro Cabrita Reis
Caldic Collectie, Wassenaar
Calouste Gulbenkian Foundation
Lucy Carter
Tornabuoni Art, Paris
John and Christina Chandris
James Chanos
Henry Christensen III
Patricia Phelps de Cisneros
The Clore Duffield Foundation
The Clothworkers' Foundation
Jenny Collins and Caroline Aperguis
Contemporary Art Society
Douglas S Cramer
Jane Crawford
Martin Creed
Bilge Ogut-Cumbusyan and Haro Cumbusyan
Daiwa Anglo-Japanese Foundation
Thomas Dane
Dimitris Daskalopoulos
Julia W Dayton
Richard Deacon
Dedalus Foundation, Inc.
The Gladys Krieble Delmas Foundation
Ago Demirdjian and Tiqui Atencio Demirdjian
Department for Business, Innovation and Skills
Department for Education
Department for Culture, Media and Sport
Anthony and Anne d'Offay
Peter Doig
Jytte Dresing, The Merla Art Foundation, Dresing Collection
The Duerckheim Collection
Isabelle and John Corbani
EDP - Energias de Portugal, S.A.
Maryam and Edward Eisler
Carla Emil and Richard Silverstein
Oscar Engelbert
Esmée Fairbairn Foundation
European Cultural Foundation
Christopher Eykyn and Nicholas Maclean
Fares and Tania Fares
The Estate of Maurice Farquharson
The Fisher Family
Wendy Fisher
Jeanne Donovan Fisher
Representation of the Government of Flanders in the UK
Lady Lynn Forester de Rothschild
The Estate of Ann Forsdyke
Eric and Louise Franck
Amanda and Glenn Fuhrman
The Getty Foundation
Antonia Gibbs
Millie and Arne Glimcher
Goethe-Institut
Dr John Golding
Nicholas and Judith Goodison
Goodman Gallery, Johannesburg and Cape Town
David and Maggi Gordon
Lady Gosling
The Estate of Alan Green
Konstantin Grigorishin
Chloë and Paul Gunn
Rokni Haerizadeh
Andrew and Christine Hall
Paul Hamlyn Foundation
Viscount and Viscountess Hampden and Family
Dr Mark Hannam
Mr Toshio Hara
Hauser & Wirth
The Hayden Family Foundation
Stuart Heath Charitable Settlement
Janet Henderson
Heritage Lottery Fund
Mauro Herlitzka
The Hintze Family Charitable Foundation
David Hockney
The Estate of Mrs Mimi Hodgkin
Marguerite Hoffman
Maja Hoffmann/ LUMA Foundation
Jenny Holzer
Rootstein Hopkins Foundation
Michael Hoppen
The Estate of Sir Robert Horton
Idlewild Trust
Cristina Iglesias
Callum Innes
Institut Ramon Llull
The Japan Foundation
Alain Jathiere
John Lyon's Charity
J. Patrick Kennedy and Patricia A. Kennedy
Bharti Kher
Jack Kirkland
The Estate of R. B. Kitaj
Leon Kossoff
Jannis Kounellis
The Kreitman Foundation
Catherine Lagrange
Pierre Lagrange
The Estate of Margaret Lapsley
The Leche Trust
Agnés and Edward Lee
Legacy Trust UK
The Leverhulme Trust
The Estate of Barbara Lloyd
Doris J. Lockhart
LOCOG
Mark and Liza Loveday
The Henry Luce Foundation
Karim Makarius
The Estate of Sir Edwin Manton
The Maplescombe Trust
The JP Marland Charitable Trust
Becky Mayer
Lord McAlpine of West Green
The Andrew W Mellon Foundation
Mikati Foundation
Boris and Vita Mikhailov
Sir Geoffroy Millais
Jean-Yves Mock
The Henry Moore Foundation
Peter Moores Foundation
Mr Minoru Mori, Hon KBE and Mrs Yoshiko Mori
NADFAS
National Heritage Memorial Fund
Nederlandse Organisatie Voor Research
Royal Norwegian Embassy
Mr Sean O'Connor
The Olivier Family
Dr John Osley
Outset Contemporary Art Fund
Maureen Paley
The Estate of Mr Allan Herbert Palmer
Irene Panagopoulos
Konstantinos Papageorgiou and Gregory Papadimitriou
Martin Parr
The Estate of Mr Brian and Mrs Nancy Pattenden
Stephen and Yana Peel
Catherine Petitgas
The PHG Cadbury Charitable Trust
Stanley Picker Trust
The Pilgrim Trust
Heather and Tony Podesta Collection
Powell Charitable Trust
Gilberto Pozzi
Cindy and Howard Rachofsky
The Reed Foundation
Mrs Frances Reynolds
Robert Mapplethorpe Foundation
Erica Roberts
Barrie and Emmanuel Roman
Helen and Ken Rowe
Edward Ruscha
The Michael Harry Sacher Charitable Trust
The Estate of Simon Sainsbury
Ms Avis Saltsman
Sally and Anthony Salz
The Sandra Charitable Trust
Fondation Saradar
The Great Britain Sasakawa Foundation
The Finnis Scott Foundation
Candida and Rebecca Smith
Tishman Speyer
Cynthia and Abe Steinberger
Charlotte Stevenson
Mr Anthony Stoll
Mercedes and Ian Stoutzker
Tate Africa Acquisitions Committee
Tate Asia-Pacific Acquisitions Committee
Tate International Council
Tate Latin American Acquisitions Committee
Tate Members
Tate Middle East and North Africa Acquisitions Committee
Tate North American Acquisitions Committee
Tate Patrons
Tate Photography Acquisitions Committee
Terra Foundation for American Art
The Estate of Mr Nicholas Themans
Robert Therrien
The Tretyakov Family Collection
Marc Vaux
The Vandervell Foundation
Wellcome Trust
Welton Foundation
Michael Werner, Inc.
Rachel Whiteread
The Estate of Fred Williams

Jane and Michael Wilson
Samuel and Nina Wisnia
Juan Yarur Torres
Anita and Poju Zabludowicz
Zamyn
Mrs Silke Ziehl
Nina and Michael Zilkha
and those donors who wish to remain anonymous

Platinum Patrons

Mr Alireza Abrishamchi
Ghazwa Mayassi Abu-Suud
Mr Shane Akeroyd
Basil Alkazzi
Ryan Allen and Caleb Kramer
Mehves Ariburnu
Mr and Mrs Edward Atkin CBE
Beecroft Charitable Trust
Mrs Abeer ben Halim
Mr Harry Blain
Broeksmit Family Foundation
Rory and Elizabeth Brooks (Chairman)
The Lord Browne of Madingley, FRS, FREng
Mr Stephane Custot
Miel de Botton
Ms Sophie Diedrichs-Cox
Fares and Tania Fares
Mrs Jodi Feist King
Mr David Fitzsimons
Mr Michael Foster
Edwin Fox Foundation
Hugh Gibson
The Goss-Michael Foundation
Mandy Gray and Randall Work
Mrs Nathalie and Mr Luc Guiot-Saucier
Mr and Mrs Yan Huo
Mr Phillip Hylander
Anne-Marie and Geoffrey Isaac
Mrs Gabrielle Jungels-Winkler
Maria and Peter Kellner
Mrs Ella Krasner
Mr and Mrs Eskandar Maleki
Scott and Suling Mead
Gabriela Mendoza and Rodrigo Marquez
Pierre Tollis and Alexandra Mollof
Mr Donald Moore
Mary Moore
Mr Mario Palencia
Mr and Mrs Paul Phillips
Maya and Ramzy Rasamny
Frances Reynolds
Simon and Virginia Robertson
Mr and Mrs Richard Rose
Claudia Ruimy
Vipin Sareen and Rebecca Mitchell
Mr and Mrs J Shafran
Mrs Andrée Shore
Maria and Malek Sukkar
Mr Vladimir Tsarenkov and Ms Irina Kargina
Mr and Mrs Petri Vainio
Rebecca Wang
Michael and Jane Wilson
The Flow Foundation
Poju and Anita Zabludowicz
and those who wish to remain anonymous

Gold Patrons

Eric Abraham
Jacqueline Appel and Alexander Malmaeus
Tim Attias
Katrina Barter
Jenny and Robert Borgerhoff Mulder
Elena Bowes
Ben and Louisa Brown
Melanie Clore
Beth and Michele Colocci
Mr Dónall Curtin
Mrs Robin D'Alessandro
Mr Frank Destribats
Mrs Maryam Eisler
Mala Gaonkar
Mr and Mrs A Ramy Goldstein
Mrs Helene Guerin-Llamas
Mr and Mrs Charles M Hale
Mrs Petra Horvat
Ms Natascha Jakobs
Fiona Mactaggart
Alison and Paul Myners
Bilge Ogut-Cumbusyan & Haro Cumbusyan
Mr Francis Outred
Simon and Midge Palley
Mariela Pissioti
Mathew Prichard
Valerie Rademacher
Mr David Roberts
Mr Charles Roxburgh
Carol Sellars
Mrs Dana Sheves
Britt Tidelius
Mr and Mrs Stanley S. Tollman
Emily Tsingo and Henry Bond
Mrs Celia Forner Venturi
Manuela and Iwan Wirth
Barbara Yerolemou
and those who wish to remain anonymous

Silver Patrons

Agnew's
Mrs Malgosia Alterman
Toby and Kate Anstruther
Mr and Mrs Zeev Aram
Mr Giorgio Armani
Mrs Charlotte Artus
Miss Silvia Badiali
Mrs Jane Barker
Mr Edward Barlow
Victoria Barnsley, OBE
Jim Bartos
Mrs Nada Bayoud
Mr Harold Berg
Lady Angela Bernstein
Ms Anne Berthoud
Madeleine Bessborough
Ms Karen Bizon
Janice Blackburn
David Blood and Beth Bisso
Mrs Sofia Bogolyubov
Mr Brian Boylan
Mrs Lena Boyle
Ivor Braka
Viscountess Bridgeman
The Broere Charitable Foundation
Mr Dan Brooke
Michael Burrell
Mrs Marlene Burston
Mrs Aisha Caan
Timothy and Elizabeth Capon
Mr Francis Carnwath and Ms Caroline Wiseman
Lord and Lady Charles Cecil
Frank Cohen
Mrs Jane Collins
Dr Judith Collins
Terrence Collis
Mr and Mrs Oliver Colman
Carole and Neville Conrad
Mr Gerardo Contreras
Giles and Sonia Coode-Adams
Alastair Cookson
Mark and Cathy Corbett
Cynthia Corbett
Mrs Ursula Cornely
Tommaso Corvi-Mora
Mr and Mrs Bertrand Coste
Kathleen Crook and James Penturn
James Curtis
Sir Howard Davies
Mr and Mrs Roger de Haan
Giles de la Mare
Maria de Madariaga
Anne Chantal Defay Sheridan
Marco di Cesaria
Simon C Dickinson Ltd
Mrs Fiona Dilger
James Diner
Liz and Simon Dingemans
Ms Charlotte Ransom and Mr Tim Dye
Joan Edlis
Lord and Lady Egremont
Jeffrey and Jennifer Eldredge
John Erle-Drax
Dr Nigel Evans
Stuart and Margaret Evans
Gerard Faggionato
Ms Rose Fajardo
Mrs Heather Farrar
Mrs Margy Fenwick
Mr Bryan Ferry, CBE
Mrs Jean Fletcher
Lt Commander Paul Fletcher
Steve Fletcher
Elizabeth Freeman
Stephen Friedman
Julia Fuller
Carol Galley
Mrs Lisa Garrison
Mrs Joanna Gemes
Ljubica Georgievska
Mr Mark Glatman
Ms Emily Goldner and Mr Michael Humphries
Ms Josefa Gonzalez-Blanco
Mr Jonathan Goodman
Mr and Mrs Paul Goswell
Penelope Govett
Martyn Gregory
Sir Ronald Grierson
Mrs Kate Grimond
Richard and Odile Grogan
Louise Hallett
Mr and Mrs Ryan Prince
Richard Hazlewood
Michael and Morven Heller
Richard and Sophia Herman
Miss Judith Hess
Mrs Patsy Hickman
Robert Holden
James Holland-Hibbert
Lady Hollick, OBE
Vicky Hughes
John Huntingford
Mr Alex Ionides
Maxine Isaacs
Sarah Jennings
Ms Alex Joffe
Mr Haydn John
Mr Michael Johnson
Jay Jopling
Mrs Marcelle Joseph and Mr Paolo Cicchiné
Mrs Brenda Josephs
Tracey Josephs
Mr Joseph Kaempfer
Andrew Kalman
Dr Martin Kenig
Mr David Ker
Nicola Kerr
Mr and Mrs Simon Keswick
Richard and Helen Keys
Mrs Mae Khouri
David Killick
Mr and Mrs James Kirkman
Brian and Lesley Knox
Kowitz Trust
Mr and Mrs Herbert Kretzmer
Ms Jacqueline Lane
Steven Larcombe
Mrs Julie Lee
Simon Lee
Mr Gerald Levin
Leonard Lewis

Mrs Cynthia Lewis Beck
Mr Gilbert Lloyd
George Loudon
Mrs Elizabeth Louis
Mark and Liza Loveday
Daniella Luxembourg Art
Anthony Mackintosh
Eykyn Maclean LLC
The Mactaggart Third Fund
Mrs Jane Maitland Hudson
Mr M J Margulies
Lord and Lady Marks
Marsh Christian Trust
Mrs Anne-Sophie McGrath
Ms Fiona Mellish
Mr Martin Mellish
Mrs R W P Mellish
Professor Rob Melville
Mr Michael Meynell
Mr Alfred Mignano
Victoria Miro
Ms Milica Mitrovich
Jan Mol
Mrs Bona Montagu
Mrs Valerie Gladwin Montgomery
Mr Ricardo Mora
Mrs William Morrison
Richard Nagy
Daniela and Victor Gareh
Julian Opie
Pilar Ordovás
Sir Richard Osborn
Joseph and Chloe O'Sullivan
Desmond Page
Maureen Paley
Dominic Palfreyman
Michael Palin
Mrs Adelaida Palm
Stephen and Clare Pardy
Mrs Véronique Parke
Mr Sanjay Parthasarathy
Miss Nathalie Philippe
Ms Michina Ponzone-Pope
Mr Oliver Prenn
Susan Prevezer QC
Mr Adam Prideaux
James Pyner
Ivetta Rabinovich
Mrs Phyllis Rapp
Ms Victoria Reanney
Dr Laurence Reed
Mr and Mrs James Reed
Mr and Mrs Philip Renaud
The Reuben Foundation
Sir Tim Rice
Lady Ritblat
The Sylvie Fleming Collection
Ms Chao Roberts
David Rocklin
Frankie Rossi
Mr David V Rouch
Mr James Roundell
Naomi Russell
Mr Alex Sainsbury and Ms Elinor Jansz
Mr Richard Saltoun
Mrs Amanda Sater
Mrs Cecilia Scarpa
Cherrill and Ian Scheer
Sylvia Scheuer
Mrs Cara Schulze
Andrew and Belinda Scott
The Hon Richard Sharp
Mr Stuart Shave
Neville Shulman, CBE
The Schneer Foundation
Ms Julia Simmonds
Jennifer Smith
Mrs Cindy Sofer
Mr George Soros
Louise Spence
Mr and Mrs Nicholas Stanley
Mr Nicos Steratzias
Stacie Styles
Mrs Patricia Swannell
Mr James Swartz
The Lady Juliet Tadgell
Tot Taylor
Lady Tennant
Christopher and Sally Tennant
Mr Henry Tinsley
Karen Townshend
Melissa Ulfane
Mr Marc Vandecandelaere
Mrs Cecilia Versteegh
Mr Jorge Villon
Gisela von Sanden
Mr David von Simson
Audrey Wallrock
Stephen and Linda Waterhouse
Offer Waterman
Terry Watkins
Miss Cheyenne Westphal
Mr David Wood
Mr Douglas Woolf
and those who wish to remain anonymous

Young Patrons
Vinita Agarwal
Stephanie Alameida
Ms Maria Allen
Miss Noor Al-Rahim
HRH Princess Alia Al-Senussi (Chair, Young Patrons Ambassador Group)
Miss Sharifa Alsudairi
Sigurdur Arngrimsson
Miss Katharine Arnold
Miss Joy Asfar
Ms Mila Askarova
Miss Olivia Aubry
Flavie Audi
Josh Bell and Jsen Wintle
Miss Marisa Bellani
Ms Shruti Belliappa
Mr Erik Belz
Mr Edouard Benveniste-Schuler
Miss Margherita Berloni
Raimund Berthold
Ms Natalia Blaskovicova
Dr Brenda Blott
Mrs Sofia Bocca
Ms Lara Bohinc
Mr Andrew Bourne
Miss Camilla Bullus
Miss Verena Butt
Miss May Calil
Miss Sarah Calodney
Matt Carey-Williams and Donnie Roark
Georgina Casals
Kabir Chhatwani
Miss Katya Chitova
Dr Peter Chocian
Mrs Mona Collins
Mrs Laura Comfort
Thamara Corm
Miss Amanda C Cronin
Mr Theo Danjuma
Mr Joshua Davis
Mrs Suzy Franczak Davis
Ms Lora de Felice
Countess Charlotte de la Rochefoucauld
Mr Stanislas de Quenetain
Federico Debernardi
Mira Dimitrova
Ms Michelle D'Souza
Miss Roxanna Farboud
Jane and Richard Found
Mr Andreas Gegner
Mrs Benedetta Ghione-Webb
Miss Dori Gilinski
Mr Nick Hackworth
Alex Haidas
Ms Susan Harris
Sara Harrison
Kira Allegra Heller
Mrs Samantha Heyworth
Katherine Ireland
Miss Eloise Isaac
Kamel Jaber
Mr Jermaine Johnson
Mr Christopher Jones
Ms Melek Huma Kabakci
Miss Meruyert Kaliyeva
Efe and Aysun Kapanci
Ms Tanya Kazeminy Mackay
Miss Tamila Kerimova
Mr Benjamin Khalili
Ms Chloe Kinsman
Ms Marijana Kolak
Miss Constanze Kubern
Miss Marina Kurikhina
Mr Jimmy Lahoud
Ms Aliki Lampropoulos
Ms Anna Lapshina
Isabella Lauder-Frost
Mrs Julie Lawson
Ms Joanne Leigh
Miss MC Llamas
Mr Justin Lobo
Alex Logsdail
Mrs Siobhan Loughran
Charlotte Lucas
Alessandro Luongo
Mr John Madden
Ms Sonia Mak
Mr Jean-David Malat
Ms Clémence Mauchamp
Miss Charlotte Maxwell
Mr John McLaughlin
Miss Nina Moaddel
Mr Fernando Moncho Lobo
Ms Michelle Morphew
Erin Morris
Mrs Annette Nygren
Katharina Ottmann
Ilona Pacia
Phyllis Papadavid
Ms Camilla Paul
Alexander V. Petalas
Mrs Stephanie Petit
The Piper Gallery
Lauren Prakke
Mr Eugenio Re Rebaudengo
Mr Bruce Ritchie and Mrs Shadi Ritchie
Kimberley and Michael Robson-Ortiz
Mr Daniel Ross
Mr Simon Sakhai
Miss Tatiana Sapegina
Mr Simon Scheuer
Franz Schwarz
Count Indoo Sella Di Monteluce
Preeya Seth
Miss Kimberly Sgarlata
Henrietta Shields
Ms Heather Shimizu
Mr Paul Shin
Ms Marie-Anya Shriro
Mr Max Silver
Tammy Smulders
Miss Jelena Spasojevic
Alexandra Sterling
Mr Dominic Stolerman
Mr Edward Tang
Miss Georgiana Teodorescu
Miss Inge Theron
Soren S K Tholstrup
Hannah Tjaden
Mr Giancarlo Trinca
Mrs Padideh Trojanow
Mr Philippos Tsangrides
Dr George Tzircotis
Miss Brenda Van Camp
Mr Rupert Van Millingen
Mr Neil Wenman
Ms Hailey Widrig Ritcheson
Miss Julia Wright
Ms Seda Yalcinkaya
Michelle Yue
Mr Fabrizio Zappaterra
Miss Valeria Zingarevich
and those who wish to remain anonymous

North American Acquisitions Committee
Carol and David Appel
Paul Britton
Beth Rudin De Woody
Carla Emil and Richard Silverstein
Glenn Fuhrman
Victoria Gelfand-Magalhaes
Andrea and Marc Glimcher
Pamela Joyner

Monica Kalpakian
Elisabeth Farrell and Panos Karpidas
Christian K Keesee
Michael and Marjorie Levine
Massimo Marcucci
Lillian Mauer
Liza Mauer and Andrew Sheiner
Nancy McCain
Stuart and Della McLaughlin
Stavros Merjos
Gregory R. Miller
Shabin and Nadir Mohamed
Elisa Nuyten & David Dime
Amy and John Phelan
Liz Gerring Radke and Kirk Radke
Laura Rapp and Jay Smith
Robert Rennie (Chair) and Carey Fouks
Kimberly Richter
Donald R Sobey
Robert Sobey
Christen and Derek Wilson
and those who wish to remain anonymous

Latin American Acquisitions Committee

Monica and Robert Aguirre
Karen and Leon Amitai
Luis Benshimol
Billy Bickford, Jr. and Oscar Cuellar
Estrellita and Daniel Brodsky
Trudy and Paul Cejas
Patricia Phelps de Cisneros
David Cohen Sitton
Gerard Cohen
HSH the Prince Pierre d'Arenberg
Tiqui Atencio Demirdjian (Chair)
Lily Gabriella Elia
Angelica Fuentes de Vergara
Mauro Herlitzka
Yaz Hernandez
Rocio and Boris Hirmas Said
Anne Marie and Geoffrey Isaac
Nicole Junkermann
Jack Kirkland
Fatima and Eskander Maleki
Fernanda Feitosa and Heitor Martins
Becky and Jimmy Mayer
Solita and Steven Mishaan
Patricia Moraes and Pedro Barbosa
Catherine and Michel Pastor
Catherine Petitgas
Ferdinand Porák
Isabella Prata and Idel Arcuschin
Frances Reynolds
Erica Roberts
Judko Rosenstock and Oscar Hernandez
Guillermo Rozenblum
Alin Ryan von Buch
Lilly Scarpetta and Roberto Pumarejo
Catherine Shriro
Norma Smith
Susana and Ricardo Steinbruch
Juan Carlos Verme
Tania and Arnoldo Wald
Juan Yarur Torres
and those who wish to remain anonymous

Asia-Pacific Acquisitions Committee

Bonnie and R Derek Bandeen
Andrew Cameron
Mr and Mrs John Carrafiell
Mrs Christina Chandris
Richard Chang
Pierre TM Chen, Yageo Foundation, Taiwan
Katie de Tilly
Mr. Hyung-Teh Do
Ms Mareva Grabowski
Elizabeth Griffith
Ms Kyoko Hattori
Cees Hendrikse
Mr Yongsoo Huh
Lady Tessa Keswick
Mr Chang-Il Kim
Ms Yung Hee Kim
Alan Lau
Woong Yeul Lee
Mr William Lim
Ms Kai-Yin Lo
Anne Louis-Dreyfus
Mrs Geraldine Elaine Marden
The Red Mansion Foundation
Mr Jackson See
Mr Paul Serfaty
Dr Gene Sherman AM
Mr Robert Shum
Sir David Tang (Chair)
Mr Budi Tek, The Yuz Foundation
Rudy Tseng (Taiwan)
and those who wish to remain anonymous

Middle East and North Africa Acquisitions Committee

Abdullah Al Turki
HRH Princess Alia Al-Senussi
Mehves Ariburnu
Sule Arinc
Marwan Assaf
Perihan Bassatne
Foundation Boghossian
Ms Isabelle de la Bruyère
Füsun Eczacibaşi
Shirley Elghanian
Delfina Entrecanales
Noor Fares
Maryam Homayoun Eisler (Co-Chair)
Maha and Kasim Kutay
Lina Lazaar
Nina Mahdavi
Mrs Fatima Maleki
Fayeeza Naqvi
Dina Nasser-Khadivi
Ebru Özdemir
Mrs Edwina Özyegin
Ramzy and Maya Rasamny (Co-Chair)
Mrs Karen Ruimy
Dania Debs-Sakka
Mrs Sherine Sawiris
Miss Yassi Sohrabi
Maria and Malek Sukkar
Ana Luiza and Luiz Augusto Teixeira de Freitas
Berna Tuglular
and those who wish to remain anonymous

Photography Acquisitions Committee

Ryan Allen
Mr Nicholas Barker
Marisa Bellani
Pierre Brahm (Chair)
William and Alla Broeksmit
Elizabeth and Rory Brooks
Veronica and Jeffrey Berman
Marcel and Gabrielle Cassard
Nicolas & Celia Cattelain
Beth and Michele Colocci
Fares and Tania Fares
David Fitzsimons
Margot and George Greig
Alexandra Hess
Michael Hoppen
Bernard Huppert
Tim Jefferies, Hamiltons Gallery
Dede Johnston
Jack Kirkland
David Knaus
Mark McCain
Mr Scott Mead
Mr Donald Moore
Mr. Axel Nordin
Ellen and Dan Shapiro
Saadi Soudavar
Maria and Malek Sukkar
Michael and Jane Wilson
and those who wish to remain anonymous

Africa Acquisitions Committee

Kathryn Jane Robins
Mr Tutu Agyare (Co-Chair)
Bolanle Austen-Peters
Mrs Kavita Chellaram
Mr Salim Curimjee
Mr Robert Devereux (Co-Chair)
Mr Hamish Dewar
Isis Dove-Edwin and Paul Ellis
Mrs Wendy Fisher
Deborah Goldman
Helene Huth
Andrea Kerzner
Samallie Kiyingi
Matthias and Gervanne Leridon
Caro Macdonald
Dr Kenneth Montague
Miles Morland
Alain F. Nkontchou
Professor Oba Nsugbe QC
Pascale Revert Wheeler
Maria Spink
Mr Emile Stipp
Varnavas A. Varnava
Mercedes Vilardell
Tony Wainaina
Alexa Waley-Cohen
Edwin Wulfsohn
and those who wish to remain anonymous

International Council Members

Doris Ammann
Mr Plácido Arango
Gabrielle Bacon
Anne H Bass
Cristina Bechtler
Nicolas Berggruen
Olivier & Desiree Berggruen
Baron Berghmans
Mr Pontus Bonnier
Ms Miel de Botton
Mrs Frances Bowes
Ivor Braka
The Deborah Loeb Brice Foundation
The Broad Art Foundation
Bettina and Donald L Bryant Jr
Melva Bucksbaum and Raymond Learsy
Mrs Christina Chandris
Richard Chang
Pierre TM Chen, Yageo Foundation, Taiwan
Lord Cholmondeley
Mr Kemal Has Cingillioglu
Mr and Mrs Attilio Codognato
David and Michelle Coe
Sir Ronald Cohen and Lady Sharon Harel-Cohen
Mr Alfonso Cortina de Alcocer
Mr Douglas S Cramer and Mr Hubert S. Bush III
Mr Dimitris Daskalopoulos
Mr and Mrs Michel David-Weill
Julia W Dayton

Tiqui Atencio Demirdjian and Ago Demirdjian
Joseph and Marie Donnelly
Mrs Olga Dreesmann
Mrs Jytte Dresing
Barney A Ebsworth
Füsun and Faruk Eczacibaşi
Stefan Edlis and Gael Neeson
Mr and Mrs Edward Eisler
Carla Emil and Rich Silverstein
Alan Faena
Harald Falckenberg
Fares and Tania Fares
HRH Princess Firyal of Jordan
Mrs Doris Fisher
Mrs Wendy Fisher
Dr Corinne M Flick
Amanda and Glenn Fuhrman
Candida and Zak Gertler
Alan Gibbs
Lydia and Manfred Gorvy
Kenny Goss
Mr Laurence Graff
Ms Esther Grether
Mr Grigorishin Konstantin
Mr Xavier Guerrand-Hermès
Mimi and Peter Haas Fund
Margrit and Paul Hahnloser
Andy and Christine Hall
Mr Toshio Hara
Mrs Susan Hayden
Ms Ydessa Hendeles
Marlene Hess and James D. Zirin
André and Rosalie Hoffmann
Ms Maja Hoffmann (Chair)
Vicky Hughes
Dakis and Lietta Joannou
Sir Elton John and Mr David Furnish
Mr Chang-Il Kim
C Richard and Pamela Kramlich
Catherine Lagrange
Mr Pierre Lagrange and Mr Roubi L'Roubi
Baroness Marion Lambert
Bernard Lambilliotte
Agnès and Edward Lee
Mme RaHee Hong Lee
Jacqueline and Marc Leland
Mr and Mrs Sylvain Levy
Mr Eugenio Lopez
Mrs Fatima Maleki
Panos and Sandra Marinopoulos
Nancy and Howard Marks
Mr and Mrs Donald B Marron
Andreas and Marina Martinos
Mr Ronald and The Hon Mrs McAulay
Angela Westwater and David Meitus
Mr Leonid Mikhelson
Simon and Catriona Mordant
Mrs Yoshiko Mori
Mr Guy and The Hon Mrs Naggar
Mr and Mrs Takeo Obayashi
Mrs Kathrine Palmer
Irene Panagopoulos
ITYS, Athens
Young-Ju Park
Yana and Stephen Peel
Daniel and Elizabeth Peltz
Andrea and José Olympio Pereira
Fondation Cartier pour l'art contemporain
Catherine and Franck Petitgas
Sydney Picasso
Mr and Mrs Jürgen Pierburg
Jean Pigozzi
Ms Miuccia Prada and Mr Patrizio Bertelli
Maya and Ramzy Rasamny
Patrizia Sandretto Re Rebaudengo and Agostino Re Rebaudengo
Robert Rennie and Carey Fouks
Mr John Richardson
Michael Ringier
Lady Ritblat
Barrie and Emmanuel Roman
Ms Güler Sabanci
Dame Theresa Sackler
Mrs Lily Safra
Muriel and Freddy Salem
Dasha Shenkman
Uli and Rita Sigg
Michael S Smith
Norah and Norman Stone
John J Studzinski, CBE
Mrs Marjorie Susman
David Teiger
Mario Testino
Mr Robert Tomei
The Hon Robert H Tuttle and Mrs Maria Hummer-Tuttle
Mr and Mrs Guy Ullens
Michael and Yvonne Uva
Mrs Ninetta Vafeia
Corinne and Alexandre Van Damme
Paulo A W Vieira
Robert and Felicity Waley-Cohen
Diana Widmaier Picasso
Christen and Derek Wilson
Michael G Wilson
Mrs Sylvie Winckler
The Hon Mrs Janet Wolfson de Botton CBE
Anita and Poju Zabludowicz
Michael Zilkha
and those who wish to remain anonymous

Tate Modern Corporate Supporters

Bank of America Merrill Lynch
Bloomberg
BMW
BP
Guaranty Trust Bank
Hildon Limited
J.P. Morgan
Le Méridien
Louis Vuitton
Qatar Museums Authority
Sotheby's
Statkraft
Unilever
Vodafone Group
and those who wish to remain anonymous

Tate Modern Corporate Members

AIG
The Brooklyn Brothers
Christie's
Clifford Chance LLP
Deloitte LLP
Deutsche Bank
Diageo Great Britain Limited
Freshfields Bruckhaus Deringer
GAM
Hanjin Shipping
HSBC
The John Lewis Partnership
Kingfisher plc
Linklaters
Mace Group Ltd
MasterCard Worldwide
Mazars
Morgan Stanley
Native Land and Grosvenor
Pearson
Tishman Speyer
Wolff Olins
and those who wish to remain anonymous